Never After, Never Again!

NEVER

Dr. Linda Frederica Walsh

tellwell

Tellwell Talent
www.tellwell.ca

ISBN
978-0-2288-8441-5 (Paperback)

Stop expecting people who have never been there to understand where your coming from.

This novel was written to set the record straight about the true undisclosed events of my life and that sometimes life is out of our control to fix, correct or change.

This novel is intentionally not edited in it's entirety precisely or totally accurately as it reflects the emotion of the contents herein, as in life as with most everything in the world, in that there are always imperfections in life as with most things in the world and we should embrace them for what they are, as not everything is able to achieve or attain perfection, perhaps even NEVER resolving or even impossible infinitesimally to be corrected or be included or be able to be corrected if even ever completely.

Especially during times of severe trauma, grief and injustice, life still goes on and on and continues, despite it, all around us, revolving in the world.

Table of Contents

FRENCH
SKI
SCHOOL
MEETING PLACE
3

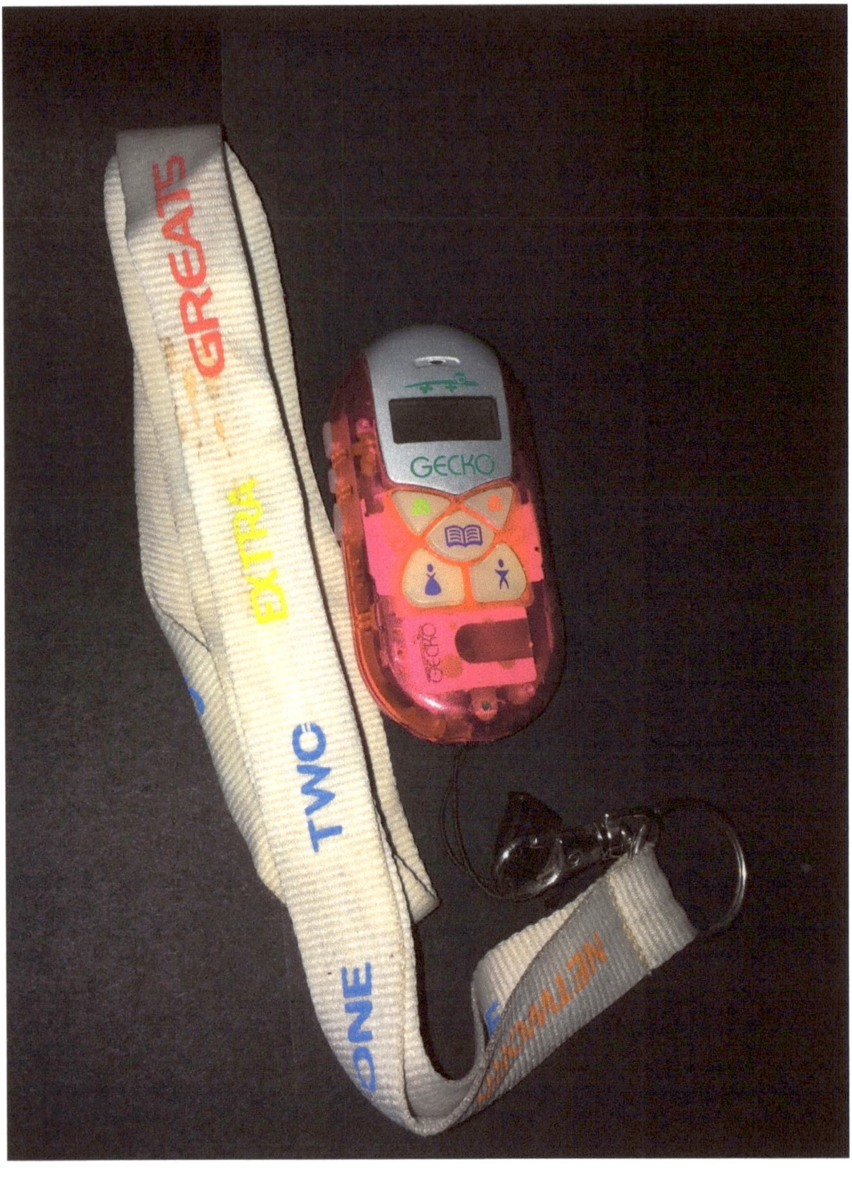
GREATS
EXTRA
TWO
GECKO

To Mummy,
with love
from Sabena
30/3/13
Freddie
フレディ
リンダ
Linda
HAPPY
EASTER!!!
うさぎ
Usagi
Rabbit

Polly as nurse
By Sabena

Kooralbyn

A CTIONEERS & ESTATE AGENTS.

LÖWENBRÄU
ONE OF THE WORLDS
GREAT BEERS.

Start The beginning at the end.

The 7th of May, 2022 and it would be Mother's Day tomorrow the 8th of May, 2022. I liked the number eight somehow it was lucky, maybe because it resembled the infinity sign but up vertical. There was Gr8, 8te, pl8, fa8, cre8, some of my favourite words among others. It reminded me of those films I liked *The Hateful Eight and True Grit* and other signs of fortitude, courage and luck, the number connected coincidently a theme with my family and personal life. It was a miserable day today freezing cold, dull, dim and solemnly grey.

We were still in the throes of the Covid Pandemic but it was slowing down due to the increased vaccinations and herd immunity that was being established but more people were contracting it but with milder symptoms hopefully due to the vaccination pre-immunity set up. Winter had only just begun and there were clues it might be mean, so it would remain to be seen what outcomes there might be. It was two -way each – way bet for someone who doesn't bet like myself.

There was a Federal Election looming, sad and needless to say but during this facocte time in Australia and the world the system appeared bizarre and chaotic, would any of them make any difference during these unprecedented times anyway.

It was not short of a miracle that I managed to stave off the dreaded virus until now, I thought I might get it eventually due to more people contracting it now, and if it could not be avoided but wasn't going looking for it. I began however to be feeling a bit like a Pin Cushion or a plastic bag with small holes in it springing tiny water sprouts leaking out fountain. I suffered severe and debilitating, a week's long duration of all the symptoms for every shot even the booster, however I was still alive which was how I went in thinking about it. With my poor immune system and respiratory allergies, I would surely have died of the Covid, so was willing to take the risk of the small chance of dying from an incident from the shot itself. I previously suffered a severe allergic reaction to a Flu vaccine in 2009 and developed partial nerve deafness totally in the left ear not so long after that the very same year. Who knows?. Since I retreat a bit more in the Winter to hibernation, and followed my usual protocols before those Covid came into play, I found without having a Flu Jab, as the Doctor said for me it would be optional, I have never got the Flu from 2009 until 2022, this present day.

The Time Capsule

I thought about these difficult Covid years from November, 2019 and they were partially a blur. However I achieved a lot somehow even though I may or might not have done, probably not during this time. Perhaps it was a blessing in disguise. It was a miracle and God somehow watching over me in providence that I wound up the Teen Talk Production program. Channel 31, would not renew our Broadcasting Licence for June 2018, due to it presumably going online fully and which would not have worked for us anyhow due to our format, small business operators wanted direct TV exposure. There was still filming from March, 2018 which required post- production for which now these programs would likely not be broadcast on TV, it was a process of months to complete the programs as we stopped filming. I also thought perhaps it also was time to stop as it was weighing it's toll on me, a burden, physically, mentally, financially and was all time consuming for little reward it felt like now, I was also no longer enjoying it, as it was becoming a job. It performed it's duty and run it's course for the time. It seemed a natural progression for me to now move on to other things in my life for myself, although it was good therapy for both myself and the kids and families involved in the interviews at the time. The program continued in Adelaide and Perth for sometime after until the programs ran out, as they were a year or so behind Melbourne.

The unbroadcasted programs I continued to save on DVD's and after much annoyance from those kids involved they would not be on TV, I began the International Streaming Channel from France (that I researched) with some FREE stuff, paying a monthly rental for the kids to access their interviews*, teen talk production.okast.tv* – that also can be accessed from the website on the PINK hyperlink at www.teentalkproduction.com.au. I looked back and thought about this monumental achievement in awe, it was the passing of a time capsule, a flickering moment in time of an era. I Made That!, 2014 – 2019, like the writing on the Melbourne trams, *Made in Melbourne.* For me it was like *Seinfeld* the show that would seemingly never end and go on forever to infinity but it did.

For me it was like the dawning of the Covid, that I premonitioned that the world would need something like the program to wake people up about how skew - whiff the world was going and that because the Covid was the impending doom that was coming, because God saw the world going so terribly *off the rails* like a train wreck waiting for something bad to happen to shake us up to reality. I also seemed to have a knack of inadvertently without thought of it of being a visionary of things, that were doomed to happen even before they happened and being persecuted for my insight. I could have been a witch with a crystal ball from the future warning of the dangers forthcoming, it could have been episodes of *Outlander* mixed with a fusion of *Back to the Future series* of films.

There were however many highlights during these years, with the comeradery of the people involved in the program and the seeming unity of people for a greater cause, the *Youth Voice.* The unique and those wonderful, special adults that I met and interviewed that voluntarily participated their time and brought something fantastical to the program and who believed and supported me.

Those intrepid and visionary people who believed in me to the hilt and who blindly trusted me and embarked with me with faith and loyalty on this voyage of exploration to create something exceptionally unique and extraordinary in our lifetime. Who never questioned my ability and fervor to deliver something Gr8 for our kid's future legacy. Delving, into the unknown territory of this indie.

It all began with the discovery of people such as Costa Anasthassiou, he seemed perpetually a single type of nice guy who was interested in innovation, and held a Photography Club for kids on the weekends, who after many knockbacks from others, saying it couldn't be done that agreed to work with me to create the original pilot being the videographer and editor, he believed in me and the concept and could see to infinity and beyond. Stefan Markworth, who's dream was to make an aboriginal documentary and movie in the outback in his lifetime. Stefan was fabulously gifted and insightful with the editing, graphics and music. They helped to bring my idea to give it's life and breath from it's inception at the very beginning. Many other crew students and members followed and their work was also invaluable.

Those adults at the very start who volunteered without question and without knowing me who participated and for some small businesses, whom we also created 1 min and 30 second TV ads shown within our *Family – Friendly* slot program.

Costa helped me to round up some of the pilot team of volunteer kid interviewees during the Summer School Holidays in January 2015. He was paid handsomely of course but his heart was always in a good place. They were a fabulous group of quality kids which I could not have picked more wisely than I casted them myself on purpose. I also recruited some from CANTEEN myself by spruiking and those kids who also aspired to work in the behind the scenes in the TV Industry schools. I mention them here individually because they are great young people in their own right with amazing groundbreaking and true tragic stories of their own at such young ages for their expose on their brave and courageous experience.

Michael Arkalis, Amelia M. (Poppy), Twins Imogen (Immi) and Tennille (Tawn), Fiona C, Natalie B (Bob), Sophia C, Mark C, Jasmina S, (Jazz), Hannah L, Morgan C, Anna Q.

Other volunteers after that episode and then following other early episodes, began also to find us and source us out themselves to become a part of this creation. The student filming sisters Brianna (Bri) and Alaina (Skin) R who wanted to travel making their own films together as a team. Brianna later appeared on an episode of Beauty and the Geek on Channel 9 which might have been filmed not long prior to the Pandemic.

Tia and Alex, with their terrific stupefying personalities, and huge singing voices at such, very young ages, so talented already.

Sponsors like Le Mans Go karts and Lazer Skirmish, Lazer Zone and Paintball and their mascot Michael Drew, who was interviewed about Le Mans, and his love for this unusual type of curating job and experience.

Spectacular Jasmine Jones, singer and songwriter extraordinaire who is well known but couldn't make it to the big time. She lived in Portugal for many years trying to be discovered and make her future fame, song (Gold) of which she is undoubtedly made of but was too obvious to be recognized.

Jaleel Y, Kristen M, Rhiannon G.

Angela Jacobsen – CEO and Founder of Oz Supernanny, who super duper Nannied Personality and celebrity Kids of Superstars in her young but ambitious and motivated successful career heights. Hinted that she nannied for the likes of Madonna.

Kylie K – Mum, Volunteer Netball Coach, Hairdresser and her fabulous gem of a daughter.

Chloe B, Abby W, Holly W.

Evan M – Secondary school teacher, Looking for Life Year 9/10 coach co-ordinator, all round nice guy, with a conscience and with a heart greater than Texas for his protégées, success in future life.

An up and coming motivated film creative was Katie Staples and her assistant, Lise Leitner who was from Switzerland was enterprising and designed her own graphics for the opening and closing for their episode – Disc 1 episode 4. Issues at School. Broadcast 03.07.2015.

I decided however to keep consistent with the original copyright logo graphics and Stefan Marthworth's – *Skyward (instrumental) version – Scott and Brendo (U- Tube / Royalty Free) opening and closing themes.*

Disc 2 - July / August 2015

Special Guests of these episodes entertwined with the fascinating stories of the youth volunteers.

Nkandu Beltz - Author, Public Speaker, Change – Maker, STEM for Women.

Fiona Summons – Dyslexia Therapist/ Remedial Dyslexia Therapy Practitioner – Alison Lawson Centre. www.alcv.com.au

Sandy Columbo- Author, Trainer, NLP, Motivational Speaker, (Eat Bigger Frogs).

Laurie Webb – RMIT/ Melbourne University Lecturer, (Accounting International study Program) and Friend / Patient.

I am not sure when I started providing the volunteer youth and adult guest speakers with gifts, but it was not long after the first few episodes were completed on the First Disc. I began with giving them each a previous disc produced for them to keep for FREE however requesting that they could purchase their own episodes once produced to contribute to the making of further programs. It then also became T –shirts, send – a – message tokens, wristbands, pens, bookmarks, buttons, lapel pins, etc. Sometimes different gifts at different filmings as they became available, FREE vouchers, tickets, discounts from small businesses, that were given as donations or in lieu of advertising discounts/ interviews and gratis.

Disc 3 – August/ September 2015.

It would be a gargantuan task for me to rewrite and boring for you guys to be bogged down in, to include every volunteer participant's names, families, all people involved in the crew and behind the scenes, my friends and those externally, but for certain they know who they are and that they remember the exciting experience.

My patient Nick Mitsios for many years and his wife Melanie, my dear trusted kind and generous friends who I told Nick about the Teen Talk Program Project program, after filming the first few episodes and he thought it very intriguing and interesting concept. He explained it to Mel and she volunteered to be interviewed about her studies and her innovative practice. Melanie Mitsios – Intuitive Medical / Quantum Medical Intuitive Graduate Practitioner. Mel provided private appointment sessions at her home. Nick was kind enough to provide a $ 1,000 donation contribution, he said to help the cause on it's way and kickstart it on its feet. I think he was also thankful and grateful of the thorough care and treatment I gave him with referrals, advice and therapy on his heart and circulatory conditions, that improved considerably with my treatments and professional advice The kind donation secured Mel a guest spot on the Disc 3 – Episode 2 Youth Learning Experiences – Part 3 and I also included a FREE ad Creation and an Advertising Package on our TV show for a monthly season sponsorship of episodes.

A few years later i gifted Nick a pair of orthopaedic footwear worth at least $ 240 to thank him for his kindness. There were few donations of this direct type but rather mostly donations in the form of advertising within the program that we provided a service of ad Creation and my advertising spots that were purchased from the station within the Teen Talk Production Program or volunteered gifts/ vouchers for the kids and their families or service discounts at their businesses or discounts on services and goods purchased for the cause.

Gifted Crew

Around about Disc 20 – I think it was Hardikumar Patel and Jarrod Brown, who suggested to me to do a Go –Fund – Me page. They were both, so wonderfully creative, innovative, helpful and injected so much artistry and enthusiasm into the program, filming, editing, graphics, IT, social media etc. There were some temporary crew that stayed with me for months and some even years, who were staunch fans and believed in what we were trying to achieve with the cause and program. Of course they were paid volunteers, as what I called pocket- money which was what I thought was also motivating and encouraging them to do their best and also learn, most of them were students looking for a break to get experience and some even volunteered for FREE. I wanted them all also to feel that their service was worthwhile and that they earned it, not being abused in the system which they said often found them interning for months/years for FREE just to get experience or even a break into the industry. I always insisted on paying them all something, what I could afford within the budget, even though it wasn't much but something is always an improvement on nothing at all. Besides there were also so many other expenses like hiring of filming equipment/ venues, and a myriad of other hidden expenses, especially as I was the sole Writer, Producer, Director and sometimes hobby self –taught fill – in filmer, since I have never studied videography or TV/ Film.

Many were very gracious and kind in giving of their extra time and efforts and went above and beyond the call of duty and they expressed wholehearted gratitude to me for giving them a chance to perform their skill in an industry where there are so many unemployed, pumping gas or in hospitality, who never managed to secure any type of work in their own career regardless of whether they were students or graduated. I felt sorry for these young creative's who's dreams unfortunately for almost all of them would almost never be realized or even for them to be able to work in the industry, let alone make any kind of a professional living were few and far between with even casual offerings. It was a sad reflection of the Industry which I abhorred but I was glad this was a hobby and not my real job.

Sometimes they offered their services having disabilities of Mental Illness, Autism, Deafness, Stress, Lack of Confidence, Terminal Illness and others. I was not running a hospital, so if their conditions were mild and I thought they were capable after being interviewed by me and performing a once of task, I would sometimes recall them or they would volunteer again themselves. If they were very keen I never excluded anyone but being a one woman army and doing most if it myself, I could not cope with liabilities unfortunately and sometimes they would not turn up or fail in minimum performance of their duties or have a tantrum or hissy fit at the beginning of filming, argue or question my direction or were in an unfit state to work, or destructive/ disruptive/undermining/ destabilizing types so unfortunately at times they were relieved of their duties early on, sometimes before they began work before beginning if necessary, I also considered the amenity, well being, safety and comradry of the volunteer participants, their families and other crew, behind the scenes members and other volunteer helpers, who might be adversely affected.

During these employee's failures, I felt terribly aggrieved by their lost opportunity and thought what if that was My Sabena, would they ever be employable or would they be perpetually lost in the system. For those who succeeded even doing a once off filming or several days/ months / years or performed tasks well, were offered and more than often supplied a written reference/ recommendation on request or to a future prospective employer or interview / promotion on the program. Others that enjoyed their time and were an asset to the team, at the Teen Talk Family would come and go re-offering their skills and services, popping in and out, when they were out of work or on holiday from study or back and forth from visiting or going home to their Birth Countries for holidays and returning to work/ study. Myself also being sometimes Technologically Challenged with pleasure would help me with tasks gladly that were not in their scope of duties for Teen Talk.

Other Special adult guests.

Disc 4 – September/ October 2015

Steven O'Connor – Safe International Melbourne Instructor/ Self Defence Course.

Phaedra Gunn- Singer/Songwriter and Steven Marshall White – Singer. Songwriter and Guitar accompaniest. The Winterfriends Band – Song (My Wonderland).

Tammi Snell and her son Ronnie, who I met through another friend of many years, was a dynamic personality, whom in various ways reminded me of Sonia Kruger, employed in Travel Sales, was currently studying to be a Real Estate Agent and already a fully licensed pilot.

Rahela Fazli – Youth Retreat Australia, Counsellor. A dynamic helpful, personality with affable approachability, bright spark.

Cathy Vesio Di Bella – Wheelz- In – Motion Body Culture/ Self Development School Youth Program. Founder/ Director/ Co-ordinator. www.wheelzinmotion.com.au

I came to know Cathy as a marvellous and exceptional woman, female leader, inspirational in her own right, who I admired in her tenacity, persistence, determination and all round wonderwoman.

Nicole Splatt – (at this time was employed with CD Chapple Labs who made our DVD's, she since furthered her career in other employment and I congratulated her for that during the time). I had never actually met Nicole who was part-time employed but Yolande always in charge at the office explained to her about the program. Every now and then I also spied Peter their Boss, who always said *What a good job your doing, keep it up!*. *Special* in her own way, Nicole suffered debilitating MS – Multiple Sclerosis and yet was highly functioning as a Sales Production Assistant and Business Owner of Jumping Castles. Her story tragic, yet also amazing and so many obstacles that she overcame, pushing forth, despite her obvious disability to continue to break the mould of what people with disabilities can achieve. She suffered many struggles at the hands of her illness and it also prevented her from having children but she described her *Fur Babies* as if they were her real life children.

Les Twentyman – OAM/ Teacher/ Director/ Founder- Les Twentyman Twentieth Man Youth Foundation. Having the unique pleasure and privilege to be permitted to interview him in person was an experience I will never forget and it gave me another appreciation and personal insight of the man who I revered as an advocate and crusader for Youth and helping them become their best in their lives. His effervescent character, enthusiasm and passion for his cause and for kid's rights, spurred me on further with his genuine conscionability and down to earth common approach.

Brad Felstead, Founder/ Director – Felstead Education. VCE program developer/ Author. www.felstead.com.au

And the list goes on as the movement gains momentum

Disc 5 – October/ November 2015.

Wesley Chamberlain 23 – Videographer Teen Talk, Actor.

Zoe Guild 24 – Promotion Teen Talk, marketing Graduate.

Lynette Fernandez 25 – Teen Talk Promotion/Personal Assistant/ Assistant Producer, Fine Art Curator Graduate.

These are fabulous youth and outstanding achievers. Lynette was my right hand woman/man or wingwoman. Meticulously organized, perfectionist and efficient, completing most tasks with ease that I challenged her with, always non –stop on- the – go, somewhat of a miracle juggling dynamo, a bit like myself. She occasionally made me dizzy with her at the speed of light approach and I worried for her spreading herself out so thin with also other myriads of projects she was also involved in, that she might be going for a train wreck, if she wasn't pacing herself or took at least a breather within 24 hrs or was to focus more keenly on less commitments but those she enjoyed more and with those concentrating, and achieving even more, rather than drowning in so much superfluous stuff. *Don't sweat the small stuff.* Eventually as I suspected and I tried to give her a hint at times from my own experience, it's very hard to make everyone happy all the time and give your all, and you have to chill, burnout ensued after her invaluable service to Teen Talk cause of many months, but she was very passionate about Teen Talk like it was her crusade of destiny, she conceded defeat and decided she needed time out. To me she was like a hybrid of Beyonce and Cher with a sprinkling of Road Runner beep, beep.

Fiona Summons, Dyslexia Therapist / Remedial Dyslexia Therapy Practitioner- Alison Lawson Centre. www.alcv.com.au What an admiral lady, changed her career and life around because of her son's Dyslexia, searching to the ends of earth for something to help him? Another Spectacular devoted mother, to name a few. Her equally adorable and bright student success story, Lisette 15.

Priscilla Monea – Business Owner/ Hairdresser – Lumiere Hair / Life Coach. Self – made woman dynamo who would never surrender to anything or allow anything to beat her or keep her down.

Dr. Helen Grogan – Medical Practitioner/ GP Western Suburbs. Those very rare BFF's that you have a lifelong bond with since primary school, we went to Genazanno together and could almost read each other's minds. They stick by you through thick and thin and are almost unpoisonable by outsiders.

Lou Smarelli – Prelli Tennis / Director/Owner. www.prellitennis.com.au I met him briefly but he sent shivers up my spine with his MC like presence and business acumen and donated a Racquet to Teen Talk as a gift or prize we could use for the kids to participate in social media activities or raise funds.

Kristine 13 and twin Alex, who's mum I met coincidentally at the Magistrate's Court about our minor matters, as I don't make a habit out of hanging around courts, if you know what I mean. We began chatting outside the courtroom, I was working on something for Teen Talk in my lap, she asked what I was doing so intently – working on a project for young people. She told me about her teen twins and the AVO she needed to get to protect herself and them. She said Kristine sang very well and she was in several school theatre productions. I invited her to bring them both for an interview. I have to say that Kristine's singing, personality and voice absolutely floored me with disbelief and incredulity.

Julia Wake- (Teens Connect Social Program/ Autism Spectrum/ Special Needs) Principal /Teacher Secondary School, Northern Suburbs. Mary Meade Catholic College, South Morang. It was actually Lukas 14, who was courageous enough to be interviewed about his Autism and perform a comedy show at the same time, a flip of the coin type of persona, who you could see never sucked lemons, *always look on the bright side of life dadum, dadum, dadum, dadum who would try to make the best out of every situation* (like the guy who sings *rid'in shotgun in the hot sun)*, who introduced me to Julia Wake, who was her student and part of the program, whom I then also interviewed about her amazing good work.

Tess Lawley 24, General Manager – Syn Media /Radio. Syn. org.au I immediately felt affinity for this ballsy type young girl, I don't remember if we met up at RMIT when I was picking up the equipment for hire or at the station when I was delivering the program each week or through other students.

Alex the Film Tech at RMIT, was also an avid videographer in his own right and trying to start up his own business, a fun loving cool guy with alot of smarts in his own way would refer me for suggestions for interviewees and give me filming tips, he liked the sentiment behind Teen Talk. We would chat and banter about film and other stuff as I was loading up the equipment in the car. It was also a round about this time that Alex alerted me our website had been hacked.

I said it's a wonder that our website was hacked with us being such a tiny cause and concern, I thought we were virtually unnoticeable but as I later discovered we were underground but we were also an Indie Power for those who followed and believed in us. Hacked! what us? Why? by apparently somebody from Canada with a message spread across the front about some actor from Canada. Go figure that! Thankfully the little pixies in the network computers at Melbourne IT fixed it soon after.

Kathleen O'Connor 23- Journalist /Reporter. Go – getter with a wholesome moral compass a bit like Louis Theroux.

Medhi Vieville 24- Videographer Teen Talk/ Journalist. His interview was heart wrenching about a growing – up post pubescent life changing experience. He truly wore his heart on his sleeve.

Melanie Mitsios – Intuitive Medical Practitioner/ Quantum Medical Intuitive Graduate. melanthia@optusnet.com.au She described her own health struggles and how she battled them.

Carlo Spada 24, an endearing spectacular personality but what would he be when he grew up. He lived in a Peter Pan, state of mind he chopped and changed study degrees like a fashion show. I wondered how he might turn out, when he eventually grew up and knew what he wanted in life? His sister Milena 18, another chip off the old block, all round intrepid sportswoman of the year.

November 2015

Tull Suwannakit 35- Director, Malvern School of Art/ Master Fine Art. Tull was a break the mould kind of guy. He wrote his own children's books and illustrated them. He was a creative SNAG! I found this gem for interview when I was spruiking for small business sponsors for our TV ads.

Bonita Sorrentino 17- Face of the Globe Teen Pageant Contestant – *Beautiful without and within.*

Alexander Nicou 22, Apprentice (Bandshop). He seemed to me a type of upstanding young guy that could weather all storms and would never be a fair weather friend. Highly ambitious and not a bit shy about it. He would have his own type Bandshop someday sooner rather than later.

Nino Zidov – Futsal Plus, Director/ Coach and his protégée Johnson 16. Both fierce about Futsal Football, and equally up to the pace of the frenetic task. I think I encountered Nino outside at the Coles, Malvern where he was putting up his own promotional leaflets for recruiting youngsters to become Futsal players. I asked him about it and I asked him if he would like to be interviewed.

November, 2015 / A Place to call home

It was about this time that we were filming in the front room lounge of my tiny flat, which was almost directly across the road from my Mum's house where I was between places most of the time. It was the first time I had ever lived on my own for a few years before it was sold suddenly like the rug being pulled beneath me, it was unfortunately a reoccurring theme of my brother's to sell my properties when he was in financial distress rather than his own first, so I always ended up skint.

I began the very first filmings at the CWA, Toorak as an experiment in their so called craftroom/ Board Meeting room, which was well lit, spacious, sparse of extraneous stuff and minimal. I would rent the room per day either Saturday or Sunday on the weekends, it however became prohibitive because of the expense to continue it for a long term basis as there were so many other expenses. So I deployed to start filming at the flat with a huge bay glass window and door at the front of the lounge room. The lighting was very good at some times of the day but atrocious at others as I found. However, we made do and people were in and out and going to the bathroom upstairs etc. it was to say the least exquisitely invasive to say the least for an essentially private person like myself. This was about November, 2015 and not long after I attended a Christmas Party and came home late to find the flat had been burglarized mainly tech stuff, liquor and Christmas presents I received valuable personal effects and jewellery. The side kitchen door was ripped off it's hinges and damaged. I had to ask my brother Freddie to help me get someone to temporarily board it up, those years before this there, no-one in the four flat tiny complex had ever been burglarized before till now. I reported it to the police but of course nothing ever came of it. *Why are people so unkind?* –Kamahl.

After that horrific incident I decided it was not safe to film in my own backyard so to speak, it was a bit too close to home as they say in the classics. So back to the drawing board again to find inexpensive and safe venues for hire for the kids, crew and families and I would have to get insurance. Needless to say I researched a string of family -friendly places, churches, schools, halls, meeting rooms, studios and alternative gigs. The most user – friendly and economical of these were among many, we continued to do repeat filming gigs. The Uniting Church Toorak, Christchurch South Yarra and De La Salle College, to name just a few. We also held our Pilot episode film launch at the meeting room beneath the Toorak- South Yarra Library where we were attended by at least forty guests. I also researched places with easy parking for the parents and central to CBD for access.

Disc 7 – March 2016

Dave Matheson – (Bandshop). Recruiting manager for Bandshop. What a larrikin character with his corkscrew curls bouncing about his forehead and neck. This previous rocker in a band of his own, tough pretence on the outside, with marshmallow bursting at the seams, sometimes they played several gigs in a night even further the way across town. He was too cool for school.

Mitzi McRae – (Melbourne Djembe), which shows white women can dance. A teacher with a heart of gold and a smile wider than Texas with wild, wild hair, brimming with. Brimming with effervescent, schweppervescence and full of bouncing beans. She was Australian who became fascinated with African Culture in her travels and met her husband who played African Drums as she danced merry Djembe to the beat of the African Drums.

She performed her dance routine and some drumming tips at her interview like an audition.

During this time an outstanding talent wrote an enthusiastically keen email letter to me, introducing her various spectacular skills, requesting to volunteer for Teen Talk. her name was Elisha Mc Call, with a humble demeanor but in a few months that she volunteered, accomplished veritable wonders. A case of under promising but delivering her offerings successfully above all expectations. She also produced and edited by herself the first official U- Tube Trailer for TTP, posted on the 22.02.2016.

A Fortunate Life!

Madeleine Parker- Hill 21, Graphic Artist animator extraordinaire who forged through her young years being the survivor of bullying.

Jess Blackman 24, who had memories of moving house so often the thought of it became terrifying.

Manav Lakhiani 19, already a mini type of blockbuster type Film Director attitude presence. Current - Farm to Fork Director/ Producer (1060 Productions) CH. 10 TV Melbourne, 2021- 2022.

Sally K Hughes, (Flute/ Music Instructor) an acquaintance that I met through my other Bestie and partner in choreography crime, Masako (Saki) Todo who wrote and choreographed Bollywood come Japanese Films Fusion and led me through the maze of the film and TV industry always talking about the Sharks and she wasn't talking about the *Great White* either, who would have been so mild in comparison to those guys. Saki loved all music, especially classical and found Sally playing flute at the Buddhist Temple. Saki said you must come see Sally Play at her concert group, so we did and brought her flowers on the opening night. The three of us often hung out together and I asked her if she would like to be interviewed she leapt at the idea, and had left her so called boring family in England to find adventure and the meaning of life having lived in Portugal for years and eventually landing up here in Melbourne. She explained she was an officiate of the The Royal Colleges of Music something like that anyhow, probably that's a huge deal but she sometimes lacked confidence in herself. During filming, I think she played some excerpts of Misty and The Pink Panther Theme.

The Hack Ensemble Band – Arthur W, Charlie W, Michael C, Harry C, Christian U. This eclectic group of amazing music performers captivated me with their own original and upbeat style. I encountered them at the CWA Annual Fair and they were finishing performing and starting to pack up on the front lawn, I asked them for their details and if they would like to be interviewed. The most spectacular sounds came from Charlie (a pretty red haired girl, bumpkin looks like Pippi Longstocking) who played the trumpet and it worked for their type of band sound. The others in the band, with their own various stories of disappointment, survival and perseverance for their craft.

It was at this time that I also came to know Carole Overmaat, the producer of Dutch TV, we would bump into each other at the station dropping off USB's for the upcoming programs weekly. We chatted briefly about each other's programs, she said her son Joerie was 14 and might like to be involved. Joerie engaged with his very charismatic type of personality, cheeky cutesy look and demeanor. I think his aspirations were to become an actor and he was in previous bit parts of Kid's Films. I think it was much later than this time that CTV31 said they were going to transitioning online. As we now know it never happened and they are still broadcasting in Melbourne to this day.

At this time however, I asked Carole about how the kid's could see themselves on TV as it was repeats on Mondays at 7.30 am of the Fridays program at 4.00 pm or 4.30 pm for different seasons. Carole suggested she was also already currently broadcasting on Foxtel Aurora as she was also concerned about the stability and the goings on at C31. She introduced me to Dirk Jonkers, the manager of the Aurora Channel, as a stepping up to have the program broadcast on Foxtel Aurora for the kid's to watch. I provided Foxtel with several months of sample episodes for them to trial and Dirk was excited about the program and said the ratings were very good from the start, but then when it came to entering an official contract with Foxtel there were obvious issues and concerns, so I pulled the current programs from continuing to be broadcast after many months and would then cease to provide further current episodes or content. It was certainly a part of the territory business of the TV and Film industry which I tried to shy away from it being fearful and because I disliked it intensely and not much from unlike the downright nastiness, cattiness and bitchiness people describe behind the scenes of the Fashion and Modelling Industry and the stuff that goes on as well. This was unfortunately not to be the only isolated incident of several dealings within the Film Industry that left me with a disgustingly bad taste in my mouth like from bottom of a cockies cage.

Disc 8 – April 2016

Bonita Sorrentino 17

Alex Nicou 22

Simon Katthagen – An upcoming middle aged videographer and easy -going fun loving type of guy who had done some collaborative work on a break on some music videos, when he was younger. Was now a statistic of young people on the scrap heap, never realizing their careers in the Film Industry, chronically unemployed and doing all manner of odd jobs to support themselves somehow to survive in life. His flopsy ginger hair that plonked on the side of his face in a loop and the deep purple psychedelic T – shirt with the plastic motif on the front of the Teenage Mutant Ninja Turtles.

Disc 9 / Disc 10 - May / June 2016

I think it was a previous participant interviewee who during their interview described their involvement with *High Voltage Rock School.* They said they attended there after school during the week and performed jam sessions at primary school halls at different locations around Melbourne. The Director/ Founder/

CEO of the school, Danniel Smith, a previous band rocker himself and they coach upcoming potential band kids. Hugh Matthews – Music Instructor at HVRS gave up part of his weekend to be interviewed by us and some of his up and coming young, raw and extraordinarily talented protégée bands to assist, help and supervise their performances. *Rage of Consent and Three Quarters Blue. Suffice to Say that you'll have to watch the episode to comprehend the full magnitude of each of their groundbreaking stellar performing experiences at the performance hall, on the day at the SAE QANTM – Creative Media Institute, South Melbourne.* They were double – billed on the same day with another group of exceptional music and singing performing youth talent from the *Hobsons Bay Music Academy. Mary Mastos Director/ Owner and her assistant Music Teacher/Instructor Irene Attard.* I found these gems in an advertisement in *Melbourne's Child.*

I was fortunate around this time to also have the acquaintance of Ms. Nik Ranger, she was originally from somewhere in the US. It might have been she emailed me with her interest, answered me from an ad for a Social Pages Promoter/ Internet /Blog/ Mail Out or on The loop or such or I bumped into her around the same circuits or was recommended. She was a master artist of many talents in her own right and dressed like a hybrid of an Emo and alternative punk style. I saw the signs as I went through that phase at Uni myself. With the Chunky platform black trendy square boots, Black Capri daks, screaming T –shirt and cropped Leather Jacket with studs. I already felt affinity with her and her dark short boyish style cropped hair. She said she was intrigued by the program and believed in what we were trying to achieve. She said she wanted to help by editing her own U-Tube Preview short video for the program herself with her own thoughts and ideas, which she did, and the crew all agreed it was sharp. The Teen Talk Official Trailer No. 2 posted on U - Tube25.11.2017. She performed some of her own filming and also borrowed some clips from us to do the short. She was also a Designer, Photographer, and Graphic Artist with her own business, she was a very accomplished and highly motivated, ambitious and achieved young individual for her age. I was in awe of her. She later on helped us with doing some Filming gigs but she always declined being interviewed for some reason, her excuse was, she was shy about her work, but who knows why? Anyway she was no cause for concern and certainly an asset to our group and the ongoing crew.

I explained to her about an incident not long ago that caused me distress, that I rented a once – off Professional Studio for a day's shoot in Collingwood, it was very dim and dingy upstairs a narrow flight of stairs, seemed a bit of a sleazy type area and parking was extremely difficult and sparse. I unfortunately hadn't researched it much or other music acts mentioned it to me because of the hurry to get interviews with the bands and music acts before they became booked for other stuff. Suffice to say the day was uncomfortable for all involved and I did not think it suitable for kids or families to attend there either. I thought it also a bit pricey due to the lack of the amenity of the place. But the worst of it all was that we were accused of causing damage to her Black Backdrop and on addition to the cost added on the cost of a whole new backdrop being purchased and installed, it was obviously opportunistic and extortion. I was incredulous but there were so many witnesses to verify for us the further cost could not be proved, as I was always meticulous on shoots to be careful.

Nik said she'd either studied at SAE QANTM before or was involved with their projects or both. She explained to me that we could request to use their Performing Theatre Hall, where there were already lights / Audio and all the accessory computer gear except for our own Filming equipment to be supplied. In exchange the supervisors/ instructors/ teachers would request work experience mentoring of their graduate students for a specified number of hours to complete their course. I contacted Christopher Mc Alpine via email at the SAE QANTUM Campus. I signed an agreement about this and it was a mutually agreeable arrangement. So I mentored about seven students over several months a music act Filming was done at the hall and other shoots their students volunteered to come and work for me at different gigs or at the other venues, churches etc. I also felt like I was helping them graduate and facilitate their career, so I was pleased to do it. I spoke to two supervisors who I was interviewed with for my suitability to mentor, I gave them some of our Program Merch Samples, we got on very well and were on the same page, then I later once appointed had to fill out reports, do comments, sign-off on their hours and timesheets and mark them with scores on tasks, duties and their demeanor. It was a lot of unpaid time consuming work but a labour of love, and I thought it quite a serious responsibility for their future lives. There were a couple of students who stood out Alex who also aspired to do comedy gigs and Ale who suffered mild Aspergers, who was a bit of a cevante in she excelled in some areas but struggled with some tasks. However she was very determined and would keep working on things until she eventually succeeded. She would correct her mistakes and often came up with lightbulb thoughts. Ale was so thankful and grateful to me for helping her, during her mentorship, she happily voluntarily continued to do both Filming shoots and editing work, offering herself from time to time and also some minor tech tasks gladly even after she graduated when she was not yet employed or in between jobs. I hoped for her she would eventually land a job that she really liked, enjoyed and was confident about and felt secure about her abilities, like she was happy and not fearful at the TTP family shoots because she so very much deserved it and was determined and worked at it despite her issues.

The others were average but they were capable and performed adequately. There was a student however who was very difficult not only personality wise and behaviour, attitude, rude, disliked by the others, lazy, disrespectful, argumentative, oppositional, defiant wouldn't follow direction, disruptive to the others working, who was coasting along doing the most minimal work possible. I pulled him up gently a few times but he became aggressive, I was forced to mark him down as it was not conscionable I thought to allow it to continue further and unfair to him in the end for his future career. He became antagonistic towards me and then made a complaint to his supervisor that he was being unfairly treated and discriminated against. Was I expected to turn a blind eye? No, but that was what he thought and planned from the beginning to pass without doing the work or hours. So needless to say, I was not reinvited the following Semester to continue mentoring other students. However, I stuck up for my rights and besides it would not have been fair to the other intensely hard – working students to pass him on a whim and it eventually would plague him on somewhere else down the track perhaps causing detriment to his career with prospective employers and workmates. It was unfortunate as it was a good reciprocal opportunity for the students, my own crew to learn. Oh, well as they say it was fabulous while it lasted and also a shame that it ended so soon for us all.

During this time I told a favourite elderly patient about the project, John Newby what a fabulous person, always giving me tips, suggestions and describing his life experiences and being tic about it. He was a very upstanding, helpful, friendly, fair and community minded person and was a ten pound pom from a long way back when he immigrated with his Italian wife in their twenties before kids. He belonged to Neighbourhood Watch and also managed and compiled the monthly Newsletter. He said he was so happy with my patient treatments and that he had improved so much during the years as my patient that he wanted to help me and thank me for my service. So he invited me to attend and said come and get your car plates changed at the neighbourhood Watch Initiative day and he said you perhaps could film it with the Sergeant's in Charge Permission if I ask him for you. It was all teed up by John, and so we attended there on site filming in front of Dan Murphy's, Dandenong Road, Caulfield. Here my plates were changed and some Families and kids were interviewed on spec ad hoc with written permission forms filled out about the day's outing. It was fun and a bit like doing a Vox

Pop, *Sam Newman Street Chat*! We also interviewed Senior Sergeant Craig Fitzgerald (Victoria Police) and the top brass at Neighbourhood Watch which happened to be John and another of my coincidental BFF 's who was also a patient and was also a close friend of John's, Norma Flowerday and their supervisor from NW, Fred Callaway.

Disc 13 - Sept. Oct. Nov. 2016

Welcome to Healthways

I think I originally Contacted Nina Simcocks from the Healthways Recreation and Aquatic Centre, 1-11 Arcade Road Mont Albert North about some gift vouchers for the kids and perhaps as a sponsor. Nina was very friendly, captivating and efficient in her manner being interested in the possibilities of their being involved in this opportunity being so kind and more than pleased to be offering assistance to the project in any way that she could with her co-operation and facilities.

I went to visit the centre and spoke to her in person and she gave me a guided tour of the facilities, she described the struggles with her husband Mark's chronic heart troubles and that he'd been forced to slow down and give up his work. They re -opened up the centre together and started a new life forward, it was a very touching story and were also in the process of doing improvements to the centre. It was a family – friendly atmosphere and the staff, were very engaging and helpful. She emailed me that same day with a mock up of the generous vouchers for me to print out and gift out at the Filmings.

It turned out not long after the visit that I organized an onsite shoot of the centre for an entire episode and also was lucky enough to interview an integral staff member Lauren Holcombe and two teen sisters who were part of the regular visitors to the centre for Youth Gym Workouts and workshops. Lauren also showed us another string to her bow with be also moonlighting as a Musical Theatre

Performer. We prepared commercial shorts for the episode and also they were sponsors in some other episodes.

Raising additional funds much required to fill the gaps plagued every step of the way for us and Lynette and the then crew would have meetings to discuss ways to go about this constantly. We thought about have a Pre Xmas Event at the centre in November, we would organize catering, have a raffle, “The Winterfriends Band “offered to play for us that afternoon, Nina donated the party room and the Bowling Lanes for the afternoon, I would pay for the Filming equipment and crew. It was a bit of a shame how it bombed it was so promising and everybody who contributed and donated their hearts were so much in a very good place that it was so heartbreaking for me to be so disappointing to them all and there very kind efforts to assist, volunteer, offer gifts and be sponsors. My patient and friend Lizz, who was doing a patisserie course at the time who I asked if she would like to cater for it as she would do some baking from her home kitchen. She said she would have but was too busy at this time but instead was kind enough to have donated a tiered fruit cake for us to raffle, among other catering donations from Toni Gledhill Catering and Runaway Cupcakes etc. It was mainly fingerfoods and things that needed a short blast in the microwave, Coles Malvern donated the water and soft drinks with a voucher they gave me from me asking their manager at the store. I also contacted the main Melbourne offices of Sunraysia and Capi, as I was already a fan of their fruit juices and drinks, whom both donated several cartons of every flavour to choose from, for all tastes. I collected the drinks, after work late on friday afternoon just before their 5 pm C.O.B from their respective warehouse and offices in South Melbourne and Port Melbourne. Not knowing these areas well, I became a bit tangled up with some streets, but arrived thankfully at my own pace just in a nick of time as they say nonetheless, and it was with a huge sigh of relief.

The sheer irony of it all and disappointingly was that I was photographed by a Traffic Camera on a main thoroughfare and also ironically there was a huge transport bus in front of me of a few metres caught on the image and so as it turned out, I contested it, as it was a faulty Traffic C Camera. What went wrong? Several of a series of unfortunate events, we failed to ticket the event as we kept it FREE to attract more families it was a FREE bulkmail out list invitation of more than 1,000 participants, families and those who were somehow involved with us and a gold coin donation at the entry to the Bowling Lanes with the first bowling game included.

Most people were sympathetic about the cause and they rallied around us. The divine retribution that no good or kind deed remains not too long unrecognized was yet once again reinforced, that quashed the disappointing doubts and I was justified in my faiths beliefs. As I had currently unfortunately become sceptical due to some other unexpected disappointing occurrences.

It all defeated us that particular day, it was maybe also to close to Xmas with people having other festive commitments and events, It was the hottest, most high humidity suffocating day that I could remember for years since. I remember I was already exhausted from packing the equipment and catering that mid morning. The car hot and steamy even though the air con was on full blast and I worried about the food melting and becoming spoiled with the long trek of a drive there in traffic. Sadly it ended up a poor turnout of about thirty people, the band came later and played a few songs but the turnout couldn't justify them playing more than a spot. Most disappointing for me was that the head videographer of my two roving crew failed to show up, who was usually reliable and responsible, and the other arrived late. In hindsight if I would have known enough then I would have tried to unpack and film it myself but it soon became evident that it was all futile there was nothing much to film anyway at this rate and those camera's are quite heavy too. It was frustrating but Lynette and I our absolutely fabulous volunteer helper crew kept up a smiley face and my faithful friends some who donated goods and services and who all turned up for a short while to support me and the project event in some way.

I hadn't countered on the packing, unpacking and packing of Filming equipment, food, drink and catering utensils, to be so time consuming and cumbersome, such hard, heavy and tiring work. The upside was the catering was incredibly yummy delicious, sorry to those who missed out, the entertainment was great with the disco music blaring out from the speakers after the band packed up. The raffle gifts I would have even kept them myself as they were all worthwhile goods, products, gifts and services. The bowling lanes kept constantly occupied even after the freebies were all used up and for those few who attended a most amazing time was enjoyed by all. I put it down to a learning experience but there really was no-one to blame that not enough people attended to have bothered to do all that organizing and hard not earned slog but as a monetary loss and as once a promotions person said to me it was like *New Websites that were retail shops with no people or following that clicked or entered them and they were empty with no number of likes on them yet.*

So many talented, promising and interesting adult youth also passed fleetingly through the Teen Talk revolving door of temporary volunteer workforce crew. Of these was Jaime Salcedo – Lopez 30, backpacking and doing Videography/ Photography gigs whilst he was travelling around Australia, he was an amazing all rounder with a flair for also graphics and design, an artist in his home country, was it Spain not unlike Mehdi Vieville 24 from France who also was doing temporary Videography and Journalism gigs as they could get them from *Starnow and The Loop and Artshub such websites.*

Of these in the very early days was Cathy Speed who was almost graduated Graphic Arts and already designed her own letterhead for invoices, such a spritely enthusiastic motivated young thing who got the brief right off the bat for our original logo that I imagined in my mind for our TTP Brand and Gabby Lovell who designed our official printed letterhead and business greeting cards. Vicky who designed our Teen Talk DVD cover and who landed a professional job the day it was printed.

Miles Eves- an up and coming small businessman Videographer. Tim Silvey who was also studying who created his own music u tube videos, who was born with a foot deformity which was not properly corrected at birth so he suffered with a limp gait and would describe the pain in his leg and feet as tortuous after a long days shoot but he was so determined and committed to being the best he could be.

The spectacular Phil Pryor who was current and a new graduate of Animation College who designed, storyboarded and created the script for his animation Teen Talk short to describe our program aim. He was a bolt out of the blue and the boy next door pin up poster, who was out of work but was bartending to make ends meet. He described his desperation to be the best he could be and prove to his Father that he could make it being an animator as a proper living making money job which he scoffed at and that he would make it and break it into the industry no matter what it takes he said to me to prove him wrong. I was all for this fierce attitude and he delivered in spades like a true professional.

Disc 15 – Oct, Nov. 2016.

There were also some outstanding adult youth participants Gaby S 17, Tori Biggs 25, Stephen Kokkas 18, Kaitlyn Thomas 15 – Singer/ Performer and Bully Zero Ambassador, Tyller Fischer 16 struggled and battled with anorexia and won through focussing on her music and song writing and met her bestie Yarden R 22 who came with her to be interviewed, sing and play their original music. Lindsey T, 22 who I saw feverishly working on something in the South Yarra Library whom then sat to eat her vegan lunch in the foyer, we struck up a chat as she offered me the armchair lounge she was sitting in as I was loaded up with bags with hard drives and other essential Teen Talk Travelling paraphernalia as I would have meetings with editors, students, volunteers and my temporary crews at my pop up office in the foyer of the Library, I became a permanent fixture there for some years.

Lindsey described her challenging life growing up in Wagga Wagga and how she was determined to turn her life around to prevent from becoming another statistic of the failures in their unfortunate town.

Mary Charlecrafte – 3ZZZ Radio Broadcaster (Assyrian and Women's World Programs) who headhunted me for a radio interview about some friend telling her about Teen Talk who was having trouble with her teenage children. This fascinating woman who lost her husband at a young age with a baby daughter and being a single mum who this was her passion project like my own and she was a professional pathologist until she retired recently due to a heart condition and was forced to ease up. We instantly recognized a common thread in each other with so many things in common. I went on her program Women's World and then later on we swapped and she came on Teen Talk for an Interview and brought her nephew who edited the Radio Interview for us to broadcast on Utube etc.

The Dynamic Duo of two sissies as Jess Mauboy would say. Jenny 16 and Kira M 17 (Chadstone Redbacks Lacrosse Club). These girls would surely become female leaders and conquer the world.

Disc 16 – November/ December 2016.

I don't remember how I got onto or came to discover the Flamboyant and out there Besties of Judith Field and Marissa Pinkus both teachers who were crusaders of public speaking for youth and speaking confidently. Consumate authors of Speech Matters and Direct Speech Books and audio. It might have been the about the time when somehow Aly Walsh also entered my social people network sphere of the Teen Talk project. Aly and I would bounce off each other, she knew loads of kids Authors as she published books – Aly's Books as she tried to turn her passion and her own kid's books into a going concern. I would in turn interview some of her current authors of kid's books, and people who helped kid's with their innovations and ideas. She also introduced me to Jade Purdie, (Be Dance Fit) Owner and Jazz Dance Instructor extraordinaire whom her daughter attended dance lessons with and so we made a great collaborative team. I interviewed Jade and Aly's daughters dance troupe and performed a segment of their dance routine for us choreographed by herself.

I thought back and look how far we have come, we were filming for a season of 13 weeks broadcasting, every day of a month for every three months season, it was about four times a year. We would shoot a full day usually Saturdays occasionally Sunday depending on the venue and the availability. It's amazing what you can squeeze into a day! Probably more than what I would have done on the usual part- time clinic days during the week, but it was all the organizing that took time.

Sometimes students were not available for shoots due to various reasons, exams, projects, holiday's, other temporary gigs, and part-time work and such like. The show must go on so trying to find alternative crew was on noticeboards, Mandy Crew and Production Hub or via referral network.

It was a long way away from that First Introductory Pilot episode where I lashed out on all expenses, Salon Mio for hair and they especially called in and booked Celeste Jackson to do a make-up session for myself to do the few minutes Introduction that Costa insisted would engage more interest. We catered a take –away lunch for the participants and families. Costa also filmed me at a Park, with a small waterfall and arena in the background somewhere around where he lived, around Heidelberg way and those areas. He was like a strict Ballet Dance teacher with a big stick tapping the parquetry floor, he made me study and repeat the introduction until it came naturally to me word for word until it was perfect with my natural expressions. He filmed in the Studio behind his home where it was in a room with a black screen and an adjoining editing suite room. Costa, also made me do several days editing in a row for a weekend, like documenting the times to start and stop at clips. He said this would take less time and cost me less for hours that he would charge and be a faster process. He also kept saying we need more money all the time for further episodes and that I should be spruiking philanthropists, it was a fact however, but I thought there was no time to concentrate to get funds now, we must just film for the time being to have enough episodes for the 13 weeks.

Since that First Episode I decided to be like *Sia* and try to maintain my privacy and work professional. So I would do the interviews of me behind the scenes asking the questions with hearing my voice. The Programming Manager at the time was Tessa Irwin, encouraging and she believed in our program spurring me on to continue at least for the First Season, then later came Caitlin Jolly. They created a couple of commercial shorts for the program from our First and second Episodes clips. Kelly Hildreth was the Manager at the Ingest Department with his other associate Matt Karimicolas who worked different shifts.

During 2016- 2017, it was also Lucy Nicol - Programming Manager West TV Perth, who was taking a hiatus from study to work and gain experience in the Industry, who contacted me about our program and found out about it somewhere in the *Buzz Feed* around. She was ecstatic and excited to have us on board. Later then came Angela Alberqerque. 2016, it was suggested by Carole or someone that if CTV31 Melbourne was in danger to shut down due to lack of Government funding like some other states previous that C44 Adelaide was another option for broadcasting even though it was interstate. Allan Lawson said to me he thought the program would engage the Adelaide audience. The Oztam ratings were successful in all states and the demand to provide more programs fierce during this peak time for TTP.

It was during those times of student unavailability that I needed to fork out more for Professional Videographers or those students who were graduated and or were starting out their business. It was either Autumn or Winter that I became introduced to Scott David Lister from those Crew Sites.

We met at another of my Pop – up temporary offices at the Palace Como Cinema Centre, Lounge upstairs, if the Library was closed or it was in the evenings. He brought his sidekick sometimes Film Partner with him, who was totally dismissive of the program and what we needed as a reasonable price for the shoot. Scott however was totally the opposite, he believed in the value and potential of the program concept and was humanitarian in his sentiment that he wanted to be involved in. Scott eventually decided to do our shoots himself without other help to keep episode costs down for us.

Scott, with an automatic affable way about him and a sort of band member/ creative look. He was average build, clean cut for an artistic type with his sandy hair in a shoulder length hippy ponytail. His eyes were peaceful and calm yet busy scanning all around him and taking it all in with interest.

He reminded me of *Peter Pan* but in a good way, like he was grown –up and sensible with clever outstanding business acumen and attractive in a comfortable homey kind of way, easy going but with a young heart and innocently child like in some other ways. I felt he was meant to be for us.

He was bursting with enthusiasm and excited for the project and asked if he could redesign the Introduction and logo, without charging us more for it. I was ecstatic about the thought, he produced a wonderful collage of participants from previous clips and an even more captivating opening. He would go above and beyond the call of duty for us, doing his best work and was kind, always being professional and treated us in this manner even though he would not be paid as much as other gigs that would of assumed preference if he was available and not already booked with us.

We collaborated well with him and the volunteer crew and we worked together for many months and then he became involved on and off helping us with graphics, commercials, promotions and uploading of our First 8 Discs of four episodes on each, onto the Amazon Books and DVD's site. He was fun loving and adorable in our Teen Talk Family and he revelled enjoying working with the kids.

He introduced me to a whole new underground world of Teen Pop Culture which I never before knew existed prior to this and learning about stuff with him on the shoots and the kids always updating me and giving me a micro view of an insight into their lives in this generation and their Teen Lives now. Scott would talk about his favourite films *Godzilla's*, I thought to myself, these St. Kilda Types, my forever after that all time favourite *Game of Thrones, Vikings, The Handmaids Tale, Riverdale and games like Magic the Gathering, Mindcraft and Fortnite etc.* His favourite topic was what would happen to *John Snow*? So eventually I made time to watch GOT – Winter is Coming! and was compelled after that to watch every episode glued to the TV sitting for binges unlike myself usually.

Later on he was also interviewed as I invited him. He confided about his time at school being bullied because he was a creative and not Sporty or Academic at his High School which was preferred. He spoke about a previous girlfriend who had sort of led him a stray and wanted him to move abroad. He decided against this for some reason as he felt there was something NQR and then met his supportive current partner who was a school teacher or some such and more aligned to his needs. He was a great asset to the program and shoots always went smoothly even if things went wrong.

In our volunteer crew at the time and assistants to the producer included Elizabeth Bridges – The Artist – Musician she coined herself with a very simple postcard that introduced her business. She was currently studying at Monash Caulfield doing Graphic Design and Media Studies. She was like a *Polly Anna English Doll* with that long wavy auburn hair to her waist like from *Picnic at Hanging Rock.* Her petite stature, with the delicate peaches and cream cheeky and freckly around the nose complexion. She was also a musical performer of I think it was mainly Violin but also Piano. Bursting at the seams with notions and carrying her notebook with her everywhere as inspiration struck. She was a terrific crew member until a bit similar to Lynette that there were too many fingers in the pies.

It was also during this time that sometimes the participants came early and lined up to be interviewed waiting for sometimes up to hours because sometimes their siblings or friends who came along with them also asked and wanted to be interviewed which I would permit if they were keen and they were with a family member or guardian or old enough to sign their own consent form.

I felt obligated to start providing food and drink so they were comfortable and not frustrated having volunteered their time for us or given up hours of their precious weekend to be at our filming shoot. I began spruiking around usually on my own but sometimes the assistant producers helping me for people to donate food and drink to our film shoots and being in the credits for it as other services. I asked the local Sushi Gallery Owner Tony, where I often before bought Sushi and Tempura Udon Soups for myself and my brother Freddie, if he would donate the unsold items from Friday avo to us. He gladly provided whatever was there by the time the shop closed and for special shooting and other events I always bought catering platters from him. Others soon donated offers too, including Brumby's Malvern, Hootsen's, Coles Malvern with sometimes vouchers for water and soft drinks etc.

The Innovative Teen Talk Crew started doing the Mail Chimp Newsletters and the Blog, and suggested content for the social media platforms and posted our clip videos on u tube and the Photos I began to take myself on the shoots as a visual record of the participant attendances and that were also posted on the Social media sites to share with other proactive, helpful content. We were rocking the boat, and we began to get more than 2,000 followers on our Newsletter mail list, the Teen Talk Vibe, I began to image that were becoming a real concern and could be self – funding. There were so many crew involved in these activities from single tasks to being months or years on board the TTP train with us, that I wish I could remember them all here, but they know who they are. Some that were integral in these activities that I recall which means they must have gave a significant contribution of days, months and years from about this time on Amber Bourke, Jialu Xu, Yolanda Zhang, Katherine Oleinikov, Jarrod brown, Michele Bolzoni, Yi Yi Wang, Xu Lu, Sandeep Threstha and so many more besides. It was a constant revolving door of media content Bees.

This also reminds me of all those essential trades and services that were involved in Teen Talk from the beginning and that were fully paid but that negotiated on minor discounts for the cause to help.

Accurate Art manufactured and provided the Teen Talk Filming Banner, Gifts for the Volunteer kid's ie. Black Rock- the wrist bands, Wizards T – Shirts, National Pen, Action Printing – Bookmarks and printing of DVD inserts, Dynamic Gifts International P/L – Buttons, Lapel Pins, Wristbands.

Some of our log lines were, *Make your wish upon a Star, Your Star Sparkling Bright in the Teen Talk Light, Make Teen Talk Great in 20 – 1 – 8, Teen Talk – Get the Low down on the real Deal, Teen*

Talk - Can you handle the Truth? Teen Talk – the Good, the Bad and the Ugly, Teen Talk – get your fix.

Hugh Fraser Allen who's dad scoffed at his son being a computer nerd tech no hoper, and hoped that he would someday get a real paying job. I was introduced to his father somehow in the neighbourhood, maybe at the local coffee shop and he owned rental properties in the area. I had thought about doing a Pop – up filming shop, but the cost was prohibitive so I stuck to the Churches. I explained to him about the project and his nephew was interested and came to be interviewed and he suggested his son for Internet, technical and computer help, which I paid him for as he needed work and money, and he set up all the Social Pages and all the links to the Teen Talk Website for us.

Disc 16 /17– November/ December 2016.

Maddison H 20 – *Maddie – Rose Music*, original singer/ guitarist and songwriter who came to be interviewed not long after she came out finally confident as being gay with her girlfriend Melissa 21. She described break out busking performers who she was a fan of like Tash Sultana and Chet Faker.

The fantastic wonder woman who is Deearne Louise Pasquali, who I don't remember how I found her but maybe through a student participant interviewee or their mum. Owner/ Dance Instructor of Deearne Louise Dancers. She devoted her life to teaching youth to jazz dance and perform especially with classes for Autistic, Mentally Disabled and Challenged kids. She came often weekly up from Yarram for her passion classes in Melbourne or the other way around I am not sure. She attended with a couple of her students and their mum's and choreographed a filming segment for their dance.

Liarra Pulle – Leech 9, who's mum was referred to us by someone she said at the Radio Station she broadcasted out of. Liarra was already a success with her own Radio Shows- Dramatic Duo /

Double Trouble Show. Phoenix FM Radio. We reciprocated and her Mum also recorded her interviewing me.

Mr. Leigh Gridley, from Oakleigh Grammar School who was involved with previous TV projects who was now a Yr 8/9 Teacher – Science / Leadership and Yr 11/ 12 Media / Psychology / Career Teacher for their Media Program. His charges that were interviewed were those particularly interested in Media or a career in the Film Industry and he said he was pleased to be involved in the project so that his students would experience it First hand to be on the set of an on site real TV film shoot. The Principal Mark Robertson was also very supportive and visionary about the Filming day at the school.

Aly Walsh from other good reviews about us from other authors soon offered up more Children's Authors wanting to be interviewed, Dallas Lyons – The Night Guardian Protectors from all things scary. I was now no longer needing to put us out there but people and kids wanting to be interviewed then came to us in droves.

Samantha Napier – Book, Stage and Screen Radio Show – Wyn Radio, whom I also swapped interviews with who also created u-tube content and described to me The Rosie Project about some guy alphabetically dating who made the Film then later wrote the book, a bit similar to myself. She juggled home and work plus the Radio show and her four boys and her partner included in here.

Claire Jensen of the Teen Style Initiative, who was an awkward Teenager being bullied about her looks and style, was a bit chubby with glasses dork, who then created her own Style. Styling and Coaching Youth, about their personal looks, style and fashion. She gave workshops and also private personal training on these, also organizing Charity Fashion Shows and providing some of her protégées as Youth Models for the shows to gain experience and confidence in themselves to project and create their own personal style and flair to be proud for others to see and be an example of what can be achieved for their future goals, potential employment and personal life success improvement. She sadly described a boyfriend who stood her up because she was too fat for him. She said it made her more determined from then on to become the best for herself in her life.

Disc 18 – February, 2017

Margaret Wozniak 12, then star quality already an amazing talented Singer/Keyboards/songwriter. *Fall 2018, Fourteen 2018 and her start up songs, West Side Love.*

Andrew Gason (Founder New Civilization Builders) – It was a pleasure interviewing him, about his traumatic upbringing, going down the wrong path and becoming swallowed up in Criminal activity at a young age. There was a dawning toll of the bells moment that he said he was arrested and he knew he was in a bad place and it would only become worse if he continued and didn't change. He then thought he would like to help other youth who were straying down to a dead end lifestyle. I think he was involved in the building trade and would help youth get back on track with their lives.

Scott David Lister – Director and Teen Talk Camera/Editor/Sound Designer.

I was also dating sporadically during the busy Teen Talk years and I would be either on Phone Dating or meet people's at the Singles Dances around the place before the Covid put a stop to all that. I think there was Mez's Lifes a Ball events. That's where I met Howard and might have danced with him, we then exchanged numbers. I might have lost my phone or some such after our initial chat. We went on a few dates coffees, dinners. I described my project to him and so he also gave me a sample of his project which he expected to become the next best thing to sliced bread in sales. It was a concept of a message in a bottle – Send A Message kind of like instead of a Postcard, it was an actual flat plastic bottle with a paper message inside and with a greeting sticker on the outside with the address label on the other side. He was trying to get approval at Australia Post and other stores. His business Subaqua Photographics, he also created fridge magnets and other types of tourist stuff. I invited him to be interviewed to help his business and explain the Send A Message to our viewers. In turn he provided me with hundreds of Send A Message memorabilia with the Teen Talk Logo, fridge magnets and buttons. I'm not sure what the arrangement was but I certainly paid for most of it and maybe he gave me some of the message bottles for free. We broke up after an argument about a dispute of his bill to Teen Talk which somehow expanded dramatically after the interview.

Sara Saunders (Children's Author: There once was an orang-utan...) this teacher and Climate Change activist and concerned parent for our future kids world, describes the impact of a sad face.

Lorraine De Kleuver (Children's Author: Adventures of Felix and Pip.) This graceful retired lady describes the trials and turmoils of her younger life and her love for Geelong and Great Ocean Road.

Disc 20 – March, April, May 2017.

Rosa Angelone (Children's Author – Rosa's Adventure House) this middle-aged lady beaming with radiance and personality taught pre- school kids and made up a story with role play and actions.

Circus Latino – Gustavo and Cecilia Barrales, this cute as a button husband and wife team with kids trying to reinvent the Big Top for this generation's youth including Tech and live at their own circus. I saw their pop –up circus advertised on a billboard not far away, on the way to drop off USB's /Hard Drives and pick up the Teen Talk Discs DVD's duplication, Dingley. On my way back, I stopped by for a visit and went around to the open caravan office as they were closed that weekday and peaked my body around to see Gustavo. I described our program and explained about it and asked if they would like to be interviewed, he said on weekends they could not leave the circus site. I then said what if we do an on –site shoot of parts of the actual Live Circus. His eyes lit up and he was excited about it.

I then went about organizing this easier said than done task that I set the mark very high for myself. Equipment would be different and roving, lighting and especially audio interference might be an issue. We'll I thought well try our best, I think we filmed the performances and then after interviewed each of the Circus Participants on their vacant stage later with our banner behind them. It was a very long day after the afternoon matinee show and after a few hiccups with the lighting we were off and running.

Hardikumar Patel hard working Pharmacist by day and aspiring side hustle videographer. He was sensible, pleasant manner and an accomplished Videographer and Editor, with Bollywood looks. I felt reassured that he was up to the challenging task at hand with Jarrod Brown who were a perfect match together, Jarrod stayed with Teen Talk on and off for our duration from whence he started with us. With his cheeky look and Denise the Menace baby face smile of Radar O'Reilly. He gave me a copy of his project film DVD that he made for his exams at Uni. It was called Two- faced, I actually watched and quite liked it for a novice Director/ Film Maker. Jarrod was pleased to help us from time to time especially at times when he wasn't working with a myriad of skills I was to discover way beyond Camera and Editing. He was also a great graphic designer, internet and digital creator. He designed our Teen Talk Posters, created u tube shorts and designed an intro for potential acquisition broadcasters, he collaborated well with Hardy and many others on significant contributions to TTP.

Not surprisingly with these consummate all rounded up and coming Entertainment Industry professionals both episodes from the shoot turned out so much more than I would have hoped.

Circus Latino - Gustavo and Cecilia Barrales

Circus Latino - Chavella feni, Ricky Aes and Maria Avaschova.

Disc 21 – May/ June 2017

Elliot Kerdel – Teen Talk Camera/ Editor/ Assistant Producer / Social Media/ Light Bulb Thinker. This unassuming, innovative, visionary and insightful young man, who fancied himself a kind of Conor McGregor – Dolph Lundgern type. Worked in the family business from teenage and Camera/ Editing were side hustle pocket money. He edited videos for US basketball games and sports. He was an avid Basketball Player in his youth but sustained a severe injury to his ankle which plagued him and he was unable unfortunately to regain his prowess and prior player status. It was a shame because he was passionate about it and it also helped him with his severe Depression at times as a type of self – therapy. He described his mental illness as rearing it's ugly head already as a youth when he became suddenly burnout and overwhelmed with working, studying and juggling his sports and side hustles. He was fragile to these relapses he explained from time to time. He often willingly attended shoots, helping out in whatever way he was required if he was available and not working for his parents. He asked me about his ankle and I gave him a FREE consultation at a clinic appointment and reviewed his medical imaging from after the initial injury was incurred. I advised him on therapy, protection, strengthening and prevention. He attended with his best friend and was very grateful of the help. It was a terrible shame after many months working and collaborating with us that he suffered a breakdown doing an upcoming episode edit that was required to be completed by another editor. I wasn't upset with him but wished he told me sooner instead of suffering in silence and trying to plug away at it regardless perhaps I could have found an alternative solution if he shared it. I guess he was maybe embarrassed and he tried to skim over it that he couldn't perform and didn't want to disappoint me. I felt for him that this thing came suddenly out of the blue to plague and undermine his usual outstanding capabilities. The best however gift and compliment that he was to bestow me with was his Captcha of the encapsulation of Teen Talk, *It's kind of fun to do the impossible – Walt Disney.* I was in awe that he admired me and saw me with my epiphany in the same light as Disney.

Live RSOM – Real Songwriter's of Melbourne. I began at some stage to receive newsletter emails from this concern, about their gigs and events which I think they must have been passed on through the grapevine from another performer I might have interviewed prior, to promote upcoming talent. I thought it might be an idea to Film a Live Gig of theirs at a Hotel, The Worker's Club Bandroom, Fitzroy and interview a few of their star performers. I would repeat myself again to say that these onsite gigs were challenging in more ways than you could imagine with also unprecedented issues. You'll have to watch it to understand. The interviewees however were real pro's and good sports.

RSOM Participants – Rachel Costanzo 20, Tanya George 23, Angelica Bredie 20, Aimee Chambers 22.

Disc 22- June/ July 2017.

Amanda Lecaude – Organizing Students. This intrepid mum who saw the need to help struggling students, get out of their losing rut. Finger on the pulse type of lady that takes no prisoners. Studious looking for her part and I think she went to France and married him to then return home. She brought with her a couple of her many student success stories as a testament that it works. An outstanding pair, of exemplary youth were Felix and Brielle, like a shining beacon in the night, I hauntingly remember her rendition of the lyrics of *Elton John's – My song written by Bernie Taupin.*

Artika Singh/ Amy Hayashi – Behavioural Autism Therapists. (Global ABA Consulting.com). After, having returned from a study trip in Canada, where they had learnt many of their skills together.

I saw their pamphlet at the local library about their holiday theatre program for dysfunctional kids.

Disc 23 – June/ September 2017.

Andrea Toronyi – At Dance Instructor. This young and dynamic dance instructor/ business woman and her protégées. She was highly refined in her dance skills until she suffered a severe injury which cut her brilliant might have been career short but she with perseverance, she recovered and was determined to not let it beat her but instead to push though it and reinvent her body and her life. After a long and painful rehabilitation to regain her strength and sharpen her known skills, she opened up her own dance school – At Dance. I could see her student Siena 11, passionate and totally enthralled in her method of teaching from the interview and how she described her teacher's enthusiasm for her craft.

Xavier Alexander 18 – Actor/ Drug and Alcohol Addiction and safe partying, crusader and activist.

Dylan Gleeson 20

Happy 18th Birthday Sabena.

Disc 24- September, 2017

Matt Schenkel 21 – Sub-Zero Sound / Sound Engineer SAE Uni/ Bass Player. Enterprising, sharp as a tack, I think I was lucky enough to get onto him because somebody else who was going to do audio, couldn't do that day so they referred me. He reminded me of a sensitive werewolf if there is such. I think it might have been our regular audio (almost graduating) final year student, Nicholas Aristia who after doing many of our shoots assisting Scott and may be also Lyndon Johnson – (Khaotic Studio Production) Audio Engineer/ Sound Recordist/ Boom Operator, preferred audio to camera and gained enough experience to be confident to do then do the audio for Teen Talk by himself. Quirky but professional Lyndon, I used to laugh because sometimes I couldn't remember his name and I would say to the crew, what US president is that audio guy named after? Franklin? Lincoln? He said he mainly worked on films but at times was involved in some TV programs on Channel 7.

Nicholas Aristia, was an instant Teen Talk Project fan and would offer to be a minimal paid volunteer student for almost every shoot except if he was on other shoots or doing exams/ projects and such. He turned up every shoot without fail and would help in any way he could but his interest was audio. He was intense, with his cheeky boyish looks and heavy thick dark rimmed glasses, and his wanting to gain as much experience as possible with Teen Talk and soaking it up like a sponge, like a child determined to master a skill at all costs. He explained to me that he came from a good home in Indonesia and that his mother wasn't approving of his career choice as I discovered was sometimes the theme for some of these Asian students who were torn between what their parents wanted for them and what they thought they wanted for themselves or at least wanted to find out.

I thought Nicholas very entrepreneurial and with good business acumen sense. He was helpful and friendly and collaborated well with crew members on a lot of shoots and defended me at times a bit like being his own mum, when we dealt with rarely a few rogues, know it all's, disruptives and lazy losers who came into our Teen Talk Crew family, which were usually once offs anyway or fill ins for other students who also might have forgotten other gigs or their projects. He was always very respectful to me and would listen to my advice and experience if he wasn't sure, with faith in me. He came from a business minded family it seemed and his Mum felt disappointed that he wouldn't have a real job money making or career profession on this wild goose chase in Australia. It was all the more reason he was determined to prove her wrong and succeed no matter what on his own merit and become something for her to be proud of, which I will confidently say that I am sure he did. He graduated later that year and his Uni Film project was shown at the Astor Theatre with other students and it was called Psyche, I spotted him some money before for a donation to help make his film and in return he gave me a T- Shirt and invited me with tickets to it's premiere Uni launch. I was so chuffed thinking about his achievements during his time at Teen Talk and we helped make him.

Julian De Boers – Si Fu (Wing Chun Bing Fa Kung Fu Academy), Martial Arts Chief Instructor. His partner Sophie Archibald – Si Mo, Women's Self – Defence Chief Instructor, who also provided a demonstration. I found this fierce duo, on the noticeboard of a pamphlet at the Uni where I hired the equipment every weekend during our monthly shoots for the season. Traditional rumour was that this martial arts was invented from several martial's for a girl to seek revenge on her previous cruel master/ fiancée who she trained herself up, dressed as a man and defeated him in battle.

Xavier Alexander 18- Actor/ Anti – Drug and Alcohol and Safe Partying Activist.

Perial Welch – Senior Nurse/ Psychiatric Assessment Manager – Specialist Dual Diagnosis. I won't give too much away about this fascinating lady and her extreme reminiscences of her previous work. Retired and suffering some severe chronic health concerns imparts her knowledge and experiences. She attended with a close friend who suffered severe bouts of mental Illness, also being her driver.

Happy 18th Birthday Sabena!

Disc 27 – Dec. 2017 – Jan/ Feb. 2018

Naomi Manyok 20, Actor.

Emmanuel Yoong Zhang 24, Songwriter, Singer/ Guitarist, BeatBoxer and pin up boy heartthrob. Describes his ultimate desire of the dream to make people feel and bring passion through his music. Emmanuel came to us through some other Asian students and friends. During this time as it happened, there were most of the students in the crew team were Asian Connected and were highly efficient and worked together with extreme smooth operation like well oiled clockwork machinery.

Nicholas Aristia, Emmanuel Yoong Zhang who after his interview also volunteered to help us on some of our shoots and also edit a few of the episodes he was involved in and a few after that. Jin – Camera/ Editing. Victor Ng – Camera. Jialu Xu and her bestie student friend, from Uni Yolanda Zhang Editor/ Assistant Producer would turn up together on some shoots and also either would attend if the other couldn't in their place. Alice, my favourite editor, who's boyfriend found her TT.

Jialu originally came to me, saying she liked our project and believed in it with all her heart and soul, asking me if I would be kind enough to be her mentor for her work experience hours at Monash. This cute, waifey, petite, Asian girl who was very humble, unassuming and talented but lacking confidence would attend almost every shoot without even asking her. She obtained her work hours and I completed her excellent report, signed her off and she graduated deserving high class honours. She also continued to help out on the shoots voluntarily assisting Camera, Audio, Assistant Producer, Internet – Utube, Social Media, Newsletter and Senior Digital Content Creator for Teen Talk for some time until she returned to China. On her return the following years, very competent and ready capable to accomplish almost everything, Jialu and I seemed to have an understanding that she would almost anticipate her tasks and knew what she was required to do without too much explanation, as if our thoughts were automatically linked. We were a very great team together and together with the others it was the Teen Talk Peak. She concentrated these times on the honing of her TTP internet skills as she was juggling other part- time work and her steady live- in boyfriend. Of course all of these high class quality students would be offered without question a referral/ recommendation or official referral letter of recommendation with the Teen Talk Letterhead.

Jialu Xu - Current, Obtained her Master's Degree in Film and TV 2022 in Melbourne and now working for a Film Distributor.

Maddison – Rose 21 (Maddie – Rose Music), who was interviewed before on Disc 16 and returned to give us an update on her progress in life, struggling to keep herself an original music performer and what it was like after her coming out after this time, deciding on a career turn detour, which will be a curious surprise to you when you watch this episode. She performs her own original songs.

Oakleigh Grammar School – Student Media Group of 2017 followed in the steps of their predecessors last year. Eight inspirational students, each with their own unique message. Principal – Mark Robertson. *Merry Christmas and Happy New Year, December 2017.*

It was the end of the filming season for the winter 2017 and most of the crew were my Asian Connection, I promised them the weekend before that since that we worked so well together, that I would shout them and buy them a dinner out for all of us together. The early winter mornings were gruelling for me and my arthritic aches and pains, but also the evenings became dark before we finished the shoot and sometimes we were still packing up and loading my car with equipment, banner, and all our accessory gear, as it was already dark and dimly lit in the church carpark. Thinking back I wonder how I managed, but I was driven by a force that compelled me to push on.

That final Saturday of the Season, the last interviewee hadn't arrived so we started packing up and it was starting to get dark, I said we'll go to the Dianty Sichuan, Toorak Road, South Yarra it was up the road from the Christchurch shoot. I think we were Jialu Cheng, Yolanda Zhang, Nicholas Aristia, Emmanuel Yoong Zhang, Li Jin Soh, Soo Wei Yun and maybe one or two others, I don't recall. Sweet Emannuel was living with his Auntie in Melbourne and he was struggling to make ends meet, so when he wasn't at Uni he was almost always doing Uber Eats shifts, but he came to dinner with us. Soo, who volunteered as Assistant Producer. Jialu and Yolanda were also sometimes assisting on Camera/ Audio. We ate a number of mixed dishes on the turning table and drank Pu Er tea. They mistakenly brought us a wrong dish and I all I remember Soo saying as she sat next to me *turn a blind eye,* but I couldn't as we hadn't ordered it and nobody really wanted it, so they gave us another in replace of it. It was a fun evening and we ate our fill of everything on the sumptuous plates and drank pots of tea chattering to each about the shoots and what they would be doing once they graduated from either side of the huge round table above the buzzing hum of the other patrons. Sometimes funny things happened on the shoots, like the time we locked ourselves out and started late, the baby screaming in the changeroom upstairs, the rap dancer who's microphone flew away, the cameras that failed to turn up and so I would have to fill in, or Jialu and Yolanda took turns, the guys who kept arguing, moving the lights around and it wasn't an improvement until I said stop and film because the volunteers participants were outside in the freezing cold waiting for hours delayed.

It was coming up to Christmas 2017 and I always gave food gift hampers to the Christmas Editors because I knew editing was difficult, labour intensive and tedious work from my own experiences before. I made up these gift bags of all kinds of goodies- mince pies, chocolate, festive biscuits, slices etc. I would see them to collect the final edits for the end of the year and they would transfer them from their hard drives onto the USB's for me, at my make shift pop up offices in the Library foyer and upstairs at the Como Cinema at my favourite spot the round Diamond Padded, Gold Velvet Lamme seat and what I termed the continuous Love Seat because it went all the way around in a huge circle being seamless with no apparent beginning or ending, it just went around and around and around.

Some of the most high quality and professional student editors who were with the program during these years and I might not have known some of them as well as those students and videographers that also attended shoots – Katherine Oleinikov, Jarrod Brown, Michele Bolzoni, Jialu Cheng, Alice Cheng Chi Man, Yolanda Zhang, Andrew Ernest Cox, Alyssha Atieh, Odin B. Fernandez, Phil Pryor, Isaac Bowen, Talib Raza, David Michael Kirkwood, Theodore Sariklis, Jean – Beau Villagonzalo, Matt Richards, Roxanne Mousallem, Jaewon Yun, Nathan Armstrong, Marius Myburgh, Joe Chamsay, Bill Chute, Melanie Potts, Joel Quick, Emma Rose Sullivan, Emmanuel Yoong Zhang, Michael

Le, Melanie Martini, Daniel Jong, Quin Fen Ong, Gabriella Asti and sorry if there were some I have not included, you'd know who you are and of course your lasting legacy is on the Teen Talk Disc credits from the Intro –pilot to Disc 41, the last.

The Animation Sequence Saga

Phil Pryor who was working on the animation sequence was almost finished with engaging, Talib and Isaac to help him with the audio as he was getting ready to go to the US for a well deserved holiday break. He was also preoccupied with juggling his part-time bartending and some other projects as well. The storyboarding was done after several versions of the script and it was the audio that needed recording, synching and tweeking. Synching audio to an animation script is very tricky. I thought of him as reminding me of a Keith Urban type with his still waters run deep, methodical approach to challenges and so he carried on with it regardless without a thought of concern about it. We were all time poor and juggling a plethora of other stuff including home, work and free time. So Phil said he would get an actor himself to do the audio script as they would be more experienced. It was unfortunate because I don't know how he found them but he would often say he posted stuff on internet noticeboards and forums and found that it worked and with exchanging information. He played it to me at the Library and we tweeked the animation script a bit, but more concerning to me was that it was spoilt by the actor's heavy accent, this foreshadowed the animation and distracted from it. This was not the only problem, I wanted it to be authentically an average Melbourne family sounding voice. It sounded far from that it almost sounded professionally exotic weird and wrong.

This disturbed me no end and I said to Phil it has to be changed, he was concerned he would be leaving soon and who would finish it. I wasn't being fussy it sounded crap and didn't at all match. Talib suggested we re – record it with somebody else's voice at the upcoming shoot at the Prahran Church, St. Matthews opposite the Melbourne Polytechnic. Talib and Isaac attended the shoot for this sole purpose. Nobody volunteered, Talib and Isaac thought it best If it was my voice, so I could be tracked down if it needed further changes or re-recordings, they turned out to be right anyhow. Not a person to shirk their duty, It was done, however there was so much background noise and interference that although my voice turned out ok despite having never having any acting experience whatsoever it was again overshadowed by all the background noise and crackling. Talib and Isaac tried to work on cleaning it up and synching but they were both becoming frustrated. To me it sounded an improvement but it was still overall crap. We all agreed it was not passable at all. Phil said there was nothing for it but to re-record it at a quiet place, so he came to the Library with his portable recording stuff and we tried the usually quiet foyer beneath, but maybe it was the school holidays and there were alot of kids and people there all bustling about busily noisy.

It was either late Winter or early Spring and still very bitey cold and considerably drizzly and wet. We drove to Malvern Library as we there were some quieter nooks there but it was the same, we were exasperated. What would we do, there was no time after this day? So we landed up deciding not to be defeated recording in my 4WD in the heavy pouring rain, doing several takes so just in case. It actually turned out the best of the previous recordings but still there was that whoosh of wind and pitter – pater of rain on the car roof, windows and doors. It was so exhausting and repetitive. We called it a day as it began to get dark and the long afternoon had dragged on, fraught with mishap. Phil, Talib and Isaac all worked on it in segments but if only we could keep the rain for the intro. Phil departed and said he was sorry there wasn't time for him to do more. Talib and Isaac, said they were stuck and neither of them could afford the time to re- record again somewhere else even if it was quieter location. So I paid them and relieved tem of their duties it was obviously beyond their scope.

Not giving up, I thought this was a super hero task and required a person with many more years experience and professionalism, even if it was costly to complete, it could not be left as it was a waste on the drawing board so to speak and all the time and effort and previous hours that went in.

I posted on the The Loop, Starnow, Crewhubs and Mandy, I'm not sure which one now anymore. I interviewed several semi-professionals for this specific task and the most sensible with many years music synching, animation and creating his own music and photographic and video sequences, on his website and running his own small business from his Uncle's home. This was Mati Obrzud, he assured me, we could fix it and that he often fixed audio things through the years and it was his job. I'm not sure if he learned his craft here or in Poland, but he had a full mini - recording studio set-up organized in an insulated padded tiny room behind his Uncle's house. He said he'd been in Australia a few years now having escaped from Poland for various family reasons, I did not enquire any further as he seemed sad about it. Mild mannered, small stature, slim and a quiet, unassuming efficient type with his razor cut stubble white blond hair and peaceful eyes but at the same time with an agitated face, that could have been mistaken for a cute singer at the Eurovision contest. There was a huge aquarium compared to the room size with all manner of exotic looking fish, angel wings and fancy tails, bright stripy colours and spots.

He said he would try to work on cleaning up our disaster final original first with his refined equipment at home. He said it was true it was impossible to clear up those pesky wind and rain sounds that hovered and yet were too minute to clean up at the speed of sound and light. It would be best he said to start again from scratch even though annoying, more delaying and more time consuming. I believed him because anyone that lived and looked after their Uncle couldn't be too bad after all. All I recall was that he lived hours away, and that I drove up there after morning work.

I drove and drove and drove seeming never to get there, it was the longest drive I'd done in years to visit someone or go somewhere. They were doing road works on the way so there a slowdown of about half an hour from destination. I know it was this side of town and I thought maybe towards Dandenong way, and when I arrived at the suburb it was a maze of cul de sacs and no through roads. It was a majestic effort for me to have arrived there, so I was of course late and almost became lost.

He was anxious because I said I was worried to drive home in the dark and we already lost time. He said to be ready for a long afternoon. He locked the door behind this tiny room squeezed with stuff. I was a bit concerned but he saw my face and said don't worry, there is no time for anything but work. I giggled, of course I could be his Uncle's girlfriends age and dismissed any worrying thoughts on this. I rehearsed and rehearsed and rehearsed and rehearsed until he said now we are ready to record and record we did over and over and over and over again, until the words kept whirling around me. He tried all manner of different recording settings and he was like a possessed maestro at a piano. We never stopped for a snack or have a drink or tea, but I sipped slowly on my small bottle of water. I think he offered me a tea or soft drink as he went to make it for himself but I was concerned I might spray or spill it over his equipment or even choke or gag on it if I drank it too quickly or hot. It began to remind me of Costa all over again except that Mati was much more patient and kinder. The repeat of the exercise was almost military like in precision and he would pick up on the various segment and sequence bits needing to be done again and corrected, so he wouldn't muck up the rest of it by mistake. The only time that annoyed me was when he only took a break for a cigie. I hadn't known he was a chain smoker, at the interview, not having smelt it on him with my acute perceptive nose. Sadly it reminded me of my ex – Eddie, Sabena's father having to send him outside to smoke because of her Asthma and my allergies. For him he said it was habitual stress release. So we chatted outside in the cold and dusk, there he was puffing away quickly with a gasp to hurry. Needless to say I was done, and the incessant smoke made me, cough, splutter and draw breath. Somehow I managed to arrive home safe and sound that evening, short of a miracle to get back.

Mati said he would work on it furiously until he thought it was perfect enough for me to watch and listen to, and low and behold he delivered like a mad scientist who's test tubes were the rainbow. It actually sounded great and I was very pleased with the final result and so it aired after the Intro. You will have to watch it to fully understand what we went through to achieve the refined version result. It is called Teen Talk and is 3 mins and 31 seconds in duration on the teentakproduction.okast.tv streaming platform. I even forgave Talib who said he was responsible for the sparkly opening stars.

Disc 28 – Feb. March 2018.

Emmanuel Yoong Zhang 24

Tayla Clavarino 18 – Rythm and Blues, Singer/ Songwriter/ Guitarist from country Sale, Gippsland Victoria. She came in like a pink powder – puff, long - haired cupie doll and sang about coming home to a place where you always belong. She sang with such emotional swagger, believing every word.

Arnold "Trigger" 23 – Born in South Africa and his black funky spiky haired dreadlocks, with an amazing story about how he came to be Australia after a topsy - turvy childhood, what a character who dared to push the envelope being experimental and delving as an imaginative entrepreneur.

Disc 29 – March, 2018.

John King Jag 23 – Songwriter/ Rapper began producing his music from the garage of his home using unusual music sounds from 16 years of age. Tall and lanky his facial features lost in the black cap.

Emmanuel Yoong Zhang 24

Chloe W 8 and her Autistic sister Madeleine W12 are a double act, bouncing off each other.

Disc 30 – April, 2018

Harry Vidovic 18, an enigmatic personality that you can't help but like, but strangely shy in ability.

Catherine Kopec 18, Music Theatre Singer/ Actor/Performer and Monash Uni. Business student. This slight young *Jane Seymour* with the set of incredible billowing pipes and range to match her passion.

Kylie K – Volunteer Netball Coach / Hairdresser/ Netball Mum.

Evan M – Secondary School Teacher/ Looking for life co-ordinator. Navigating Technology, in schools.

Disc 31 – May 2018

Joe Hoffman 29 - Teen Talk videographer, quirky Englishman in Oz, bounding with enthusiasm struggled with keeping up at school and feeling lost as a child to upcoming aspiring Indie Director/ Producer/ Videographer and Photographic Journalist, who on his adventurous roving travels abroad met his American beauty of a girlfriend and who looked like he sprung out from the Blondie and Dagwood cartoons, affable and down to earth, fun loving determined to make it his own way.

Happy Mother's Day!

Matteo Mazzella 23- Smooth dark haired attractive reminiscent 50's rocker look, Animation Film Graduate, growing up in WA, with mild Autism issues. Imagined, Created, Directed and Produced his own animation *Learning Difficulties* inspired by a classic work *Dante's Inferno*, that captured him emotionally and whom he reinvented featuring his own little person's fears and life struggles.

Happy Mother's Day!

Jeffrey Li 12 - Original Instrumental Music Producer and synthesizer creative, plays his instrumental.

Maddie – Rose 21

John *King Jag* 23

Happy Mother's Day!

Naomi Manyok 20

Chiarra R 14, suffering with severe anxiety and having to learn from home, her colourful paint brush artistry an escape for her into her own fantasy world and cute fierce rapping duo brother, Gianni 9.

Happy Mother's Day!

Disc 32 – June 2018.

Matt Vaughan 37 – Kiwi Hawthorn Rugby Senior Coach. MV Corporate Health / Owner/ Trainer.

Alec Potts 22 – Archery Instructor/ Olympic Medal Winner and that you can do it, if you believe?

Joe Hoffman 29

Matteo Mazzella 23

Bonus - Introductory Pilot Episode.

Disc 34 – July/ August 2018

Solange Anglaret 29 – Author/ Model /Beyond Borders. Describes her own travel catalogue, with a chapter for each country and brings it to life with her tiny soft toy mascot in a literary *Travel Guides.* She talks frankly about growing up with plaguing food allergies in France and managing them.

Mish Arndt – Mish's Dishes Cooking School. Her ray of sunshine delight, cute as a button daughter Jamie 12, hip hop break dancer, humanity visionary about our responsibility to care for others.

John King Jag 23, Tayla Clavarino 18

Disc 35- Oct./ Nov. 2018

Charise Katz – Owner/ Founder/ Author, KML (Kid's Magic Life) Music Theatre Company Group.

It came to pass that my friend at the time Sally K. Hughes, whom I was introduced to by my bestie Saki. Sally said to me she had recently joined a Theatrical group, which she was composing songs for and performing her flute and singing. There were a few other Young adults in the group who were recruited on a semi- volunteer basis by Charise, and were also music performers and Theatrical Performing Artists, who were out of work or dysfunctional or struggling with mental disabilities and that were trying to stimulate and broaden their resumes by doing various types of fill in the gaps and temporary work. Sally was doing some few and far between casual gigs at the time at the time with the piano, and keyboards, I'm not sure at the Umbrella Lounge Bar with the Owner, man for all seasons Temo Zorella whom recommended her to Charise as another professional addition to her music troupe.

Charise contacted me through knowing Sally and asked if herself and her group could be interviewed. I thought this a cute suggestion and why not?, the more the merrier. It was very time consuming and arduous disrupting our kid's interviews routine but we interviewed them in about almost one to two days in duration. They brought their instruments, amplifiers and music rhythm desk to be set which was already hours in preparation itself without us even doing our own setup.

I felt an immediate empathy with Charise, a lady who was following her dream and passion, a person after my own heart and trying to turn it into a reality, a real tangible entity not unlike myself. She was however more canny and devious than myself in her work practices than myself and very sharp. As I have said before I loathe that side of the entertainment industry the ugly cockroach killer side, but obviously she'd already been involved in this industry for many years, so maybe she became that way out of necessity. She was also immigrated from South Africa within the past decade, I was kindred with previous South African Jews as I admired their determination, work ethic and nause.

Charise, who's fine features I thought similar to a Jackie Collins look alike, described how she began KML after divorcing and coming to Australia and developing a rather unusual chronic severe malady which went on for some years until it eventually burnt itself out of her she said. She was so weak and struggling during this time that she invented KML out of her imagination. She wrote stories about KML and songs to accompany them with visions of her theatrical show becoming mainstream. It's a shame but I think it was a bit childish for our modern day progressive kid's now but perhaps an even more daggier sort of version than *The Wiggles*, which I thought quirky and that my generation of little kid's would have liked way back then when there was *Adventure Island* and *Mr. Squiggle*. It was sort of that she missed the boat somewhere and was stuck in a kid's time warp of *Dr. Who*.

Daniel Amondola 25- Actor /Singer/ Musical Performer (alter ego Leprechaun at the end of the rainbow).

Roberto Socciarelli 30- Italian born, Drummer and musical performer, slumming it out in Oz.

Lachie Ryan 21- Puppeteer / Bass Guitar / Musical Performer with his own demons. (alter ego the puppet, Bentley).

Abigail 11 and Asher 9, delightful young bright enthusiastic children who's Auntie was Charise and she trained them up, honing their gaining experience and involved them in her musical productions.

Sally K. Hughes- Flute Player/ Singer (Alter ego grieved Maid Marion Maiden playing and singing)

Fran Brett 20 – Pianist / Keyboards.

Bailey Dunnage 21- Guitarist.

Ryan Rhys 25- Singer / Musical Performer.

Naomi Feng 25 – Make –Up Artist, Behind the Scenes.

Nat Limdasakul 23- Videography Editor/ B.A. Screen and Sound, Rogue Light Productions.

Encore - Judith Field and Marissa Pinkus, spectacular teachers and educators and their spotted purple mini dinosaur. Described their own out of body experiences which were chilling to hear. Marissa, who also learnt firsthand about the brutal cruelty of apartheid after hiding a black SA. Children's Authors of Speech Matters and Direct Speech giving kid's an edge for Audience Speech.

It was about this time that I thought about presenting a weekly Friday night event music session at the Umbrella Lounge with a small entry fee going to the proceeds to help supplement the ongoing TTP expenses. Temo although a nice person I found, trying to do everything himself but there were areas of the Lounge's operation that suffered badly because of this and negotiating terms with him was an absolute nightmare. He was so set in his ways that his obstinacy caused early abandon of this very short lived experiment in collaboration between his cafe world and TTP music sessions, almost before it started at the first opening night and the second Sunday's following musical performers failed to attend due to having difficulty negotiating a fee for their music performance. Alas Teen Talk Plans and opportunities foiled again due to circumstances out of my control.

Disc 36 – Oct. / Nov./ Dec. 2018

Yvette Dunand – Owner Costume Wonderland. (Alter ego The long eared White Rabbit). What a vibrant real life version of the animation of Alice In Wonderland with her flowing long blonde hair, fantastic figure, sparkling smile and eyes. Her real life adventures were going to her best friend's Nonna's house as a young girl and the Nonna providing them with baskets of left over materials which they designed and created their own dolls clothes. Later on she became involved as a make-up artist and costume designer at Channel 7, NSW and after that flash of lightning ride deciding to settle back home and open her own costumery shop.

Marcus Traumanis – (Alter ego The Mad Hatter, who was the Long eared White Rabbit's sidekick.) Marcus was Yvette's current boyfriend of several months, her partner in Alice Wonderland crime. His story about from being a small boy superhero to wanting to be a super hero the best ever cop. His career dramatically and what seemed for him overnight cut short at an early age due to illness.

To my ecstatic and astonished surprise they turned up a little late but in full make –up and costume regalia and I was gob smacked with delight at the sight of them and she went to so very much effort.

It was kismet that not long after arrived some young cutie pies that I interviewed previously in 2016, who happily returned for an encore interview, Naomi 7 and her little brother Kingsley 5. Naomi made a beeline for the white rabbit and the mad hatter, and it was as if they like suddenly stepped out of a picture book with Naomi so adorable in her mini Alice outfit in the front and the long eared white rabbit and mad hatter hovering above her. It was perfect and absolutely meant to be, happening at that moment in time.

Gail Barton – Owner/ Teacher (Gail Barton Art Studio). This brave, determined mature lady was mesmerizing with her blonde bob locks and rosy, beaming with health complexion. With a familiar face that made you think of Olivia Newton – John and that you immediately loved and you felt you were at home and comfortable with. Who knew that she was in Cancer remission for about a year or so longer? Actually I knew but not much, as my clinic patient

Peter used to go to her classes after his appointment with me. He said what a breathtaking teacher she was and that he learnt so much. I often said to him over the years, that I was looking for a hobby outlet funnily enough as my earlier life was always revolving around mainly work and it would be a good social and creative disruption. So her name and number were on a slip of paper on my desk always on the, to do list of non- urgent. I might have in passing said to Peter, do you think Gail might like to be interviewed even I haven't met her yet. She was beaming with excitement at the interview and I gained another dimension.

Candice Wong – Owner/ Teacher (Vibrant Art School). This cheery, young and vibrant adult just like, the name of her Art school. Incredibly grounded, dressed like she was at a country fair but exuding imagination on a mission to impart to her young students knowledge and another vision of art. She brought with her, three of her young protégé to demonstrate the versatility of her insightful mind. Erin 13, Tarika 12 and Ayma 12 all individual, and with their own style of artistry in their own right.

Jen Webb – Owner/ Teacher (Port Art Studio/ Melbourne Art Classes). This polished, and professional lady with a grand presence, meticulous in her detail with refining skills rather than the composition. Like an opera singer or fine wine that improves with life experiences and the journey. Her equally talented young students Eric 12 and Zane 12, their art, truly inspirational and fantastic. All very individual, unique and original ways of teaching art to students and the result is astonishing.

Susan Yarrow – Owner (Gourmet Kids Cooking School). Susan absolutely delightful with her joie de vivre and fun kids cooking experiments, there was a glimmer of Edwina about her from Absolutely Fabulous as she effervescently described the things the kids would create and her being lost for words for the kids that artistically put their own individual spin on the basic recipe and I smirked and chuckled as I broke in with *their own treasure* perfectly exact she said their own treasure and so was she I thought in that moment in my mind an absolutely exact perfect treasure that broke the mould. There were swords, wands, happy faces, butterflies, zoo animals, love hearts, lollipops and initials.

It's amazing what a coincidence that Sabena went to a Birthday Party of a friend of hers from Loreto Mandeville Hall at this lady's cooking school. She would have been about six or seven years old at the time and either during 2006 or 2007. She arrived home in a constant chatter about what she'd made and how much fun she had doing it. So busy and preoccupied with the horrors that were looming and lurking all around me that it went through an ear and out the other, other than she'd had a terrific time and thoroughly enjoyed it. I remember this was during this time because only a few months later that year indelible on my mind was that on the 13th day of September, 2007 when the trauma of Sabena being ripped away from us. From us being her loving home with myself, mum and Freddie, and her immediate family since 2002.

Of course this has nothing to do with Susan who I never met before as there was only just enough time to have dropped Sabie off inside the front door quickly and waved her off to pick her up at the end of the party. During these days it was rush, rush, rush, rush hectic all the time with no spare minute for pleasantries or saying hello to the other mums which was a shame they never knew me. It wasn't the good sort of rushing either but the desperate consuming type of work, home and court. I should have been paying more attention that busily distracting day to find out what she made and created at the cooking school her favourite things were in this order love hearts, wands, happy faces and butterflies. Sabie could always bring a cheeky smile to my face with her tiny fairy love hearts she would draw on the sticky note paper and hide them in precarious places like on my pillow and chair or in more blatantly obvious places for constant reminders or day to finds like stuck on with the fridge magnet with things like I love you Mum, love heart or Mum your the best, love heart and other endearing stuff like king Freddie's chair, sticky note still stuck to head of the

the King Arthur, GOT wooden chair in the Dining room love heart with an extra piece of sticky so it wouldn't fall off when actually the king might be sitting on it and the pictures of fairies for Nonna, love heart. I still get those pangs of that sentimental jibber – jabber that more often than not brings an instant tear.

Will Billings – Driving Trainer/ Instructor. This young man, was a bolt out of the blue, with his twighlight wild werewolf looks and his larger than life bravado and likeable naughty personality. He described his already short life journey as a horribly confused and tormented rebellious youth, who's on the wrong track life turned around when his Uncle asked him to help at his Driving School. He said it opened his eyes to invest his bounding energies into something worthwhile and purposeful career. He also dabbled and moonlighted in the Cosmic Rain Band and in audio and videography. He said he wasn't sure why he rebelled against his father who was a successful professional and was oppositional but he wasted many years of resentment on this, until now he was also studying law, happily married for a few years, least likely to commit with a number of little youngsters at his heels. Later on that year he would also volunteer to come and help us with the filming and audio of the Feel the Love Tribute Concert in memoriam of Steven Marshall White, a previous TTP interviewee and member of The Winterfriends Band which was held around June, 2018 as a cause event for TTP.

Disc 37 – Oct. Nov. Dec. 2018

Tamera Francis 21 – Teen Talk Social Media and Digital Content/ Communications and Management Graduate / Journalist/ Model with a presence and brilliance of something exotic and Sade, Smooth Operator coming out of Rio De Janiero about her. Something very sophisticated beyond her years.

In this Hallmark DVD there are also excerpts from the Feel the Love Tribute Concert of the Young Performers Competition who were judged and given trophies for the various top star performances, who were chosen by myself and invited to become part of the concert and the TTP star performers. Yuvaraj 16 and Bala Prakash 14, Tayla 14.

Margaret Wozniak 14 (Fall and This Time – Original songs). Songwriter/ Singer/ Keyboards.

Sevim 14, Caleb 13, Naomi 7 and Kingsley 5.

Lyla 15 (Seperate Ways – Original Song) /Acapella. Singer/ Songwriter.

Oakleigh Grammar Youth 2016 and 2017 – Mr. Leigh Gridley Yr 8/9 Teacher/ Co-ordinator / Science/ leadership. Yr 11/ 12 Media / Psychology/ Career Teacher.

Mr. Mark Robertson – Principal.

This was our second year of doing a shoot at Oakleigh Grammar, towards schoolies and the end of final term. In December 2016, we had done also a school tour of the grounds and the Year 9 chill out rec – room space, science lab., the Year 9 *Dreamcatchers* classroom the ceiling totally full and covered decorated with these lucky fluffy delicate ornaments the students made themselves. I think it came originally from a tradition in Canada from the native Indians there to bring good fortune. We were well organised, whilst Scott and myself filmed the kids in the rec room, the other camera began doing a roving shoot of the grounds and rooms, we then all went together on the classrooms school tour.

In December 2017, we set up in the school auditorium as the Principal thought this more appropriate, more private and less noisy. The camera on this shoot was from Feathered Films, a once off gig because most of the known crew were not available, but a few helpers. I remember us having to climb up several sets of narrow stairs to carry the heavy filming equipment but we were guests of the principal and so we thought we must suck it up and follow directions. It was long haul with the equipment and then setting it up onto the performing stage, and we were at least a couple of hours behind schedule the students were getting restless and there was schedule interference. The auditorium was difficult to shoot in because of the audio acoustics and the conflicting hall lights. It was an exceedingly tedious and laborious shoot, that we were all frustrated and exhausted by, having to rearrange lights, constantly check acoustics and move props due to also outside window light, some students schedules were disrupted, suffice to say we all finished very late that day. The highlight of this filming however was even though we filmed less students, the content was eye- opening and poignant. It was snap shot of their school life and some of their personal challenges. The most memorable of the interviews was a courageous girl struggling with Juvenile Rheumatoid Arthritis since a tween and it's drastic affects on her and another who suffered a without warning panic attack at school and thought there was something very severely wrong with her own health.

I thought about this girl with the sudden panic attack, who needlessly struggled with high levels of chronic anxiety at very minor or low exposure to a triggering stimuli, or exceedingly sensitive. Sabena was always a fragile and extremely severely sensitive child to minor emotional stuff which most of us *shake it off* like the time when her school friend called her stupid, who was surrounded by cruel older brothers who taunted her and she didn't mean it or when her friend went to another friendship group. She took these things very personally to heart and the depth of her emotion would sometimes last days and weeks about her brooding over these every day to day school stuff things. Would Sabena be suffering anxiety like this girl now or even worse still? It brought me back to that day of her traumatic sudden removal from the Family Court that sombre, dismal and miserable day. She was removed from us, her family myself, mum and Freddie and her school and performing arts friends. All those things she held most near and dear, that were most important to the cosmos that revolved around Sabena's fantasy world with the rosy coloured glasses and the sunshine lollipops. It was the 13th September, 2007 it was probably a Friday because we'd also been though our hearing from the day before Thursday and they'd most likely contrived to have her with them by the weekend. It was her birthday just about two weeks ago on the 28th August, 2007, she'd turned eight years old. That was almost 11 years ago now, and she would now be 19. The hot pink scooter with the silver and white tassels coming out of the handle bars like shiny streamers and the flashing light, it was covered in thick dust on the front veranda a constant reminder to me that she was not home. She had never hardly ridden it in those two weeks except once with her friend Sophie and me another time with me to go for a walk to park at the Primary school with the huge park behind, this is where I actually met Debbie Byrne from Young Talent Time fame who was playing with her own children in the park, we exchanged pleasantries as the children climbed the small rockery. How freaky and coincidental is that?

That day at the family court evil was plotting and without warning and unbeknownst and oblivious to it was myself, Sabena or my family. An execution of sorts, with innocent lambs lead to the slaughter. There was something of a sinister air in the atmosphere that day but I was still incredulous to the events that quickly followed in those few hours late afternoon on that dreaded Friday. She would not be coming with me from the Family Court that afternoon on that horrific fateful day. I think if we would have any of us especially my mum, of an inkling of what dastardly betrayal and evil treachery was to occur that day, Mum might have warned me to have kept her home but I obeyed.

Sabena as if we were going to a party or outing wearing her current favourite rosy pink soft wool hoodie with sparkle written in script on the front from silver sparkly layered sequins and her bottom frilled pink/ purple vertical tube striped Barbie type velveteen skirt, with denier thick white stockings and patent black leather Mary-Janes dressed up, smiling and beaming as if she was going to be in a photo portrait or something exciting like that. Sabena loved posing and role playing for the camera.

To me I thought this much worse than the stolen generation, they were removing her from her happy home, many friends and a good catholic school to go to a unknown scary life, far location, dingy flat and crowded public school. The separation anxiety almost struck me the next day, as Sabena and I were almost always inseparable like twin sisters except if I was at work and her at school. I suffered at least six months with severely disrupted sleep, nightmares and melancholy. I refused to give in to the anti-depressants they were pushing onto me always as an easy fix. For two reasons Mum had suffered post natal depression and described her severe reaction to them and that I also due to my health studies I believed they were a longterm unhelpful and dangerous crutch. So I continued to go to grief counselling and therapy for years after than the duration of time it was ordered by the court of a year maybe. Sabena unlike me with my robust resolve and resilience, a very fragile and superciliously sensitive emotional state was not provided with any counselling order.

I often wondered how she was fairing and coping with the shock of the reality of it all, suffered anxiety or melancholy worse than me and it soon came to pass that I discovered Sabena was struggling crying every night into her pillow and severely despondent suffering with PTSD for many months not eating well and disrupted at school. She became so run down with grief and chronic sadness that her immune system crashed and she contracted a virus, about 6 months after leaving my care. Her dad filled with remorse allowed me to chat to her a few times after the terrible incident, Sabena described the horrendous throbbing pain in her head and the burning high fever that went on for two days to me, that she screamed and cried out because she said it felt as if she must be surely dying. During these two days she wasn't seen or taken to a doctor. I thought this tremendously cruel and abusive to say the least. She said they lied and told her the fever would break and then she would be better straight away again. Of course if she was at home I would not allow her to go even a day without seeing a doctor, because Sue, a friend and her husband, that I strangely met through Eddie, my ex when we first met, was a paediatric nurse and said that high fevers for any length of time in children would fry their brain. I also knew this to be true from my previous studies and that if their brain was without oxygen for several minutes that they also could die or be brain damaged and other even worse catastrophes. So although Sabena would never make a fuss when she was sick, I'm fine mummy, not to worry me, I nevertheless always saw a doctor if there was a high fever, trouble breathing with her Asthma or she wasn't be responsive, improving and her usual eating and happy playful self, for peace of mind.

She must I believe have suffered similar to like a stroke or paralysis from the virus as an allergic reaction. I knew she had developed Bell's Palsy because even though I hadn't seen her for many months after until the drooping dropped eye and surrounding muscles almost nearly resolved after many months. I was eventually permitted to visit with her and she gave me pictures of her deformity laughing haughtily as if it was a non-event and never actually happened and it disappeared and was gone. The pictures were horrific and shocking to me and one third of her face was limp and drooping her eye at nose level, the piece de resistance was that she was doing an Elvis hip pose with her right arm up in the air, like a Rock Star spoof send up. It was incidentally the right side of her face that was damaged.

These days I have reconciled myself that there was nothing I could have done to stop, prevent or help it due to the dastardly cruel circumstances and also what I didn't realise then, the damage was not at all superficial but that it also had affected her in other intellectual capacities, causing her to have Autistic behaviours and being more dysfunctional and disabled at another insidious level which I didn't comprehend or reached at that time. She sounded different on the phone as if a piece was missing from a mind jigsaw puzzle, she was often confused and couldn't seem to remember the fun and happy times at my mum's house with us and couldn't recall or had difficulty recognizing friends. It was as if the brain damage she sustained erased everything from before the tragedy happened. I was severely disheartened, crestfallen, broken hearted and despondent, that she mightn't know me.

Disc 38 – Oct./ Nov. / Dec. 2018

Ross and Ramona Headifen – Youth Environmental Awareness featuring Beach patrol and love your street. They described it was about saving our planet for future generations and sustainability. This retiring couple who began to make it their lives work and purpose to volunteer themselves and also help to recruit youth to help them clean –up the beaches, which they were dismayed and appalled by having a sashay on the foreshore to find they couldn't help but start to tidy it, up it was awful. I met these intrepid kindred couple at a radio interview I attended it might have been triple RRR, and somewhere around Fitzroy or Collingwood, chatting to them in the green room behind the scenes and couldn't help but notice Ramona's heavy American accent and her engaging broad smile from ear to ear. Ross, who was also very mild and knowledgeable previously having also worked as a professional engineer. They were a most fabulous captivating dynamic team together, as I sat there after my interview, watching theirs. I was very pleased to have made their acquaintance at the radio.

Amal Aboud – Eid (Teacher/ Children's Author/ Mum) *My Muslim Mate.* Such a pretty, pleasant, patient, and sympathetic lady wearing a paisley headdress scarf with two very small children of her own trying to bring our kids together in community peace and also bridging the cultural gap for the littlies to understand different cultures from her own previous teaching experiences in her book.

Susie Kliman – Teacher/Social worker/ Author and Breast Cancer Survivor. This mature attractive lady, *always look on the bright side of life* kind of person, makes me think of Goldie Hawn, and takes us on a journey. Never surrender, take no prisoners, make the best tasting lemonade from whatever comes your way. Dotting on her grandson and who's obsessive fascination for shoes gave her the idea of *Jonathon's Thongs*, a quirky, funny, cheeky children's book about some Thongs that come to animate life. On the flipside is her spoof funny adult book, sending up the reality of Cancer in her *Surviving Cancer* Guide. She also delves into a bit of her ancestry and her own family's previous holocaust escapes.

Mohua Das Gupta – Coach/ Member (The Coaching Institute). I met Mohua through my bestie Masako (Saki) and Sally, who I attended with them some events at the Buddhist Temple in Maribyrnong. I would pick –up Saki and drive us there, it was a long way not knowing the area. There would be chanting, singing, discussion groups and sometimes Sally played her flute at the end, every person brought a plate for lunch to celebrate the occasion to share with all the other members. Mohua felt there was something incomplete in her life beyond raising her sons and became a member of the Coaching Institute to enlighten and improve her life in more ways than the obvious.

Jude Perera – Accountant / Teen Author (The Beast). This mature friendly, sympathetic man with those, Yul Brenner, cheekbones and oval features that could be stern and kind at the same time. He speaks glowingly of the country he was born in, and that a trip reminded him of its vast beauty. He reminisces about youth in his home country, combining both in his Teen adventure book. I also admired him for stepping out of his usual comfort zone and deciding to follow his passion to try his hobby writing skill and put it to the test, sacrificing, taking several months off work to actually do it.

Disc 39 – Oct./Nov./ Dec. 2018.

Nova and Nicole – Soul Link Studio (Trauma Memory Therapy and Eradication). These two amazing young mums who's mission impossible is to find a solution to traumatic early incidents that cause detrimental behavioural and long term emotional effects on especially young children and adults. They came together as a common goal from experiences with their own young children growing up. They describe this method of therapy at the source cause, the youth describe it and it's trapped away and locked out of their subconscious minds so it does not linger in their thoughts reeking perpetual havoc and rearing the ugly monsters head when triggered by similar stimuli again.

Walter Trupp – Owner / Teacher. Trupp Cooking School. Author – Wholefood Kitchen. This tall mature interesting, intellectual man, who followed in the family restaurant business but wanted to discover more. Working in many of the top hotels around the world in his early career and settling in Melbourne with his unique take on food is fuel, our diet shapes us and his Beetroot Chocolate Mud cake that is a favourite for young and old, both healthy and decadent, a recipe for his students.

The Bowls Club Elsternwick.

This was an event that was instigated from a suggestion of Phaedra Gunn (Singer/ Songwriter) to pay tribute in memoriam to her music partner in crime Steven Marshall White (Singer/ Songwriter/ Guitarist / Audio Technical Engineer Expert) who was taken off this planet much too soon from a rapidly developing aggressive cancer to which he lost his life and succumbed ultimately less than a year after its diagnosis. I previously interviewed these kindred music spirits in August 2015 and they sang their song together from The Winterfriends Band – My Wonderland with Steven playing his guitar and also assisting our crew with the music audio. I found this band playing in a Bar just off Greville Street, Prahran at an afternoon Sunday trendy music session, where I attended with my then current boyfriend of a few months, Allan. We both liked music and art and were out for a winter constitutional of a breath of fresh air, brunch and to check out this easy - going avo music session upon this groovy, psychedelic chic bar. When we arrived there it was almost at the end of their spot, but I liked their style and got a card.

The event was actually held in July, 2018 about a year after Steven's passing but there was a lot of difficulty with the synching of the music performances in the audio that it took many months to complete by various collaborative professional editors that I engaged due the student's difficulties. In essence it was a good thought but it also required many months of preparation and organization.

Phaedra and I shared the burden of this endeavour, she asked around about a volunteer venue and recruited bands and singers that were also mutual friend's of Steven and her own husband and kids to help. She knew a place where they made glass award trophies for the best upcoming TTP talents. Phaedra designed black and white, posters to be printed up. The event was set up on Eventbright or some such, and I gave fifteen FREE entry tickets to friends and helpers. Phaedra sold her tickets separately and there would be tickets at the door on the night sold by her son at the door. The music audio amps and mixing desk were set up by Phaedra's friend Greek George, who knew Steven and collaborated with him before on other projects and he wasn't here to do it with himself now. I donated a set of discarded amps which were from The Rebar and George said he could fix them.

I organized the best of the Teen Talk Talent performing prior interviewees, the volunteer donor sponsors, vouchers, services and goods for the silent auction, the discounted donated food catering, the master of ceremonies speech, the hire of the filming and specific audio equipment, the videography crew and some of my behind the scenes regular helper volunteer paid crew, mail out newsletter, social media and digital content advertising of the event, professional post – production, professional editing and DVD production costs. Sponsors were also thanked on social media.

Thanks to Sushi Gallery, Thai On High, Illy's Cakes, Elsternwick Bowling Club, Aim Archery, Springpark Golf Club, Romeo's Toorak, Hobson's Bay Music Academy, High Voltage Rock School, Djembe Melbourne and many more other vouchers and gifts from previous interviewed adult sponsors. I also donated bottles of champagne, skin care, accessories, Sport memorabilia, Trike Bikes and more.

Masako attended as well as some other of my other friends. Masako also introduced me to her agent, who was Wayne Cuthbertson of the Boulevard Agency and she explained to him about my program and she thought he might be able to help me promote it to other broadcasters etc. Masako was in the throes of writing her children's book, and also doing an ethnic video treatment concept. She previously produced choreography for Bollywood films and was writing her own musical. I was fortunate to have known Masako from an AWG Christmas Party where we became instant friends. Masako liked me to attend her frequent meetings with Wayne to discuss progress of her projects, these previous few years as she saw me become more involved in Teen Talk, worrying about sharks. We met a few times at their office in Lennox Street, Richmond upstairs but they were moving out. I was introduced to his part- time agency partner and associates Anne Young and her partner Andrew.

Feel the Love Tribute Night Concert performance – Part 1 including excerpts of performing Teen Talk Production best of youth talent.

Feel the love Tribute Night Concert performance – Part 2 including excerpts from volunteer adult bands and music performances of the latter part of the evening.

Greg Steps- Original Song (Under the Radar), Jane Cameron Original Song (The Sea Knows his Name), The Phosphenes Original Song (The Window), The Winterfiends – Phaedra Gunn and Steven Marshall White (2018 In Memoriam) Original Song (My Wonderland).

Disc 40 Jan. Feb. March 2019

This is a compilation DVD of our best interviewee youth for the term of the program and encore return updated interviews of youth, and youth talent, with some current interesting adult favourites.

Happy Valentine's Day – Sabena!

Disc 41 March, April, May 2019.

This is a compilation of our best Youth Interviewees, encore Youth return updated interviews and youth talent for the term of the program.

Masako, Wayne, Anne and Andrew attended with their free tickets, to support me, Andrew unfortunately was wheelchair bound due to complications of his severe Diabetes but was still was very determined that he would attend the performance, no matter what. Andrew said he was very proud of what I achieved and was happy he made an effort and came as he enjoyed it immensely.

The evening was a success, but to me it was a blur, getting but glimpses of the real audience experience. I was thoroughly preoccupied and torn between supervising the filming and video, supervising the volunteer help with the organizing the silent auction, trying to greet my friends, supervising the youth talent and organising their performances and stage/audio requirements. From the early morning that Saturday in the dead of Winter organizing and setting up of the layout, Filming equipment / audio / mixing desk/ amps, Silent Auction items and labels, Talent Prizes, Decorations, food storage and preparations of setting up the tables, serving trays, picnic dishes, plastic cutlery, serviettes etc. and for the Catered Sushi, Handmade Spring Rolls, Curry Puffs, other finger foods and the Flourless huge Chocolate square Mudcake with 150 Episodes on it. It was such a full day's work and Phaedra checked in much later in the day to have a music audio test on stage. I snuck home quickly after she arrived, to come home, have a bite to eat, shower and get changed into something more presentable for the occasion within the space of an hour to return to be in time to greet the youth for their upcoming performances in the early dusk of the damp, crisp evening.

I recall a previous youth interviewee who said that her teacher saw her student's interview on TV an afternoon after school, pleasantly surprised and she congratulated her, that she was very pleased. The teacher was impressed with the program and she might also have recommended the program to some of her other colleagues. This was how I think I also became acquainted with the music teacher Lynda Watkins, who also coincidentally was a friend of Sally's. Lynda organized for some of her students to be interviewed on the program and some she also helped them prepare their performances for the Tribute Night, training and helping them with rehearsing prior to the day. Lynda attended with her partner, to support her students and to also encourage their performances.

You'll just have to watch the performance, to see which youth talent performers and performances were judged the best youth performers and that won the top prizes and encouragement trophies.

Anne, business woman (Senior, Steadfast Eastern Insurance/ partner, Boulevard Agency) but compassionate lady and loving Nan, devoted to Andrew, with his own Insurance business and pulling out all the stops to get Andrew there and to keep him comfortable for part of the duration of the night. I was so much in gratitude for their encouragement and support, I offered Andrew a free consultation at the clinic, but I feel he was maybe too housebound and too debilitated to accept, and too late perhaps, after that night.

I asked Wayne especially to do a speech as the Master of Ceremonies to introduce the program to the audience, and with consummate ease, minimal preparation, spontaneous with his natural flair and savoire faire, in true Bert Newton popular style (who unfortunately passed away from us too soon before his time, incidentally not too long after his leg was amputated in May, 2021, a lost talent), who's short speech was a congratulatory highlight of the evening, and he also nudged me gently and it would be best for me as founder/ CEO/ Director/ Producer/ Writer of TTP to say a few words on being so chuffed and so thankful and grateful to all the contributors to the show and to all the prior volunteer youth interviewees, their families, our sponsors, our constant flow of crew and helpers that made it in Melbourne possible for Teen Talk Production' celebrations of 5 years of filming and broadcasting, 41 DVD's and 150 Episodes, with more than 1,000 participants on our data base and that my original concept idea went from being imagination to becoming a real reality.

Hope Springs Eternal

Wayne was like a warm, soft comfortable hug, charming, fake it till you make it kind of smooth criminal, born in Tassie with connection to some privileged business family, Tassal Salmon. Monogamously, and also happily gay and with a partner. There was a glint of John Wayne about him and air of lilting tone of phrase. Wayne would jokingly say to us that he was an Aries, a leader not unlike myself and being born at midnight on April's Fools Day only made him perhaps point five of an idiot hopefully. During this time that I knew him he unfortunately was plagued with various continuous ongoing health issues which required them to be a survival priority for him to attend to beyond work and all else. It was concerning and disturbing to me however that none of Saki's projects or works were seemingly probably never coming to fruition or ever being realized, even though Wayne was her agent for many years. I cannot comment on any of Saki's works as she was very protective of her content and I never read any of them myself.

Saki came from a well heeled, privileged, aristocratic family in Japan. She was previously successful as an editor of some magazine in Japan before coming to Australia, meeting her estranged husband and having her three now grown up children in their twenties, whose father retained custody when they were young. I don't know the full story but it was familiar. Saki's brother who remained in the family business in Japan, as I understood from Wayne helped support a huge amount of her artistic hobbies, experimental imagination and creative pursuits.

Wayne, well I think it was a matter of past performance is not an indicator of current performance. He would always mention things he previously delivered on like Schokolade, a previously successful entrepreneurial venture. Saki pointed out it was difficult to find an agent who cared, who would back you or who took you on board without previous successes or credits and Wayne was also a close friend. Wayne would say one trick ponies, were easy to come by, or was I, as I began to doubt my abilities and achievements, as many knockbacks proceeded and continued to proceed for years. You couldn't help liking Wayne anyhow, he would make me smirk with his quips, *were a motley crew, aren't we!.* Wayne said to me in confidence once that he needed Anne because of her backbone, as a softie deep down he often also got burnt sometimes as well as his creative's, without her scrutiny. Saki and I agreed that Wayne was a bit shifty but maybe that's what it took in this industry to get in but that he would eventually come through for us someday and just like this bullshit industry, never.

Masako waited in vain and with hope as the years went by but nothing ever came to be for either of us. It was only fraught with emptiness at every turn. Charlatans, of the industry it was always glass, smoke and mirrors and I wondered how the industry survived like this and with those snake oil salesman wagons.

Masako and I were besties, and she encouraged me to continue pursuing my creative outlet, giving me advice and all manner of contracts from privacy contracts to crew confidentiality and registering my content etc. Saki thought my talents wasted at the clinic, as she didn't have much time for Drs. She however disregarded this part of my persona, and would ignore my health advice suggestions. Saki would call me at least once a week about stuff to touch base, as I was also juggling the clinic. Saki also always endearingly, trying to matchmaker me with her single Japanese, Indonesian and Asian male friends, as she thought me admiral, and deserving of a partner of real worth in my life. She boggled that I had settled for a loser like Eddie, and not at least some person of high standing.

Masako's current partner of at least a decade after losing custody of her kids, was Arthur Lovring, who came from NZ and was a tradesman with his own business, who she also tried to promote him. I never met him in person because they'd moved to regional Victoria, soon after they met, long before I met Saki, as he disliked city life, but she could never say enough good things about him, her soul mate and that he supported her through the difficult years of her divorce and parental alienation from her kids by their dominant and stubborn father, who kept them at ransom from her.

Masako was a constant high maintenance social butterfly, flitting about everywhere and anywhere that was of consequence to her, she went on trips to Japan at least twice a year for a few weeks. We would invite each other to celebratory events as they arose and Masako often was given free passes. She was generous to a fault with gifts to her close friends for every holiday occasion or birthdays, she was very old school, always well mannered, polite with good breeding and so thoughtful towards her friends. It was a bit of congratulatory whimsy, but Masako brought a beautiful bunch of flowers to an opening night of Sally's orchestra group performance and for me when, I received the Higgins Community Award 2016 from Kelly O'Dwyer and there was the presentation night event at the Malvern Town Hall. These were kind of Masako things to do, that showed her recognition. In turn as Masako for some reason gave up driving a decade ago, I would if I was not working be her exclusive designated driver, if I was not working of course, I would also sometimes pick up things for her, and If she wanted me to accompany her somewhere I would without question, if I was available. We reciprocally shouted each other get together lunch's about once a month and we exchanged best friend occasional gifts to each other, as I do with my other close friends. She supported me and tried to help me in my creative ventures, I would help in return if I could like referring her to a graphic design illustrator that I knew of, for the children's book she was working on as her latest project. We were so close there wasn't almost anything that we wouldn't do to help each other.

I confided in Masako that the community station C31 was going online and they weren't renewing our broadcasting licence for June 2018, because they thought it would not be suitable online and some editors at the Ingest Department complained to me that we gave them too much work because our submissions needed sometimes to be corrected with editing by them before being ingested with the others, to become up to standard specifications. It was true that I could not afford to always get professional and experienced editors, some students were excellent, others learning. However how would these graduating students ever learn their stock and trade, if their weren't people like myself to give them a chance to prove themselves gaining real work experience, being a community station I thought they should be a bit more lenient and understanding of this. So what the young student editors made a few minor boo's from time to time and it was I thought easier for Ingest to fix them but they became grouchy and began to return all the USB's to me for the specific editors corrections, even if minor, it was actually better for the students to learn but this also interfered, delayed programming schedules, sometimes causing repeats of episodes and dramas.

It also now became a problem because there were various editors working on episodes to finish our post – production from the previous season's filming and these would now not be broadcast from June 2018. The kids and their parents, adult participants often sent me emails to find out when likely their episodes might be broadcasting on TV, to within a month and so they were terribly, angrily disappointed when I explained that there was now no more broadcasting platform in Melbourne. I thought it was such an incredible shame that they would not see their actual interview episodes.

This was now an urgent situation, so Masako introduced me to her friend Taka from Japan, who was successful at producing international video games for at least a decade and dabbled in promoting entertainment stuff too. She would then try to get myself, herself, and Wayne to collaborate with Taka to help find us a new broadcasting platform. I also tried myself beating on many, many doors to be perpetually rejected from many commercial, mainstream and all other sorts of minor streaming platforms. Taka came up with a great idea I thought about format of the program in Japan and Asia. It could be licensed to these countries to make their own versions and also our episodes subtitled. It sounded good in theory until Taka asked for us to invest in his current games project in the process. I thought this a future possibility but it still didn't solve the kids in Melbourne watching their episodes. I began to think maybe promotions help exposure would find us a new home or even a big agent.

It was a very heart wrenching time for Masako after her partner some years younger than herself, met his untimely passing. Masako said he often went out with his friends after work on Friday for a few drinks, she said he always liked a bit of a piss on and why not, he seemed in good physical health. She came back to their regional home after having lunch with me and doing errands in Melbourne, to find him spreadeagled on the bed unconscious. She said to me she wasn't sure what to do or who to call because she was in such stunned shock about it. Not knowing much or precious little about health stuff, she attempted to try to give him CPR on the bed, but he was unresponsive. Masako said she then rang the ambulance and he was already passed when they arrived regrettably. The ambulance crew said that he had most likely suffered a sudden, acute fatal heart attack failure.

I asked Masako why she hadn't called me but she said she didn't think of it at the time. I said to her for future reference that you need to give people CPR on a hard, flat surface to be effective, any how he might have already been passed by the time Masako arrived home as she wasn't sure he was still alive. Arthur Lovring, her partner passed in 2017 and there was discussion to have a burial in NZ.

Masako sold their home and eventually returned to live in an apartment off St. Kilda Road, Melbourne because Masako liked to be close to all the action and city life offerings. We became even closer than before. After selling their home, she had nowhere to stay and I would have put her up with me for even for a few months but the on suite bathroom wasn't working in the other bedroom and I was always fussy about sharing bathrooms with other people with my allergies.

I thought about it and introduced Masako to an ongoing friend, who I had previously dated for a few months. I knew Ian, built a loft room up in the attic of his house a few years before as when we were dating he showed it to me and offered for me to stay there, after some of his annual house parties on his Birthday, Australia Day, Queen's Birthday as he was a staunch monarchist and also Jewish. Ian fancied himself as that hulky guy from the Fast and Furious but in reality he was more of a bald uncle Fester from the Addams Family. I also thought he must have had a deprived child hood in Poland as his parties were like afternoon to evening children's parties as if he'd never grown up in a time warp. So she went to stay in the loft for a few months at a discounted fair rental as Masako was my friend. Sometimes I wish I hadn't introduced Masako to Ian as he was always trying to get her to patch us up again, which I found exceedingly annoying as I felt we wanted different things in a partner and he was so awfully commitment phobic anyway, that he'd managed to keep himself purposefully single.

It was tragic how Masako 69, in June 2018, passed not much more than a year after her partner Arthur, and returning to Melbourne. It was an incredulous shock to me having to find out from Wayne about what happened. I talked to her on the phone a few days before, when she said she was getting a meal delivery service with prepared packaged home meals which was more convenient for her busy life. She said she'd ordered too much and there wasn't enough storage in her freezer and asked to use my freezer, unfortunately due to my allergies and I didn't go out much in Winter I was stocked up. Her distressed son found her after 24 hours on the cold tiles of the kitchenette still barely breathing and trying to stay alive but unconscious. Masako would have lived forever if she could have and so such a fierce will to live was instilled in her. She was taken to the Alfred Hospital and apparently suffered a sudden massive stroke. She was on life support.

I went to visit her a day or so after when I could and chatted to her as if she was conscious and her feet and legs were so cold and lifeless that I brought some cream with me and asked the nurse if I could massage them for her. I would be the second last time I would see her alive, I returned the day after next and the staff said to me that her condition improved slightly and she gained a second wind with vital signs but not consciousness. The doctors recommended pulling the plug after a few days, that her imaging showed severe brain damage and even if she recovered she would most likely be in a vegetative state. I felt sorry for her three kids in their twenties about this heavy decision that was forced on them. I begged them to keep her going for a few more days in the slim chance something might happen, like those amazing medical story miracles. Alas I saw her an hour before on the day they pulled the plug at which they would have a departing chanting ceremony of her Buddhism group of friends and family around her hospital bed. I didn't attend because I was upset that I wanted to be celebrating her alive and as she was not as a lifeless corpse as she would be after.

In my mind I could still feel the dainty icy to the touch of Masako's fingers as I held her hand in the hospital with those fat sausage blisters on her thumb, second and third finger, usually those for cooking, on both her left and right hand which I assume she must have accidentally scalded herself at the time as she was having the stroke attack. The thoughtful gifts she always brought for me and Sabie, even though she knew she wasn't with me or hadn't been for some years. Like mum, she tried to keep up my morale and say, you will keep them and give them to her whenever you will see her again or when she will come home to visit you or even stay. I often tried to ask her to take Sabie's back and give them to someone else but she would not hear of it at all. So I kept the cards and gifts.

The funeral was a Buddhism Funeral at the Crematorium in Springvale, I knew it would be a big deal and that the kid's would do their best to put on a show to impress for all those many upstanding people who absolutely loved and adored her and who's lives she was fortunate to have touched. It was for this very reason and also because like them pulling her plug, I preferred to celebrate her life. So I went on strike and refused to go to the funeral and I'm sure that Masako would have accepted. The worst thing of all, I thought the irony that Masako so particular about her work, the kid's couldn't get into her Laptop or her phone without her passwords, and so even though they cleaned out the tiny flat, they couldn't find any reference to them anywhere, or to any medications or Drs. Not having any of her contacts available they were forced to rely on Wayne for most people's no's.

I'm not sure whether Ian knew that Masako passed and it wasn't my place to have him know either. Ian I'm sure he would have been there with skates on, as he always never would refuse a free invite. Adele was on the list of my all time favourite singers and Ian played her day and night till I hated her. The shows he liked like Breaking Bad and the huge portrait at the top of the kitchen bench which I found distasteful each time I saw it, of a 60's girl with flick up shoulder at the ends hair and a brightly rainbow coloured face made up of a jigsaw puzzle of pieces of what might have been a patchwork of what seemed chards of glass. It might have been after another of his biannual trips to the Philippines and other Asian countries, where it was likely purchased, it could have been 2016, as I was still then invited to his parties as a friend. I wondered if he somehow knew something about Sabena's mental illness, suicidal thoughts, mutilation and self harm which came to light after she was admitted to The Royal Children's Hospital for suicidal idealization and tendencies, around about November, 2013. I never said anything about the portrait, as I felt it was to spite me as a constant evil reminder of 14.

The Carnival is over.

The Feel the Love Tribute Night was our last Teen Talk Production, Hoorah!. I was still mulling about Sally and Charise, days after, their betrayal and mutiny of a preordained event for a flash in the pan gig. Having been organizing the event for many months prior I asked Charise not as a favour but to give them practice experience and a hand up exposure, since they hadn't done a gig in what seemed to them forever, to do a single spot of her performances, once the kid's performers arrived at dusk for their and some of their young families entertainment on the night. It would be a novelty too! I have two minds about this, that I might have done the same thing myself, as it was minimal paid gig as opposed to volunteer spot gig and because it was a once off and most likely wouldn't come again. Sally's excuse was that it was her first real gig since having joined Charise's troupe and they were actually being paid something to perform, I maybe would have paid them not to perform as my dad would have said if he was here now but that's a bit funny harsh. Later I was to discover this was Sally's stock standard excuse if she thought she might get a better offer, like she shafted and ditched me several years later for a Christmas lunch that was already booked as both of us were estranged. For Charise I guess it was nothing personal it's business, but I to this day Sally who was previously a close friend, could have offered me a raincheck at another time and at least apologized for her appalling rude and disloyal behaviour to me being an upper stiffer lip pom and all that such stuff. She could have even asked Charise if they would do a spot for us after their gig finished in the afternoon, but maybe the logistics of it all would have been too difficult and also them being tired. These are the things I would have done, if it was me in her place. Alas no one else has taken over my body thus far. There performance was a flop, with a few stragglers of an only audience to play to, which must have been disappointing for them. The irony was that, as it turned out we didn't need them at all, since we had lots to do in precious little time and we were already behind schedule with more kid's performers than we actually expected would turn up on the evening. Our concert was a resounding success, the hall full.

Somehow also somewhat annoying to me was that Phaedra at the end of the night ended up with most of the proceeds and I would end up with most of the payments. Phaedra keeping, at least two – thirds or more of the proceeds, which she was supposed to have divvied up fairly between us. I never saw the full amount of proceeds from the entry door fee or for that matter the Vintage Guitar and other top selling high end items at the Silent Auction all which were controlled by Phaedra. Totally ripped off man!. On top of all this later on down the track she threatened me with extortion of the bands and performers filming rights to try to ban me from editing and using my own filming. Again that dog – eat – dog side of the entertainment industry, get them before they get you, which reared its ugly head, jumping out of the closet like a horror movie monster without any suspicion of it happening and totally oblivious and unawares about it. These incidents caused me to shudder with despair, it was like comparing a car salesman's attitude to that of a specialist brain surgeon's conduct, as they say you can't ever compare bananas and oranges with those ruby red apples.

I wondered about Sally being single and on her own here in Melbourne, Australia after having abandoned her husband and English family, whom she described as boring and staid as bat shit everyday of the week and yet despite this her dear kind mother always sent her gifts and clothing, which she always proudly wore. In fact the version of her story seemed to me to be highly illogical. It was a bit like the thing about Pam film, there was other stuff hidden in them there hills and her obsession with Buddhism which I never quite grasped, as mostly Asian people were Buddhists. She often said to me that Buddhism saved her from what I thought, I had loads more bad stuff than her. She encouraged me to chant with her and attend meetings dragging me out also in depths of winter. It was her belief and Masako that chanting solved almost everything in life, so with all my shit Sherlock I gave it a good college try. A loyal true friend ironically, that was a member of The Soka Gaki Buddhism Institute (Nam- Myoho – Renge- Kyo), this is the chant. Admittedly I tried to get into it but I didn't get it for one and two it didn't seem to have any magical lasting powers on me, myself. It was chanting the chant over, and over and over, and over, for several minutes both morning and night, maybe it was something to do with the rhythm of the chant and the pattern and melody of the words that seemed to soothe people and all their issues vanished disappearing into thin happy air. I thought there must be some scientific or logical explanation for its strong belief system hold on all these seemingly staunchly loyal followers that it worked for Well it was not apparent to me at all, and nobody can solve a problem like Maria. Sally and Soka Gaki were to be a fair weather friend to me, despite the books I bought, meetings attended and chants I did. Anyhow give it a try if you like, and see if it works for you, it does apparently work for million, millions of people around the world.

The Exposure Trap

There would be some other monsters in hiding that were lurking in the wardrobe in the coming months, it resembled those horror films where the scary thing keeps coming back no matter what. Contracts would be terminated for no specific reason and my reputation tainted and damaged too boot. It was about this time that I thought to find TTP another broadcasting platform for the previous and yet unbroadcasted episodes, that perhaps media exposure would help to get us out there and maybe even an agency with more clout and resources would also come to our rescue. I thought this a sensible investment during these months and I was determined to find us a solution.

I recruited a Promotions Agency from Sydney, they weren't the most flash but other inquiries I made to many other places either wouldn't take on such a small project or were asking for inordinate amounts of big scary money. I thought for what we needed in a campaign was to get us out there. So the contract was for a short term of three to four months as it was a monthly fee for services. The campaign commenced from September 2018, it was doing well and we were starting to get invitations for Radio interviews, our press releases began to show up on online papers and forums, we were gaining momentum fast, we were getting attention to the cause from various sources. I don't remember but I thought it was actually working and the industry would rise to the occasion. I think it was by the second or third months press release was due that the one person promotions manager was very late that month with preparing the press release and began to become argumentative about nonsense stuff as if she was purposefully trying to sabotage her own project. I was concerned about the delays and excuses, as time was of essence, and her sudden changed aggressive and unco-operative negative attitude. So I raised my concerns and my contract was terminated after of course having paid the third instalment in advance, which wasn't chump change for us but several thousands. I thought it a lot of money for what they really do by all accounts but then perhaps your paying for their connections and their weaselling about, all roads lead to Rome. I was mortified I had done that month's instalment money, with no promotional work or Press release. It was terrible for me not being a gambler to see our precious little money go down the gurgler without much reward for it as in outcome, results or the exposure required to achieve our goals. Dumped in midstream without much of anything to show for it up to now and with nowhere else to go from here, and no more dosh to spare on it. Well as they say in the classics it ended in tears but I refused to have squandered that money for the third instalment and so I decided to fight and so I filed a complaint to the Office of Fair Trading and the efficient officer mediated a partial refund of that final months monies, well something is always better than nothing salvaged at all and nothing ever solid or good comes without much effort invested, it was long haul but we got there.

The Hacking Stalker

It was bad enough dealing with all that crap outside but then it came from my own ranks. I thought how fortunate I was until now that every youth that was involved in producing digital content was for the most part decent, diligent, trustworthy, loyal, co-operative, efficient, respectful and honest. Those who were lazy and who didn't deliver, or failed to turn up and weren't stayers simply vanished of their own accord. I would usually make up short agreements on paper for their term of engagement of usually many months and we would mutually agree on work to be done and payment per month. Until it came to pass after the previous debacle that we were now even shorter on funds for social media management and sustainability of the Teen Talk cause digitally. So I tried to pull on the purse strings and tighten the budget for this. As Mark a family friend of ours loved to say pay peanuts and you get monkeys and in this particular case but not all cases, he was right.

I think this young overseas immigrant might have also been illegally working here but I wasn't sure. I recruited Social Media people by phone interview and sometimes in person at my pop up offices. Her English was very broken and I barely understood her at times, but she seemed keen to do the work and happy to work from the comfort of her home for the amount agreed upon mutually. The first few months she was very efficient and I tried to help her with finding content and explaining as best I could my directions via email and suggestions for suitable helpful youth content to be posted. She began to start posting dark and not age appropriate content and doing stuff that wasn't requested of her, I thought she might have been experimenting with her craft but it was strange and sinister. She began to threaten me with posting worse stuff and asking for more money until I told her I could not afford to give her more than agreed. The bomb dropped she changed the password and hacked the Facebook and Instagram, defacing and posting nasty and defaming untrue comments about me and Teen Talk.

This torture went on for weeks and I wasn't sure what to do, so I posted no cheque for that month, hoping that she would tire of the tirade and eventually give up and stop doing it. She was holding me to ransom and said she wouldn't stop until I paid her that month and another few months in advance it was escalating and becoming worse out of proportion. I asked around what to do and eventually reported it as cyber attack to a police government agency. I even rang the Moorabbin Police to try to make her stop and they went to home several times to give her a warning and they urged her to mediate something with me but she refused to do so. Instead she elected to report me to the Fair Work Ombudsman government agency to which I had to defend myself against this rampaging extortionist and vandalism perpetrator of what I tried to keep wholesome and sacred, helpful, useful and entertaining media content for our kid followers and their families.

Why me? Why me? Why me? Why me? I don't know why, it was as if I was being singled out and that she was being paid by someone to cause the torrent of digital trail of destruction and damage for spite to the detriment and demise of everything we'd done up until now and accomplished. I felt hopeless and helpless to make her cease in any way, shape or form that she could come to reason. How to fix this without her? So I re-interviewed again to find someone to start from scratch again.

I found someone kind and good very quickly who was also distressed and dismayed by the ongoing slander. She was sympathetic and supportive of my plight and myself being significantly tech challenged. I think she asked me even for a bit less in payment and said it was more of a hobby for her to gain more experience. It was an angel from heaven, she and her internet fairies in the computer. She waved her fairy wand and managed to change the password again and block the vandal from posting. I think it was Xu Lu was her name, and I was so eternally grateful to her and it was truly a miracle. The bad news was the fresh social media pages were never the same again after. Lu Lu as I would call her as her nickname tried fervently to regain the stature that our previous social media enjoyed, but alas the perpetrator broke something more than the internet tarnishing my and Teen Talk's reputation in our followers eyes. We were cleaned up but the public no longer trusted. As for the vandal, it turned out I was telling the truthful version and there was no substance to her illegal person's complaint and in fact that she owed me more money for having to pay someone else again to delete the defaming, defacing messages and restore and start totally new FB pages again.

After that bizarre rogue attack of terrorism, I was in despair and shaken by how quickly things turn on a dime, as what my friend Bronwyn Trimble, and renting neighbour would say. She was a former Model turned Motivational Trainer, whose face was severely damaged and injured after a near fatal car accident that required massive reconstructive surgery. Her previous partner was Len Thompson with two daughters, Laura and Emily. I occasionally babysat both of them Emily who was a Annie look alike became an International model and her older sister with pretty features became a primary school teacher.

LuLu tried her very best to try to resuscitate interest in the FB, but the historical loss of how far we'd come was gone. I never saw LuLu in person but on the phone she reminded me of the little girl in the textured red pullover waving at her mum from an apartment window who was in nurse's scrubs and natural suede jacket looking up at her at the corner of the street – *NAB more than money* or those young, cute, dainty girls who glided onto the stage floor of *You are the one*, format show. LuLu after several months, finishing her studies and it might have also been in the early phase of the Covid pandemic, would return home to China. Jialu was also sporadically helping me with the quarterly Mailchimp Newsletter *Teen Talk Vibe*, digital creation and maintaining the bulk data base, later she would also assist me in also implementing a primary and secondary school data base, to go out to Victorian schools. Some young students, aspiring journalists and digital content producers wrote short blogs about Teen Stuff with links from the Newsletter and these blogs were also posted on our website. Jialu also returned to China around about these months.

Money eventually dried up in addition to previous incidents I described and I could not sustain the cause as a hobby, so I shut it all down once these loyal volunteers were on their way home, of course many, many, many others before came and went on their way to a future career. So to all those numerous creative's who contributed in some way, shape or form to Teen Talk and believed we could make a significant difference in youth lives, I say Thank-you, Thank-You, Thank-you and you all know who you are and this is probably but a short list of those who were involved.

Georgia Pike, Samantha Davenne. Tykeisha E, Linda Shi, Vicky Lim, Asha Khan, Ella Di Marco, Xiao Wu, Scott Robertson, Elle Curran, Elisha Mc Call, Emily Lederman, Alex Zmau, Nik Rossi, Jeremy Tay, Alex Zemtsov, Matt Field etc.

I began to be concerned about somehow keeping the kid's interviews for posterity and for future generations to view them, the Teen Talk Time capsule of Youth lives in Melbourne for the span from 2014 – 2019. The best way I thought to keep treasured memories forever safe, accessible and free to all, was at the Library, so I contacted the State Library Victoria and gave them permission to catalogue Teen Talk Production DVD's memorabilia, 1-41, 14 Seasons and 150 Episodes of which I provided two copies of each for their archive Audio- Visual department of the Library, currently being renovated. I also approached some University, College and Polytechnic main libraries but there content of this type was submitted in digital form so they could not accept them, I would have like to have dispersed them in Primary and Secondary School libraries but it was the stock answer.

Duff, as I cheekily nicknamed him (Simon Duffield), was usually a pit stop for me for questions about filming and stuff, he was somewhat knowledgeable about this area as he'd dabbled in this as a hobby for the past decade, but there was always his employed everyday work to fall back on. I met him strangely and coincidentally at a singles night at a tiny dimly lit dingy corridor bar at the Windsor end of Chapel Street that I attended with my bestie Audrey, before her mum became gravely ill. It might have been organised by Fun, Food and Friendship singles group that we became members together. We sat cramped on the side benches that finished up at a end in a corner patch of handkerchief dance floor. We chatted, he said he was separated becoming divorced from his high school sweetheart wife but still saw his few children Tweens or younger. He described them drifting apart as partners and not getting on, wanting different things. It sounded to me the run of the mill adage, as if it was midlife crisis wandering, FOMO or a scene from the seven year itch classic. Apparently he was now lost in the dating quagmire of quicksand of wanting to root anything around.

I was attracted to Duff, but very concerned about his situation. Born in Australia of English ancestry, he spoke coldly of his wife, blaming her for almost everything which I thought terribly unfair. I don't feel that he was particularly attracted to me although we dated a few times, but he was after a freedom fling thing which was I guess to be expected straight off the bat until you went around driving the same dead end again and again. He shacked up with someone as I suspected very quickly.

We remained however good friends for several years exchanging filming tips, thoughts and ideas, getting together for Coffee or lunch every now and then. Sunburnt Films was his hobby moonlighting indie film production company, in his spare time he was also writing a script for a feature film concept that he wanted to make and had already made his own comedy – drama short film. He introduced me to various organizations AWG, SPA and ADG for filming and artistic creative's, urging me to register my IP officially, and collaborate with a credited professional producer, which I agreed might be the way to proceed and was staunchly firm in his belief that viewing content was now in the future only of benefit if it was somehow in digital form on the internet. I thought about my *Maroon 5* friend, as every time I heard their songs on the radio (Sugar, Girl like you, Memories and others) reminiscing to myself, I wonder how Duff is doing, as we also drifted apart as friends, as he enjoyed his single freedom. So, I bought a recent edition of the industry book Encore that was a directory of all types of industry creative's and began trawling through to find any connected person to help me or give me advice or guidance, agencies, producers, directors but many of them were no longer operating. Those few professionals that were still in business were swamped with requests and would not be taking on board any other prospective or projects. I also kept business cards that I networked at social media industry functions like Johnny McConnell, but they all proved dead ends for me. No wonder a huge majority of creative's suffered mental issues.

I found however John Hipwell, this producer who also lived in Melbourne, I might have spoken to him on the phone, trying to describe what TTP was and we exchanged a few emails. I decided to go to his office/studio home in the Inner city suburbs after clinic that morning, it was a dreary dismal Winter's day and the nav on the iphone was going haywire with all the no through roads and those annoying streets that have partial barriers, so you have to turn around and get in from an adjacent street at the other end. Well I became tangled in these doozies of streets and it was an absolute maze, it began to get dusky and misty, I rarely became lost but I was for at least some hours, so I back tracked several intertwined suburbs and found it before it the dead of night came, thankfully I always have my trusty Melways in my car seat back pocket, as an emergency backup plan. He wasn't there, drats after all that, and so I never met him in person but I dropped him some samples of the program in his front door return and then came swiftly home for obvious reasons. I received the knockbacks I was now getting used to and expecting that he was preoccupied with other projects. He commented on his emails that he wasn't sure how he could further my situation anyhow, except that he also said you have to get it up online somewhere. We of course had preview and short clips clips on utube but not whole episodes, he started suggesting shorter episodes or segments online which I was unconvinced about and I thought it would spoil the continuity of the episodes and besides staff again to have to do it and all that jazz razzamatazz again. It made no sense to me.

John was kind enough however to have given me an initial response and attention, and I was grateful of even this minor guidance. Where frequently as many years ago, I was a casual in a call centre and for almost every sheet of lists of people to call maybe a couple would wait and listen to your short spiel before they abruptly hung up. So the strike rate was very, very low. I would from time to time send him a short email query about things, I was concerned about with respect to the program and he always politely willingly responded with a curt email, usually after a day or so.

I'm not sure exactly where the NFSA popped up, I might have been slipped this brain wave on my Encore ring around or more likely as previously discussed, it was more like a friendly Library teacher at the Melbourne Polytechnic College that suggested I contact the National Library in Canberra for catalogue items. Thinking about the kid's, posterity, perpetuity and Australian content, it was an excellent idea. I contacted the National Library but they only archived written material, but that originally made Australian content should be preserved in any form. She then referred me to the National Film and Sound Archives, Canberra where I chatted to Jeff Wray and he said it was most welcome and be a very interesting and worthwhile addition to the Australian content collection. There was a glitch in that they regrettably only accepted audio/ visual materials in digital form nowadays. He asked if the content was saved anywhere and being thorough as I was usually, all the episodes were saved and stored on external hard drives on both regular and compatible ISO International broadcasting standard formats. I posted the hard drives in two sections, DVD 1-20 and then 20 – 41, in case something went wrong, with my permission forms, and a few episodes that became corrupted, I resent them on Individual USB's. It was done. I was pleased with myself for finding a bit of a solution but also that I was contributing something of our countries kid's culture.

The time capsule was archived and catalogued but it was still bothering me that the kid's could have direct access to their broadcast and particularly their unseen and unbroadcasted episodes of 2018. I was in the process of renewing my subscription memberships and as I was having some difficulty online at the SPA, some sites rejected my email as invalid on forms and so I then couldn't proceed. Brad Taylor at the SPA (Screen Producers Australia) was very personable and welcoming to members, he would process the renewal personally and was ever ready to provide information or facilitate the obtaining of guidance in the industry. Willing to be of service, I might have in passing asked him about the broadcasting issue I was having. Streamings the answer, I knew about live streaming of events, (in real time, early June 2022, The Queen's Platinum Jubilee 70 year Ceremonies celebration), I previously thought about live streaming for the Tribute Concert but the cost was inordinately prohibitive and even though I discussed it briefly with Peter and Yolande at the CD Chapple Lab, the cost and complexity to me was decidedly totally unfeasible and not viable. What was streaming, streaming? I was enlightened that it permitted audiences to watch stuff they liked at any time they wanted, being TV generation I watched things then and there or not at all.

Relentlessly I searched the internet for small streaming service platforms, I started with Melbourne, the costs were prohibitive and provided for only large platforms of broadcast content, other states similar. It was a record on repeat again, it can't be done any other way, and no-one wants to help me, so I will do it my own way. Frankie, Ol' blue eyes was right, why can't I and there's nothing you can't do in New York (Alicia Keys), and there were many actors these days writing, producing and directing their own films. I was starting to get used to this industry attitude, so I would play by my rules and do it my way or not at all. The google search continued for the elusive answer to solve it.

I was at the Magistrate's Court, coincidentally with my alternative and spiritually minded friend Norma as a, support about an AVO intervention order against a boyfriend of five months duration and another two years of pain and suffering after that. In the waiting area with my iphone, as Norma sat with me and she was strangely spooling cotton tea bag threads so they could use them to crochet for her volunteer charity work at the church or some such other worthwhile organization, she was involved with. I wasn't sure what she was doing and then I asked her, she explained in her alternative way and I continued searching but started using alternate search words and phrases. Hip Hip Hooray, I struck a site providing independent and alternative content video streaming service with various packages from mini to huge. Maybe, it could be done, after all!. I was ecstatic, turned off the phone and popping it in my black leather satchel and electing to help Norma with spooling.

Arriving home that afternoon, I looked into it more closely and apparently they were in France. I remembered Elliot sending his video editing Basketball things to the US. I found the how to and now it was but how? The platform was called OKAST and the principle innovator was Simon Le Deaut, as I was clueless and knew virtually nothing about this stuff, I would call and get him to explain it to me. The hours time distance caused havoc and we kept missing each other in phone tag and following up with emails to synchronize a specific time. It was a deep but smooth heavy French accent that he spoke a bit topsy turvey broken English with but somehow we managed to communicate between English, my fluent Italiano and petite francaise. It sounded like it was feasible but I heard the words echoing from him*, but you needing to someone to uploading the content for you.* I began to get that sick stomach churning feeling again, having to involve other people again and hoping they delivered. I explained my position and so Simon knew I was tech challenged and I understood nada, nothing! Ok, I said leave it with me and I will email you if I decide to continue with the uploading project. I pondered on it for several weeks. Simon sounded an enterprising young man in his thirties and he was sympathetic to our cause and plight, I also said I was old enough to be his mother, so he answered that he would try to help us as much as he could, without extra charges to get it up. This was the best I could do to get streaming of the unbroadcasted episodes, that still not seen the light of day, since they were edited into episodes from the filming in 2018. Feeling conscionable, and obligated that I should deliver to the volunteer interviewees and youth audience these promised episodes.

I posted, searched and interviewed yet again for this task on those entertainment sites like before and maybe also on *Indeed* to describe in more detail what kind of specific task needed to be done. I vaguely remember there were few replies for candidates for this fiddly specialised technical task. I interviewed them on the phone until I found Sandeep Threstha, professional graphic designer and video editor, who was running his own small business doing video edits of commercials and utube stuff for business and cause brands, he was also employed part-time elsewhere at a company, his wife also worked with him there. He understood the brief immediately and I sensed he knew what he was doing, so I interviewed him again in person at my occasional pop up office in the Prahran Library lobby. He exuded this Zen kind of aura about him, calm, efficient, peaceful, and a silent achiever all rounder. He was here a few years from Nepal and I visualized him sitting in a temple on the Himalayan Mountains in the lotus position praying with his tightly cropped neat dark hair perfectly in place, tidy and pleasantly cheerful, content with the simple things in life, like the cheeky grinning guy on the Bega cheese 2022 commercials on TV. We negotiated a reasonable payment agreement for hours spent in instalments of work progressed, uploading and the design layout for the graphics of the streaming site. I kept faith that he seemed decent and would deliver timely as promised. Sandy, as he endearingly liked to be called, said he preferred doing tasks for causes and such, contributing to the improvement of our society. He was currently doing some graphics and edits for *Sisterworks – Work Empowers Women.* I appreciated his benevolent attitude and nature. I introduced Sandy to Simon for collaboration and they communicated very happily and productively only asking my permission for things about my authority about decisions for our particular Streaming site and basic requirements. Sandy performed his abracadabra, sim sala bim, open sesame and uploaded the episodes, it was sometimes fraught with ticky tacky tech glitches but he always managed in his own zen fashion to overcome whatever the issues were, nothing phased him. Consulting with both Simon and myself, calmly getting on with it and plodding through it systematically until he completed certain parts and also get me to review it and to check and see, passing it as that he was on track and that those parts were up and running accordingly. He was similar to Scott in some ways, always willing to help and be of service above and beyond his duty to make it happen, with the Kevin Costner attitude taking from the rich to give to the poor.

He said he could only upload a certain number of episodes due to our tiny package, so the priority was those unbroadcasted and then we mutually chose a few others that we thought outstanding.

I was to pay a monthly rental fee to OKAST which was equivalent to my basic Foxtel package per month, in turn I asked Simon if the youth audience could access some FREE previews and select episodes as other sites were full rental. So on our site, he was kind enough to accommodate us with either rental monthly or subscribe for seven days for some FREE stuff. Rentals attracted further income for Okast with us receiving a very minute percentage from the actual EURO 9.99 rental fee which supposedly would be paid into our nominated account through Stripe until Covid interfered. I haven't seen any razoo at all since to this day deposited into our account. Cest la vie, Com si com ca. But doing it for kids and taking it for the team as Robbie W would sing, *I'm loving angels instead.*

It was also after our broadcasting licence was not renewed after 2018, that Matt Field from promotions at CTV31, emailed that our ratings were the highest for the years 2016 – 2018, and he suggested that to obtain detailed figures of Melbourne, Adelaide and Perth contact OZTAM and I fee would have to be paid to obtain the detailed ratings statistics lists for the states involved in airing. From memory Adelaide was the highest followed closely by Melbourne and Perth, for those years. I tried to use this information to pitch to other broadcasters before approaching OKAST but either never received responses or the responses were its not appropriate for our current programming. Foxtel's Brian Walsh, Viceland, ABC, 7Two, 9 Gem, 10 Peach and now there's shake too. Disney and some other streaming platforms too, but I either couldn't get in or there was no direct contact available or they weren't permitted to accept unsolicited materials in any way, shape or form.

After winding down everything and now that our streaming site, was up. I was done for the most part, trying to flog the dead horse. There were other projects that preoccupied my mind that I would retrieve from the backburner. I decided to a short introductory course, on scriptwriting in Winter of 2018 and then later in the

Summer a short memoire writing course at RMIT. From 2018 to 2021, I wrote three film/ TV series scripts and one film treatment. May 2021, I completed my Part 1 of my memoire NEVER, published by Caidex Communications, Brian Dole Principle and his right wing man Carl Segnit who typeset, secondarily proof read and realized my visualization of the front and back.

Teentalkproduction.okast.tv

Ybidda, ybidda, ybidda that's almost all the teentalk story folks! (Bugs Bunny, Rex Hunt)

4T2HOT – for teens to help other teens.

Your star sparkling bright in the teentalk light!

Make your wish upon a star –

From the youth whisperer.

SPA Party

I received an email about the SPA Screenforever Conference 12th November, 2019 and with a reasonable income from the clinic available then. I will make a last ditch effort to ready, steady pitch! my folly to them. I might have paid for a day and a half, it went for three but couldn't afford time off real paid work. Preparing as much as possible, I emailed John for some tips at what to do there, so as not to waste this maybe once off opportunity. So I pre-booked and bid for huge and such terribly fierce demand for Roundtables and Pitching guests. It was at the resplendent Crown Conference Centre Complex, Southbank Melbourne. Most of the hoy poloy I couldn't grasp, so I attended sessions and talks that kept my interest for a few minutes and stayed for the duration alternating between many floors, escalators and opposing speech rooms. I made a few *industry acquaintances.* I even tried to work the room, swapping cards, advice and networking connections of people whom some were known celebs and others. *Who are you? Alice in Wonderland.*

I managed to snag a few Roundtables with Stuart Baxter EntOne UK, who skirted past talking about formats shows so my ears pricked up, that I was interested. Dan Jinks USA producer of American Beauty. Claire Mundell UK Synchronicity Films. Pitches, it wasn't quite my lucky dip either Que Mihn Luu ABC, Brown Johnson Sesame Workshop USA, and Ben Ulm ITV Studios. I brushed past the likes of Rachel Griffiths, Director – Ride like a girl, giving her some sample DVD's for her kids and Sue Maslin – Dressmaker and Lisette Atkins, Unicorn Films - Celeste. It was a lollyshop of semi celebs and a very much scaled down wee version of watching the Academy Awards or TV's Logie Awards.

Pitches were hard, sharp and fast, so I practiced the best part of the day with new acquaintances with their own take on how to manage the witchy pitch, until my sessions were up. They came and went in a flash before my eyes and I tried to chuck a bit of everything I could think of in here and there, Teen Talk Production, Film Scripts – Soul, Bizarre Triangle and Sparkle. There were a few of the ITV shows that stuck out for me and they were up my alley on similar veins. I spontaneously made up a few things on the spot for Ben Ulm and to my astonishment he said *already filming that for the next season to switch it up.* Finally I landed up contacting Stuart Baxter a few months later, alas I ended up with his staffer Sophie and again, nothing was to come of it, as everyone was on a different train of thought.

In the lobby of the Crown waiting for a Taxi to go to the Netflix Opening night drinks, sitting on the arm of the white leather lounge, I said *where are the Taxi's*, she said *there aren't any available.* We chatted about her films and she'd amazingly won some BAFTAS. In her UBER which she prepared earlier, from experience, I briefly described my various projects to her but her thoughts were somewhere else, she said she thinking about what her kids in the UK were up to. It was Clelia Mountford, Merman Films UK. I sent an email to her office, for which I received a generic standard reply, on the lines of not interested and were too busy with our own stuff anyway, so don't bother us. The conference gave me the courage and gave me hope that there were other possibilities out there if you looked for them but they all crumbled into sand in my hand, once the daylight of reality struck me, that I would probably never get through that elusive industry door that made magic.

The finale of the conference was the Screen Producers Australia Awards at the Forum Theatre, a beautifully decorated grand lady and the Amazon Prime Video Gala Party After, even though I found these industry people a bit dippy whippy flippy, they knew how to organize a fab bash and have a ball. It was the most fun in years for me, food absolutely ace up to gourmet fingerfood high stars. Drinks overflowing and not the darn cheap stuff either, Music Performers, Disco and dancing, shaken the groove thing all night apart from a break to network people up and get more yummy grub and piss on. Boogieing down with the likes of Jason Taylor, Futurism Studios, US. Somehow, I stumbled myself to an after party recovery nightcap at The Atrium Bar and then a few kind people waiting out the front who helped me, pour myself into the first available Taxi to home. That fleeting moment in conference time was over. As a reminder I have my passport photo pictures of the night in my fav red dress.

Behind the Scenes

There was a flashback frenzy and I saw the orange synthetic fringed mats on the chunky wooden carved tables of The Lindentree, that Edith Eberts chose when they were running it before he died and Mum and Dad then took it on. Mum hated them and so she summoned me to a task of searching for a whole lot of gabardine material that was that rich royal red colour that was stunning against the deep rich wood stain. I brought home samples to test on the tables and found our material at Spotlight. We measured, cut and Mum sewed hundreds and hundreds of those red mats.

Those heavy beer barrel tub stool chairs with the red vinyl padded upholstery that were so cumbersome to move she rallied me and Freddie up to twist them around so that she could vacuum underneath at the end of a hectically busy night before at The Tree. Mum Vacuumed because she was the fastest at it, and she said we dilly dallied at it. I would wipe the tables, change mats, re stock fridge, check the ladies for bodies forgotten and the men's etc. later in Rebar times the Indian Guys would help me clean and sort out the lavatories. Freddie was always mostly doing bar stuff, stocking etc.

Some of the weirdest people from Foster's Home of Imaginary friends, staff and customers alike. The Tassie Davs and Bazza the body – builders on steroids, the Russian Bisexual lady with her huge alsatian, Gregg and Dean, the divorced homeless brothers, of which Gregg was Fred's lackey help. Wolfgang the Werewolf wolfie with a grizzly Adams beard who proposed to me and then went to live rural in The Patch, Tall Giant Helmut with a little boys face and white fine wispy hair who scarred his hand in a trade work accident who painted the German Liebfrauwein bottles that became flower vases when empty, crafting them with flowers and Edelweiss and gifting them to mum and me. He might have been a bit of a fan of me as he also gifted me a locket with a head shot of me in it before he eventually returned to Germany. The white Rabbit, we called her who seduced unwitting married cops on the sly. Ennio, Lindo the Italian brothers and Paul Ross who were Freddie's friends, but always constant appendages around the bar. Skoda and the other Indian helpers who Freddie ushered about getting them to do whenever and whatever needed to be done. Short stubby Hans, who was a larger version of a ventriloquist doll with the checkered English cap that made him look even more of a dick. Dad chuckled at times at home coining him *Hans mit der langer schwanz*, the German rumour about Hans was that he met at The Tree, a Nun who recently gave up her vows and was now shacked up with Hans both having been single most of their lives. Hans apparently broke something around the bush area with his ginormous dongle and something was operated on, so that it wouldn't happen again. *It won't be long now!,* It was hysterical stuff that you couldn't make up if you tried.

No wonder Dad called it a Circus and the Circus was always in town at The Tree. The Huge Irishman, laird of the castle, shiny dark slick haired Frankenstein but more attractive leprechaun giant. He wore those double gold breasted Irish coat vests and with his fob watch chain dangling from the vest pocket, very dashing something out of an Irish picture book. He dressed in Irish costume on occasions like St. Pats day and he once gave me a felt Irish harp shaped dress pin that was handcrafted, as a gift, that I hung on my bedroom above my bed and cherished, it was true Irish. He would crack sick jokes, one liners and Knock knocks at me in gest and laughed at them himself with a Santa's Ho Ho Ho. His favourite that he repeated every time he came and I would always smirk at the punch line. *What did the cat say when they cut off its tail? It won't be long now,* in his thick heavy heeping Irish cut with a knife accent. I don't think he and Hans ever became introduced because our Irish laird sat on a table for two aptly beside the band stage and Hans Up at the bar. Those were the days my friends we thought they'd never end, we'd sing and dance forever and a day. There were many, many more of these astonishing characters, reminding me of another of my fav films of all time *John Merrick – The Elephant Man,* that escaped the dreaded cruel Freak Show. This film was sensitive like our characters and always brought a compassionate tear to my eye. These kind funny endearing characters that wore their heart on both sleeves and to me extended family. Since this is a brief flashback, you will just have to read my NEVER novel – Part 1 of this proposed memoire trilogy to read about the other hijinx and shenanigans of the other Tree Circus patrons.

What's the Time Mr. Wolf?

2018 sometime late sultry February In Melbourne. A blast from the current past made an appearance. It was a Saturday and I was having my usual long sleep in sojourn until at least 11-12 am that morning. I dragged myself to the kitchen bleary eyed, checked the mobile as a habit and saw these early riser messages about why I wasn't answering the phone, because of course I was asleep. In my hand it rang again and I picked up the call.

It was my friend James, whom I dated a few times before I cancelled his contract but remained so so, luke warm friends. He made these stupid three month contracts with girlfriends, that they would be exclusive for the duration only. I thought him rather a madman. I was a free spirit, nobody's chattel. It was all rather amusing to myself that his young girls actually agreed to this outlandish beastial behaviour, but I would not suffer such utter nonsense was *Helen Reddy's – I am Woman*, all for nothing then. I wasn't a women's libber but it was something out of the dark ages a bit like Henry the Eighth, another stark raving mad Englishman. Probably enough ranting and raving about that so we agreed to disagree on his contract caper.

Why don't you answer your phone? He stormily shouted down the phone. I was too embarrassed to say I was still sleeping in son of a gun. Well I have answered now anyway and I almost hung up the phone at his rudeness.

I heard him out because I hadn't seen him in virtually years and was curious. I occasionally sent him an email greeting for his birthday as friends do and on festive times to touch base and keep in touch, of course I never knew where he was at for any given length of time, he flitted around with his mining show gig, between Vietnam, China, Singapore, Sydney and the like. What the devil was it he wanted after all these years? I certainly lost interest a long time ago and thought he must have been shacked up or even could be married to one of his contract concubines. It was so freaky, people don't just come back into your life like that, at the flick of a switch. That limorous crush which I felt at the time I met him years ago was all but extinguished with the perpetual neglect of an unwatered plant.

I'm back in Melbourne he said for a few days, and I would like to meet up with you today, I said when today, Now, he barked the order down the phone line. Why not? so I dressed speedily and met him at his fav corner cafe shop. Douglas, who was his wing –man might have been there to for a while. Douglas was his go to man for everything and anything, like a PA, he wouldn't do a step without him. There was another odd friend of his that he acquainted me with also, Sylvester Finbarr Nagle Esq. MM Mediator Practitioner, always dressed like an Irish prince, who I tried to solicit to help me mediate but he said he wouldn't take on such things especially Arab family matter disputes. He was an Irish prankster and thought I probably dodged a bullet that I never became entangled.

James was sitting at his favourite window corner spot table with these orange stretch jeans and black crew neck pullover and his hair fluffed up in bouffant bleach quokka style, wisped around his face. Was there something flickering there? Like a silly schoolgirl I tippled my tea onto my red and white stripey sailor shirt long sleeved crew top, specifically between the cleavage of my breasts as if it was done on purpose, bad things always happened when I wore white tops, I needed a bub bib.

He cheekily spied down at my top and said to cheer me up even more, that will stain you know. It became darker and darker as it dried and we chatted about rather nonsensical stuff of no consequence that I can't recall what. James offered Douglas another coffee and Douglas says no thanks, I'm off now. His eyes looking everywhere except my stain as he was polite just like that. That coffee shop was about to close up, so was there something he wanted to say to me now Douglas was gone. He said we should continue our chat at the Laurent opposite as they were open longer hours. I tried to guide him to a conversation where I thought it was going but it never went there. Sitting in the Laurent at the corner table for two he orders himself a croissant with butter, a small bottle of coke and another tea for me. As they arrive, his phone rings and he answers it straight away which to this day I find so exceedingly rude if it's not urgent which it wasn't I knew because I heard Liz Fleetwood his number one fan on the other end talking jibberish as verbal diahorrea about nothing, I was thinking scatty ditzy Liz, was more up his alley and she was also quite comfortable and availably divorced, I felt a soft spot for Liz, picking up her girls deb dress and going to her regular psych. She was a bit too high maintenance for me as a true friend and another planet wavelength.

It wasn't a quick chat either it seemed it went on for ages so I drank more tea and wished I ordered a marmalade sandwich to take up the slack of time to distract me, like the Queen with Paddington. I knew she fancied James but I wasn't sure if he was into her or not, they'd been friends for years too. It sort of ended as it began with nothing in hand but a catch up and the conversation went decidedly downhill after the phone incident, he arrogantly left his half drunk Coke bottle on the table and I said pick it up, people in Mexico would kill you for that bit of precious Coke and said a loud No.

My hopes for this unfruitful friends reunion were all but dashed, so I nudgingly suggested dinner, No he was off he said to meet up with another male friend of his whom he was collaborating on for a project and they were going to dinner and a film after, like a date. I also thought this weird and that if he cared about me enough he would have taken a raincheck or at least made an effort to have taken me out for a cosy dinner before he left for wherever he was flitting to next up from Melbourne. So there it was another nothing day, that was so disappointing, it was the neverending story with Bowie. Know I fully knew now that sadly this guy was a total Dick and a jerk and I simply lost interest. He wasn't at all chivalrous but the opposite of Dick Chateau fame. No, he belonged to the liz's and Bella's category of men and he should stick to his concubines and not bother me further, as he would hopefully later find out for himself I was way beyond his league, and I would give him a run for his money and bang for his mean buck, like you say it best – Ronin Keating. It was then and there that I decided that I would let this infatuation drift away, as he took me for granted.

The Lockdown Years.

These were actually very productive for me apart from actually earning money and working. Ironically I got things done which I probably would never have got a chance to do otherwise. I fought the developers to the left of Mum's house who were going to build a COVID monstrosity design with their entrance to the building and lobby in the front of my kitchen window along the side footpath with less than two metres distance in between. Through, VCAT and the Supreme Court during Covid. It was worthwhile I think because I sort of got a win in that the council pushed for an amended acoustic walkway down the side and the developers then put up the house and land for resale with permits and plans as it now stands, but it was a lot of time, money and effort for me these years.

The KOORALBYN sign, that I designed for the letterbox column in front of the house. There was a thirties sign there before but some schoolies ripped it off with also a coach column light that dad had to re order and buy when I was still at Uni. They were similar to the Spring St. Parliament House lights. That one was more of a gothic house sign style but it was a brass cut out sign. I wanted it to not be the same but similar on those veins, so I designed it in cursive and in cut out brass it was also different from the run of mill house signs on plaques, it was controversial in our street but it was an original for the house I thought and I gave no hoot if other people weren't impressed with it, similar to the father in The Castle film. To me it was elegant in its simplicity, grace and style in its form.

The Alice in Wonderland garden setting that I decorated the front middle garden with at the footpath with resin figurines it was similar to a shop installation and passersby could see the story. The kitchen pantry creation, in the wasted corner space on the opposite side of the old classic kitchen cupboards style. The master and instigator of this was Cain Hamill of Nu- life carpentry. I was very pleased with the result.

The Kitchen galley aristocratic heavy solid wood swinging chunky door that dropped off its hinges with the other development excavations on the right four metres from my driveway from the streetscape. Quirky Swedish Adam who was a handy man, I found on Indeed I read his resume of being a boat builder in Sweden and I was sold and he delivered splendidly as with some other tasks until the Covid anxiety struck him. The Antique American 12 seater dining table, made from that curly grained antique wood that Mum and me bought together at an auction at Aingers in Richmond while I was at Uni. The pedestal leg posts of which also fell off during the development on the right due to the vibrations and movements of the deep excavations. I found Jamie Allpress of Allpress Antiques to repair it, as Mum would have been mortified to have seen it damaged.

There would be further house repairs, some organizing and declutter, plus vintage precious memory photos retrieved and restored of the family, friends and The Lindentree, Freddy's and Rebar. Personal photos were done at Pro Lab South Yarra and the Memory Cards in the Cameras that were the still images of the kids, crew team and guests at the filming interviews, that I photographed myself, of thousands that were developed and saved on external drives and USB for posterity and infinity, at Photobee, Malvern. There were literally thousands as Jimeoin says and these were developed at Photobee, Malvern. Being during the Covid and having nobody to help me, at the time of picking up the TTP photos, I bought a USB from them and asked if they could help me transfer the Never novel onto the USB as a digital copy.

Central heating went down next and it was the stark middle of Winter, it was two weeks of having to wait for the service and another two weeks for the part, guess, the longest without heating, with all the hydronic and bar heaters all on at once to keep the damp from the door with a chill on the edge. New Pool pump as this was dragging, leaking and without suction, causing difficulty to also vac it and so it went on these months. It reminded me of the time my patient Denise who's semi retired expressing her dismay at everything breaking down around the house once and when you retire.

The day another handyman came late, due to the earthquake of some reasonable magnitude, to repair the twist on the column boundary side of the driveway fence where it snapped top and bottom due to the torsion of the foundations during the excavations, securing the gates. Sleeping soundly, before he arrived the entire ceiling shook above me and rocked from end to end of the room, the chandeliers jingled. Not grasping what was happening, thinking that's a dirty great big possum banging about in the ceiling. Occasionally they were getting into the roof for shelter and fighting, screeching, noisy and bully bandying about. I chuckled as the tradesman said his ute skidded off the road due to the tumultuous motion. These security measures became crucial on finding the column buzzer seized and the gate hand lock super- glued and thought people going mad. Replacement buzzer repair and securing the gate lock, it's a shame people behaving badly.

Other later handyman repairs included securing outside doors, statue base and concrete garden seat repair, relocation of the Persimmon tree and planting of the way outgrown the potplant avocado. I moved the Persimmon as it was not doing well and would soon die off to the concrete foundations. The 3X3 M, Cubby House, Wendy House, Tiny House, Bungalow, Hutchey, Studio apartment, whatever you call it, was an early pre – COVID idea to supplement home expenses. There was that small wasted patch of garden in the South – West corner of the rear garden that I would have turned into a veggie garden. Boarders, otherwise would be too difficult to navigate with allergies and so on. This construction that should have been finished within weeks or months went on for years during the COVID and five builders later, due to the engineering being incorrect for the concrete foundation from independent soil test results, of the company that I purchased the kit home from, that was supposed to be all inclusive of all materials, permits, engineering, foundation and appointed builder. I was at my wits end sorting out this colossal mess, excavations required were far too deep for standard practices, there were other issues getting machinery in, getting the dirt out, getting a builder to do it.

So I researched other engineering systems on the internet and went on a ring around until I discovered the Surefoot System and then emailed Barrason's for engineering. What's happening with the The Parthenon as Nick, my patient charmingly described it, went up a few weeks after the foundation was finally achieved, with the current builder, coincidentally also Nik, a principle of (Rebuilder) who also agreed that this would require other alternative engineering to be less cumbersome. It was fully completed and appointed by April, 2022 having the intention and commencing from mid 2018.

Merrily pottering about doing things in the garden in the more pleasant temperatures on days, I had savaged the rear garden Olive tree as it was overgrown and bushy, interfering with other shrubs, it was almost overhanging the pool, until Norma said *why don't you pick your olives? What Olives?* Low and behold the tree was heaped with olives, that mum had been trying to cultivate olives for some thirty years unsuccessfully, they were runts of the litter until I came to almost decimate it. We collected bags, Norma trotted off with her bag and so I researched to marinate them, gave some to some Greek and Italian patients to do their own concoctions, that year my own olives were yummy. At the same time I was also trying to cultivate Avocados because I adore them and they are costly. The first avocado plant was planted beside the Persimmon along the right boundary fence, doing well, I continued to experiment planting many pots with plant grown from discarded avo seed pip. There is a whole ring of them now around the little mannequin piss, boy with fish concrete fountain, pride of place in the centre of the front garden, all flourishing at their own paces and some passed.

I was getting somewhat used to this COVID cockamamie lifestyle, until the dreaded M word came up. There was a dark vertical streak on my right big toenail which came up suddenly over 5 months during Autumn and Winter. I scrubbed and dug underneath but it was embedded in the toenail. It was increasingly darkening with such speed and intensity, all the length of the nail which concerned me, so went for three opinions, to have it checked. It was a rare animal, not your common garden Melanoma but a Melanonychia on all accounts, they all said surgical biopsy was urgent on it. So it was done on the 20th October, 2021, Norma drove and picked me up from the day surgery clinic, and Freddie said he was getting terrible cabin fever and would be pleased to drive me there and back for a dressing change to have a break away from his wife and three year old daughter for a few hours. He brought me home and I prepared some lunch for us and we chatted about almost everything. The results being decidedly with my usual luck inconclusive and that I must have to die from absolutely friggin' everything possible. We will have to wait on the final outcome of that dubious procedure, and that aching persistent incidental nagging throbbing night pain on the front shin of the same leg, I hoped I was early enough to have been onto it before it went farther afield faster. All those months from February 2019 having been sporadically dating online, as it became a daily COVID activity.

The script writing course thankfully was completed during the Winter, 2019 and the Memoire Writing Course of November, 2019 both at RMIT. I began to write in the dreary, bleak Winter months, not much work, can't go out, what to do? feeling, as I was bored of clearing drawers. Like a woman possessed I have written to this day, three film/ TV series scripts, first memoire novel *Never,* and a treatment for a futuristic dystopia society envisaged as a concept feature film or TV series.

My Mum and Dad to me were the epitome of True Love until before Dad succumbed to an attack of Spinal Meningitis which was to alter his behaviour drastically like he was someone else entirely. The late life crisis ensued not long after, it was the beginning of the end, of his poor life expectancy and maybe like Dad, similar to Sabena tracking badly with her Dad (The Arabo) Eddie, as my Mum used this term interchangeably and Bon, her stepmum (Mop), but Mum said that it wasn't over yet and gave me hope that things might yet turn around.

Why was it True Love? Dad explained to me about his girlfriend English Glady's before he met Mum, a bit chubby, whose legs were like elephants stumps and she walked with a decided hobbled limp to one side. She was a very nice lady Dad would say but there was something NQR, about her vigour. He began concurrently dating my virgin conservative Italian Mum, who spoke a few English words. Dad fancied Mum at first sight, and so he saved up wages for a month to invite her to High Tea at a posh place that was in fashion to impress her. They came home from the High Tea in hast as my Mum was feeling ill, to my dad's flat which he shared with Philon, his close accountant, Dunera ship friend and wingman who introduced him to the Fitzroy Church Social where the girls were smashing.

Dad says to Philon, I am besotted with this girl for serious, what do you think? Test her he said cruelly, tell her you can't have kids, Italians won't have that? Stupidly, and wastingly, over thinking, the simple situation. Mum answered that she would manage to overlook that for his intentions. Mum then embarrassingly and humbly trusting explained her malady and that she forgotten thingies in her purse, he would have to rush her home. Practical Dad said I won't hear of it I will pop to the pharmacy shop for you. There it was, dad broke up with Glady's, who was waiting on a different story and Mum and Dad were married within a few months, after with what Mum said was exactly five pound between them and her own discarded potential other keen admiring suitors, who were also courting her avidly concurrently with my dad. Dad's address label stickers since forever with both him and Mum on them, on the top line as a team and on the line below proudly in letters *Kooralbyn.*

Kooralbyn- Home to the Valley of the Copperhead Snake. / Void in the house

After Mum's passing in December, 2010 there was a void in our home and an ugly dynamic between sorrow and grief for both of us and Freddie's own narcissistic and his controlling boss power attitude over me. Things stalled along after the funeral, my overseas residing sister failing to contest the will and Freddie to my concern behaving as if he was the King and boss of Everything, even of myself. However, I was not Mum as I was my own independent person and said we should finalize matters. Freddie rebelled at the even bare thought of this as if the idea exceedingly repugnant, so I felt he was still suffering the loss of Mum, whose beanie he would sniff and keep on the bedside table. I was struggling and suffering too but to keep prolonging the inevitable would be even more difficult. I gave him the benefit of the doubt and give him some time and space about it, until he comes around. This went on for some years until I realized, Freddie would always be controlling the money. Things would probably never change, if nothing was done and I would be at his mercy like a Britney Spears conservatorship for the rest of my natural life, and he would try to reassure me by saying I will always look after you for Mum no matter what. Thankfully I woke up as Sabena 14, was admitted to the Royal Children's Hospital, Melbourne in November, 2013 for self – harm mutilation and suicidal idealization. It was obviously a critical circumstance for me and I said to him I will need some money if I need to take it to court again and appeal for intervention for Sabena's well being sake.

Bull by the horns.

Freddie snapped after mum's passing and he strangely became more aggressive and power hungry. I felt trapped and frustrated, and our communications became strained, when once we were such a team. I was more than jack of being bossed around by Mum but in a guiding way, Eddie (The Terrorist Arab), and now Freddie. Mum called Eddie also Saddama as in Sadam Huissen, as he looked like him too. Mum was able to put Freddie in his place when he was out of himself, as he took heed of her critic. Freddie was on top of the world now, and he wouldn't listen to me with his thoughts about mega construction plans that never came to fruition or were never realised after the plans were drawn up.

Having now been stalled for years, I confronted him one more time with no response and then went to see some local lawyers, the next day, who were not much use, perhaps under resourced and then relocated to a larger city firm, they were on the ball writing letters, making enquiries immediately. Our day to day life together in the same home became excruciatingly, always walking on eggshells. He received the first lawyer's letter and said to me *you're not real are you*, trying to intimidate me. He was trying to get me to stop pursuing this avenue and cut it off in its tracks, to keep his control. The second letter, after the midday mail arrived I was in the clinic, that backed off the kitchen with a hospital curtain screen, at the rear of the house when Freddie stamped his foot and screamed FF'ing B! or something similar in a gruff and abusive tone. It was embarrassing for me and the patient was genuinely also concerned for me with this outburst. The patient asked if I was alright, and ignoring him, continued as if nothing happened and he then left after a few minutes, I'm not sure what reaction he thought he might get from that. He never returned again that day until evening time much later.

The ensuing letters caused a tumultuous revolt in anger and similar to a Battered Wife Syndrome, and abusive Domestic Violence situation, who can't get away, I would be punished by walking in to the kitchen before Dinner and whacking my face, in a fit of rage, unawares and my glasses tossed across the room and not being able to see and find them, as him chasing me about the house and me running for cover until in the corner I held up my hands to stop him, his temper now at its peak. I was afraid of these, be very afraid, that the anger might get to exploding point that he injured me. This mafia agro tough guy behaviour occurred rarely with Freddie, but he never disrespected Mum, but somehow I was different. I saw it momentarily now and then when he was bossing about the Indian helper workers at the bar, hitting them, kicking them or punching them, if they were too slow or made a mistake, it was slavery all over again. If it was torture, I would have intervened but it was only enough to shake them up usually and show them whose boss dog. I was abhorred but made no fuss, not to perhaps inflame the situation, puzzled by what I was seeing and incredulous, gasping. This was totally opposite to the happy go –lucky brother and the pretend Freddie who tried to please and get on with all and sundry almost everyone or the best Freddie with his random acts of sweetness, who always came to the rescue like a superhero and delivered as the cheeky boy with the Cadbury bar gives the crying girl on the bus the offer of his chocolate, what a sacrifice.

It became intolerable me working and living in the same house with him and I was powerless to do anything, nowhere to go and no money to go somewhere else to reside, I was stuck suffering. After many pairs of damaged and distorted eye glasses later, minor cuts and bruises, I would then try to avoid him, but where would I go at dinner time in the dark, especially in Winter. I began to drink more than usually now and then, so I could get to sleep, to forget and wondering if he would attack me at any time, the concerns for Sabena churning over and over in my mind, bad combinations that fuelled the fire. There was an incident, when I escaped to the car and drove to my then boyfriend's house, staying for a few days. The attacks became more sporadic and being soused I was more useless and helpless, which irritated him even more, with him screaming abuse at me, and worse broken drinking glasses and bottles were also involved in the mix. Make it stop, then until the day the chard of glass went up into my throat, as I was sitting on the kitchen chair, it was minimal penetration and so my carotid wasn't slashed, thanks to god. He called the Ambulance and it was a minor laceration, patched up on the spot but there was blood splashed about and my blouse and towel soaked. I asked some girlfriends for advice, *even if it's your brother, you have to get an IVO or AVO,* I don't know the difference myself and buy new locks for the gates and doors, lock him out.

It Became like a messy divorce, War of the Roses saga, he would come home when I wasn't there and took stuff, from Mum's safe in the wall to which he had the key to, knew what was in there and then locked it again, he locked all the rooms with doors in the house so I couldn't use them, again no keys until the IVO finally came up through cops. The other reason also I was concerned about obtaining an IVO against Freddie was his cop friends at Prahran, so I went to Richmond instead. He came to collect his stuff in bulk and he brought a security guard to supervise, so I asked a friend too. I felt however mum's good spirit was also always lurking about the house guiding and protecting me. I called locksmiths to break open the safe and the make me copies of the all the house door keys. It was quite a performance, what was going to happen next? I began sleeping with a crowbar next to my bed and the mobile, after the interim order, he wasn't permitted in my bedroom, but that was no help and then I applied again with further information and was granted IVO, him out of the house. They were jumbled scenes out of *The Good Wife and Nightmare on Elm Street – where's Freddy?* and sounded *Toxic – Britney Spears.* So I continued the legal battle, certain that I might end up homeless or on the street should I not defend myself or *Fight for my right to party – Beastie Boys,* colloquially, be tossed out on my ear without a leg to stand on and not being given what was my birth right and without a home or razoo. I stayed in Mum's house, Freddie stayed in a flat of his apartment block and his building complex in St. Kilda, with the corner building being Summerland Mansions.

The wake

I wondered why I never twigged that Freddie might do this awful stuff to me. Mum's funeral was a celebration of a life well spent at St. Anthony's Hawthorn, her and Dad being founding members. Freddie and I, with attention to each detail down to singing and music, that we thought Mum well deserved recognition of her life. Sanae, my Japanese friend, who lived a few streets away from us, was a mother figure to us, supporting us with suggestions and organizational arrangements and lending us her maid, studying nursing Hiromi to help us, organize a wake. There was a celebration at our house, with a small shindig of close invited guests after the best hospitality royal funeral ever, overflowing with so many people and Freddie even organized for the video tape recording of the Church Funeral and Procession. Mum and Dad would have been so proud of the both of us united! In the entrance hallway of the house there were a few guests and my sister chatting. I was busily getting people settled with food and drink, helping out to keep the guests happy. Freddie joined them with a cop buddy and then I brought out a tray of food for them. Someone asked me about the exquisite mahogany stained wood carved panelling around the walls in the entrance hallway that went almost to the top of the of the ceiling with a wide ledge. I certainly, not seen anything like quite like it in any of the stately National Trust houses that I visited before, so knew it was original and unique. I purported that the owner and builder of the quasi stately home was a well heeled timber merchant from the Kooralbyn Valley in Queensland, where he lived part of the year logging timber I assume. He brought the timber especially to Melbourne himself to have it made up. He also ordered particularly and bought the best English and Scottish accessories for the house adornment. I was pleased that they appreciated our house as much as my family and how Mum cherished it. My sister, having turned up somewhat coming from Turkey and late to the funeral, and then dragging her luggage with her to our house, plonked at the bottom of the hallway staircase which was still there that same guest evening. She megaphoned, blarring into my face, *Why are you still in this house?,* nastily with toxic venom. It was a rhetorical question but I thought to soothe her, as the cops glared and was silly enough to reply. *Because I have lived here nearly all my life and now due to my unforseen circumstances work here too!.* She turned into a savage beast, screaming hate and then in a flash dragged me by the hair across the room and me dropping the tray. What was this? I shrieked as my head was tugged, Freddie then grabbing her suitcase and tossing it into the front garden and then proceeded to extricate her from me and then threw her out the front door after. That bitch on wheels is never coming into this house again, to be sure, I will make sure of that and there it was and I always thought he was defending me during that moment in our sibling lives.

Aberrant Neurology

This was the epitome of low, as I thought of Mum not having seen Sabena for more than two years, Eddie not wanting her ever to come to the house, as Mum always sat hawklike on the veranda balcony keeping a watchful eye on everything around her. Eddie absolutely hated my Mum. Mum's last time of seeing Sabena was that day in September, 2007 after which she then suffered the febrile Illness paralysis months later. I don't remember if I elected not to show Mum the disgusting snaps of the Elvis hip pose, sagged eye. They lived in a flat in East Bentleigh then, and she went to school at Tucker Road Primary, where they sent me newsletters, results and school photos of Sabena as I wasn't permitted to go 100 metres of her school or my agents etc. Eddie done that too, as he said I might harass them at court. I even spoke once or twice for a few minutes with the Principal, Stan Oakley who was more than sympathetic to my extreme circumstances and series of unfortunate events, he described having concerns about Sabena and her worrying behaviours that were disruptive to the other children at the school, that commenced after her sudden viral illness. After this they soon moved quickly to a brick Veneer in Sydenham, on the other side of town around Keilor somewhere where she attended Keilor Downs College, Principal Stuart Andrews. The principal pleasant enough to me after a once off truncated by staff conversation said Sabena 12, seemed isolated, reclusive and lost at Keilor Downs College and voiced concerns about her emotional well – being and suggested the father and stepmother were in significant denial, about Sabena's state of mind. Since Eddie and Bon never permitted me to visit with Sabena more than an hour or two, I couldn't understand the nature or extent of her neurological impediment and what triggered these disruptive behaviours which I never personally observed myself apart from that her thoughts were confused. Of the few annual visits Eddie and Bon (Squash faced Not attractive as Miss Piggy) would drop her at our local coffee shop and Romeos' Bistro and return in a couple of hours or even invited themselves and at always my expense, never offering. I thought they might even ask me for their petrol money to come to visit someday. I never complained. I asked Eddie sweet as pie, as Mum came out of hospital gravely ill from both bowl and kidney infections and she was very weak if he would allow Sabena to visit her for brief while even for a few minutes, and he said a flat NO without even hesitation and he also refused her to attend the funeral. These were not the only vindictive streaks of Eddie, later on he refused me permission for her school and medical records.

Not certain how I discovered which Medical Clinic in Bentleigh that she attended because it wasn't the same clinic that Eddie and I attended many years previously when Sabena was a toddler, that was in Mackie Road. The male doctor that treated Sabena was morose about my prying into the incident. He tried to passively paint me a mental picture of her condition as best he could and what may have happened without actually providing factual information, which he said regrettably and remorsefully that Eddie would never permit it. Genuinely being concerned as practitioner to practitioner, as I was known to him through my own clinic in Carnegie, from several years ago.

I think Mum thought it was not as serious as it was and solaced me that children recover from most ills in given time and recover. We agreed however that Sabena was deceitfully lulled and lured into her residing with Eddie and Bon, without retaliation, with her believing it would be a short fun holiday and joyride for a few months and then she would come home. Sabena seemed excited and happy at the thought that she would be a real bridesmaid at a real wedding, her loving fancy occasions, at her Dad's wedding and they would all be going on a Qld trip for the honeymoon. Then the reality hit that she appeared content enough initially until the months dragged on and she became despairing, rundown, vulnerable and debilitated, her immune system crashing at the slightest tiny trigger.

Alice In Wonderland

Before Sabena began at Keilor Downs, she still dressed pretty, cute and prissy, with ribbons, bows, headbands, combs, sparkly things, with attention to detail, and themes of vibrant bright colours of a symphony of hearts, flowers, Butterflies and those silver sparkling with glitter dainty ballet pump shoes, she appeared normal for the most part to other people, myself and Freddie, being together for short bursts of time and we were also oblivious to the extent of the neurological damage that was seething below the ingenuous surface causing the bizarre and aberrant erratic behaviours that were taunting her. Sabena's fav place in those seemingly early happy days to have our visit was, The Pancake Parlour in Chapel St. Before she went to live with them she would beg me to make her pancakes on any holiday occasion, me cooking up a big stack, for most of the morning and so she eagerly ate them for brekkie, lunch and tea for a day or two until they were all eaten up without a crumb or morsel left at all. She grinning and laughing with me and her Uncle Freddie.

Always forever ordering the Alice in Wonderland Pancake, that Pink might have been eating in her music video, with lots of hundreds and thousands, sprinkles and loads of other yummy delish gooey stuff. Hot chocolates all round with pink and white, marshmallows that Sabena bounced them up and down with glee with her spoon to get them melting and oozing with froth. Another place we sometimes went was the Quaff, simple but gourmet food for their three course lunch special and that was my favourite and Bruce the owner was attentive and welcoming.

Mostly it was Romeo's being local, reasonable, fine family fare, popular and also open all hours for coffee and food, and once we saw Bronwyn our prior neighbour there and introduced her to Sabena. I tried to engage Sabena with people that she knew to remind her of when she was younger like Sue and Lucinda, Mum and daughter patients of the clinic, who Sabena thought Sue's shortbread the absolute best only problem she made it rarely. Affectionately me quipping then nicknames of Sabie Beans and Lucinda's Mum of her sweet peas. Freddie if he could make it and was available and our sister Hilda, one or twice, on her bi- annual travels to Melbourne. I should have realized then that my sister was a traitor as she defended Eddie of whatever I complained about blaming me without even having ever known or seen him, like Mum deduced him instantly from looking into his eyes and he always looked away in deceptive shame.

The show goodie bag.

Planning busily the day before the visits to make the most of these rare opportunities to visit with Sabena, and make it heaps of fun, It was the show goodie bag or Felix the cat, happy bag of tricks to love her and cheer her up. I encouraged her to draw and sketch, after we finished lunch for something for me to keep as a precious keepsake of each of our visits, and also because she liked doing it for me. So armed with various coloured papers, Faber – Castell and Kimmie Junior textas and markers, stickers and other bits and bobs. At this phase she mainly sketched Japanese Manga girls with their huge dolly eyes with sometimes Easter or Christmas themes of singing cheeping chicks, tiny birds, bunnies, trees, flowers, bees, hearts, eyes, me and her together and the odd words she learnt at school written in Japanese. It reminded of preparing for a Joey Scouts crafting session. The pictures began to become a more increasingly gloomy and insidiously sinister with the girls now having eye patches, flowers and hair dangling far down over one eye. Kind of girly versions, of Jack Sparrow. Every time I brought her a gift to take home with her of books, clothes, and other cute stuff, she was into. I would always bring my favourite still Olympus and Mini Minolta cameras to take snaps of us as a memory that contained bought film in those days to have to get them processed.

I never imagined that years later I would be taking photos of other people's kids to bring out the emotion of the interviews and for their show and tell of their most favourite item of which, a nine year old interviewee said her it was her devoted Mum, goofily sweet and so absolutely adorable. The kids also taught me to take pictures of everything as it was their shortcut way of recording all manner of things and stuff without writing and that you could learnt almost anything on u –tube if you tried, like another young teen who almost corrected her speech impediment by practising on it. Sabena's dress, behaviour and attitude began to become even darker, bleaker, grungier, butch and morbid, one day it was a bikie girl from the Hell's Angels rebellious type of angry, tough girl look. I wondered if the injury severely impacted her and that maybe it had resolved or morphed into something more psychologically deep seated from which I first thought. It certainly wasn't *jolly good* anymore as my temporary boss Colonel Patten, of many years ago often said to me who passed of a brain tumour sadly before retiring to his project dream home in Provence was realized. Justin Beiber, June 2022 contracting Ramsay – Hunt Syndrome similar to the symptoms of or what they now say replaces Bells' Palsy diagnoses of that that time. After Sabena 12 moved to Sydenham, was about the time the walking dead zombie of her personality appeared in sketches, dress and attitude. She morphed into something not now recognizable to me as my previous daughter, it was very disquieting to me and I hoped it was a passing teen phase or trend, as my Uni days as a punk emo. She pretended to be too big for giving me a hug and kiss on the cheek, after her visits and instead leaned on Bon if she was in attendance as if her groupie. Eddie the tyrant, began to say it was now to far for them to travel here and I would have to always go there from now on and visit Sabena on their turf near Watergardens. Visits became strained and infrequent due to my own busy work schedule then and their being exceedingly uncooperative and negative. I wasn't good with that end of town, not knowing it well and going round and round that Ring road that was a Bermuda Triangle force, and some of the people were weird and scary so I wouldn't go by myself and also I needed a witness and a friend in case they might do a swifty shifty on me at their house, as I had to pick up Sabena there. So it wouldn't be three against one, if they tried to pin something on me to stop me.

Sabena began wearing eyeglasses before they moved to Sydenham, wearing her long shoulder wavy and wild, auburn hair at our Romeo visits she would chatter and chipper about loving all cute things Japanese, Hello Kitty, Manga, the language, the country she wanted to visit the most. The worst part of the visits for me and I think Sabena too was saying a tearful Goodbye after the blink of an eye in time, we spent together. It was separation – anxiety all over again, and I would console her by saying we'll see each other again soon. For days after I was also melancholy and morose and sometimes I was relieved not seeing her for months, so that I recovered emotionally, as I would forget and be distracted by the other circumstances in my own current life.

Sometimes it was the same with the 10 – 20 minute phone calls on the weekend, I kept a brave face for her well – being, but I was worse functionally after speaking to her at times, it was so strained with them always spying on us and Eddie either hanged up on answering me or if he was annoyed about where the conversation was going. I tried to ring her at least early on every two weeks and later on at least once a month on the weekend as Betty Kotler, my grief psychologist suggested to show her my love and be there for her or abandon her if it was too draining for me emotionally, which I thought worse and because it was a devoted mother's duty to give her child hope, love and support for her future life, as I was brought up. Eddie and Bon also never encouraged her to ring me, not even on my Birthday, Easter or Christmas, the onus was always on me in fact I think they even discouraged her answering me and seemed irritated by the fact that I kept calling no matter what and if they ignored me enough I would disappear from her life, hopefully.

I wondered why Sabena couldn't take the initiative herself even if they disapproved, like usual rebellious teens and it was painful, but I now feel she wasn't capable to do, due to perhaps residual autism or similar disparity since her tragic incident. I was reconciled now maybe that she perhaps wasn't functioning enough to do stuff on her own anymore and there was nothing she could do about it helpless, under their rules and their roof. So she gave up on me and went the easier route to please them so she would get whatever she wanted like video games, music, internet time, favourite sweet treats and What's App and We Chat with her friends, which I technology wise wasn't savvy about. Eddie and Bon eventually disconnected her mobile those years and Sabena would say things like don't ring me on the landline so often or only ring me during the holidays, as if she wanted me to go away and not bother with them at all. These things were hard for my ears to hear and my heart to swallow and I felt heartbroken but there was by the same token, also nothing I could do under the difficult circumstances anyway myself being powerless.

In October, 2014, obsessed and distressed by Sabena's terrible hostage situation, I began fervently to write letters, after I read the article published in *The Australian on 27th September, 2014 – Fugitive Parents,* to the Attorney- General's Department, then Chief justice of the family court Diana Bryant from 2004 – 2017, and all manner of government departments and agencies I could think up and looked up on google, to enlist outside help about her plight, receiving generic answers of no consequence. Every now and then Derryn Hinch frequented Romeos' and I thought about telling him about my situation, or was it already too late for that at this stage, damage was done, but he might have been having issues with Jackie Weaver at this time, which was unfortunate so I thought not to bother him, ironically in the TTP years I was also to meet the funny, tubby lady from The Gogglefrocks TV program and she said her daughter might be interested in being interviewed for TTP program, however I never heard from her after that day.

Sabena's tastes in music also radically changed, which were from in this order, Let it go – Frozen, Ellie Goulding, Kelly Clarkson, Lily Allen- Sing Song Ching Ching, Sia, to Rita Ora, Mabel, Dua Lippa and K-pop, after she began attending Keilor Downs College.

Prince Charming

It was less than two months since Mum's funeral in February, 2011, that I went on my first date with James. I saw him at a singles party of Mez's at the Sugar Bar. He was wearing a very loud screaming Hawaiian shirt, which you could see a mile off and my friends Audrey, Rosemary and I thought this an absolute hoot. Later I was to meet him again at Sezanna's cafe a few weeks later and he asked for my mobile number and we exchanged them, I thought him a bit of a geeky dag but that was ok. He rang me not long after that and asked me on a date. We would meet for dinner at Kanpai in Chapel St. and on arrival he brought me a medical mask because I explained to him I suffered from allergies. I thought this a sweet gesture but said to him I have my own thank-you which are specific filtration masks from 3M, he said to me keep it anyway, so I thought it might come in handy someday anyway, so I kept it. After dinner he said, as he walked me to my car, weirdly, I have locked myself out, I can't find the keys to my place, as he walked down from his place in Armadale for exercise to keep fit. He said I will go home and return later and meet you at the Claremont Hotel, with that bit sleezy reputation of cheap floozies, I said no thanks that's fine I am going straight home.

Puzzled, what was it, I struck here, first date sex, No I don't think so. What a drongo dick? What sort of girls was he dating before me? Surely, they were either too easy, scrubbers or desperate prostitutes. I won't do that, That's not it. He hinted he preferred Asian girlfriends, but said he also was attracted to exotic sexy types like middle – eastern, Sabah with whom I also became acquainted later on with her and her 18 year old daughter, after she also moved on from James. I was in a fashion flattered but I was brought up a good conservative catholic Italian / German girl. What was he thinking, I certainly wasn't desperate or dateless, thank-you very much, so was a bit insulted that he thought so lowly of women, to have what I presumed would be a one night stand on the first date. I drove off speedily thinking hopefully I will never hear from him again and he will move on to more of his type.

He wasn't particularly my kind of guy anyway that I would be attracted to, I wasn't keen on ginger haired people, with the lighter tinted bleached streak at the front fringe for a start, he also towered over me a bit because my heels weren't that high or maybe I was wearing my chunky black buckle boots. The ginger hair made me think of bad tempered Scottish people and cruel, English Henry the eighth. With an average build, not very toned and he said he'd been in the military and wore headphones a lot due to his army injury deafness in one ear. I wasn't that keen on Military, jump how high, preferring tradies or preferably academic intellectuals or self – made men ambitious and motivated. I was unaware he would be likely to return to call me again as Big versus Carrie on Sex and the City. Those guys that annoyingly turn up on and off, whenever they want, you at their beck and call, uninvited and unexpected, as if you are perpetually available, without notice at the drop of a hat, usually as you are already dating someone else. What a damn nerve and cheek? I always thought Aiden the best of the lot in the series, he was my top fav. Make an appointment and queue up in line matey. The second date which I should have refused was dinner with a couple of freebie film tickets he was in possession of, Star Trek. He fancied himself as a bit of a know it all spock but better. His looks to me, a cross between Chuck Norris and Donald Sutherland, not to insult them.

I was a fan of the historical Star Trek series and films with William Shattner and the original cast but not so much of the modern versions. I became more involved with the Babylon 5 TV series and Hitchhikers guide to the galaxy, Red Dwarf and similar trendy stuff to these. So the film wasn't too bad and he behaved well during the screening as a perfect gentleman does. I drove us both to my tiny flat, as I was feeling that tiny sparkle again and maybe he'd done a once off silly mistake previous. It was not yet totally dark as we arrived. Opening the front door after fishing for the keys, I turned to face him on the top of the few steps below the landing entrance and bending down he dove into my face zoning in on my lips at a rate of knots. No, I was wearing my classic tight white tube skirt and black sheer, collared v- neck blouse with the flared arm sleeves and small side splits. It was an automatic instant dive and duck response, this happened before without asking permission. I felt his deep disappointment and seething resentment, but yet again I was more disappointed by his second date faux pas antics. My dad rest his soul if he were alive would have said he was a clown.

Beyonce – If you liked it you should have put a ring on it. We were back again to the young Asian girls and Prince Charles cheating on Diana, Andrew later also had dipped the Royal family into disgrace. These issues flashed passed in my thoughts, but my own devoted mum before her passing was worried about my future prospects and advised that even if you have a difficult suitor who seems promising for your life plan, try to please them. So I sacrificed my principles for James and instead of slamming the door in his face that was another natural instinct, I looked up with a sweet smile and said, would you like to come in and chat for a short while. His eyes pricked up and we sat on the chocolate brown velvet Jacobeen rattan lounge. I explained that it was not long since Mum's passing and I was still in shock. To me he seemed both privileged and very spoilt in his domineering manner. He described his own mother's and sister's passing an ultimately untimely tragic sudden death. His only living family being an uncle in Queensland whom he visited with annually and supposedly an illegitimate daughter he was supposed to have sired in his younger days that was not proven, living in his house.

These sounded more compassionate in nature and so giving him the benefit of the doubt I leaned into him a bit and spotted the daggy white cotton singlet hiding beneath his shirt collar. My dad wore singlets similar to that, the metal shirt sleeve armbands, colourful trouser braces, spectacle string and long white socks with his shorts, Freddie being more up to date T's.

James softened temporarily in his attitude we cuddled playfully like children without kissing, him trying to give me solace. He then suddenly stood up and said I'm off now it's getting very late. Should I drive him home, no I will walk he said, would you like to walk with me to the end of the street. It was a pleasant evening and I agreed, we continued to chat happily together, all the way on Clendon road his shortcut to Armadale, walking past the stately houses, arm in arm, him pointing out he admired the grey houses, why are there so many grey houses I thought, I much preferred them white, cream and beige to my taste. The constitutional ended as we parted ways at High St.

I wonder now whether James was aware of my Freddie predicament, probably not, of him holding the purse strings of Mum's money from me, Britney's conservatorship. 'Cos regrettably your mind always ticks over much later afterwards, in hindsight. It was my own money he was withholding from me. He hinted to me on our walk that he went every day to Sezanna's at 3 pm after he wound up his work and met all his friends there, until they closed at 5 or 6 pm. My life however continued to be constantly busy with something or other and weekdays I worked some days afternoons and evenings those hours for my own needed income to pay my own bills and on weekends I simply forgot, preoccupied or became more preoccupied with Sabena stuff. He Invented a Caterpillar. Mum encouraged me to date before passing as she believed that I deserved and she wanted a proper real life partner for me, who would help me, succeed the empire, ambitious and motivated. About the frequency of every few months I would coincidentally have to go to the pharmacy or do some errands on my few avo's off, out of my hectic schedule and pass Sezanna's, waving to him at his window seat and motioning that I was too busy to stop today but once or twice I stopped there. Somehow our polar different worlds and schedules were not colliding or even aligning with the stars. We were now definitely in the friend zone, he never called me up for another date after that even.

Queensland Sojourn

It was a particularly treacherous Winter of 2014 not dissimilar to 2022. I was fretting about Sabena almost constantly. My dear friend Angela called from Brisbane, Queensland asking if I would babysit her house for a month or so while she attended an Obgyn conference in Spain, at which end she was to walk the Camino with Vincent her young teen son. Freddie agreed and said it will be good for you to go and be distracting. The holiday began horribly with Freddie getting me late to the airport, he was always late to everything and never bothered about it. I was however frustrated, that I missed the flight and becoming increasingly agitated. They were trying to get me on the next flight but I was wearing my allergy mask and leather gloves maybe they thought I was a bit of a nutter in those days. They presumed me weird and a trouble maker at Qantas, requesting me to get checked by a doctor for my blood pressure or some such rot they made up, later on the return flight they would make it up to me though, treating me with kid gloves. We were there for hours, Freddie patiently waiting as he wanted to be sure I was safely on the plane. I eventually saw a doctor there, who examined me and I was passed and yet, the Staffer unapologetically said I still couldn't board the current flight. So I flung my three quarter empty water bottle at her in absolute disgust, Freddie thankfully soothed and smoothed her down, he was tops at stuff like that and but I said I was going to go back home. I don't know what Freddie said to her in the window corner away from earshot, but voila I was on the plane.

I loved being in Brisbane at this time of year, I babysat Angela's house that was about 10 minutes walk from beautiful crimson flowering Southbank walk on the river and bridge to Brisbane City. In her Queenslander there were also two female young student boarders from Brazil and Chile. In the backyard, the chickens and the white cat called Sunday who left the dead rats on the back kitchen doorstep, presents which I wasn't appreciative of. Yuk, and those birds that pooped continuously on the front deck. That creepy bat, that hovered in the tree at dusk which freaked me out, with a Hendra agenda. I was to make the boarders dinner every night except weekends and help them with their laundry, bed linens and such. Angela preparing and forward thinking left me a float for groceries. She explained about the dying chicken on its death bed that she cuddled to keep it alive.

They were very pleasant girls, keeping to their studies after dinner until I worried about them not coming home after a weekend party till early Monday morning, I was worried I said why didn't you call me or leave me a note. I hadn't yet called the police as didn't want to cause a false alarm. On their birthdays I bought them both cakes, with candles, cards and little souvenir presents and made their fav dinner and my own Spaghetti Marinara and poached Salmon fillet having a mini party. On my weekends off, I went to visit my Queensland friends from Melbourne Irene and Stewart Meek in Broadbeach, went to Redcliff, the gigantic Cupie Dolls were sadly gone and Ipswich, in my rental car, where I stood outside listening to some school eisteddfod. I was fascinated by those stately hilly houses. I visited with my uni friend, Caroline from Moffat's Beach and we went for Sushi and gelati in New Farm at the Re del Gelato. I lunched with my Queensland friend Janis at the Hari – Krishna Cafe in Westend, and she and her teen daughter Kirsten came to Angela's house for afternoon tea. The aromared, hippy next door neighbours who I desperately had to enlist help from to shut off the smoke alarm as It went off nonstop after I cooked some chops and sausages in the greasy top griller for a change for the girls as I mainly cooked fish, pasta and vegetarian meals for all of us usually. The family on the other side that Angela said could help me bury the chicken or pests would come. I tried to talk sweetly to the sick chicken each day but could not bring myself to cuddle it with beak phobia.

I loved walking to Brisbane through the Southbank almost every day, doing shopping and errands, going to the Library and visiting all the galleries and museums. My favourite places were Fortitude Valley and New Farm with trendy cafes, restaurants, clubs, hairdressers and trendy fashion shops, that I went by bus for the day. I also went clubbing a Saturday at a trendy club in Fortitude Valley that I walked to and from the Club in high heels but it was a fun night of dancing and amusement, people were dressed up from Eaglefarm in their racing clothes gear, the girls worried about me. Visiting Petrie Terrace, for the galleries and exhibitions, the Barracks and The Paddington Antiques and collectables centres for jewellery and vintage clothes. I would always be home in time to cook the girls dinners and I also helped them to improve their English language skills from my celta course.I also would do all my chores every morning until the sun was toastie on my body and then I went out for the day. So everyday feed the chickens with food scraps, take something out for dinner, sweep the deck and I eventually washed it for Angela of the built up poop. Feed the cat, do the laundry, hang the clothes, sweep the floors and wash down the kitchen benches, I had to lock the cat out in the mornings as he pranced all over the kitchen, cooktop and benches which I washed with disinfectant and wiped down with meth spirits. Sunday hated being locked out until I at least prepared dinner and the kitchen was at least sanitary for that, he would begin to rebel, chasing me about the house and hiding anywhere and everywhere, breaking stuff on a rampage but I shooed him each day early afternoon with the broom to go on his expeditions, he eventually conceded that I was his senior and after worming and delousing him of ticks and fleas, began the rat presents on the doorstep and licked his lips at the left over fish scraps. We came to a mutual understanding standoff.

I managed also to degrease the griller and stock up the fridge and freezer for Angela's return. I began to then also use my own money the last couple of weeks as the float had dried up for food, groceries, toiletry and laundry items but figured that was fair. I also wanted to thank Angela, so I bought her a hydroponic heater for the girls for the very chilly frosty mornings and a vacuum cleaner from The Good Guys. The TV was broken and Angela said she left it purposefully unfixed like that as it distracted Vincent from his school work. I watered the plants every day without fail, recycled the food scraps and the various recycle bins I organized and sometimes had to supplement the chicken feed with dry food if there weren't many scraps. I swept, washed and cleaned the house everyday like a regular home duties housewife. I always crossed my way off the hundreds of minor tasks, errands and duties on Angela's daily list before even doing the stuff that I volunteered to do to make Angela's house better, cleaner and easier for her to manage after she returned home from Spain. During my short stay there I also strangely received correspondence from Allan my lawyer boyfriend of several months of suggestions about my inheritance dispute at the Supreme Court and Family Court matters about Sabena. I already had my own representing lawyers at this time about Freddie and that he was poking his nose into my personal affairs unasked and I felt uncomfortable about it. We began to become conflicting in our own views about things and found him to be too interfering.

I became acquainted with Janis, the speech pathologist through Angela since Angela was a Obgyn Nurse Matron at the Mater Hospital, Queensland. She introduced us I think because Janis was a single mum with Kirstin and the issues with her husband were not dissimilar to the issues with Eddie. Kirstin, her young daughter also suffered with the 50/50 shared visits with her father who was also mean, domineering and narcissistic, Kirstin returning home to Janis's traumatized by emotional, physical violent and sexual abuse. Janis was struggling to navigate the Queensland Family Court. Her situation was a step up, as she managed to retain full custody of Kirstin somehow until she was 18 years old. However during these years we at times compared notes about our unbearable scenarios.

Kirstin, an attractive 14 year old teenager, with a happy disposition and bright green eyes, long blonde hair, she could have been a young Taylor Swift or a real life Alice in Wonderland if she was dressed in costume. After Janis and I lunched at Westend, there were some kitschy shops, we widow shopped and I bought Kirstin an Owl T-shirt and matching skirt for Janis to gift her, as Kirstin was an Owl and animal lover her mum said. Janis and Kirstin visited me at Angela's for tea to thank me. I also asked her about those weird oversized yellow passionfruits in Angela's front garden, were they edible, I never in my life saw a yellow passionfruit apart from the usual smallish purple wrinkly type. Oh yes, you can pick those and eat them she said, so those that weren't dropped on the ground rotten or bird pecked, I picked and the girls ate them for breakfast on cereal and I made fresh fruit salad, but to me they tasted somehow different from the purple passionfruit a bit more tart funky. I waved goodbye to Brisbane, dreading that Storey Bridge which grasped me into its tentacles, and I went round and round endlessly trying to work out where I could get the turnpike off, only to return to the entrance again, I wondered if it was especially designed to keep people staying in Brisbane. Somehow after some time doing the circuit, I must have followed other cars with a huge petrol bill.

King Freddie

Mum must have been still alive when Freddie proudly obtained his Divorce Certificate from Sally, he was so relieved and happy, or she probably would have asked for even more money. We spent months through the court, I attending the Family Court with Freddie to help and support him. Not long after however he began suffering high levels of anxiety and having these psychotic paranoid episodes and wouldn't leave the house at all, terribly dysfunctional and obsessively peering out the windows and doors for agents Sally supposedly sent to spy, stalk, injure or kill him, who were following him everywhere he went, for a chance to accost or attack him. I was concerned about his state not knowing if the allegations were true or not but he certainly believed it himself, and this bizarre behaviour went on for many weeks until I forced him to come to the Psychologist at TVMC. Thankfully after a few sessions he seemed to have recovered back to normal with sleep medication.

It was early Autumn, after mum's passing in 2011, Freddie was until then preoccupied with renting the St. Kilda apartments to backpackers and managing the Rebar, and renting the small front shops. My conscionable lawyer cousin Romano with his wife Sandra and stepdaughter Melissa, invited us for a fancy Lobster Dinner in Carlton to cheer us up and also Hilda who was soon returning to Turkey, and suggested we should go away for a few days to chill out after the aftermath of the past months.

So Freddie and I went to Queenscliff for a few days, and we were very united as a team during this time, staying at a splendid Antique mansion / home B & B, Lathamstowe House, with various opposing rentable rooms upstairs. The lady of the house very welcoming and ready to please, retired here with her husband to renovate the mansion and start up the B & B, it was her life's dream and she also experimented and dabbled in gourmet foods and would cook us up fancy breakfast delights.

Months after this Freddie seemed to snap out of his grief and regain a new weird vigour for life. He became more involved with the Liberals having fierce ambitions of getting into politics, through his friends Bob Hodgkins and John Dorey, his GP. Freddie gleamed as he said he was lobbying and rubbing shoulders with the likes of Kelly O'Dwyer, he would come home and boast of his status.

Freddie knew Bob from the Prahran Police, as they went from police brutality to firm friends with my Dad and Freddie after an erroneous, now funny incident at the bar. They would go to police lunches and dinners together, fishing/ camping trips and Freddie was introduced to other current or former police officers like Duncan and John Wills. Moira Wills, his wife was a patient of my clinic already for many years from Malvern, John began having health concerns and he began to attend with his wife.

Moira's, now grown up daughters also attended Loreto and she was very proud of how they turned out, as she saw Sabena in her uniform after school, at the Clinic reception with Jean, the receptionist drawing pictures and practising writing patient's names on files until we went home. In fact I encountered them both a day picking up Sabena from school attending a grandparent's day there together. It was a far cry from Eddie suddenly removing Sabena from Loreto without my permission or notice at the beginning of the second term of Grade 1 for her to attend Tucker Road Primary approximately six months after the final family court hearing in 2007. I continued to pay for her the Loreto tuition fees until then, with Mum's help, regardless of where Sabena was residing. I was powerless to prevent this as he was given residence of Sabena temporarily under the current orders. It would be a blazing signal of even worse possible things to come, lurking around the corner.

I felt betrayed and disappointed in Loreto having the school counsellor, testify against me at the court. Why would they sabotage their own student and also a former student, myself who they were supposed to nurture and protect. Incredulous and in disbelief to what was happening, I also saw the other mothers and daughters distance themselves from us, once no longer residing with me. Many years later as Sabena was attending Keilor Downs College, I was approached and invited by Loreto to contribute a memorial commemorative tribute engraving on the stone steps of the glade gardens. This was similar to a building fund donation, Sabena having a difficult time, I thought to contribute and Freddie agreed, thinking it might be helpful and at least be a memory of her happy time there. I'm not sure, If I could afford to have both of our Names engraved then but definitely Sabena's name is engraved there as I went to visit it like it was a headstone and photographed it. So in essence I moved on from the resentment, anger and disdain that shrouded me after their mistake.

Freddie increasingly flashy, on top of the world, with a new navy BMW, a member of the prestigious Halo Coterie of the St. Kilda Football Club, attending all manner of lunches, dinners, sporting events, corporate social meetings and events. Donating huge funds, purchasing expensive tickets and buying or bidding in silent auctions for various precious football, and other sporting memorabilia. There was a quick and incipient sinister change in his behaviour, becoming more empowering and grandiose. He was more money hungry and greedy than ever before, the epitome of selfishness, self – centred, self- absorbed, arrogant and narcissistic. He was turning into a horrible beast that I didn't like. I was mostly home these years with a mundane schedule working in my clinic and plodding along day by day that I partly ignored Freddie's behaviour as a part of a phase of the grieving process that passed. It never passed but worsened and escalated into him several times in a year going on these two week trips with the Football Club not locally but to Canada, New Zealand, USA, Aspen and Boulder Colorado and also by himself for a few weeks in Europe and Italy. I managed and looked after the household during these times he was frequently away from home, and exorbitantly shopping and spending on myriads of stuff in a frenzied binge splurge, but with Freddie paying the house bills.

During this time it was also a complete body, health, fashion and image total makeover getting ready for his foray into becoming a politician and high flyer. Duncan suggested for him to diet and Freddie never deprived himself of anything food wise. He suggested he keep a small bottle of gone off cream on the top shelf to remind him of his diet, well it worked and Freddie would shriek if I tried to throw it out many times. His teeth were shining and veneered to upgrade to model cosmetic standards. The new insatiable fashion spree after the trim and slimmed down version of Freddie which I never saw before appeared, and accessories of every description, from Henry Bucks, Gucci, Gant, Politix, Trevor West. Boss, Polo Ralph Lauren, Toni and Guy etc. He denied himself nothing it was a mania.

It was like keeping up with the Kardashians, I being more grounded due to work and study never bothered much about being big noted and went about my usual day to day activities and business. I tried to warn him about trying to keep up with the lifestyle of these high flyers and big wigs, who were so far ahead of him financially, corporately and well connected but he was lured in, hook, line and sinker into this seemingly magical world of seduction, decadence, debauchery, extravagance, indulgence and hedonism. Where supposedly you could have whatever you want for the taking? It was like Gatsby saying to Nick, Old Sport and I was worried it would end badly for him going sour.

Reminiscent of JR and Bobby Ewing in Dallas, Bobby trying to uncorrupt, the self -possessed JR.

It appeared to me as if Freddie's new found lifestyle was increasingly unsustainable for the longer term. However, I never complained and sometimes reaped odd benefits of free footy and racing tickets for me and my friends. I never went to the footy or the Melbourne Races, even rarely Caulfield but enjoyed a once –off Ladies Day with my hairdresser friend KImmie that I was introduced to by Sanae, who at my haircut we both said we'd never been to the races, so it was done. I even spoke to my friend Maggie Sefton, who I chatted with at the singles night at Churches where we both commented on the disparity of the poor quality of men attending and that the women were far their superior in every way. Maggie lived not far in South Yarra in a tiny house, she was retired but previously worked at the ABC for most of her entire life, meeting her husband David who also appeared to have gone on a frenzied rampage similar to Freddie and they were divorced. She advised me that Freddie may become more aggressive towards me, if I stood in his way in any way, if you know what I mean. She suggested that if he backlashes on me that I should lock him out. I heeded these experienced words but never acted on them until the beatings came after contesting the will.

The Dating Merry- Go Round.

It was around August, 2013 that in hindsight now I think Freddie was trying to distract me from annoying him, a bribe so to speak, about tidying up the will and settling between us. I actually believed that he wanted me to sort out Mum's aristocratic house in Italy that he would inherit. I was serious about my task and followed up everything about the house, like an executive on a business trip in Italy only taking time out to visit relatives or do some site seeing around. Effervescent young not long married Silvia, Mum's house neighbour, who said I must go, here and there with her and see with her the statue workshop of Antonio Canova and visit the tourist villas in the area of Treviso. Not being able to fly for extended times due to my allergies it was part Emirates and part Princess Cruises – Ocean Princess. Whatever happens on the ship stays on the ship! That would be another interesting saga in itself. Maybe some tidbits, the onboard crush that never eventuated because I figured out later he was gay, the many married fling proposals I never took up, the pirates taking over Petra and we couldn't stop off for the tour, the day I was left behind in Santorini and the dinghy's that came back to look for me after the others left and there was a head count on the ship. The stop off in Mumbai at the Elephanta Caves where we all, passengers and crew developed both a respiratory and gastro virus, that I was sick for at least a week, and the staff that attended with us the South African, Cape Town brothers that were brothers from a different mother. I supect it may have been mould induced as the caves were magnificent but damp and seething dripping with leaks everywhere and mould and moss hugging all the walls and ceilings. The two or three weeks where the ship's satellite went down and nothing communicative worked as in internet, email, mobiles. This might have been unfortunately around Sabena's 14th Birthday and was unable to contact her. On returning home, I continued contacting Sabena but only speaking to her for shorts bursts as Eddie hung up. I was blissfully unaware she was undergoing some kind of severe mental meltdown and none of them ever let on anything was wrong. She was school refusing, severely depressed, with high anxiety, self- harming, mutilating and having suicidal idealization as they now say, not tendencies. She was apparently going downhill fast on a steep ski slope and nobody could stop her from crashing. I continued about my daily life, knowing that she probably was very unhappy but OK.

I was trying to stay out of the house as much as possible these years to avoid Freddie for obvious reasons and so I became a member of Solo Singles, Maggie said they were quality professional men and women who were all university educated or academics. She wasn't eligible, not gone to Uni, but insisted that I try it. It became a bit incestuous after a couple of years with me dating Ian and Allan for several months on and off and only a few dates with Mark, Phil, Jacques and there might have been a few others in the mix also.

Before this phase I was phone dating when it still existed and going to Mez's lifes a ball Singles nights with my girlfriends, the Sloney – Poney, Dogs Bar, Rah Bar, Barney – Allens, and the Abel Tasman Dutch Club events. I picked up single Murray, Murray up at the Sloney who was an accountant and professional swimmer aspiring for the Olympics. A bit of a boozer but we immediately hooked up after a few dates, this was very weird at this juncture because this is around the month that I sustained nerve deafness in my left ear, they suspected it was either a virus or allergic reaction. I think I was sick for a few weeks and neglected to check my mobiles, but there were hundreds of messages and voicemails from Murray to which the final saying he was dumping me because, I was cheating on him and ghosting him as they say. I thought this rather hilarious of his self – sacking. I believed him and it ended. Seeing him months later at the Sloney, he was dating a cancer victim and I explained what happened and we were still chummy and chatted at other music venues and events. Peter was country and into farming, divorced not long ago and I suspected as before after some fling time fair – enough but I wasn't go down that road my health was also precious as my principles. So I think after a few dates he became bored and moved on which was That's Fine.

Chris the teacher turned lawyer, living in Caulfield with Irish ancestry who was phone dating, with whom there was the blind date, us finally meeting up at a cosy nearby Indian Restaurant from his flat. Believe it or not he accidentally wee'd himself under the restaurant table, at the moment my Tandoori Prawns arrived. He alighted to go to the toilet, jeans there was a huge soaked penis patch.

I should have walked out then and there, from my first instincts but being involved in health you are understanding and have compassion that these mishap incidents sometimes happen. So I stayed. Dining out a few more times, there was a classy, trendy restaurant in South Yarra, Bistro Gitan, serving French – Spanish influence fare with a modern twist. We might have argued about giving a tip, so I gave it $ 10. Hospitality people deserve their money especially providing prompt, helpful, correct and efficient service.

It was a weekend in Winter, and so Chris wanted to see his favourite shows on his flat couch, he orders Thai takeaway of a Thai Beef or Chicken Satay for himself and Prawn Pad Thai for me but without the peanuts. He was irritable and snappish should I now and then interrupt his viewing concentration, they were topical news items and controversial doco's. It was as if he was shusshing a school child. We drank a bottle of red wine that I brought. I might have been late 40's to early 50's during this phase, this is to provide perspective. I don't remember if I slept over that or another night but I'm not a fan of Futon beds on the floor especially those of cheap and uncomfortable quality, with a black foam mattress and matching doona. I always carried a couple of condoms in all my purses, likely expired. Sometimes with condoms, stuff can leak out if they slip, so you must be careful. Chris 's physic was about my height but very slight not toned but probably a bit scrawny runt towards Jockey status. I was average weight but curvy, It was my impression he preferred skinny blondes, so I felt shy with him, not being his usual type and pried my clothes off under the doona. He commented how silly, him throwing all his off with speedy abandon, he wasn't exactly body beautiful for even a nudist beach himself. It was ironic. Perhaps resembling, a young Michael Parkinson. His face was pleasant of an Irish Choir boy but I was attracted to his sympathetic fun loving nature, his empathy for causes and doing the right politically correct things by people, fighting injustices and such, most of all. Our ages were not dissimilar and we hit it off from the first date.

Chris considerately informs me he will be away for about a week, maybe it was Tasmania. I requested that he please bring me back some small keepsake token from where he'd been to see if he would remember and whether he was thoughtful. Whatever people gift you, should be reflective of themselves, as that's how I gift or try to. Well, here it was definitely the thought that counts. I pretended to be pleased but I was deeply disappointed. It was the lack of thought of my personality, that bothered me, it could have been any cute thing, but it was a costume, hard cheap plastic sky blue graduated beaded necklet with a large heart dangling of it compared to its size with some gold plastic flecks on the top corner. It would have been something a child of three would choose from a school fair or Target toys little girl's dress up jewellery outfit. At least he brought back something. It seemed to me that with my complexion the red palette or strong bright colours showed up my features best but muted blues, greens and greys were suited more for blonde complexions, although there were a few vibrant Royal blue clothes in my collection, for a change. Even, Sabena would have tossed it as it was too tacky for words. It didn't at all suit any of my own fashion and tastes, in any chic costume bling. Never mind there might be more other good stuff about him instead, I thought.

It was always the same theme with these perpetually single, commitment phobic paranoid lost guys that missed that nuptial boat many, many moons ago, there was no hint of the slightest idea of how to treat a lady. Also he was from my generation too. Regardless, I thought to surprise him, he'd acted a bit evasive and elusive since returning, by turning up unannounced at his flat with some take –away, as a Friday night treat for him, after work only to have him shoo me away from the downstairs buzzer gate, being angry, irritated and rude towards me. He lashed out at me explaining to make me go that he was now dating an older work admin colleague from his office and he now has herpes. High Times at Ridgemont High!

Disgusted, I left that night never to return again, I saw his true colours and the older blonde lady on his arm at the Rah Bar, some Sunday evening that a live band was playing, I attended there with my girlfriends Audrey and Rosemary. He was a fan of the peninsula, swimming, country music festivals, St. Kilda FC, the 60's free love era, Rock n Roll grunge music and Stevie Nicks. Maybe not too much in common between the both us, with his Peter Pan Syndrome, stuck in a time warp. So with *The Rake* it ended as badly as it started, a wastrel of a life that should not be glorified but gawked at in awe.

Not in any particular order are the following and be reminded these were only significant dates. Robert, the tall lanky Australian, a few shaving nick papers and he was Norman Gunston, he might have been of Scottish / Irish Ancestry, the upside was he owned his own humble small daggy house in an outer south eastern suburb and a couple of cars in the driveway. He was a bit nerdy but nice. He was very easily aroused and excitable at the tiniest caress or stroke with a high libido drive. Mild mannered accountant by day, and vintage car enthusiast for hiring the car out for films and events. Doing some reno's on his home on the weekends, he was married for a few years in his youth and was domesticated. His last girlfriend was a corporate but spent always much far beyond her means and couldn't keep up.

No matter how gentle he was with me, as kid gloves I constantly developed these continuing rashes. I surmised that there must have been something of a minute parasite insect nature in his house and on his own body which he was obviously immune to but I wasn't. He worked diligently and sometimes on weekends, being overloaded with work and his bosses appeared to be slave drivers and horse whippers. We sometimes made dinner together at his house. Having a reasonable income in those days, I could afford to pay and go to conferences, so I booked this double room at the golf venue in Lorne and invited him to tag along arriving on Saturday avo. It was a fun day and a bit after the conference closed up for me and he surprised me by booking a table and buying us both a pristine delicious gourmet lunch at their exclusive elegant restaurant. It was shortly after that he was also cheating on me, record on repeat, with someone he encountered at his work, his eye becoming infected. So thankfully again, saved by the bell and I was to leave the scene of the crime, never to return again.

Gary, perhaps of polish ancestry, as I encountered him at a party at Ian's place, who knew him from current legal circles. Gary was more my type in looks with his dark hair and rugged George Lazenby, and suave Timothy Dalton features. Previously a boat salesman, who was separated from a long standing partnership with her having young adult kids, but however, never married. He spoke of it acrimoniously briefly and skirted around so I imagine and gather, there was some damage done. He also worked casually supervising at the Sports Stadiums whilst building his practice on weekends. He was a huge fan of all things sporting, the first person who comes to mind is *Eddie McGuire, good old Collingwood forever, they know how to play the game,* Freddie turned family traitor many years ago. There might have been a couple of dates, the first at the Laurent cafe in South Yarra and another, until he emailed me and said he' been offered a sort of legal internship in Adelaide and was hyped. Gary departed for Adelaide a week or so later and we emailed a few times after that until it fizzled.

Taylor Swift 2014 – Shake it off!

Looney Tunes

On my way to return home, it was necessary for me to order a taxi to Singapore Airport departures, on the 15th October, 2013, because of the magnitude of my luggage. At the information counter a attendant helped me because I required two trolley carts for it. It was oppressive sticky, hot and sultry day, as mum and Pina from Italy described it perfectly *Soffaco* – suffocating or Choking. At the departure counter I was requested to repack my luggage and send some of it off by parcel delivery.

There truly was heaps of stuff but in my defence most of it was gifts and souvenirs for family and friends, I left some of my personal belongings behind giving clothes to Italian family and friends. Some of these were favourites but I was sick of them or outgrown them and suited others more. I gifted a travelling friend, Sarah George an English Lady, whose husband was a financier and they owned a hotel called The Unicorn Cublighter which their son was the manager, some of my clothes that were in good condition and stylish but because she was trimmer than me, would be more suitable and flattering for her, showing off her figure as they were particularly snug and hip hugging. Eileen and Stan Beer were also travel friends from the US, Eileen a slightly more robust figure than me, I gifted some accessories and costume type classic antique French inspired jewellery that she remarked to me an evening she very much admired. I previously bought these at a specialty shop in South Yarra which then disappeared after about a year later. There was a fabulous array at a low price.

Somewhere in a room I repacked the gears into several boxes, which were quite expensive due to their weight and off they went, strangely they were to arrive before myself and Freddie picked them up for me. There was an issue with my phone card and so the attendant helped me buy a temporary phone card for the airport phones and I called Freddie from the airport and also might have left a message for Sabena on their landline phone. As in Italy I offered him a tip but it was seen as bribes.

It was not long after I arrived home, that the reality dawned on me that my credit cards were now all maxxed out, and the appointment diary was now sparse of patients. There was a locum, few years graduated young male student, who replaced me for the duration of the trip but Freddie was concerned about him, and they argued about something and he left a bit earlier than his time was up. In the clinic, I wondered what hi jinx happened as I found broken glass behind the medical trolley, instruments broken and some gone missing and some damaged electronic equipment. Freddie's feedback was they thought he was lazy and weren't happy about their treatment or his behaviour towards them and went somewhere else until my return or if at all ever again, as patients. There was so much to be sorted, fixed and prepared for before I was to have patients in the clinic soon. The sorting of the will came back up with Freddie. Boxes, luggage, clinic, cards all in the mix.

In the Clinic, picking up the landline, a spied a chard of glass that was hidden beneath the desk and thought I will have to remember to get that later on. It was the RCHM – Royal Children's Hospital, Melbourne admissions. I stared at the glass blankly, whilst she asked, it might have been Karen Daly, *Are you the biological mother of Sabena? She's in a terrible state and been admitted to The White Department for severe anxiety, chronic depression, Self – harm mutilation and suicidal idealizations. You will have to come down and fill out some forms about her so we know her full medical history.* Chills went all the way down my spine as she said this and for a few minutes I was cotton wool fog.

Eddie wouldn't permit this, maybe there was no choice because of hospital protocol and their rules. Between 2009 and 2013 I sought out all kinds of mediation programmes. He almost always refused except for Cabrini Centrecare Counsellors, Uniting Church Connections, Prahran and which he later cancelled indefinitely and the Melbourne Relationship Centre. In early 2014, he must have been concerned about Sabena because he agreed to attend a shuttle mediation. The lady mediator, worked on him patiently and sweetly for almost two full days until an agreement plan was reached. It was as if I could almost taste it happening. The next day he sends an email to the lady, that he refuses to sign the typed up agreement and no longer agrees. Thwarted again, this was always the scenario and never changed, I must have collected at least five government certificates of mediation impossible with this client Eddie.

So I attended the RC Hospital after the 8th November, 2013. I filled out the forms and was asked questions about her birth and early health in my care and if she exhibited prior symptoms in the past. Both parties were kept separated across the large alcove area and I never saw Sabena that day. It was funny in my mind because before Mum's passing, she said to me in partly jest that if she lived with Eddie and Bon that would be enough to send her looney tunes, let alone what Sabena must have to tolerate and contend with between those two nitwits, like the hilarious film with Jim Carey and Jeff Daniels - Dumb and Dumber. Sabena most likely was the most intelligent of the three.

Mum and I, whilst she was still alive, often speculated together during these years that both Eddie and Bon were bisexual, certainly to say the least, unusually strange circumstances. My mum, Idelma Maria albeit being brought up in a small Italian village, San Zenone Degli Ezzelini, Treviso (TV), was pretty switched on and also an intuitive and perceptive Pisces, her predictions and sleep talking were usually spot on.

I was brought up however with the notions of rosey coloured glasses, Icy - Pops and happy sunshine smiles, so it was difficult for me to comprehend these things and I couldn't even reach the depths of the terribly bad, evil and horrific thoughts, images and conceptual ideas of the consequences that would be brought about by these revelations.

Sabena's (Nina, my mum dubbed her), real fears of ongoing sexual abuse from both of them as their stooge pawn, trapped in a terrifying and sicko threesome act, constantly trying to keep her perpetrators at bay.

They were ugly, weird bedfellows and suspiciously Bon, resembled a butch squashed - faced Miss Piggy and Eddie, a mildly androgynous bagged -eyed mean expression, Saddam Hussein (Mum coined them the Mop and Saddama). The Salvation Army throng defending them and shrouding them under it's expansive wings. Freddie also concurred that sinister and *Stranger Things, 2016 Mystery - Horror, were going on with Sabena and the both of them.*

Bad Guy, 2019 - Billie Ailish

Unbreakable (2000) Thriller

His Dark Materials (2019) Fantasy- Drama - Mystery

The Nevers (2021) Sci- Fi Drama

Superfreak, 1981 - Rick James -Album: Street Songs

Bizarre Love Triangle, 1986 - New Order

Album: Brotherhood

Easy Lover, 1984 - Phil Collins and Philip Bailey

Invisible Touch, 1986 - Genesis Album: Invisible Touch

Another Day in Paradise ....1989- Phil Collins Album: But Seriously!

Whiter Shade of Pale, 1967 - procol Harem

The Village of the Damned (1995) Sci- Fi Horror Director: John Carpenter

The Exorcist (2001), Horror - Thriller Director - William Friedkin

Truth is Stranger than Fiction!

Ripley's believe it or not!?

It was no wonder that Sabena was struggling now in that state in those damning circumstances (and whoever else wouldn't be - Dr. Phil)

Mum tried to console me that Sabena would come home again eventually and that until then that as she grew up and became stronger, that she would be more able to defend and protect against both of them and and be able to fend them off all by herself.

Mum's own shocking gruesome horror story of her youth about the insane, deranged village idiot who interfered with two very young little twin girls, that tragically died almost instantly afterwards. The urban myth that my Nonna, Romana described to my own mum as a child about the concerned, wise and superstitious village priest of the day who banished the evil unrested souls and spirits from the village and not unlike the Pied Piper possessed them and led them into a very deep valley, outside of the village, exorcising them to remain there and not to be able to leave and not to be bothering the innocent village residents again from then and that day on.

My grandmother on my mother's side, Romana named my own mum Idelma after and from a book she read. She was apparently very strict, but in a good way, and my mum, her younger sister (My Zia Wilma), and her older brother, (My Zio Evelino) would chaperone them if they went out and the girls were not allowed to go out after dark themselves or especially on their own or not in a group, or without their brother in tow, also especially during the war years too.

Their older sister (My Zia Dirce), oddly was at this time in a nunnery, almost about to take her precious vows, which she then not long after abandoned and relinquished and then later on left the order entirely. It was suspected she was having an affair with a priest- It was such an awful shame, disgrace and lose face in the village catastrophe matter and her mother, almost never recovered from this scandalous fact and was devastated by it and her leaving the order - but that's another story in itself!

My own mum said her own mum was so strict to the point where if she disobey her mum and it was serious, that she wouldn't speak to her for several days at all, as punishment and my mum said it was even far worse than any beating she might have got.

My Zio Evelino, as a young adult man with a good heart but sadly, a coward of sorts. He hid from being conscripted for several years, for doing two years in the Italian Army, only to find that when the Germans took over, apprehending the village to ransom, that to expunge secrets of escaped of escaped Jews and the like, also to keep the townsfolk in line The discipline was that one young man, was chosen once a week from the village to be shot, gunned down in cold blood in front of the whole village to be onlooking and be warned. It was very cruel to say the least. Nevertheless, despite these and other unpalatable circumstances, pillaging the village and raping young women and men, Romana (My Nonna) elected to still take the risk and hide an entire Jewish family during these years, for months during the German invasion, in the granary attic loft above the house in Via Beltramini (Villa Beltramini), where her sister Romilda lived, whom when young was the local midwife for the whole village and much revered for her being so kind.

Gen Y and older generations relevation epiphanies! Present and past

Say Nothing! - Flume: February, 2022 feat MAY - A, Album: Palaces

Every Side of You - Vance Joy: June, 2022

Cloudy Day! Tones and I: June, 2021

Things take time, take time! - Courtney Barrett: November, 2021

Meanjin - Thelma Plum: august, 2022

Magic - Julie Jacklin Album: Pre Pleasure: August, 2022

Thousand Miles- The Kid Laroi: pril, 2022

Growing up is ......Ruel: December, 2021

FutureNever - Daniel Johns: April, 2022

Not Pretty Enough - Kasey Chambers, 2001 Album: Barricades & Brickwalls

On a Bad Day - Kasey Chambers, 2001

Album: Barricades & Brick walls

We're all gonna die someday ....kasey Chambers, 1999 Album: The Captain

the Devil's inside my head ...- Kasey Chambers, 2008 Album: Rattlin' Bones

Apparition of those too soon passed requiem!

One Song - Archie Roach: February, 2022 Album: My Songs 1989- 2021

Archie Roach dies of natural causes, 30.07.2022, Warnambool

I know I'll never find another you .. - Judith Durham, The Seekers, 1964

Georgie Girl - The Seekers, 1966

A world of our own .. the Seekers, 1965

Wild Rover - The Seekers, 1963

(The Carnival is Over...) Album: Introducing The Seekers

Judith Durham dies 05.08.2022 of natural causes, Melbourne.

It's because I love you ...- The Master's Apprentices Album: Choice Cuts, 1971

Glenn Wheatley, Bass Guitarist, Music Entrepreneur Extraordinaire

Linda Linda - The Master's Apprentices

Album: Masterpiece, 1970

Do what you wanna do, be what you wanna be.....yeah Album: The Master's Apprentices, 1988

Glenn Wheatley dies 01.02.2022 of COVID complications, Melbourne

Escaping - Margaret Ulrich, singer and songwriter. Album: Safety in Numbers, 1989

Only my heart calling ...Margaret Urlich, Album: Safety in Numbers, 1989

The Horses - Margaret Urlich, Iconic accompaniment vocalist to Daryl Braithwaite, 1990 Album: Rise

Margaret Urlich dies 22.08.2022 of Cancer, age 57 - NSW Highlands

I felt even more pressured now, to sort things out financially, this might have been the time around I commenced legal proceedings against Freddie, and should it be necessary I would appeal at the Family Court again. Temporarily it was also reassuring to know that Sabena might actually get the desperate help she needed. It was some years before that I suspected that she might suffer depression, for two reasons living with them and also Eddie's medical history of depression. When she began going through the early phases of puberty and beginning to be a walking dead, I begged Eddie and Bon to get her counselling help and I even researched their Salvo Centre St. Kilda for counselling services for her but they never and with all their Salvo connections and resources. She was from May 2013, I was explained by the hospital staffer attending the school counsellor as her behaviours were escalating at Keilor Downs College, as school attendances became increasing more erratic, disturbing and she refused to attend school from June 2013. As far back as 2010, she was having some behavioural issues, interfering with her study and was attending the school counsellor.

December 2013, turned up suddenly that year from a day to the next and there was all this shit going down around me. I continued despite this to attend the Solo's Singles and Charities Plus functions because these were the only things that cheered me a bit up during this solemn phase. It was somewhere at a hotel in Fitzroy or Collingwood for a dinner, that I was to become introduced to Allan, who sat beside me on the long dining table of about 12 Solo Singles guests of all walks of life. I knew Ian, before him at these functions and but he wasn't there that particular evening so I wasn't aware that they were also acquainted before me but after we started dating Allan also attended Ian's parties too, but Allan never hosted parties and at his Party, Ian said to me, Allan is always so very terribly grumpy, unfriendly and nasty. I said, he doesn't seem to be when I'm around him tho.

For her hospital treatment Sabena is prescribed RCH counselling services weekly and several heavy and strong adult type medications for various conditions described and diagnosed in her state. Before attending the RCH she might have been referred to the RCH by the counsellor at the Sydenham One medical clinic, where I was also denied access to her medical information files.

Zonked Out

Sabena is prescribed Fluvoxamine and Ritalin, increasing in months to adult dosages after attending Alasdair Vance, Head Academic Child Psychiatry, RCH Melbourne. It was concerning me to that at such a young age she would be prescribed these drastic medications. Particularly my family medical history on both sides, of being highly sensitive and allergic to strong medications, as also inherent in my own self. It was a mixture of pain killers, anaesthetics, cortisone, anti-depressants and sedatives. I wondered what other allergy traits she might have developed these years apart from those not too dissimilar to my own. Sabena exhibited gastric symptoms similar to her own father and sensitivity to chemicals, food allergies and EMR, we would react similarly on exposure to these stimulant triggers. Nobody was listening to me, and her father and stepmother shut me down every time I brought up the subject of having improved symptoms after having become a member of AESSRA and seeing a particular environmental allergy specialist, Dr. Colin Little. It is my opinion even to this day that Sabena was misdiagnosed and the medications appeared to make her incoherent, dozy and dopey on the phone and on the odd occasions I saw her worse than ever, she was a very scrambled zombie.

6th March, 2014

Extract from Alasdair Vance Report.

In summary, Sabena presents as a14 year old student with a clear moderate severity anxiety and depressive vulnerability manifest as a developing dysthymic disorder associated with a range of anxiety difficulties driving school refusal behaviour and inattentive type ADHD symptoms along with oppositional defiant disorder.

Sabena will be reviewed annually by the Academic Child Psychiatry Unit or more frequently as required.

Supposedly I assumed that they might know what they are doing, although they discredited my allergy theories as a multifactorial combination effect mixed with the severe anxiety or cause of, and that perhaps a short term course of these medications up to a minimum of 3-6 months possibly would settle down these and take that extreme edge off of her, so then other therapies instigated. I thought that this temporary zonked out escapism existence from the looney tunes of her environment might even actually be beneficial in the very short term at least to lower her anxiety.

It' s not that difficult to pinpoint around the time span that her behaviours escalated and she became more despondent and debilitated, checking –out of life, probably from the commencement at Keilor Downs College among other scary scenarios that I also imaged were occurring at home.

Mid 2012, because she was still travelling reasonably well then, Sabena on the phone describes to me her disconnected and faded kaleidoscope memory of her previous Loreto primary friends, National Theatre Ballet School, Stage Left performing arts school and Bambini's Talent Agency, which she revelled in these types of activities in my residential care. Sabena in spurts remembered hating her swimming lessons and always dodging them at school because her ears became sore if she forgot to insert her ear plugs from her swim tote. Sabena was separated from her bestie Sophie since their eight year old birthdays, I hoped that a reunion with Sophie might reignite her and spark her memories of the fun times and happy days. Phillipa, was very understanding about the current difficult circumstances and I organized a reunion, having Begged Eddie and Bon that it would help perhaps to bring back her joie de vivre to have a routine change to good memories in her life. Of course with Eddie always strict conditions, so Bon came along to chaperone the visit with Sophie.

It might have been early Autumn, I was sure that Phillipa would be pleased to have a break from her own Bakery items and both the girls who were keen on sweet treats would love it equally too. I booked a high tea table afternoon at the prestigious Gables on Finch, Malvern for five of us, Phillipa, Sophie, Sabena, myself and tag along Bon. It was a pristine and elegantly renovated mansion veranda and garden setting.

Maybe it was Easter or school holiday time. It was many months since I had seen Sabena myself, and I was shocked, she was fully developed with a curvy figure, voluptuous breasts, past shoulder auburn wavy hair tied with a black satin ribbon high on the top. She was wearing an adult young lady's black flowery dress with bunches of red palette flower motifs pattern with full buttons up and deep plunging v- neckline. She was a full blown young miss no more a little girl or child, but she also could have passed for at least a 16-18 year old, if you weren't aware. Sophie in comparison was a young svelt straight up and down, underdeveloped tomboy or beach surfie figure, with her short denim cuffed shorts and an embroidered white cotton shirt top with splits and Mao collar. Sophie with her short cropped Annie coloured flame hair was still in tween zone and they were polar opposites apart now as compared to twins from different mum's. Sophie commented on seeing her WOW, look at you! Phillipa's eyes also widened marvelling at the extreme transformation from a little girl. Bon was the mole and monitor guard, interfering and cutting Sabena short if there were entering touchy subject or taboo subject matter. It was a pleasant afternoon spoilt by being on tender hooks with Bon the entire hour or so. I felt vibes from Phillipa that she found it annoying to without warrant. Sabena and Sophie were now on different path trajectories and no longer was their common bond. That was to be the final time that Sophie and Sabena would ever meet again and so also their sweet childhood end of friendship. Sabena never again returned to visit the South East Suburbs after that.

Much later sometimes on and off, during these years speaking about her anime sketches, current favourite games and K pop music, some tidbits of taboo information sometimes slipped through instantaneously. Our conversations mainly revolved around her hobbies and this was to steer her away from topics that would end the call abruptly with a hang up or punishment of not answering my calls on the answer machine for weeks and months from Eddie. Sabena began to become very defensive about this but on a few different phone calls an insight into her life in Sydenham was revealed, *I have to lock the bathroom door if I shower these days mummy as I get so scared. They increased my medication dose again. At Keilor Downs College the kids are from different backgrounds and some are a bit rougher than she was used to before at Tucker Road Primary.*

Several months after the hospital admittance on the 8th November, 2013, she appears to be suffering symptoms of adverse side effects of the medication complaining of cold feet, fogginess of her thoughts, sleepy all the time, constant tummy aches and becoming more agitated and paranoid. Sabena unusually begins to avoid her phone times with me and Eddie is constantly saying she isn't up to it and call, only in the school holidays because she is so overwhelmed during this cure phase. For me terrible to say, it was actually therapeutically of benefit to me, than strained artificial pretence conversations and watch out for those walking on cracked egg shell moments that killed the happy mood and tone between us, mother and daughter bonding moments that caused Bon and Eddie to become jealous and hang up in spite, hoping Sabena would stop enjoying our interaction.

Extract 1st May, 2014

Jo Winther

Senior Clinical Psychologist – DNP

Mental Health Service

Royal Children's Hospital

Sabena is a 14 year old secondary student who was referred for treatment of her worsening social anxiety, social withdrawal, school refusal, self-harm behaviour, as well as panic symptoms. Sabena was initially assessed in a standardized manner within the Academic Child Psychiatry Unit and referred to the Developmental Neuropsychiatry Program for Cognitive Behaviour Therapy and medication treatment.

Upon assessment Sabena described school refusal behaviour, social phobia, panic disorder, generalized anxiety disorder and dysthymic disorder currently being at a clinical level of severity.

Sabena presents as a 14 year old student with generalized Anxiety Disorder, Social Phobia, Obsessive Compulsive Disorder symptoms and Depression driving school refusal behaviour, self-harming behaviours, rule – breaking behaviour and inattentive type ADHD symptoms.

I have been involved in working with Sabena since October, 2013 with an agreed Individual Treatment Plan goal of reducing her depressive symptoms by undertaking 10 Individual Cognitive Behaviour Therapy sessions and discussing medication options with Dr. Vance. We recently reached our 10th individual session using cognitive behavioural therapy which has been focused on mood regulation skills training, anger management training, anxiety management training, problem solving skills, assertiveness and social skills training. We have also discussed her educational difficulties and developed a plan to assist Sabena to return to school. Please do not hesitate to contact me on 9345 4666.

Extract 6th March, 2014 (In the father's affidavit – One year follow up assessment is also included)

Sabena Lazar – DOB 28/08/1999 (Age 14 Years – UR 1461973.

From a temperamental point of view, within the first year of life, no Chess and Thomas vulnerability factors were noted to be in the clinical range. Motor, speech and language developmental milestones were within normal limits.

Current neurological subtle signs examination revealed evidence of fine motor coordination difficulties alone. Cognitive examination revealed average full scale IQ, superior level verbal comprehension index and average perceptual reasoning index with no significant visuospatial is to verbal IQ disparity. Reading was at the 63rd percentile, spelling at the 95th percentile and arithmetic at the 27th percentile, indicating no specific language learning disorders. Assessment of higher order executive function revealed evidence of decreased span, adequate spatial working memory abilities and visuospatial memory encoding and retrieval abilities. Sabena's parent reported significant symptoms associated with managing her, in particular obsessive compulsiveness anxiety and interpersonal sensitivity.

Be aware that I was not privy to these reports before the court hearing being the applicant in the proceedings at the Federal Circuit Court of Australia in December 2014. The father banned all contact between Sabena and I from October, 2014. After this and various other factors occurring simultaneously during this phase, I lodged an appeal for full residence of Sabena at the Family Court it then being transferred internally to the Federal Circuit Court, being self – represented due to lack of funds and writing my own affidavit, obtaining advice at various family legal centres, Clayton, Oakleigh, Port Melbourne and St. Kilda and I was urged not to enter an appeal due to the weight of prior orders. Also note in the extract that the father whatever Sabena' s records or documentation, she is known by Sabena Lazar not the name change that Justice Brown indicated in the orders many years before, a hyphenated version of both parents surnames, My family surname and Eddie's surname.

The Awakening

Being overwrought, distressed and severely concerned about Sabena's well being at this stage from the day I received the call from the hospital during early November, 2013. Professor Alasdair Vance is the admitting attending professor but Sabena is monitored, every two weeks by the attending clinic counsellor Jo Winther.

Riptide – Vance Joy.

Extract – Private Notes Biological Mother.

May, 2014 – The biological mother makes further enquiries at the hospital about the treatment and is concerned about the severe adverse effects of the medication and lack of any sign of significant improvement in Sabena's condition which is rapidly worsening and deteriorating ongoing day by day. The hospital provides basic information but is restricted by the father and the previous court orders they say legally preventing them from providing further assistance and information. I try to go to the Mental Health Complaints Commissioner and Health Commissioner Ombudsman for advice but they are restricted by the previous court orders and the father's reticence to give permission for further investigations or another professional opinion.

I'm not sure if I remembered how I discovered more about Sabena's self – mutilation and suicidal thoughts. It could have been in the beginning from Freddie who went to visit with Sabena without informing me that December, 2013 whilst we were still on reasonably co-operative and civil terms. That was to be the last Christmas that we spent time together as brother and sister as I prepared us a Christmas lunch reminiscent of before mum's passing with all of our favourite fine fare foods.

- King Lobster
- King Prawns
- Avocados
- German Style Potato Salad
- Italian Style Fruit Salad
- Warm salads of string beans, zucchinis, pumpkin, broccoli and cauliflower.

Generational home recipes

Bought Recipes

- Panettone
- Traditional Fruitcake
- Mince Tarts
- Shortbread
- Brandy Butter and Custard
- Lemon Curd
- Anything with 75 % or more to 100 % Dark Chocolate, yum!

My perennially Favourite christmas fine fare foodstores are Laurent, Baker's Delight, Phillipa's, Haigh's and Koko Black depending on the previous years affordability and budget.

A penny saved, is a penny earned -Eddie McGuire Millionaire Hot Seat Ch. 9

The following year 2014 and after that on Christmas day, Freddie spent Christmas with his ex- wives and both his daughters from each wife and their respective families, Sally with her young daughter Katia, and Lucinda with her teen daughter Claudia. Freddie and I were never to spend another Christmas together again after that year.

Melancholy, teary, distressed and extremely distracted myself Freddie sympathetically revealed that he went to visit Sabena on compassionate grounds, as an Uncle's Duty as it was to go to Uncle's Day at Loreto in Grade 1. He said they were extremely sucking welcoming and that Sabena wanted a treadmill for Christmas which he was generous enough to provide on the day. He said she was a shadow of her former self and that he was shocked, thinking it was probably for my own best interest not to see her in that state. Sabena's eyes were sunken deep beneath her thick rimmed glasses and her mood exceedingly sullen for her. They naggingly requested to *borrow monies* from Freddie and if he could also get them a car. Freddie was annoyed, irritated and disgusted by their reaction to his friendly visit and never returned again after that to their place. Mum always told me and Freddie to avoid giving them any money as they surely continued to return for more and more each time as if it was a ransom or ongoing extortion bribe to lure us to believe, that I might have hope of increased visits or get further contact with Sabena.

Sabena was dishevelled in appearance and described to him in confidence that she was severely depressed, with issues of despair to end her life, cutting and scarring herself on the face and body with various sharp and pointed implements, small kitchen knives, Sharp jewellery objects, razor blades, whatever she could get hold of or find around the home and that her Dad's matches and cigarette lighters helped cause skin burns that she inflicted on herself in the bathroom, every time going in to pretend to brush her teeth and sitting on the floor after she locked the bathroom door. Eddie and Bon began to lock away all items in the home that might be used as a weapon of torture. Eddie was still chain smoking and there was the Greek concrete planter which he procured, whilst I was in Hospital many years ago, which was outside the kitchen full to the brim with cigarette butts.

Horrified and traumatized by this information, I was hurt, frustrated and fearful of what might happen next with Sabena. Not being able to get to sleep for hours on end with negative thoughts repeatedly churning around in my mind I began to experience these recurring nightmares every night, and waking up in fright shivering in the ai, wee small hours of the morning. Freddie hearing me shriek out, *Please Teen Talk*!, *Please Teen Talk!*, from his bedroom, waking him. It was always the same nightmares the hospital calling to inform me that Sabena was dead or that she injured herself or damaged herself irreparably and be tragically amputated of some of her appendages.

Gangs of New York – Daniel Day Lewis in fine style.

I arose after a particular nightmarish and scary nightmare, mulling over what else I could do for Sabena, because it was so far out of my control with these prior court orders. Frantically, I already contacted the hospital and various other institutions that I researched, rang around and googled. I begged the Hospital coordinator that I be permitted to have some involvement and participation in Sabena's hospital care and intervention for example attending some counselling sessions together with her. Sabena, always a little miss congeniality, during her younger years with me, never complaining and submissive, complacent about being unwell, which was very concerning to me even then or not wanting to make a fuss about things she was always very shy and introverted about things that bothered her, brushing it off – I'm Fine Mummy! I'm Fine Mummy!. Perhaps it was the attention to her severe allergic Asthma she dreaded, that was brought on suddenly and without any sign or warning by chemicals, pollutants, some foods, insects, stress, swimming, excessive cold and sports exercise at school etc. Sabena's spare puffers were in the school office fridge if those in her school or tote bag ran out during extra curricula and other strenuous activities and hobbies.

What about a book to draw attention to these concerns in our upcoming future youth? But this would not get the urgent exposure to the mental health and climate change environmental problems affecting our youth out fast enough for Sabena to get urgent help or other young people. What about Radio? That might be remembered for 15 minutes and then simply forgotten in days without any government organizations standing up and finding tangible solutions for our kids now.

Any type of TV interview or lifestyle doco, was the speediest and most likely way to attract attention to immediate social issues and gain huge audience exposure, that the consequence being finding help for our kids on the outside of the faulty system, that kids fell through the cracks, and never returned from the brink. That morning I was possessed and on the laptop, with my concept epiphany or light bulb moment and I wrote a short paragraph synopsis of an idea for a Teen Talk Production pilot interview doco program.

I rarely but sometimes watched stuff on CTV31, Like hard times don't last people do, Regional Italian Cuisine, The Dutch show, the money and worker's compensation shows and sometimes the classic Oz Umbrella films. They were scouting for new show concepts and programs for their current programming as this was being advertised. Well, I presumed it wasn't going to be easy or was a very long shot, and go large or go home as American people often quip. So I would have a go and try to pitch the idea, to what I thought would have the least rigorous TV standards and might go for a once -off doco to fill in the social conscious and community gap of educating and family entertainment. I never bothered about whether I might fail or not, as I knew squat about the industry but my hospitality background always kept me in good stead with tasks out of my passive comfort zone.

The Birth of Teen Talk.

Confidently I marched up to the Station and spoke to Tessa Irwin the current programming manager co-ordinator probably youngish, in her mid to late 20's who was very encouraging, open minded, lateral thinker and the idea resonated with her automatically. You will have to fill out a program proposal form for your program to be assessed and formally accepted for your broadcast licence. Not even dawning on me what all this might further entail with devil in the detail if I would succeed. Tessa informed me that my program proposal was well received and what the youth needed now.

Pleased that I was accepted, but wondering what do I do now and go from here. *Occam's Law, the most likely or reasonable explanation is the correct and simplest. – Dr. Phil.* I was sure it might not even get up, so wasn't too bothered. How stupid of me I assumed, that the station facilitated the filming and production of the program. I was wrong. You're on your own. You know, Tessa remarked you have to submit your own Pilot program to be assessed as appropriate programming.

TV Reality

So I also pitched the program to enlist help at every station, every streaming service and visited the Disney office at the Channel 10 building at the Como Centre. Most of the time I couldn't get a foot in the door or it was the stock standard reply, we don't accept unsolicited materials or it's not suitable for our programming schedule at this point in time. Maybe I was too much out of my depth and that I should sensibly simply abandon the whole project. I even contacted a cured patient Ian, previous senior TV producer, Southern Star TV, for Channel 7, who I had not seen in years to find another professional producer contact to refer me to for guidance. Ian produced some episodes of Blue Heelers and other programs for Southern Star TV programming. Mum, Freddie and myself were all fans of Blue Heelers and at a time it was her all favourite program with John Wood and Lisa McCune. He referred me to Natalie, an upcoming junior producer again it always came down to money, money for scripting by her boyfriend, money for pre – production, money for crew so on and so on.

It wasn't particularly an appropriate phase for me to be spending my own meagre savings, the overseas trip credit card debt expenses and bills, the instigation of legal proceedings for the will, the Sabena Issue etc. There was no regret for me however about having spent the money abroad because I wasn't going back there anytime soon and I wouldn't be going back that far for the items I would deeply regret not having purchased there and then at the spur of the moment in travel mode. I purchased many things for family and friends and always thinking of what Sabena might also like.

- Italian Fairy Figurines (le Fate)
- Italian Fairy Books
- Venice Harlequin Masks
- Murano Glass watch from venice.
- Italian T-shirts, shortie pyjamas, clothing and costume jewellery
- Hello Kitty merchandise from Italy, Dubai and almost any other country.
- Dubai Souvenirs and memorabilia for her Middle East Dad's roots (Sabena's other favourite Disney film was Aladdin and Jasmine)
- Something cute and memorable from every country that I stopped at on the way.

At a particular timeline during these years there was a court case I was involved in at almost every court level except for the High Court of Australia and I won't keep my fingers crossed for that either.

- Magistrates Court
- Family Court
- Federal Circuit Court
- Supreme Court
- County Court
- VCAT

Certainly I couldn't ask Freddie for any money as he would not even give me it for an Appeal for custody of Sabena, that's why I represented myself wherever I could to manage matters.

After months and months went by and Natalie failed to turn up at a lunch meeting and was flat to the boards with work, in the beginning she responded to my emails and then nothing. I also searched for other producers but they were either swamped with projects or out of business or changed their career pathway. Perhaps it was divine intervention because I wasn't going to be pigeon –holed by their plan for my program and have also to pay too.

It was several weeks where I pondered heavily about whether to continue the project.

In the end I decided it was for the greater good for youth and for the world community.

I would allocate the minimum of $ 7, 000 – 10, 000 from my savings to produce a project pilot program and that it would be a once –off lifestyle documentary feature program.

Field of Dreams – Kevin Costner "Build it and they will come"

My previous casual receptionist and friend, who was unemployed at the time, years before I went abroad was optimistic, quirky, spirited and genuinely believed you could do anything if your heart was in it. Simone received a parking fine outside the clinic unfairly and I thought about to try writing a note to help her on behalf of her workplace and for her to contest the huge fine. The parking fine was cancelled and Simone was so thankful ecstatic as her husband's work hours were also then cut back. We also arranged to spend a holiday day visit at a light lunch with Simone, her daughter Adele and Sabena (both around 8 -10 Years old).

We organized to meet at La Parissiene Cafe, South Yarra a very tiny bakery and cake shop, and the girls both loved the Rainbow Magic Fairy books and Katy Perry songs, so they gifted Sabena with a couple of the miniature fairy paperbacks. Adele (now 15 Years old), the only child with a genuine ingenuous naiveté and being painfully shy and a bit awkward was encouraged by Simone to be in the program after I invited her to be interviewed on my program many years later on TTP Disc 3, 21.08. 2015.

Firework – Katy Perry
California Girls
Roar
Teenage Dream

There were also some other inspiring people that I met sometime before I started the program, Priscilla Monea who I visited for a haircut at her salon Lumiere Hair, ambitious and motivated a veritable dynamo business woman, NLP Life Coach- Neuro change, single mum with two autistic young children. She said to me there is nothing you can't do if you just try.

I was so enthused by her brilliance and attitude, she was also invited to be interviewed TTP Disc 5, 23.10.2015. Priscilla was also kind enough to donate some vouchers which my friend Roberta Jack was fortunate to win in some raffle competition at our Bowling Function Party.

Eye of the Tiger
The Rythm of the Night

Misha, that I became acquainted with through being an AESSRA member. She started her own business making products for people with chemical sensitivities that were Chemical Free and her partner Dan who also imported some products to help people with MCS. Misha suffered and struggled most of her young life with MCS and also her own daughter Cassandra was affected too, people not understanding her condition at all being frustrating. It was her mission to educate others about MCS and to pass on her knowledge of how to cope with it in everyday life with MCS strategies, aids and products that enhanced their life. In exchange for some of her products, I discounted her daughter's treatment accounts at the clinic.

Fed up with waiting for something that might never happen, I would be my own producer. So, I searched for professional videographers all of which weren't interested in the project and it couldn't be done, it was a recurring theme, until I stumbled upon Costa Anathassiou.

He was a consummate all rounder and was sympathetic to the project cause and values.

Filming of the introductory pilot began in January 2015 and it was aired on 12.06.2015. I assumed that I was done and that would be my contribution to Sabena and the Youth. After the broadcasting that week Tessa congratulated me on the audience success feedback and then in another breath said now you only have to make another 12 episodes to complete this season for your annual broadcasting licence. It was a complex order of circumstance.

TTP – Descriptor Summary 2016

Mission Statement: For Teens To Help other Teens. 4T2HOT.

Teen Talk Production – a series of interviews involving brave youth from 9-25 Years talking about their feelings and experiences. It is a platform to give teens a REAL voice in these virtual technology generations. I hope it becomes a useful tool for teens to connect and communicate about the issues that affect them during the interview they try to impart some useful information to help other youth and each other.

It's about a MUM who started and created Teen Talk out of so much love for her daughter, that her heart ached with pain and she would have horrifying nightmares about what terrible things might eventually happen to her daughter! Her daughter who was with her father and stepmother from age 8, suffered a mental breakdown at just 12 years, was self- mutilating and with suicidal thoughts and actions. Admitted to the hospital, Banksia mental Health Unit, immediately placed on several severe adult dosage anti-depressant medications and counselling for several years. She is almost 17, and only marginally improving or getting better.

The MUM myself was inspired to help other youth even if she couldn't reach out to help her own daughter during this time. The beaurocracy and what the system offered was useless. Even if I help just one other child it will be worth it. But also to help other youth who are struggling not just with Mental Illness, but many other issues. Her daughter who was always shy, introvert, reserved and timid kept things to herself, not confiding or asking for help, not to be a bother. I woke up one night after a horrific nightmare that the hospital called me saying that Sabena suicided. I woke screaming, Please Teen Talk! Please Teen Talk! Get it out! Express Yourself.

She needed to express herself and talk about her issues and problems to heal. The first step to healing starts with a Teen Talk! February 2014, wrote idea for the program synopsis that very early morning. An Epiphany! I was then driven by passion to realize this idea to fruition. Introductory pilot program filmed January, 2015 accepted and broadcasted on CTV31 from June, 2015.

My vision for the logo was to represent the Teen Youth Community using a wheel of Umbrellas interconnecting. Umbrella's symbolize rainy weather and reference those times when we are worried, confused or face issues beyond our control. The sticks of the umbrella remind us to hold on and stick together, while the hook represents you or a group of youth, as in connecting with you. As a community we can help each other to get through it together with strength. It is also hopefully a springboard to bring change for the better to improve resources, services and systems. We should be the heroes of for our youth for the future!

I dedicate this to my darling daughter Sabena, whom I will love to eternity and beyond, no matter what, which sparked the passion and inspiration to drive me to start and create this project. Teen Talk helps youth by giving them a voice to learn improve, grow and make their future lives better. The first step to healing starts with a Teen Talk! Love MUM, Dr. Linda Walsh.

Why we are useful and how we can help, offering a type of one of a kind original communication system for our youth. Without effective communication there is breakdown in families, relationships, self- esteem, addiction, abuse, bullying, illness and many other issues contributing to the damage to our youths personal lives and futures.

Why the system is not effective in helping our youth and the need to provoke change?

We can listen to what they are trying to tell us as well as what we don't hear at times.

We as adults can try to understand them better and help them from knowing what are their thoughts, actions and behaviours are about not just having contempt for them.

To teach them to Beware of bad social media and the internet as the advice may not always be good and confide in someone you trust, BFF, your MUM, teacher, and stand up for yourself, be assertive, be strong and stand your ground until it gets better or something changes and gets done, don't be intimidated, frightened or embarrassed or give up hope!

Sisters are doing it for themselves.

It never entered my consciousness as I never reached there to that level of negative destruction that would see my daughter so debilitated and vulnerable to harm herself.

All that we see or seem is but a dream within a dream – Edgar Allan Poe.

My Brilliant Career, The Piano – Sam Neill

Another day in Paradise – Phil Collins

Geoffrey Rush, Craig Mc Lachlan, John Jarrat, Robert Hughes – Violence, harassment and sexual abuse of women and children. 2022

Neighbours finishes 10.06.2022

The perpetrator

It is strange to think back now but I was actually pleased about Eddie marrying Bon. I considered that this might actually help him to become milder with respect to having visitation and connection with Sabena. I even tried to befriend Bon but she seemed jealous of my interactions with Sabena, so this was not helpful for our mother – daughter bonding. The spiteful actions of ceasing all contact with me in October, 2014 and disconnecting their landline altogether and changing their phone number in 2017, the police check that I called in to Moorabbin Police station who called the Police on the North West Side to see if Sabena was alive in late 2014, that they would not permit them but stood behind Sabena at the front door to see her and then dragged her quickly away without any information about her health or well being. The Salvation Army whom I desperately called for some information about her whereabouts due to the sudden phone disconnection and all cease of contact, also I thought maybe they also moved suburbs without informing me about her welfare.

The legal advice that I received was not to go to appeal in 2015, and that it was suggested to me that time would heal all wounds and that my ex- partner would eventually come around to providing a normalized contact for me and my daughter, whilst forgiving and forgetting his bitterness and revenge.

Eddie was chronically unemployed even after having married Bon, having the excuse of a back injury in Sydney in his 20's as a labourer and also his ongoing anxiety, bipolar and chronic severe depressive illness. Eddie continued chain smoking regardless of his Diabetes diagnosis for several years, he was ongoing on and off on medications such as Prozac and Effexor.

Extract from My Affidavit 15.12.2014

As a consequence of the child's current condition and the Father's bipolar illness, neither have the ability and the capacity to be rational and impartial about what is in the best interest of the child.

That the cause of her condition as diagnosed, is a consequence of Post - Traumatic Stress Disorder (PTSD) and Parental Alienation / Separation Anxiety Disorder Syndrome.

The child was told by the father that she was taken away from the mother's care because she was a bad mother and is now resentful towards myself, without mental closure for her well – being.

Past behaviour is the best predictor or pattern of future behaviour – Dr. Phil.

For me it was as if Sabena's hatred, Anger, Resentment and Abandonment issues were increasingly worse. This was also mixed up with grief, guilt, moroseness, Impending doom, helplessness, futility, powerlessness and hopelessness for her current desperate never ending isolation and paranoid circumstance.

After the retrospect brain damage she was never quite the same, there was always something lost, confused or missing in the jigsaw of her brain's mind, a blank page. It was like she forgot everything up until she went to live with them and I gradually learned to reconcile this, to live with myself and to be kind and forgive myself that it was not my fault.

A momentum of which her potential was never fully realized or even been recognized.

Why me? Why me? Why me? Why Me? Why me? because God Knows I can cope. I thought of my dear Mum calling him the Arabo or Saddama Hussien, a deranged man.

Watching the repeat of a heart wrenching film many years ago, reminded me of, but a much more improved, ingenuous, honest and a more simple, mentally disabled and autistic, retarded version of Eddie, it was called *I am Sam (2001), with Sean Penn and Michele Pfeiffer.* This man tries to regain custody of his young daughter after a one night stand with a homeless, addicted street woman. My favourite scene that is indelible in my mind is that he would routinely everyday without fail go the ihop (International House of Pancakes) for his breakfast. Who is Sam?

It was ironic because of how much Sabena loved pancakes and life's basic pleasures.

I can't feel my face when I'm with you but I love it – the weeknd

I don't want no srcubs –TLC

Don't let the sun go down on me – George Michael

I won't back down – The travelling Wilbury's

On the road again – Willie Nelson

Dirty Deeds done dirt cheap – ACDC

Mummy your the star twinkling day and night in my life – Sabena WL

Stay – Bic Runga

Once the wheels are in motion it's too late!
Video Games – Lana Del Rey

The Jabberwocky Celebration Dance.

It must have been December, 2013 that I sat beside Allan at the Solo's Christmas Party, we chatted constantly, myself not getting a word in to chat to the others at the table for 20 people. There were several fascinating and interesting people at the dinner at a rustic pub in Fitzroy or Collingwood. I exchanged a few numbers with both the male and female sex. Allan kept my attention most of the evening, butting in at moments, chatting to the others.

By early January 2014, I received no call from Allan as I thought he might call because he was glued to me all the evening. Not my usual modus operandi, but because he seemed pleasant enough I decided that we were in the 21st Century and girls could also call guys if they liked. The thought of seeming to be being too easy, bothered me and was keeping me from calling. My life was pretty ordinary those months with all the shite going on in it and the world too. So why not? At worst we could become friends and stay in the stuck companion friend zone galaxy like Ian, who he already knew from Solo's previously, whilst connecting with other people, who introduce you to also other people which is helpful for your social life and also you might stumble on Mr. Right or your true life's forever after partner to eternity and beyond. Anyhoo, it was worth a shot! So I made the call.

It was true as Ian said, he sometimes had the grumps about him but mostly with me he seemed quite happy. We began to interact quickly after attending also some other Solo events separately. Then we dated exclusively because Allan began to be annoyed by other guys at Solo events trying to chat me up and drawing my attention away from himself. Looking wise he wasn't my type but he was attractive nevertheless in his own way, probably even more distinguished in his youth. Of definite Scottish ancestry, several generations Australian, from his surname and his family crest. It was uncanny how these cold Brits made a beeline for me, as moths instinctively drawn to a flame. Best described as a wrinkly faced and sparse white haired, Brian Keith look alike but in his mid 70's or even a few years older, I never knew his true age because he lied about these things and similar because he was very conceited and selfish or cagey and dodgy about some stuff evading revealing too much.

For the most part he was Old School Tie and often said *seems to me* this or that. Both being classical kind of people of a similar genre, there were many activities we enjoyed together and had in common. It was a bonus that he actually owned his own house in Brighton and drove a Mercedes silver type 4WD. We dined very frequently, High Tea at Studley Park, visited stately mansions (Labassa), art exhibitions and galleries of even the tiniest size, attended lectures and cosy concert recitals. In our honeymoon phase he mostly paid which I thought very chivalrous compared to loser men who began Dutch, on first date and never saw me again after that. I repaid him in kind by doing thoughtful deeds of buying him groceries, vitamin supplements, checking his leg and foot X-Rays, treating his ankle wound at the clinic, helping him with his Diabetic and other polypharmacy medications, home duties and the like. We seemed to being getting on absolutely smoothly. I was so very hopeful! I felt I found somebody comforting during the turbulence with Freddie and Sabena's debacle.

There were a few other guys that I also fancied from the Solo singles, Mark and another his name was David, both perpetually single and we chatted at another previous event, David discovered I was a Downton Abbey fan and he surprised me It was touching at another event in January, 2014 at a Collingwood Hotel with a

Downton Abbey mini paperback, *The Real Downton Abbey* – so very utterly thoughtful. Don Burke also happened to be there that evening and I think, he may have got a selfie with him.

I ceased attending Solo events once we began dating each other however Allan hedging his bets continued to go to events, not sure if also the Solo events but certainly Bayside Singles going on bike rides, walks, film and theatre nights, dinners and belonging to a book club.

Places with Solo's

Niche on Bridge, Copperwood, Glenferrie Hotel etc.

Places with Allan

Laurent, Romeo's, Dainty Sichuan, Red Wok, South Yarra Trattoria, Quaff, Oriental Teahouse, The Little Ox.

On his birthday, an Aquarius I reserved us a table at Da Noi, fine Italian cuisine and exquisite dishes handcrafted daily, different menus, white truffle seafood linguini was a signature dish and cleaned our palates with regional Italian Prosecco. I paid as his birthday gift.

Later on he was to also surprise me with an evening at prestigious Sails on the Bay, Brighton with amazing spectacular marina views it was modern taste fusion Australian fine food fare.

Films we watched were at the Dendy and Brighton Bay, The Palace Cinema- Como with their Italian, Spanish, and English themed film festival functions in the upstairs and downstairs foyer areas. Films – The most memorable the Dallas Buyers Club with Matthew McConaghey, Turner, The Book Theif, The Grand Budapest Hotel, The Wolf of Wall Street, The Monuments Men, Carol, The Invisible Woman, Brooklyn, The Immigrant.

The Ian Potter Museum of Art – University of Melbourne for Art Exhibitions and Classical Concerto Recitals.

Sometimes I researched events on the weekends on Only Melbourne – What's on Melbourne and it might have been the Pawn and Co. Bar where I dragged Allan to have a trendy brunch and then chill out at this lazy Sunday afternoon twilight band jam session where The Winterfriends Band was playing who were then interviewed on TTP - Disc 3 August/ September, 2015 with Steven Marshall White on acoustic guitar singing together with Phaedra Gunn their own original song My Wonderland.

Home base was usually his modest classical quaint weatherboard house in Brighton, where the first front room was the bedroom and all other smallish rooms off this narrow arched hallway branching off to the west side the fourth room was the lounge room with the 80's tan leather four seater couch where we watched TV, cuddled, caressed, and playfully cajoled. The house would have been more appealing without all the thick clutter in the hallway and part of the lounge room his bicycle pride of place leaning on the inside of the front door as you entered to remind you of its presence. Pieces of Art on the hallway and lounge room walls and floor. The bathroom located to the left of the house and the kitchen to the right at the back. The house was a bit musty and the shower a bit dingy and mouldy with the piece des resistance the back kitchen door hanging by a thread on the top hinges, so there was a gapping gap at the bottom that overlapped leaving a gusty breeze to enter through it. The kitchen was obviously unused for a long time with papers and business cards strewn everywhere, rat scats on all the shelves and bench tops, unusable dirty moulding pots and pans, greasy and rusty stovetop, oven, griller and small 50's vintage rounded shoulders small fridge. The rear was a squatter's dive hovel place. It was shocking and disgusting but I thought he can't live like this and I decided a particular long weekend to clean up the whole damn kitchen mess so we could use it sometimes and perhaps even cook now and then. I spent two full weekend days on the project, washed and sorted the fridge of stale, shrivelled, expired and mouldy food, as well. With a trip to the local grocery store I bought cleaners, disinfectants, cloths, cleaning equipment, Tea Towels and groceries to stock up the fridge. I lined all the shelves and drawers with the Tea Towels and then placed the cleaned crockery, cutlery, pots and pans on top of them. Another full day a week or so later I also elected to do a sprucing once over in the bathroom and shower. Allan never helped me with these tasks but came home to have a peek now and then to see my progress and then we went out for dinner at the local pub. I said to him, shucks I don't even have time to clean my own kitchen and fridge this well, my kitchen however was tidy and hygienic for the most part though unlike his and you could also cook and eat in it, with some few stray dishes in the rinse sink.

The neighbour on the right John Wall (75 years), passed the following year, so it was being auctioned off by his niece Pam Straw, as he was single with no children of his own. I was concerned about another development on that left side of my Mum's house and asked him to attend the auction where I also spied my brother with his current new partner, but they never spoke to me. Allan was a costing lawyer with his own small business working from the second and third rooms of his own house. I since found out he also owned several other investment houses and properties in his area and around Australia. Of course, I hadn't the money to buy it, but thought it might be a good future investment for him and maybe I could purchase it from him once my will settlement eventually might come through. I was too scared to bid myself but he never bid also either and eventually it sold privately to some Chinese Investment property developers, which I was dreading that as a worst case scenario. I was however deeply disappointed, it was a terrible blow. That fateful day, I cooked for him in my own kitchen lunch before the auction serving poached aromatic whiting sliced in the sauce with pre blanched potato and mango sorbet, another time after that with poached aromatic Salmon with steamed sautéed vegies.

Early on after dating a about a month or two he offered me his house key voluntarily and he said just let yourself in on Friday afternoons after work if I am out elsewhere and not home. I was pleased he trusted me with his house key and why not, I made it sanitary and habitable after all.

Cover me in sunshine

shower me with good times

Tell me that the world's been spinning since the beginning

and everything will be alright

Cover me in sunshine

Pink and Willow Sage Hart, February 2021.

Most weekends I drove to his house and a few times he stayed over here at my house from Saturday evening to Sunday afternoon. Our intimacy during these months was more touching, affectionate and loving rather than purely sexual.

It was endearing how he left me notes on a whole piece of white foolscap paper in huge printed biro capital letters outside his front door, people from the street could almost read it, if he was out Friday afternoons or while he went out on a Sunday morning to get a paper and a coffee whilst I slept in.

Be back in 5, 10 or fifteen minutes - A, Gone to get a coffee, see you later - A Things like that.

Allan's front garden were two different sized hankies on either side, tiny patches with no driveway and a narrow cement path to the front door, the back garden in comparison was all over grown with high grass and there was enough land to have a another small house behind. I arrived a Friday evening to find he planted these adorable little red and pink pansies all along the edges of the path, he greeted me at the narrow veranda landing step and pointed to the pansies, as proud as punch of his work, very pretty I said but why haven't you pruned that overgrown shrub at the back of them. Always an early riser in nice weather, he must have mowed the back lawn and pruned the shrub whilst I was blissfully sound asleep, on cloud nine. I heard him come in and shower changing into fresh clothes and turn the kettle on for a cup of tea. He was exceptionally hygienic in his person and he changed his sheets at least every week without fail embarrassingly even more often than I do. As I gradually arose, I showered and then we made our way for our mid morning constitutional to Cafe Bliss in front of the park and beach, where we ate brunch and later walked further on to the marina.

I became introduced to only three of his friends, Margaret and Guy a nice friendly couple around our age who also lived in the area they were polar opposites in personalities but matched perfectly. Guy was a semi retired College lecturer. For some reason their teen granddaughter was residing with them temporarily, I'm not sure of the issue. I immediately felt close to them, them however keeping aloof but we never became closer than having a few light lunches and a chat at nearby cafes together, Margaret would say, you must try such and such soup or those Portuguese Tarts are the best.

Allan's Cousin Pastor was already waiting at the table as we arrived in Allan's Merc. It was around my Birthday or Easter, sometimes unfortunately my birthday also fell on Good Friday too, it was somewhere in the far outer suburbs as it seemed a long drive for the evening passing through Balwyn. I wondered how people might find this restaurant unless they knew where it was, the food was Lebanese but it was even much more spicy, tasty and delicious than I had ever eaten before. He was a contented but also a cheekily funny pastor, chatting about his congregations works and at the end, saying *see how we pull up tomorrow morning.*

Allan loved Italy and was enthralled and admired all things Italian, they were up on a pedestal for him. Italian women were very beautiful, sexy and captivating he exclaimed as he grinned gleefully with their curvy voracious and voluptuous breasts and smooth bodies. I imagined a fresco of Da Vinci's art with those floating figures. Of course there were classical Italian beauties who were representative of this Mona Lisa, Gina and Sophia. Every now and then, I spied him momentarily peering down my sneaky peeking cleavage. I was pleased about my heritage and European looks and the thought of it made me feel sensual. Allan's dream was to retire to a Tuscan village in Italy and write a fiction novel, cliché some film with Angelina Jolie and her husband Brad Pitt – *By the Sea.*

Allan knew about the circumstance with Freddie and he agreed I should get a restraining order after I arrived at his house late a Thursday evening slightly battered, beaten and bruised on my face and arms. I told him about me contesting the will and that Freddie's plan was to tear down Mum's house to build a six apartment building complex, of which he promised to offer to keep one for me to live in, for the rest of my days. I heard all that before and I was still always back living in Mum's house. He began to advise me to write a chronology of events leading up to the contesting of the will, I was thankful of his suggestions but I didn't like him meddling in my personal affairs or interfering. I already had lawyers retained and signed a disclosure agreement but he was adamant that he would attend with me at the barrister's initial meeting which I was uncomfortable about since I only knew him for a few months, I felt the barrister's vibe suspicious also, he also scrawled a few notes for her. I printed out the chronology on his home printer as it was faster than my own and then he said we must drop it to the chambers for the barrister to peruse before further discussions ensued about how to proceed. He urged we should drop it off immediately at the clerk before COB Friday but I disagreed It can wait a day or so until I can get a pink ribbon for it, important legal documents and files were always strung by that pink legal ribbon, he had a piece but it was too short to reach. We argued about the pink legal ribbon detail but I left his house and proceeded the next day to buy similar. *Grumpy Old Men,* wasn't my document important enough to have a pink legal bound ribbon, he laughed saying it wasn't important and why should I have to be such a politically correct person.

Allan asked me about my baggage and I described to him my worst fears and concerns for Sabena, and how I would use the money from the settlement to appeal her residence and custody issue. Allan apparently was on reasonably good visiting terms however with his daughter Susan, who regrettably suffered with Kawasaki's Disease and couldn't have children but was happily married for many years to an Asian man and they both had working contracts in London for some years, so they had lived abroad for some time. Allan described how he was also entering a family court application against his son Brendan to obtain visitations with his small grandchildren in Canberra. I helped him to prepare his affidavit and also wrote a short summary affidavit of my own to support his case, which we lodged together. Later that year I lodged my own self - represented application and affidavit of appeal, without his offer of support against Sabena's father contesting residence and his only help was to suggest to include exhibits of photo's, personal notes, emails, cards and Sabena's sketches drawn especially for me.

Allan sadly suffered a few chronic health issues Diabetes, Bipolar and Manic Depression, Thyroid, Sleep Apnoea, Knee Arthritis and maybe some others I wasn't even aware of. His main medications were Metformin, Seroquel and Thyroxine. Despite all our heavy breathing and petting, he never became obviously aroused but was always revelling in the soothing feeling of the sheer splendour. I suspected that he might be impotent as happens in some men as a side effect of Diabetic medicines. Not bothered at all as I was mutually enjoying our amorous moments together, and I even said to him to even reassure him, I am more than happy just to be loving you nothing more is needed.

I'm too sexy for my cat – Right said Fred, 2007.

My worst fears of his meanness was recognized when he said he was getting quotes for painting and repairing the front veranda and cosmetic house facade, that was ironic as I said, why don't you repair the damaged kitchen back door and crooked corner foundation of the house, as an urgent priority instead. He neglected to answer this. I thought it was perfect common sense myself, in Summer months it was fine with a slight cosy breeze wafting through the house except for the cockroaches and insects coming in which was pesky but as the weather began to cool it was draughty and very freezing. There was the split system in the lounge room but it wasn't enough to cut the dampness and it was necessary for me to coax a lot to even have it eventually turned on frosty cold days. With my respiratory allergy I struggled with the coldness and easily developed bronchial conditions.

A particular day I enquired about his ex- wife, he explained he was studying Law at Melbourne Uni and working part-time as a clerk in his young days and that his wife was the first woman that came along who grabbed him to have sex and he was hooked by it. Marrying at a youngish age for a man, Allan remarked he wasn't sure that he actually loved her but she soon became in the family way. His previous wife, now also with two children became increasingly nagging, financially demanding. They were not long divorced after that. He never spoke about other relationships but was chronically single it seemed.

After several months of our cosy companionship, this weekend at Allan's house he was grouchy and irritable for some reason. I brought near me, take-away fish and chips on Friday evening for us to share together, so we needn't have to go out. I usually prepared my small overnight tote for the weekend with my satin pyjamas, change of underwear, toiletries, medicines and vitamins etc. He always preferred me to go to his place rather than come to my mum's house although I offered. That morning his mild sleep apnoea startled him abruptly and he was restless, jumping about, irritable and erratic. He couldn't get back to sleep even though I spooned him to try to calm and soothe him, again being good sound sleepers that we all are on our Mum's side of the family I wafted off into oblivious dreamland, while he was still awake counting sheep. As usual he was up early, I don't know how much he slept that night but I faintly heard him showering and slam the door, to get his coffee.

Sometimes there were bugs on the front window side of the bed in his bedroom and bed, and I began to get bitten with these rashes showing up a few days later, so sprayed the bedding lightly with aloe vera, after he left in case he might tell me off because he never was being bitten I was. I always brought a few muesli bars or snacky type things for breakfast that I could eat after he left as he was gone for some time until he returned at brunch. It was starting to get brisk on these early Autumn mornings, It was a Sunday. I consoled him about the night before and suggested perhaps those CPAP machines might help. He returned only for a short while obsessed with urgency, scrambling to search for scripts in his bedroom drawers whilst I was buried under the doona. What the hell are you doing? I said. I requested Viagra from the Doctor's last week and I'm going to get it.

Oopsy Daisy!

In my tote there were always a few muesli bars and some kid's size orange juice boxes, I usually swallowed my tablets in the morning after Allan left for his coffee. Saturday morning I noticed I finished my daily HRT tablets for Endometriosis and Ovarian Cysts prevention. I had been without them before once or twice, for a day or so and nothing terrible happened and then recommenced.

In the ruckus of Allan rummaging his drawers in the bedroom then I decided I might as well shower. We ate brunch at Laurent and straight after he drove like a man possessed to a Pharmacy that was open in Glenhuntly Road. He raced in and out and in his car we returned home at breakneck pace.

It was a particularly freezing day and a lazy day that was appropriate for staying in bed for most of it. We arrived at his house and he said, *let's go back to bed and cuddle.* It was even far too cold to tolerate sitting on the coach in the lounge room with the split system on and watch a film, with the blustery icy damp air seeping and streaming through the crooked, tilted and hugely gapping kitchen back door. It wasn't even secure as it couldn't be locked or shut due its heavy slant overlapping.

So we did. Allan switches on the kettle for a cup of tea and brings it to his bedroom, sits on his side of the bed beside his chiffonier and proceeds to remove from the pharmacy paper bag these light blue lozenge shaped tablets which I recognized as Viagra, Freddie tried them once or twice after his paranoid phase of

Sally's stalking. He said that he hadn't found them particularly useful and seemed to only elevate his blood pressure and make him dizzy.

Allan, please don't use it, there's no need and besides I explained they have been known to cause heart attacks in patients with other co-morbidities especially those with Diabetes and heart issues. He tended to be grouchy, stubbornly obstinate and tenaciously resistant to reason now and then as I discovered as it was more revealed to me after the argumentative saga about the pink legal ribbon.

Defiantly, he swallows it. *I want to do more than just cuddle you.* He annoying begged, coaxed and coerced me constantly that afternoon that he wanted to have a try. I instinctively thought it a bad idea. Being sensitive of him and thinking it might also be an ego thing, I eventually gave in but the immediate urgency of it all was very disturbing and unsettling to me, it was as if he was taking bets. Why was it that men wore their flashy bright tight red jocks on the day they think they will have their conquest or might get lucky, it was an indelible throwback from the fated evening with Aussie Irish lawyer Chris.

Of course you usually have to take it as with these medicines about an hour before to have an effect. I thought well nothing will happen immediately, feeling extremely uncomfortable about the situation and then he will probably conk out eventually and have a snooze as he often unawares dozed off into Noddyland. He was doomed to failure and disappointing humiliation, after he became slightly aroused with my soft stroking, light caresses and hugging of his torso and then it instantly flopped about without warning. *Have a nap and we'll try again later on* I suggested. He became exceedingly frustrated, irritable and angry with himself and so he persisted to my dismay. I wasn't at all enjoying the interaction now as it was becoming very pressurized and uncomfortable. Eventually he managed to my relief with it, with it up for more than a few seconds and he went for it. Personally I never felt a thing myself but he was sure he accomplished something and I let him believe it, it was even more real and believable as he spied the tiny spotting of my breakthrough bleed on the bottom sheet. What a dang nuisance, it was so very terribly embarrassing for me. He was to have another attempt very early the following morning as was his fleeting morning glory and I departed in the very wee early morning to get a few hours rest in before starting work at the clinic.

We slumped into each other and he slept dreamily but what was all that urgent fiasco about. He awoke some time after, startled with his jolting to reality sleep apnoea bouts. I was by that time a bit annoyed and remarked what about the kitchen back door, I hope you'll get it repaired before this Winter. Disgruntled, he said *what if I don't?*, pig-headed as naughty little schoolboy to his teacher. I laughed jokingly and said it would be reasonable grounds for severe physical and financial abuse with an instant divorce ensuing.

Franks Red Hot Sauce – I put that on everything!

Sadly, he actually meant it and instead of it being promptly repaired before our next encounter, the front facade was lovely and painted but alas the back door swung farther apart. I was disappointed in him not listening to me and being disrespectful as it was a very huge deal and bone of contention for me, nonetheless and he knew it. Despite it, regardless he ignored my consternation about what I felt was his continuous misguided pattern of mistaken priorities and his blatant disregard for my health and wellbeing being neglectful and abusive, not to have repaired it but being haughty, arrogant and shallow painting and repairing the cosmetic front facade first and not the back door.

I regularly in passing trying to help I would check Allan's prepared daily medications tray from the pharmacy that was brazenly obvious on the lounge room coffee table, he seemed to have been failing to keep up with the Diabetic medication as some tablets were still in their slots from many days past before. He began to have these rages for little or no reason, confused, argumentative, erratic, abusive and behaved in a deranged manner. I previously experienced this horrifying unstable, mental illness caper with Eddie before and I wasn't keen on revisiting those potentially violent and verbally abusive seizure moments that seemed to last for hours especially when you are afraid and can't escape. It was happening all over again. Allan behaved increasingly more aggressive towards me, however he never struck me. He accused me of stealing his wallet and watch, only to find he only misplaced them, a few hours later. He became even more gruff, and emotionally abusive, flying off the handle at almost any little thing that wasn't right and deflecting it onto me, it was Dr. Jekyll and Mr. Hyde, who was it to be today, lying about his whereabouts on weekends he wasn't available for me to visit, increasingly more self- centred, self- absorbed, narcissistic and selfish than his usual conceited self. He was a very *unattractive man* during this phase, Mr. Crotty who at uni, my best friend, a different Chris, we said unkindly about this practice clinic patient that we wouldn't touch him with a barge pole as he was dirty, aggressive, kicking, shrieking and destitute.

It was becoming too excessively cold and intolerable for me to visit his place anymore and I would no longer stay over but left before he went to sleep, sort of a strike action you might call it as I was concerned to become sick and ending up with a bronchial condition or pneumonia because of my immune- compromised, respiratory allergy status. Somehow he failed to comprehend my fears and was blaze about it, even though he complained himself and grizzled about his arthritic knee in the cold and the limp was getting worse, he would have to get it operated on eventually at some stage. I however invited him to stay over at my mum's toasty cosy house instead but he was reluctant to drive here because he was either too tight, too lazy or also because he said he was a bit miserable with the Winter himself and slept in, on his own bed much later in the day on those frosty mornings.

Allan became suddenly oppositional to whatever sensible stuff I might have suggested, I should have got out then and there, as our love fizzled. It was to be a short and bittersweet romance ending in irreconcilable differences. Mum would have said have you scraped the bottom of the rubbish yet again, I wanted so much to make her proud of me and have a proper supportive partner for life.

Would I be so bad if I could turn you on? Mouth – Merril Bainbridge 2012.

Shallow Hal –Gwenyth Paltrow, Jack Black 2001.

Game of Thrones – Winter is coming, Bend the Knee 2011.

Run too fast, fly too high – Janice Ian 1979.

Robin Hood – Cate Blanchett, Russell Crowe 2010.

After Alice slew the Jabberwocky,

The Mad Hatter does the The Futterwack

or Futterwacken Dance.

Fairfarren (Farewell may you travel far under fair skies).

Star Trek – 2009 Chris Pine.

Star Trek Into Darkness – 2013 Chris Pine, Benedict Cumerbatch.

Pinestars vs Cumerbitches – The Graham Norton Show.

I arrived after work, early evening on a particular Friday at Allan's house after several weeks break away he greeted me at the front door squeezing beside the bicycle leaning on the narrow hall wall. The tumultuous kerfuffle, barely lasting more than a few minutes but slower in motion in my mind. Instead of bringing me into the lounge room he elected to have me stand in the hallway beside the doorway to his bedroom. He was jittery with irrational hysteria, he spoke like a runaway train and said he booked a holiday to go to Turkey and then London to spend time with his daughter Susan, this June for a month or so. Margaret and Guy would be accompanying him on the trip, I asked him why he hadn't said something before about it. He answered he knew I wouldn't be able to afford to go with them anyway. This grated on my nerves somewhat, but that's not all folks, and then the next bombshell hits, the icing on the cake, he said and I have also been seeing a previous old girlfriend lately again. I glared at his Dan Murphy's outline shaped jaw line face gobsmacked at the turn of events. I'll be needing, my house key back thanks, he blithered. Both of us facing each other at the bedroom door at a Mexican standoff, I walked a bit further down the narrow hallway arched corridor, he blocking me off at the pass. Not knowing how to react as I was stunned, I walked back towards the bedroom and angled myself, quickly removing the said keys from my car key ring and throwing it onto the end of his bed. I asked if I could have a look to see whether any of my belongings were there that I might have forgotten from a previous visit and then without warning he grabs me by the elbow and tosses me out of his house, just like that, as if tossing rubbish into a bin.

Don't Call Me Baby – Madison Avenue, 1999.

You don't own me – Lesley Gore, 1963 (Ad for Si perfume with Cate Blanchett), 2019.

Miley Cyrus and Liam Hemsworth - Married December, 2018 – Divorced, January 2020.

Miley Cyrus – Slide Away 2019, Midnight Sky 2020, Nothing breaks like a heart 2018, When I look at you 2010.

Liam Hemsworth – The Dressmaker 2015, The Hunger Games 2012.

Could've Been – Tiffany, 1987.

Rolling in the Deep – Adele, 2011.

Johnny Depp and Amber Heard- Civil Defamation Trial, Fairfax County Virginia 11th April – 1st June, 2022.

Johnny Depp – Pirates of the Caribbean, Australia Visit March, 2015.

It's a small world after all, it's a small, small world – The Sherman Brothers, Disney Park Music, 2018

Billie Eilish – Bad Guy 2019.

You've lost that lovin'feelin' Whoooa – The Righteous Brothers, 1964.

It must have been love but it's all over now – Roxette, 1987.

Wuthering Heights – Kate Bush, 1978.

Total Eclipse of the Heart- Bonnie Tyler, 1983.

Don't go out tonight, it's bound to take your life, there's s a bad moon on the rise – Creedence Clearwater Revival, 2007.

I 'll show you a sunset, if you'll Stay with me till Dawn – Judy Tzuke 1979.

Battle Scars – 2012, Choir 2019 – Guy Sebastian.

Break Free 2018, 7 Rings, Boyfriend 2019, Thank-you next 2019, Greedy 2021 – Ariana Grande.

I'm with you 2002, Girlfriend 2007- Avril Lavigne.

Rupert Murdoch 91 and Jerry Hall 65, Divorcing after 6 years of marriage, June 2022.

Summertime Sadness 2012, Blue Jeans 2012, Young and Beautiful 2013 – Lana Del Rey

Flame Trees 1984- Cold Chisel, Jimmy Barnes.

It was simple *All Men are Bastards* Diary 1992, Pan Macmillan Publishers Australia, cartoons copyright Rebecca Pannell 1991, some girlfriend gifted me this and I was to keep it at my bedroom desk to be a constant reminder to me not to be sucked in again.

It was the same raw deal over and over again, I thought of James and his Bella's (The petite pretty Asian girls he collected whilst away and brought home), from wherever he'd been and was Vietnam, Hong Kong or Sydney, I most likely called him around his birthday the 8th November, 2017 we were still on reasonably friendly terms and permanently in the stalemate friend zone. Why should I bother, until then I never?. He blurted out, how silly, in his hoi polloi speak, he'd forgotten to pay his rates whilst abroad something went askew with his computer reminders or weird online failure. He then made some stupid comments supposedly to be funny and rehearsed to impress, but they were daggy, sick and dumb, they made me heave a despairing sigh. He wasn't a comic that's for sure, I pulled out heaps of things spontaneously from time to time without even realizing, they'd come out that were much more amusing. He said he wanted to go on living forever and be frozen, Cryogenics if he passed and so that he might be resuscitated for another round or go at life, be immortal as such. I said I wasn't particularly keen on a second round the first round for me was more than enough, yep. Maybe he needed increased time to continue with his world travelling collections.

I saw indelible flashbacks come to mind of the film Vanilla Sky 2001 with Tom Cruise, Penelope Cruz and Cameron Diaz. Tom Cruise who is David suffers a severe facial injury in a car accident and is then inadvertently caught up in a cycle of buying eternal life, switching between his girlfriend before the accident and the current rebirth version girlfriend. Will the real girlfriend, Please stand up whomever she is? Not a fan but kooky enough to have to watch it to the very end to find out how the whole mess ends. I hinted to James that I would have much preferred to spend the money on a real life diamond. You would have to end up usually buying them yourself because you'd never see any from these type of guys. This was to be the final phone interaction I was to have with him until the shocking surprise visit in February 2018 that sealed the deal for me not to waste any more effort.

N: DVD's 2-20 $20-
14MM SINGLE DVD CASE SEMI CLEAR
1-14-1-C2.A
QTY: 100 PCS
20-29 $10-

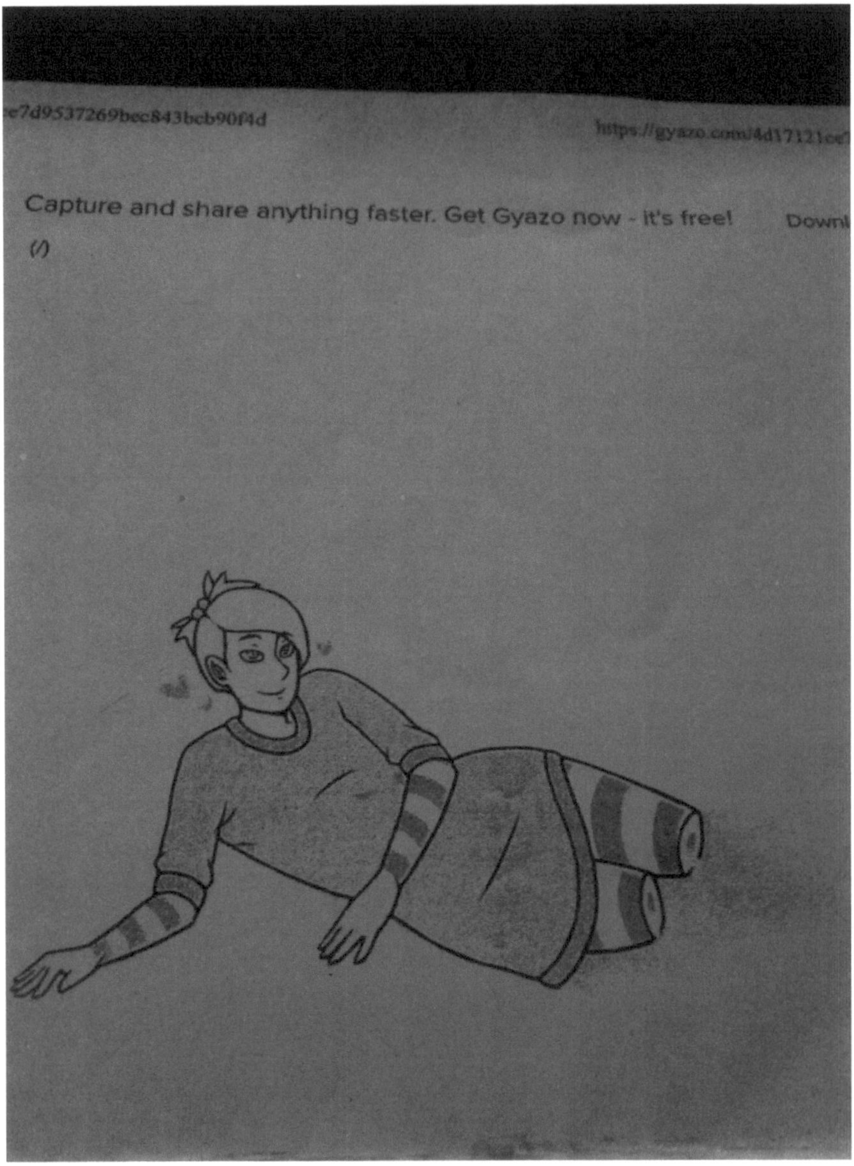
Capture and share anything faster. Get Gyazo now - it's free!

Teen Talk
PRODUCTION
FOR TEENS
TO HELP
OTHER TEENS
4T2HOT
N: DVD's 2-20 $20-
14MM SINGLE DVD CASE SEMI CLEAR
1-14-1-C2 A
QTY 100 PCS 20-29 $10-

WELCOME

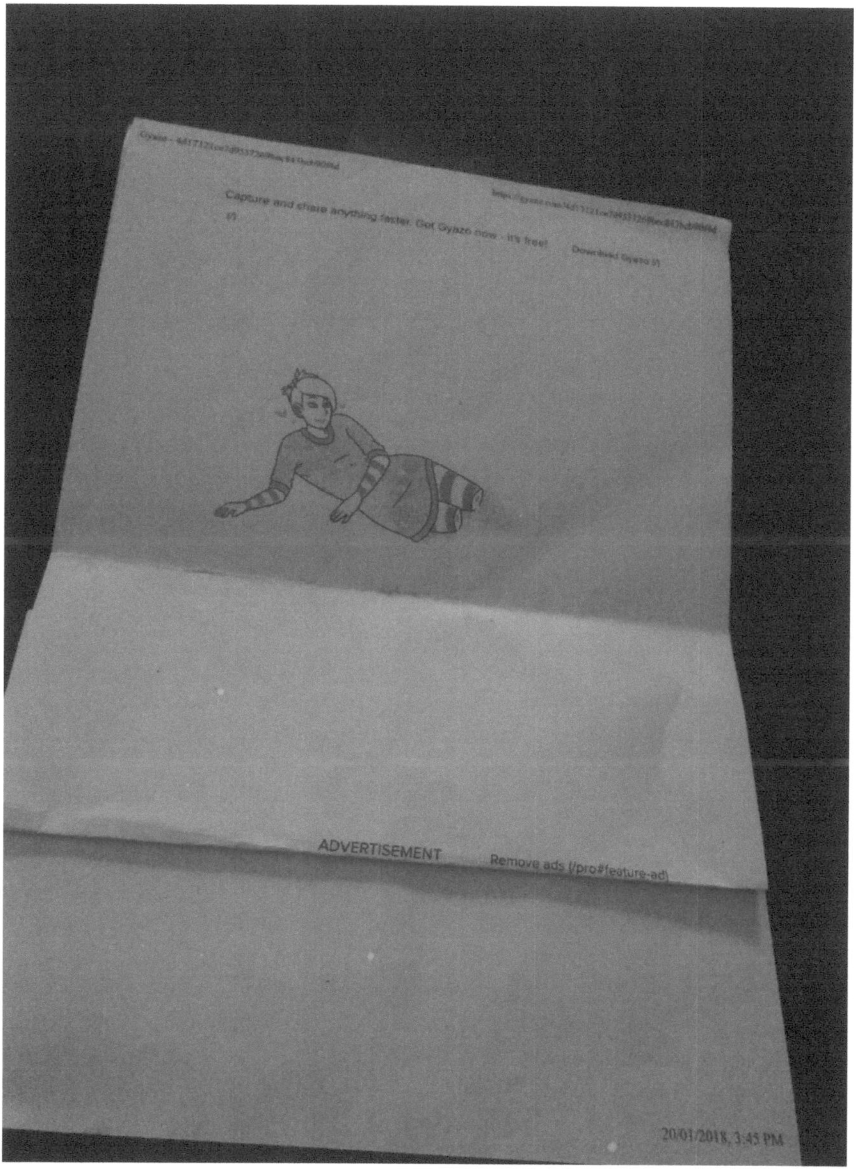
Capture and share anything faster. Get Gyazo now - it's free!
ADVERTISEMENT
Remove ads (/pro#feature-ad)
20/01/2018, 3:45 PM

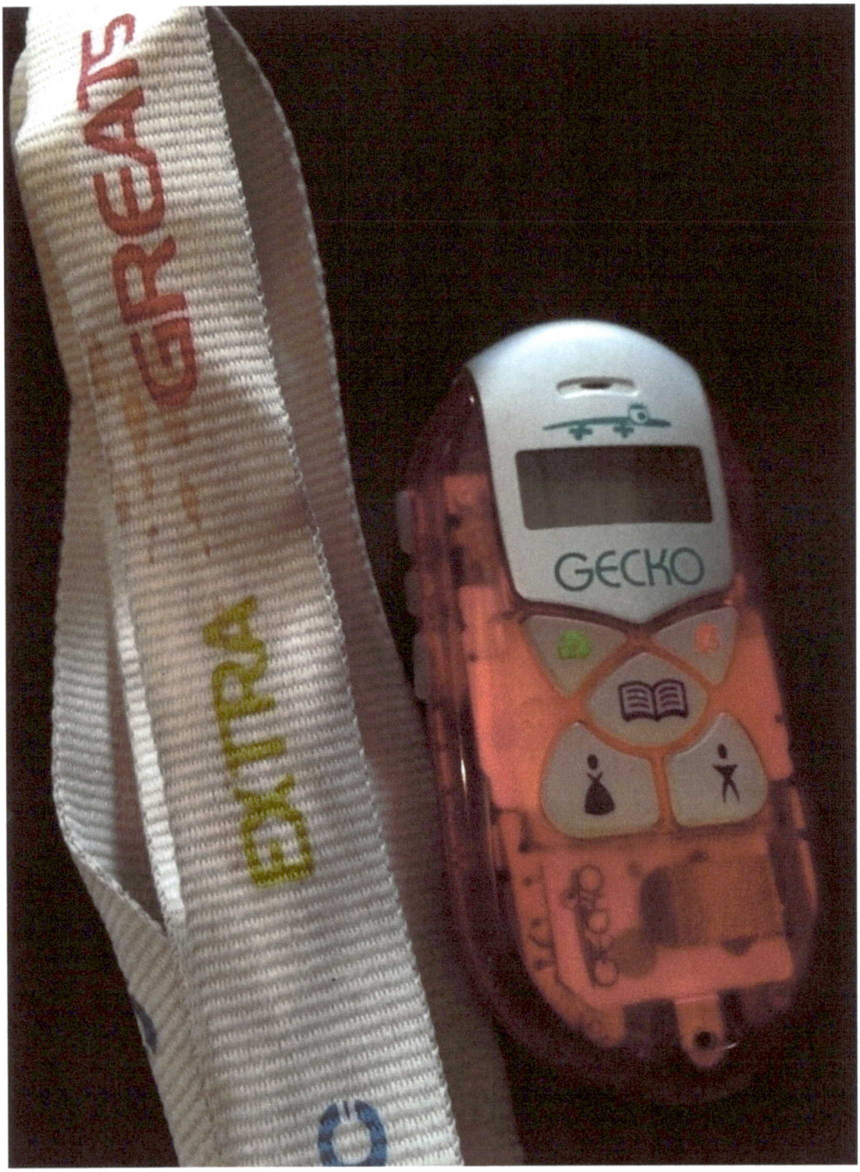
GREAT
EXTRA
GECKO

PART ONE
HEY!
TEEN TALK
DAUGHTER PRESSES BUTTON

FOR TEENS TO HELP OTHER TEENS
Teen Talk PRODUCTION
FOR TEENS TO HELP OTHER TEENS
FOR TEENS TO HELP OTHER TEENS

A Cautionary Tale.

Easter holidays, 2014 at a Watergardens shopping centre Pizza – cafe Freddie drove me to see Sabena. Bon arrived late with Sabena, she was always driving that second- hand beige squarish metallic sedan. What a waste of effort it was for me to have bought Eddie all those driving lessons and obtained his driving licence when I was expecting with Sabena, as he never drove these days. I brought Sabena her gifts, cute stuff from Singapore, Dubai and Italy, according to her previous likes. Sabena seemed somewhat recovered and calm but was very much out of it, dazed and Bon monitoring her every word, even when Freddie tried to engage her in distracting cheeky chit chat.

Eddie was as usual not in attendance as was the pattern these past previous few years. I guessed probably most likely he was at home malingering in his regular occupation of playing video games, surfing the net or downloading porn thumbnails of young children with animals and in erotic ass poses. I once caught him myself doing this, in the early wee hours of the morning, at my three bedroom weatherboard house that I bought for us in Bentleigh, that later vanished from me because of his gambling debts, whilst Sabena, two years and I were deeply in slumber land. I woke with a parched dry mouth and went tiptoeing to the kitchen not to wake Sabie up and then I snuck up behind him in the tiny squeezebox study downloading these disgusting and abhorrent thumbnails of very young children posing for porn. He said that he came across them by accident, accidentally on purpose that is because I never did and besides you would have to know to find them especially.

Later in 2005, just before Eddie met Bon at the Salvation Army Store in Bentleigh, for the original court case the Moorabbin Police confiscated his computer for evidence about his taste in porno habits. He was living at another co-workers, of his Sophie Woods, back outhouse room where Eddie was camping free for a few months until he moved onto Bon who was a Major and the manager there. He was strangely sort of tipped off and there was a hint of this maybe happening a day before and I assume Eddie erased it as quickly as he downloaded it.

It was during these months after that I invited Eddie to attend that was my final try at a two day long and intense, totally failed mediation session for Sabena's sake at The Melbourne Mediation Centre in the city. I felt for the shuttle – mediation lady because she gave it all her effort of at least six pages of compromising notes and a plan forward, she drafted and prepared it as a proper document only to have Eddie refuse to sign it and cancelling it a few days after it was finally drafted and emailed. So close yet so far away. The lady landed up as usual providing me with a government mediation failure certificate and she said she was sorry that it hadn't turned out for Sabena and he might regret it.

After this mediation failure however with which brought a lot of sensitive topics up about Sabena's health and well being, Eddie became somewhat milder and less damaging in his approach towards my contact and my visitations with Sabena, Freddie said, he suspected it was some remorse or guilt on his part for what was happening with her. Eddie began to be more encouraging of my weekly weekend calls and somewhat less bitter and acrimonious than he'd ever been all these prior years.

Conversations were strained with Sabena, as they were both listening in on them and cutting her off in case she slipped up, her state was sometimes confused and distraught that she made no common sense at all to me, I was becoming increasingly worried about her or Eddie said she was having a bad day and to call back again perhaps in a few weeks and then eventually call the next school holidays.

The next time I was to actually see Sabena again was in September, 2014. I had arranged this appointment several weeks before, since her real birthday was on the 28th August, (Virgo), like my dad. I attended with my bestie Norma, to which Eddie uncharacteristically humbly also agreed to. Norma drove us there in her car and it was a maze to find, those tiny squirrely streets ending in cul de sacs. We arrived about 15 minutes late, Eddie with an aggravated stare as we knocked on the front door. It was always his first comment, YOUR LATE, not pleased you arrived here safely or Sabena will be happy to see you, but consistently negative. We sat on their couch for a while as Sabena wasn't quite ready to go out yet. He moved us onto the kitchen bench where Sabena was sitting crouched beside the back glass door and window. I had spent the past week preparing to cheer her up with my Felix – bag of surprises and show bag goodies and armed with Birthday Card, Flourless Chocolate Mud cake, stripy candy cane Candles and a matching huge number 15 Candle, books, Italian fairy figurine, clothes, Phillipa's fancy biscuits and some manga designs that I bought previously from the Melbourne Oz – Comicon Convention that I attended for the first and only once with Masako during the June Winter.

Sabena was wearing a sloppy loose fitting navy tracksuit with a hoodie top and a white T underneath it, like a boy's outfit with a white stripe down the legs. Her freckly pocked pimply scarred nose and cheeks, her mousey brown thick fuzzy tousled hair with some lighter streaks through it and boofy at the ends sticking out the sides fly away bad hair day teased style and parted flat at the top in the middle. It was rough, wild and woolly, unkempt. Her eyes dark sullen and sunken, peeking above the thick dark rimmed glasses with her left elbow and chin in hand, in the thinking man position. Her body puffy, swollen and bouncy like the Michelin Man ads. Her face decidedly deeply sad and melancholy depressed.

I tried to crack that Sabena smile that was somewhere inside her but it was a chore and not forthcoming with only obtaining a corner lip smirk, a light gone out lifeless and blank zombie.

I was a bit embarrassed in front of Norma as they never as much as offered us even a glass of water, so after a while Norma sparks up and says let's get this party started, so I unpack all my wares as a packed party in a shopping bag. Norma seeing my despair, she helps me to engage her in assisting me with placing the candles on the thick chocolate icing of the cake and to light them all up, Norma being her most fun loving self and I start singing to her with Happy Birthday. Eddie and Bon contemptuously looking on as if we were farcical but we cracked yet another smirk.

We all have a slice of my cake, after Norma asks Sabena where the snack plates and cutlery are kept. Norma tired of waiting for her cuppa to never arrive to wash down the cake, suggests we three go for a walk to the park across the road and then go to Watergardens for her much needed latte. During our walk I ask Sabena if she liked her gifts or if she wanted something else for her birthday instead, yes she said but I need a bra mummy, why wasn't Bon helping her with that kind of thing. There was nothing for it we would take Norma for her coffee and get you some under gears too. As we return from the park Eddie doesn't resist us going to the shopping centre for refreshments. We settle down for a latte, a tea for me and hot chocolate with pink and white mallows for Sabena.

Sabena appears to brightening up to her usual cheery disposition and is becoming more open with us, still having bouts of disorientation and confused thought processes however and going blank outer space on us now and then. Concerned Eddie might blast us for being gone too long and sending the possie out for us, I say to Norma let's get her some needed intimate apparel, we search at the Myer, K mart or Target whatever and there are only small sizes, Sabena also doesn't know her size and refuses to go to the change room with some pretty suggestions we pick for her. I then suggest we should preferably go to the specialty Bra shop and get her fitted correctly after all. I was a bit the same build as Sabena with a small back and voluminous breasts so sizing was an issue. We find the Bra's and things shop, Sabena is having difficulty choosing so Norma and I pick her a smooth hot pink contoured bra with a ting satin bow at the cleavage with pants duet, perky for a young lady. Sabena enters the cubicle by herself and the attendant goes to search for some suitable sizes for her. The attendant aware of bashful young teens passes her the bra and Sabena says she is poking out the sides a bit and it's not right and puts her T back on top and the lady attendant measures her with the T on. The attendant goes off to search for more generous sizes, going towards D – F Cup. The attendant says she might not have all the sizes in stock for this particular model of the bra. Sabena calls me in to help her undo the bra and says she is feeling embarrassed by the whole thing, so I step inside and I help her lift up her T and to my total shock and horror there are numerous cutting and burn healed keloid thick scars on the inside of both wrists, underarms and those soft fleshy and exquisitely tender around the armpit breast areas. I was incredulous my mind not believing what my eyes were seeing, Sabena must have seen the horror in my face and she motions me to undo the bra and says I want to go now and let's get out of here please mummy.

Norma returned us to Bon's brick veneer ground floor house. There was no time to explain to Norma at the shop but she sensed something untoward happened. Norma cheerily chatted away to distract Sabena and then she soon forgot and disregarded the incident. We returned to sitting at the four seater wooden table beside the kitchen bench and Norma passed Sabena her birthday card that was on the bench beside all Sabena's heaped medication boxes. Why don't you read your card and check out your gifts? said Norma. Sabena proceeds to pull the card out of the envelope, I'm not sure Norma knew about my party trick that I learnt from my dear friend Countess Zoritza, Don't get mad get everything, kinda gal.

Surprise! The fun little metallic sparkling rainbow coloured confetti stars popped out spilling onto the table and the floor and Sabena breaks into giggles gleefully, as if a Christmas cracker gone off. Bon snarls, as who would have to pick them all up again. Sabena's frizzy ends fro bobbing about and we all look down at the floor, Sabena shaking a few stars off her white thick – soled sneakers. She then proceeds to remove stuff from her goodie show bag, several books, I asked her if she liked Mary Poppins, it was a small classic hardback, I don't know if she remembered the Disney film from years ago, watching it with Mum and me. She said she was in the midst of reading a James Bond book at the moment, I thought this strange for her young generation nevertheless, not The Hunger Games. Italian clothes, Italian fairy figurine- Mini Alpes and Hello Kitty various cutesy merch and the Manga design pictures appeared, her eyes brightening up as a flickering minute semblance of the bouncy Sabena of yesteryear.

Alice In Wonderland – Disney Original 1952 - The lazy Obese Caterpillar smoking a Turkish pipe – repeating over and over, Who are You? Who are You? Who are you? Alice laughing heartily at the odd creature.

Cats and Rabbits were dressed in shoes and hats and trousers and the flowers would talk for hours and hours in a world of their own – Sabena's favourite part rewinding it often on the DVD player at my Mum's house at seven years of age, and singing merrily along with the words in the song.

The sequel of Mary Poppins Returns was first announced in September, 2015.

Pink – Just like Fire, 2016. Alice through the looking glass.

Pink - Just give me a reason, Try 2012.

Pink – Get the party started, 2001.

Pink – Who Knew, 2006.

The kid's sized under the sea themed quilt blankie that they gifted Sabena at SECASA in 2004 – *Especially made for you by the patchworkers and quilters.*

Pink – Walk me Home, 2019 Hurts 2B human.

Sia – Chandelier, Voices 2014.

Sia – Elastic Heart, 2013 – The Hunger Games: Catching Fire.

James Reyne – Reckless – Electric Digger Dandy, 1991, Hammerhead 1987, Errol – Sirocco 1981.

I described in the car to Norma on the way home, the very real horror of the spectacle I witnessed in the bra shop and then she understood. Norma answered, Sabena's hug with you was long and tight.

The Empty Man, 2020.

IT, 2017 – IT, 2019 Chapter 2.

Superstition – Stevie Wonder, 1972 – Talking Book.

Sledgehammer, 1986 – Peter Gabriel - So, remastered 2012.

Damien - Omen II, 1978. The Exorcist – 2001.

The temporary IVO in 2005 I urgently frantically obtained from The Children's Court on Sabena's behalf in lieu of Sabena's disclosure of molestation because I could not get a suspension of contact order fast enough to protect Sabena against Eddie, to cease and suspend visitations and the process in the Family Court was slow and arduous, and I would have been slapped with contravention of the currents orders from Eddie going against me.

Still reeling from the shock of the visit, I spoke to Helen my long term bestie from Primary School days at Genazzano about Sabena's case. Dr. Grogan's, Western Suburbs GP, opinion was that she offered that we would visit together and try to ascertain further information about Sabena's mental health status. A few weeks later in October, 2014 Eddie agreed to me visiting with Dr. Helen Grogan. So he must have been noticing things with Sabena were taking a turn for the worst not turning the corner or so to speak after many months of medications and two – weekly counselling at the RCHM. Eddie was given two weeks prior notice of my visiting with Helen and that we would be arriving somewhere between 1-2 pm probably closer to 2 pm depending on traffic and so forth. We arrived in Helen's car slightly before 2 pm with them having ample warning about our visit day and ETA. To our amazement Eddie at the door said Sabena is still in her bed. Helen answered at this time of day. I guess he thought that would shoo us away, for another day but no I wasn't having precious busy scheduled Helen dragged all this way without seeing Sabena at all. So I stepped around Eddie and waltzed in to find her bedroom. Neither Eddie nor Bon surprisingly stopped me or even blocked me.

Sabena with her hair peeping out on top from under the doona, I pulled up at the doona and Sabena in her crushed Jamies with her hair all teased and dishevelled a bit sort of Tim Minchin style hybrid of Yahoo Serious electric shock fuzz. Helen poked herself around the corner of Sabena's bedroom door and then decided to leave me with it and go and sit in the lounge and wait for the outcome. Sabena looking ashamedly up at me, as if a little child, who'd done a naughty and then her eyes immediately peering down at my feet. Why aren't you ready yet?, I said. There was a resounding silence and then forza, common let's get you up and dressed. So I proceeded to facilitate Sabena. I sat on the corner of her bed and brushed her hair delicately until it was smoothed down and then tied it up in a ponytail and I got her to choose some clothes to wear. It seemed as if I was dragging the listless zombie up a steep hill and there was a constant mild retaliation to my nudging encouragement. It felt as if I was there for hours, it might have been only half an hour in total but a long haul nonetheless. It was a hard slog to get her the slightest motivated. Helen waited patiently on their front lounge couch but could hear my whispered coaxings, come along now, as we walked down through the kitchen. Helen was gobsmacked by Sabena's altered states of, out of it, Tara persona. Helen threw me a side stare with her eyes and we both knew exactly what she thought.

I suspect this was during the stage of her psychosis where Sabena became most agoraphobic, basically avoidance of people and the cruel world outside. The tag along monitor guard, happy days, spoiler alert who always invited herself and grabs Sabena at the elbow and says I will drive me and Sabena down there. Sabena was silent, but she seemed reluctant to come with Helen and myself also. So, I let it go. In hindsight analysis, there may have been various issues at play here, Sabena at the height of her agoraphobia preferred then to have

- Bon came along in case Sabena was panicked or felt she needed to leave at an instant.
- Bon would have come along anyway regardless of our mother –daughter re- bonding.
- Bon was to eavesdrop on what Sabena might say or what Helen and I might say or ask her.
- Bon knew that Sabena wouldn't leave and would feel more secure whilst she was there to.
- Bon was always invidious of Sabena's and my interactions together and overly vigilant.
- Bon interfering causing breaks in our conversation about her health, school, and hospital.

It was the 19th October, 2014 as it read on my CBA credit card statement, at Di Caprio's Italian restaurant in Sydenham. Bon arrived with Sabena and they both alighted from the beige Keens Mustard metallic sedan as Helen and I walked towards them from

Helen's canary yellow mini Fiat. We sat at a row of wooden cubicle bench tables that usually seats six people, three on each side. Bon sat on the closed end of the bench on the left with Sabena at the open end and Helen was directly opposite Bon and I was opposite Sabena at the table. Sabena was distracted, dopey and muddled. Helen and I tried to make the best of the situation hoping to make Sabena feel calm and settled. I don't remember what Helen or Bon ate for their lunch as I was fully focussed on Sabena's needs. Sabena ordered herself the creamy Funghi homemade potato Gnocchi and a hot chocolate, I always ordered my favourite staple Spaghetti Marinara with a cup of Lemon English Breakfast Tea. Sabena for the most part was very reserved and sadly solemn. She was very low key, but I thought best not to push the envelope too much, she'll feel pressured. Sabena was a crazy sweet tooth as was since I knew him her Dad, perhaps before he was ultimately diagnosed Diabetic when they moved from Bentleigh to the North – West suburbs of Sydenham. I asked her if she wanted Dessert, she said she was full but we shared it, the waitress cutting it and placing it on two plates for us, this was way before the COVID and customer service was probably at its peak during this generations decade. Knowing Sabena's and my similar tastes, it was most likely flourless Chocolate Mud Cake with Berry Compote or Pancakes. Helen and Bon almost simultaneously ordered two Cappuchino's to finish. Sabie or Saa-beee, as Katia her little cousin used to say, then mentioned to me that when she was still attending at the Keilor Downs High School, Bon would pick her up and they would go to the cake shop, with her consistent favourite being the Baklava.

Sabena then sat in her slumped current standard fed up, sensitive pensive position of her left hand cupped over her left eye and her elbow on the edge of the table. Helen was exceedingly thoughtful these days as she came from an Irish descended family with seven children and close ties to all her siblings. Body language, our concerns for Sabena's wellbeing resonated. Helen brought out a small gift wrapped surprise for each of us, even Bon as it was getting very close to Christmas time anyhow. I of course already gave Sabena all her birthday gifts at the previous visit. Sabena at this visit seemed to be fading deeply away into a nothingness melancholy of despair and was also apathetic to everything she knew and loved the most, particularly these after the hospital incident, visits I wasn't even able to sway her to be the slightest bit interested at all, in doing a sketch of some of her fantastical magna imaginings for me, like before. It was as if her thinking was in arrested development mode, lost her lust for life and such that everything that happened prior to that day was forgotten or erased. All of these concerns about Sabena, the hopelessness of the circumstances and situation she was in sent me into a diving tailspin. I asked her, what she might like to do in her future for work and she answered nurse or medical attendant, I wondered that wouldn't she rather follow her graphic design passions. Sabena said she admired Jo Winther, her psych counsellor at the RMCH that she trusted and was significantly attached to her, as she reminded her of me, sometimes in her own way. Helen also seemed astonished by her current occupation choice. Helen then said it's very difficult working in health emotionally and also physically demanding. Oh my, how could she ever possibly be capable do those kinds of studies or occupations with all her current myriad of disability issues? Agoraphobia, anxiety, panic attacks, delirium, she wouldn't even be able to learn to drive or get public transport by herself let alone go to college or have a future career. Sabena needed a lot of heavy sorting out before that was even remotely ever to be possible. I personally couldn't see her coming to anything resembling a happy life or future on their watch.

During all these visits and all previous visits I always brought my camera and also we all posed for phone photos. Now, many years later I fatedly lost all of Sabena's photos from 2013 onwards on my iphone and there were also some mini pocket pictures of hers of previous visits, the single eye copy sketch, love hearts, Sabena's fantasy park etc., of course I was all too consumed and preoccupied with all that was going on in my life that unlike me at that moment, I never eventuated to get the photos developed, the phone had accidentally fallen out of my bright mini red leather backpack that the latch failed to close properly and it must have flung out when I slung the thin strap over my shoulder, I had just left these Camberwell hairdressers. I even drove back after I arrived home to search for it but it was gone, I rang the Camberwell Police for lost property but they were only in possession of iphones 6 or 6 plus and my model was the iphone 5, so they weren't my iphone.

Lemony Snickets a series of unfortunate events.

I was forced as was my catholic upbringing that as a biological mother I was obligated to do something rather than see Sabena languishing and floundering in this awful messy state of decline.

Extract from Fax RMCH.

12 November, 2013

Confidential

Karen Dally

Dear Linda,

Thanks for your phone calls –apologies we have been missing each other.

We can arrange an appointment for you to meet with Prof Alisdair Vance to discuss the results of Sabena's assessments.

We have appointments available in the last week of January on a Tuesday or Thursday.

How about Tuesday 28 January at 11.00 am?

You mentioned you may have other questions, please feel free to fax/email or leave a phone message and I will get back to you?

Thanks,
Karen

After that several appointments were scheduled and then also cancelled, in the end it may have been Karen who explained to me that Sabena's father withdrew access for me to obtain all medical information.

In the Keilor Downs Secondary School report Sabena's attendances are very erratic from May 2013 and she stops attending formal school in June 2013.

Mothers' Notes 27.04. 2015

Several months after the urgent hospital admission Sabena continues to self – mutilate and is also suffering severe adverse effects of the medications. Her breasts increased several dress sizes and her body becomes swollen with severe fluid retention. Her breasts are tender and uncomfortable. She is unable to find intimate apparel and is increasingly concerned about her body image and self – worth. She describes problems with insomnia and then severe lethargy, apathy, drowsiness, incoherent and confused / laziness state during the day. She also describes headaches, stomach aches, bowel and urinary problems. She describes extreme coldness of the hands, legs and feet. She expresses feelings of severe isolation, hopelessness and futility. I feel empathy for her as I feel she unduly suffered and struggled all these current years with fear, submissiveness, intimidation, shyness and insecurity. She loses all her friends as she no longer attends school and becomes agoraphobic also, although some distance learning begins. Her self – mutilation and suicidal idealization worsens.

May, 2014 – The mother makes further enquiries about the treatment at the hospital and is concerned about the severe effects of the medications and lack of any sign of improvement in Sabena's condition which appears to be deteriorating.

The hospital provides basic information but is restricted by the father and the previous court orders they say legally preventing them from providing further assistance or co-operation.

I try to go to the Mental Health Complaints Commissioner and Health Commission Ombudsman for advice but they are restricted by the previous court orders and the father's reticence to give permission for further investigations or another professional opinion.

On Thursday 18 September, 2014 I made a phone complaint to the RMCH.

Extracts RCHM Log

25/09/2014

Mother responded saying that around April the father had already provided permission for mother to be informed about daughter's treatment. She is happy for Jo to contact her.

30/ 09/2014

Mother called again with some concerns. She says the hospital has duty of care and that the hospital will be liable if something goes wrong with her daughter. She is happy with the way I handled the problem, but not now the treating doctor/ clinician. She reckons the prescribed medications might end up killing her daughter. The father might have custody but it is still the hospital's responsibility.

It was a previous patient (KW) of at least ten years duration, a Gen Y or Millenial, working part-time as senior Lab Tech for post-graduates in Science and also doing developmental research on a new type of pharmaceutical antibiotic, who years later described that their funding was cut drastically during the pandemic. She explained to me the undesirable shift that more money was being spent on hi turnover usage drugs like anti-depressants or lifetime daily drugs than short- term antibiotics or cancer medications. Her promising collaborative research unfortunately came to an abrupt end, just as the paper was almost finished, with no interest to resuscitate the new antibiotic and after losing her temporary contract tenures, she found a remote job with a Pharmaceutical Company and also moving to the western suburbs, with her partner, at about the same time. Among other things she introduced me to her generation's pop culture diet osmosis of *The Handmaid's Tale,* Vikings, Google Pixel and the Sisterworks cause.

It was also confirmed to me, by also other sources that exorbitant funds were being expended on drugs of dependency than drugs of cure. As with anti-depressants, pushing them onto youth as a quick fix and if they became hooked early as teens, it could become a life-long dependency or at least 20-40 years or more unless they wean them off them after short - term use or until they eventually suicide or die.

My work colleague at the Royal Melbourne Hospital in my late twenties and friend who's husband decades before retired from Pharmacy and they both moved to Broadbeach, QLD.

(SM & IM).

Her husband (SM) also affirmed and explained similar to these facts, to me whilst visiting with them for a day trip during the Queensland Sojourn of Winter, 2014.

Ironically during this time, I went to see the Film Dallas Buyers Club with Allan at the Palace Classic Cinema, South Yarra. *Dallas Buyer's Club (2014) -Matthew McConaghey,* Jennifer garner and Jared Leto. Director - Jean _ Marc Vallee.

Agnes Girdwood – Carer Consultant for RCH Mental Health.

I wrote emails voicing concerns to alert various staff including Karen Dally, Agnes Girdwood and Dr. Ric Haslam – The Director of Mental Health at RCH. Agnes tried to liaise between Karen, Jo and Ric for an outcome.

It was déjà vu all over again, on the 2nd October, 2014, I wrote a letter about urgent Family law Reform to the Attorney – Generals Department, 3-5 National Circuit, Barton ACT 2600 and Australian law Reform Commission. Those many correspondences I mailed out before on 27th September, 2007. The Hon. Ann Bressington, Legislative Council, Parliament House, Adelaide SA 5000. The Hon. Peter Costello MP Malvern. The Hon. John Howard MP, Prime Minister of Australia, Parliament House, Canberra ACT 2600. Diana Bryant AO QC, Chief Justice of the Family Court of Australia, Melbourne. I wrote to whomever I thought might be able to help not only for Sabena's sake for whom it might be already too late but for the many other parents and children trapped in a broken chaotic archaic Family Law System that wasn't at all working for them but against them to the family detriment.

I discovered some other helpful people on my Family Law quest for justice. From the Website Kids In Distress Australia Inc. Information and papers. Paper on the internet Australian Government – The Attorney Generals Department 24th September, 2003 - Inquiry into Shared Parenting by the House of Representatives Family and Community Services Committee Family Law Council Submission. Paper by Dr. Elspeth McInnes, June 2002 and other were available on the internet of many personal tragedies to children as the case of a child Joe and his mother Sarah in WA. I wrote an email to Elspeth asking her advice about my circumstances at that time and she responded with suggestions. Bernadette Docherty became best email friends from Sydney through Bravehearts, having her own Family Court Issues about her young son. Dr. S. Caroline Taylor, author of Court Licensed Abuse 2004, whose book I read, admired and I wrote to her at Ballarat University, other books of hers are Surviving the Legal System, Social Death and Sexual Violence. Council of Single mothers and Children where I became a casual office volunteer, ABC Radio National – law

Report and there was a conference in Brisbane on the 28-29 June, 2007 Shared Parental Responsibility in Australia's Family Law System that I found out about during those previous Family Court years.

Extracts RCHM Log

07.10.2014

From Dr. Ric Haslam CC. Agnes and Jo.

Jo, we should revisit the Family Court Orders relating to parental responsibility, which I recall sits entirely with Eddie. We should be clear in our own mind that S herself is Gillick competent and if she refuses her mother's requests for 1) Information 2) Second Opinion 3) Influence of care and her father is supportive, we can safely continue to refuse to accommodate Linda.

I sent even more letters from the 7th October, 2014 - Family Law Council, Justice Connect and the Victorian ombudsman.

RCHM Log

Agnes Girdwood

Repeated emails from Linda were answered on the 21st October.

Dear Linda,

I understand your frustration but at this point I don't see any avenues for you to explore other than perhaps make a formal complaint.

As promised, I am forwarding you the complaints/ feedback form, but you can lodge a complaint in a normal letter as well.

Consumer Liaison Officer

Quality Unit

Royal Children's Hospital

50 Flemington Rd.

Parkville

Victoria 3052

Or Fax (03) 9345 4650

Or Email.

So I wrote a letter on the 22nd October, 2014. Complaint of lack of duty of care and neglect.

Extracts Letter

I did not receive a response from the hospital for some time and so then I was advised by other organizations to make direct contact with the Consumer Liaison Officer to liaise with the treating clinicians for a resolution or better outcome. I did this officially on the 18th September, 2014 on the basis that my daughter is suffering significant adverse reactions of the medications, and her condition is deteriorating each day, this is not an appropriate or expected outcome considering that the medication is being administered at the maximum recommended amount for adults of Fluvoxamine 200mg/day, to be reviewed at alterations for 10 weeks post adjusting and Ritalin 30 mgs/ day.

It is my fear as a caring devoted parent that my daughter is dying each day in silence and she may either commit suicide as an indirect consequence of the medication, she may come to irreversible harm or even die due to excess amount of the medication or during heavy sedation with an acute medical emergency of the ongoing cumulative adverse effects.

Despite the fact that my daughter was ordered to reside with her father since 2008, my daughter exhibited no signs of mental illness whilst in my care for nine years.

I have never suffered from mental Illness fortunately, however her father suffered bouts of Bipolar and severe anxiety which were treated with Prozac and Effexor whilst my daughter was an infant, he then rehabilitated for a time but he is now relapsed the past few years. My sincere belief is that he does not have the faculties to be making appropriate choices for my daughter's well – being let alone for his own self-care at this time.

Regardless of draconian and outdated orders from 2008, the law is to ptotect children and young adults from harm, since circumstances do change in people's lives and life is a continuum, the utmost consideration should be the ultimate interest, recovery and well – being of the minor. At this time her future prospects may be death or chronic ongoing mental illness, lack of skills and formal education, unemployable, perpetual welfare recipient, destitute and homeless. It is erroneous for the hospital to suggest that they are devoid of any liability for the minor if the minor comes to some irreversible damage or tragic death as a direct consequence of their actions, or lack thereof ie. Neglect of a patients ongoing care in which the outcome is they suffer severe personal detrimental injury or tragic death, due to unfortunate circumstances which could have been avoided. In this case the default is the safetynet, if the residential parent is not of sound mind, the hospital cannot negate its responsibility to the minor being treated, in fact this creates more responsibility for them to ensure the minors' safety.

The reasonable person would suggest that they are not to ignore the signs and symptoms of a patient at imminent risk as a result of their therapy just because they relinquish and believe they are devoid of all humanitarian responsibility for the patient's outcome, care and life, due to extenuating legal circumstances and / or ill informed determinations made by mentally incompetent persons.

I don't remember receiving an official response to this letter perhaps it was still coming in the process until now. I wondered if also the hospital was intimidated by Eddie both because of his long history of mental illness and also his background before arriving in Australia in his 20's of fleeing his hometown of Baghdad, Iraq for political reasons escaping violent and sexual abuse at the hands of both his stepfather and then later his guardian uncle.

There were frequent venomous response emails from Eddie to my pleas to Eddie and Bon to do something about Sabena who was on an exceedingly bad trajectory moving ever forward.

In the jumble of my memories during this ugly phase were Sabena's favourite biscuits in childhood melting moments, Yo Yo's, shortbread and lush caramel or chocolate slices, Bon's Bung knee and she was due for an op Sabena said, unusually for Sabena or most unruly and gregarious teens, her stark sterile teen bedroom now bare of happy or fun stuff, some of the books I gifted her these previous years, *Pip the story of Olive – Kim Kane, Along for the Ride- Sarah Dessen,* thinking like a bird in a gilded cage she was hardly there for their amusement or entertainment in their dull nothing lives.

Mother's Notes (After October, 2014).

I ask the father for permission to visit with Sabena for Christmas he refuses. I am so concerned and worried for Sabena that despite negative legal advice that it is a waste of time and a hopeless case, as a mother I decide to try and fight for my daughter's life and file for variation of orders.

The father was antagonistic towards me for doing so and he punishes myself and Sabena by preventing phone contact and I have not seen Sabena since October, 2014.

During 2013/ 2014 – I made various attempts to notify Department of Human Services, Child Protection Unit about my concerns for Sabena but no-one ever investigated.

2015- I asked the Keilor Downs Police, to do a welfare check and attend at Sabena's home, early this year as I spoke to he once, she answered the phone and as her voice was very strained and I was worried for her. They said she was alive, but that I should get a medical opinion of her state.

(Extracts have been copied precisely as written from my notes without embellishment or alterations.)

Either a patient or friend suggested for me to do a welfare check since I was so very concerned about her, I wasn't aware of these but sometimes I was told they were for frail elderly and high risk persons. So I rang Richmond Police Station as I wasn't knowledgeable about that side of town and their systems, they contacted Keilor Downs Police, who they then said would get back to me direct of the outcome in a day or so. Keilor Downs Police rang me the following day, so reasonably prompt for those years, pre – covid before there was no customer service existence, services still worked and were available, Ambulances and Emergency services weren't at system crisis breaking points. (July, 2022).

The police officer said that the father answered the front door and would not let them enter inside about the matter or to see Sabena and that the father rather brought Sabena to a gap in the door. I asked if there was any information about her appearance or mental state of mind or behaviour. He answered that he could not comment and it was not up to him to give me further information other than suggest that a medical opinion should be sought by myself. To be fair he said they saw Sabena but for a fleeting flash of a second and then she was sent away by her father without them even having spoken to her at all.

I felt justified in complaining to the various authorities and the RCHM and I even contacted the Independent Mental Health Advocacy for advice and information before I then soon after self - represented myself for this type of appeal called variation of Existing Orders. I drafted and prepared without help my own Initiating Application (Family Law) and it was lodged and filed by myself on the 11th December, 2014. My lawyer friend Ian, witnessed it, who I dated a year before and then on and off. Who's Slovakia now? But his ancestry was Polish, but it's in the same neighbourhood and close enough to it too.

Ironic that the word justified was three attempts on google, 1. Justified – Film 2. Justify paragraphs 3. Justified – word meaning in that order of appearance. Dr. Phil quotes, Don't be a right fighter, would you rather be content in your circumstances or be a right fighter but this situation is also different because we have a child's well – being, freedom and long term future at stake in the balance. It was to me survivor and into survival mode to get the Sabena back on the live life train.

The Variation of Orders would hopefully at the hearing dredged up more light and information on Sabena's cosmos, that I was not privy to before and the hospital would also be on notice that there was a duty of care and responsibility on their part for Sabena's well – being and health without regard for the medical adverse reactions, or the medical principle of first do no harm to the patient.

It was so wrong on so many levels and of course for me a rollercoaster of myriad opposing emotions.

At this point in time it was of my opinion that the benefits of her non- improvement were not worth the risks of not monitoring the dosages adequately, altering medications or weening her off the medication within months or a year, rather than being dependant, addicted or developing a tolerance, being on it for years or worse as necessary for our life's entire duration. Another example of our freaky family health and genetics is my late onset Mum's Diabetes, they must have changed her medications and even dosages at least a handful of times with various Doctors, I even became frustrated and made an appointment for her to see Endocrinologists at the Diabetes Centre at the Caulfield Hospital before her severe adverse effects eventually settled and she was able to function eating and sleeping well almost normally again.

From previous personal and other family member's court experiences, so many years later, appeals of various sorts have known to have been successful despite blistering odds which were not at the least in their favour. So I continued on my quest for the scales of justice which were definitely MIA, many moons ago and as Norma liked to often say after some of her encounters, The Law is an ASS.

Just Keep Walking – INXS, 1980 Album INXS.

Hotel California – Eagles, 1976 – Album – Hotel California.

Harley Quinn: Birds of Prey, February, 2020.

I've been everywhere, man – Johnny Cash, 1996 – Album – Unchained.

Is Don is Good!

Feels and looks good off as well as on – Delmonti Suits.

Megalo, Megalo, Megalo! Franco Cozzo, the furniture icon.

All you need to know is the location of the library – Albert Einstein

This girl is on fire – Alicia Keys, 2012. New York! New York!

I'm Every Woman – Whitney Houston. Bodyguard, 1992.

On the road again – Willie Nelson, 1980 Album – Honeysuckle Rose.

Total Control – The Motels, 1979. Album – Motels.

Cheap wine and a three day growth – Cold Chisel, 1980. Album – East.

Oh Yeah, of course I was Kookasnatchas and awkies every now and then during these few years but then what semi normal person wouldn't have been anyhoo and dealing with those pesky Eddie and Bon sort of people who were contemptuous haphazard guardians of Sabena who I had to pander to.

Ray Liotta Dies. 27.05.2022 (Age – 67) Notorious for Goodfellas role! Mafia Film.

Initiating Application (Family Law) Variation of Parenting Orders, Appeal filed at Family Court on 16th December, 2014. Court Date for 23rd March, 2015 at 9.45 am. Affidavit affirmed on 15th December, 2014 at Melbourne Registry lodged for the Federal Circuit Court of Australia. The affidavit was witnessed by my bestie for many years, Justice of the Peace, Norma Flowerday. Norma Flowerday apart from being an avid volunteer worker for many organizations and surviving a husband or two and a few partners, she also dabbled in retaining her first husband Albert's, a previous Policeman, Insurance's work sideline afloat.

Extract Mother's Notes.

March 23rd, 2015. – Initial Hearing Court. Appointed ICL – Ms. Maria Kourtis- VLA>

April 22nd, 2015- Interim Hearing Court.

Lampe lawyers – VLA – acting for father, Melissa Scarfo.

ICL – another attends hearing Ms. Helen Vickers.

Outline: Rice and Asplund argument.

Chronology.

Affidavit ICL requests.

Mother's chronology log notes end here.

I thought about Jo Winther, who sounded a reasonable person with similarities to myself as Sabena described her, and her being bound by her superior Professor Alasdair Vance. It brought back haunting ghastly flashback memories of my thesis supervisor at Melbourne Uni. at the Department of Anatomy. Thesis lodged, November, 1988. Gordon Campbell who was either the absent minded professor, MIA or perpetually in absentia, so during my thesis year when I needed him, I saw him about twice. His wife Susan and partner researcher explained to me that he was engrossed in their research work and chortling that sometimes she was required to make an appointment herself.

I felt desperately alone and lost for direction during this year and would go as a final resort I sought out other students supervisors' in desperate search for guidance, solace and help, and some direction they felt pity on me, (Dane Alcorn, John Bertram and Roz, who married for the first time very late in life and then retired at the end of that year, even though their projects were very different and they didn't understand, they helped me wing it somehow. John Manderson, Howdey Cowdey as I nicknamed him, was the co-ordinator for all the students but he also tried to help as much as his time allocation to me permitted. My fellow students also felt my abandonment pain and frustration and so my bestie Sharon (Shazza) and I was Linda (Pinda – eater) facilitated my getting through that horror of a year which seemed it was a gaol sentence four times longer with Paul, Simon, Christine and some other junior supervisor/ researchers such as Giuliana and Callum.

Matruschka Dolls

There was also loads of other behind the scenes stuff that was going on those frenzied and frantic years. The Scout Group that I joined not long after Sabena went to reside with her father and Bon, that I ran the Joey's Mob and I also helped David Stidson, 2nd Prahran Troupe Leader with the Cubs and Scouts now and then. I explained to him about Sabena and why I became a Scout Leader to help children learn and develop them into strong adults by providing them with life skills and motivation to do good things. I asked him to write me a letter of reference, he said he didn't often do but since he'd known me for several years and after Mum's passing he wrote me a character reference dated the 21st February, 2011. Somehow my membership was accidentally on purpose made inactive, I suspect on the 9th August, 2011, I tried to re- enter a few years later but I was not permitted for some administrative reason.

Extracts Mother's Current Affidavit, 2015.

3. That I seek to rely on my previous affidavits which were affirmed on the 15th December, 2014 and the 5th may, 2015.

4(b). That I worked with helping youth of various ages for at least the previous (7 Years) and for 29 years in my professional work duties, in various capacities and have a lot of patience and empathy for them, I have a working with children's permit for at least 9-10 years. ie. Scouts (Vic.) Youth Leader of Joeys and Cubs groups for 5 years. Volunteer Council of Single Mother's and children (CSMC) for 2 years, CWA, Country Women's Association (Vic.) for 2 years.

I also studied the CELTA course at RMIT / RMIT training for 12 weeks in 2011, for youth learning English as a second language. I have since voluntarily helped several non- English youth prepare for their English language assessments. I studied from March, 2011 to February, 2013 through the La Trobe University and obtained my Pharmaceutical Prescribing Licence for my scope of practice on 27th March, 2013.

Annexures and Exhibits some included with the affidavit and some exhibited at court of the Joey Scout Working Folder, Scout Letter, Letter from Dr. Helen Grogan of Hoppers Lane Clinic Werribee dated 28.05.2015, Keilor Downs School attendance record for Sabena from May 2013 and school report for Semester 1 of 2013, RCHM Letter, Letter to the Attorney – Generals Department, Legal Organizations and members of Parliament, Hospital Email Logs, My Doctors and Specialist Reports, previous Psychology and Psychiatric Reports of me and Sabena, Emails to Eddie, Sabena's Sketches for me, Photo's, Family Dispute Resolution failed Certificate. In fact almost anything thing, that illuminated the long saga.

Eddie's Affidavit sworn 1st June, 2015 – Annexures and Exhibits, Emails to and from Eddie and Sabena, Eddie's emails to and from Karen Dally and Jo Winther, Emails to Dr. Helen Grogan, Email from Trang Phan, Year 10 mathematics teacher- Distance Education Centre Victoria, Hospital RCHM Brief Annual Review Summary Reports dated 6th march, 2014 by professor Alasdair Vance and Jo Winther, short extract from the failed Mediation of the six page recommended notes mediator plan. Affidavits were also filed of Professor Alasdair Vance and Jo Winther and the current ICL for Sabena.

I first met Ian at the Solo's Singles Christmas 2013 Dinner-Dance Party at the Russian restaurant Matrioshka's in Carnegie.

I remembered it was a fabulous night, thoroughly enjoyable, delicious food and dancing to the Russian Band entertainment. I was wearing my favourite Bright Red dress that I bought years ago on the Australia Day weekend in Launceston, Tasmania it was reminiscent of the elegant and flatteringly flared at the top of the hips, figure enhancing dress, of The Woman In Red fame with Gene Wilder and Kelly LeBrock, 1984. At the end of the night after too much indulgent dancing eating, drinking and carousing, Ian and I pleasantly chatted on opposite sides of the table invited me to visit his home for the best ever cakes in Caulfield and cuppa tea time afternoon soiree.

Cakes, Dicks and Mary – Jane.

Ian could have been a Kojak look alike, Telly Savalas played the detective character with an alternative novel approach, in the 1970's. If you could perish the thought to imagine Kojak wearing a bright Hawaiian Leisure shirt, beige deep pocket cargo shorts and thick sandwich thongs. Ian's cute and adorable mini Victorian single storey (Hansel and Gretel House) was almost at the bottom of a steep hilly street behind the cemetery as it so happens. The garage and driveway under the front door tiny terrace and wooden stairs, the house was well appointed, maintained and almost totally refurbished, it was polar opposites or a stark contrast to Allan's house. His home law office in the front first room of the long spotless Hall, I know this because he witnessed my pharmaceutical endorsement documents. There might have been two smallish bedrooms, two smallish bathrooms and a small lounge, living area TV, kitchen bench and Kitchen area all opening out onto a short deck with sliding glass double doors and the Japanese inspired garden patch with a coal heat cauldron and a tiny fishpond moat with a mini temple and bridge replica. It was very impressive and I marvelled. Also there was the loft upstairs extension that he 'd finished not long ago with the pull down wooden rickety staircase going up into the hatch in the ceiling, that Masako rented for a few months from him from my recommendation.

Let me entertain you – Robbie Williams, 1997 Album – Life Thru a Lens.

Slumdog Millionaire – 2008 Director- Danny Boyle.

Ian was a perfect host that Saturday afternoon, he prepared by buying the assorted sampling of cakes, he knew about my allergies, and they were in the fridge, he made us both a cuppa of mild English Tea, I with a slice of lemon and Ian his with both sugar and milk. The huge cinema size screen TV at the front of the sliding glass doors with two black leather flex recliners sideways in the living TV area. There was a huge long sound bar on top and bottom of the TV. He played Adele songs mostly and then we chatted and on some other after dinner evening dates we watched Breaking Bad and Better call Saul.

There were also quirky eccentricities to Ian, his fluoro Lime Green Honda Jazz with the press button key, the oriental massage, dental and cosmetic surgery tours to the Philippines or Thailand and other exotic places at least twice a year with his long time best friend Tony, wingman. Tony mostly needed dental and Ian also wanted skin and eyelifts done too. Things he often said to me like Not Today or Not for You, which irked a bit and signs around his home like Happy to spend every dollar of my client's money. Something similar to that was at an Arthritis seminar I went to that Dr. Stephen Hall quaffed - I can put up with any pain my patient's can tolerate. At times he was quite inventive, funny and charming but there was that mean, nasty cheap side that popped out unawares without any warning or notice. The Bat Lights that he bought to light the deck for his outside parties that were magnetized. The I'm just not interested phase when he became quickly bored or things weren't going his way. His ingenuous and endearing parties on his birthday or patriotic holidays (Queen's Birthday etc.) days several times a year, that were like a kid's afternoon or early evening parties with mini chocolate bars, lollipops and candies in bowls with chips, cheezels and twisties. Poppers and streamers, confetti and party treats and all for after a late Lunch of Pizza, Sushi and KFC then cakes and peoples own bringing plates. I must have been a kind of a muse for him because he improved somewhat later during our dating on and off years. He once even paid Sally to dedicate and to play a few flute songs for me at a late evening party of his. I always thought I looked ravishing in that Red dress with a combination of my swaying feminine wiles. At his birthday parties singing – You look like a monkey and you smell like one, two. After I started dating Allan later, Ian later said he would see Allan at the local Lawyer's meetings which were for professional points for qualification credentials.

An American Pickle – 2020 Directors – Brandon Trost / Dylan Meyer

Geronimo – Album -Bombs Away! Sheppard, 2014

We didn't start the fire – Billy Joel Album – Storm Front 1989.

The image of Ian's kid adult parties made me smirk, and I reminisced about my first Joey Group 5-7 years, the Halloween and Christmas parties I organized in the drafty, dusty, damp, musty and mouldy vintage Scout hall at 2nd Prahran, were I wore my allergy mask all the time and the Joey's just accepted me. Painfully timid, embarrassed and shy Sam and Eric, who I encouraged and they become more confident in their abilities each scout meeting, getting their stripes and badges for skills tasks. The crafts I created for them, my favourites the tiny paperTee Pee's and Police and Emergency Services badges replica's. The Fern Gully, nature Film evening about conservation. The excursions I organized given permission from the board to The Studley Park bend nature reserve where the ranger warned about some few poisonous mini beasts and don't touch them, The Potter's Children's Garden at Botanical Gardens, The St' Kilda Road Art Gallery Tour and Ripponlea House. The tour person at the Gallery describing to the kids who sat on the floor of the gallery about Picasso's Weeping Woman significance, lime acid green and purple paintings of universal suffering of Picasso's partner Dora Maar, his muse, a passionate, strong and intelligent woman.

Black Velvet – Alannah Myles, 1989

90 years ABC – June 2022.

Paper Giants: The Birth Of Cleo, 2011. Asher Keddie plays Ita Buttrose.

Offspring, 2010.

New Chair ABC – Ita Buttrose 27th February, 2019.

New CEO BHP – Mike Henry 1st January, 2020.

Tara – Gone with the Wind.

I became acquainted with Sarah from the UK travelling part way by herself without her husband, as partnered evening dining guests on the Ocean Princess cruise, 2013 with Ruth and Elliott Beer from the USA. I couldn't have asked for anything more than to be paired up with these exceptional people. It was a fabulous surprise when much later on 15th November of that same year, Sarah was passing through Melbourne and called me to spend time and visit with them. It was a shocking November of that year and Sarah bitterly complained that it was freezing cold and rained every day they were here, getting on and off the trams. I regrettably said to Sarah that this was a particularly bad terrible November weather season. She remarked it was even worse than English weather to date and would it be like this every year. Sarah and Steve George both visited Kooralbyn and I showed them around the house and surrounds, Steve was also here on some minor business as a Bank Financier. I invited them for lunch at the Quaff Restaurant whilst it still existed in those precovid years. I shouted them at the lunch special menu and said that I hoped they would return the favour when I visited the UK or might be accommodated at their son's pub. They were both very pleasant people, and liked Melbourne but they really couldn't bear this Melbourne weather that was even worse than theirs in the English countryside. I wasn't able to convince them it was unusually bleak for this year.

Art Imitates Real life

Heartfelt thanks to those who believed and trusted in me from even after 2007, during and against insurmountable odds Dr. Simon Forbes, Winsome Thomas, Dr. Barry Kenny, Dr. Simon Gillian, Dr. Robert G. Adler, Dr. Nick Siemensma, Dr. Colin S. Little, Dr. Betty Kotler, Dr. Michael Jones, Dr. Richard Baker, Dr. Ben Srikumar, Dr. David Bornstein, Dr. Emily Walsh, Dr. Alan Molloy, Dr. Gordon Ku, Dr. Denise Fraser, Dr. Meredith Day, Dr. Jadwiga Kapusta, Dr. Martine Burger, Dr. Jane Healy, Dr. Chris Sherman, Dr. Tanya Shnider, Dr. Andrew Allan, Dr. Katie Stout and those doctors who also collaborated with my clinic during my years of practice at Carnegie, its surrounds and Malvern. Dr. Henry Monkus, Dr. Mark Lipzker, Dr. Barbara Bloch, Dr. Andrew Patrick, Dr. Diane Patrick, Dr. Leslie Segal, Dr. Steven Kalfas, Dr. John Kioussis, etc. etc. etc. etc.

My friend Norma also witnessed some of my literally 100's of Pharmaceutical Endorsement documents as she was also a JP and my former patient Laurie Webb, who was an accounting lecture at RMIT who fallen into some inadvertent legal and financial distress due to his daughters and their respective partners. Ian also witnessed some of these various documents during those two years and a bit prior to Mum's passing in 2010, of my La Trobe study and the many patient log book medicines cases studies. It was incorrigible to me that he was sometimes in a child's mind of taking selfies of just about anywhere. He even said that some man slid off a high cliff with those extendable selfie holders and fell down it.

Extract - Acknowledgment of Thanks.

I have recently completed my qualifications for assessment for Board Registration Podiatric Endorsement for Prescription of Scheduled Medicines (2012).

I gratefully wish to acknowledge the participation, co-operation and helpful assistance of all those involved, for which I am sincerely appreciative of their time and valuable efforts of the following on my behalf.

Ie. My Supervisor, Knowledgeable Professionals, Pharmacology Advisors, Specialists, Professors, Nurses, Receptionists, Staff, Referees, Associated Universities, Hospitals, Teaching Clinics, Private Clinics etc.

Dr. Helen Grogan, Iramoo Medical Centre, Werribee.

Mr. Andrew Kingsford – Podiatric Surgeon, Admisitrative Assistant – Ines Durand. Surgical Theatre -Sir. John Monash Private Hospital, reception, nurses and staff.

Dr. Christopher Mc Cormack – Chief Senior Dermatologist. Dr. Alexander Chamberlain and associates. Clinic nurses and staff – Eileen Wynd, Michelle Molloy, (Stephanie Mascaro).

Associate Professor Richard Mac Isaac and clinical practitioners. Diabetes and Endocrinology Clinics, St. Vincents Hospital, Fitzroy.

Professor Kenneth Myers, Victoria vein Clinic. Nurses and staff- Hannah Tilli, Janet Hargreaves. Senior Vascular Sonographer – Amy Clough – Victoria Vein Ultrasound.

Mr. Michael B. Bruce – Vascular and Endovascular Surgeon. Cabrini Medical Centre. Wound Clinic Nurse and (staff), Andie Carroll (Sarah).

Mr. Gregory William Self – Vascular Surgeon. Southern Vascular, The Epworth Centre. Clinic Nurses and Staff – Ann Gniel, Julie Ashcroft, Robyn Tolley.

Dr. Wendy Stevens – Rheumatologist.

Professor Ange Romas, Barbara Gemmell – Specialist Clinical Nurse – Scleroderma and PAH Clinics. Scleroderma Clinical Department 3rd Floor, Daly Wing, St. Vincents Hospital, Fitzroy.

Mr. Mark Gilheany – Podiatric Surgeon. Jane Tennant – Podiatrist. East Melbourne Podiatry. Staff – Sarah Schrader (PA), Lesley Ryan, Jean McDonnell.

La Trobe Bundoora – Dr. Adam Bird, Podiatry Department- Margot Hatty, Nikki Frescos. Mr. Paul Jeffrey – Legal Services, Stephanie Chard – Equality and Diversity Centre, Cliff Picton – Ombudsman.

Professor Louis Roller

Dr. Jenny Gowan

I should have also included Debra Randa of the Disability Discrimination legal Service but she wasn't involved in my studies or my case studies clinically but instead played a much more important and crucial role in getting me study equality and appropriate care for my allergy and respiratory disability. She also helped me again later on with discrimination at the RMIT Celta course about my allergy mask and wearing it in and during classes and also providing me with appropriate equipment of an air filter and adequate ventilation in other classroom teacher and practical student areas. Without whom I would not have been able to embark or succeed with either of these study courses.

The only thing I could say about the Celta course was that I was bitterly disappointed and treated so very unfairly and was not supported by either the teachers or the staff at the RMIT Training Building. Ross, a teacher then was slightly more sympathetic and lenient towards my disability but he also said I would never be able to teach English as a second language to a classroom of international students wearing my allergy mask, which I would remove from time to time for short sessions of personalised speech sessions with the individual international students and for their assessments etc. I thought Ross, a very kind, dynamic and entertaining character who made the teaching English lessons fun and If I were you... and his obsession with the Rastafarian Cultural Revolution and who explained to me the mouth sounds and the prepositions that foreign students always invariably forgot, left out or made the same repetitive mistakes perpetually without practising their English enough with other pure English people. This he suggested could also become a lifelong affliction as the other teacher said was fatally flawed and occurred sadly with Spanish language and Vietnamese language speakers.

Seal – Crazy – 1991 Album- Now! That's what I call music.

No Woman, No Cry – Bob Marley and the Wailers. 1999- Album – Live at Maritime Hall.

My most memorable log book pharmacy endorsement cases were with Mr. Gregory William Self, I probably spent about two half –day sessions at his clinic in The Epworth and unlike other practitioners or specialists whom it was the nurses and staff that mostly more or less supervised me, he was very thorough spent time and individually described and explained each patient case together with me and the patient also later on in his office. He was an affable man, genuinely open and helping character with many Volunteer and Donation awards and certificates on his office wall, desk and shelves without the God complex syndrome. On Norma's dining room walls there were probably just a few more frames than his.

The pictures of his family and children were in pride of place on the front corner of his office desk. I learnt a fair bit on those two short days with him, the nurses and staff filled in the other gaps.

He also measured my calves for compression stockings and maybe they gifted me a light denier air hostess pair. I admired him because he was patient, sympathetic and compassionate, I wondered maybe because he went to school at St. Kevin's College that I also spied on the wall, he was probably there before my brother's radical class years there. He was a down to earth fair dinkum good bloke. I felt more than comfortable and trusting also referring some of my severely vascularly compromised clinic patient's into his specialist care for opinion, advice or therapy, as he would look after them.

The Joker

I chatted to Mark at a party of Ian's and we also dined and dated a few times, he lived past Southland so I never saw his house. He babbled something that he was previously retired from the Defence Force in an administrative role. He always wore geeky checked shirts of different colours and grey office trousers. He was a mean type of frugal person as necessary but he was never scungy with respect to me, on the contrary he was always more than kind, grateful, well mannered and generous. I also treated him at the clinic as a once off fix patient and he said I must take full payment for it and as it was an infection of the sort, I was to have to prescribe him some form of antimicrobial, so it was just as well.

A particular evening we dined at a restaurant called Tinto who was owned by Maria, who I was at primary school at Gennazzano, Kew with her sister and her husband was also the chef. I was curious to try their various Spanish inspired flavours and she was also a twice annual patient as she sometimes couldn't get time off helping out at the restaurant. The menu was exquisitely Spanish influenced Portuguese style gourmet with various alternative daily menu items. My favourite was the South Yarra Trattoria for either lunch or dinner, where they made the best ever Spaghetti Marinara in Melbourne, they prepared, deveined and sliced their King prawns into cute twirly swirly spirals, and the servings were heaped on for the families of all ages, it was consistently good, packed and busy. You would never get a seat there unless you booked or arrived very early unfortunately the over 35 years family owner suffered a heart attack so it closed down about a year or so before the Covid struck.

We arrived back early those evenings and so Mark and I would come home to my house for some glass of red wine, sweet or tea and we would watch TV or Videos of Brideshead Revisited on the couch, it was unusual that I never found that particular video of the four again. Every time I sat next to him I developed these raised rash wheals over my whole arms and torso, I said to him he must have ticks. His cat or cats were in place of a girlfriend, his sole companions, a previous girlfriend many, many moons ago became bored of him after some months and simply left him like that.

It appeared he was unfortunately terminally unsuccessful in the obtaining a steady partner or girlfriend department. It was a damn shame, a waste of a potentially good sort of decent wholesome living man. I asked if he would mind to delouse the cats but he lied about this and he never did, I think he was concerned it might be harmful to them, so that was thoughtful for the cats however but the persistent rash was so annoying and irritating for me that it was sending me a bit batty without sleep. It happened a day that I had enough and said that what if he was to choose between me or getting rid of the cats and there was no answer forthcoming. So there it was thank God for me, the cats won but we continued to remain on friendly terms. It was the geek syndrome of non-commitment over his cats.

Ian also suffered from the perpetual bachelor loser men's affliction, commitment phobic single – Peter Pan always a child never ready to commit to a full adulthood partnership relationship. He used the excuses often that he was an admitted coward, scared and everybody he knew was already divorced anyway, that he was also polyamorous more like polygamous and cherished many ladies. It was a bit complicated but I wasn't bothered about it as we remained on and off companion outing, dining and firm film friends. I assumed his other whatever explicit needs were actually being satisfied and obviously met elsewhere, or on the massage tours. Apart from some of these weird cons that didn't sit well with me, and that I did not agree with, we were bosom buddies, both loved Spaghetti Marinara, rarely argued and enjoyed similar stuff and with loads in common about most things in life.

It was a bit of a triad at some stage with Ian, then Allan and then Mark all seemingly vying for my attentions. I wasn't particularly impressed or flattered by the thought of these curly, shirley and mo show or the Moe, Larry and Curly of The Three Stooges. Ian's Birthday was mid – September and he said once that I missed out on his 75th Birthday Party extravaganza, the invitation still on his fridge. I forget exactly how old they were because both Ian and Allan always lied about their age like women are supposed to. All three were probably around the same vintage of years 76 – 78, but Mark was the most best preserved and Allan was the least. Old enough to know better, too old to care, as it was written on Tanya, my accountants favourite Tea Mug. Ian was a Virgo and Allan was an Aquarius and I probably hadn't dated Mark long enough to find out.

Somehow I re- encountered Allan after being estranged for many months, it might have been even at Ian's Birthday party at his house in September, 2014. We even both turned up separately to Ian's Australia Day afternoon party in 2015.

Allan seemingly to want to remain pally with me, seeking me out here and there again. If he called on me this time however it would be decidedly different, I would not have intimate relations with that low life scumbag cheater. Allan also used the ploy that perhaps he could help me retrieve some costing monies from the fees of Michael Maplestone from the 2007, Sabena court case, from the outdated cheque books and invoices, alarm bells should have rung the Ambulance chaser. We never explored this, but I also remember him saying he scored an easy $ 300 cash from a new client, who needed urgent and desperate legal advice, late on a Friday afternoon. We dated a few times as plutonic friends sporadically and infrequently on and off over several months until it was St. Valentine's Day, 2015. He hadn't tried anything on so far and then Allan invited me to an early film and supper after. I bought him a card as he already seemed to have everything he ever wanted heaps of clothes, watches and lots of things that were much more costly than I could afford to buy.

I drove to his house in Brighton and but I thought several years later to gift him some TTP Merch because he wouldn't ever get these anywhere else, a T-shirt and some of our original first rare DVD's for posterity and eternity. I noticed since from before he returned from being abroad that year that at the end of the arched hallway was a rather large new painting leaning on the heap of other smaller paintings in the squeezed crammed hallway to the lounge. I thought it the ugliest thing I had ever seen of all his other weird eclectic art collection. It was a very distasteful abstract of a grey astronaut or alien figure, it might have been from a popular sought after artist but I wouldn't have had it in my toilet. I asked if it was new, he said yes that he bought it for a steal at $ 15,000. I gasped and almost collapsed of heart failure, I would never have spent such money on a frivolous extravagance like that but rather for Sabena's current court pending where I was self –represented due to severe lack of necessary urgent funds. I hoped it was a famous artist. Ironically he said he was a bit annoyed about me spending so much time on weekends preparing for my program pilot project with Costa the videographer for which we scheduled to film in the January 2015, school summer holidays, so would go to his house in Heidelberg for our meeting preparations. Why would he be jealous of our work project collaboration weekend times when we were barely going out together anymore. He gifted me a scarf and small black leather handbag that he bought whilst in Turkey. Some night we even watched an Andre Rieu Video together in my house on my lounge couch.

We leave together in his car on this St. Valentine's evening and we get to the Dendy Cinema Brighton. I don't remember what he wanted to see there. We get to the cinema counter desk and he pays for himself and then horror of all horrors, twilight zone time, do do do do, he says you pay for yours were going halves from now on. What a nightmare monstrous action to do on St. Valentine's Day without warning it almost even peaked that time being stood up on New Year's Eve years ago. So I left and went home in disgust. After all he'd done to me, it was screaming Vanilla Sky and Cryo all over again. It was a bad toxic marriage and acrimonious instant divorce on repeat, like the film of Elizabeth Taylor and Richard Burton. Liz – The Elizabeth Taylor Story, 1995. Drawn together like moths to a flame but it invariably always ending in a wallow of tears and yet another divorce.

Joker, 2019 – Joaquin Phoenix, Robert De Niro Director – Todd Phillips.

Maybe your too smart for yourself Mr. Stephen Hawking?

The Intentional Great Resignation.

The King is dead but the Queen is alive – Pink, 2012 Album – The truth about love.

The Staircase, 2021 – Colin Firth and Toni Collette.

Not the Same as it was – Harry Styles, 2022 Album – Harry's House.

Know when to hold them – The Gambler, Kenny Rogers 1978.

When Marilyn Monroe called Jackie – Biography, 2013.

Monty Norman 94 dies 12th July, 2022, iconic James Bond composer.

There is nothing like a crown for picking it up and putting it down.

James Caan – Actor 82 dies 8th July, 2022. Tempestuous Sonny in The Godfather.

Start Again – Conrad Sewell Album – Life, 2019.

As a previous potential boyfriend once quoted me years before the first family Court case hearings – keep going forwards don't ever go backwards – Trevor.

Do a Trump!

Fleeting moment of bliss.

Pave paradise to put up a parking lot – Big Yellow Taxi, Counting Crows Album – Hard Candy, 2002.

It's miserable inside!

It's too good to be true and it's too bad to be any good too!

Meatloaf dies 2022, 74 years – I'd do anything for love. Album – Bat out of Hell, 1977.

It's difficult compromising!

Don't judge me about my past I don't live there anymore!

So foggy, yet so clear!

Madonna – Express Yourself 1989 and Vogue 1990 Album – I'm breathless. (don't go for second best baby, put your love to the test)

Britney Spears conservatorship from her father James, ends 2021.

Buying a stairway to heaven – Led Zeppelin 1971, Movie – The song remains the same...

The windmills of your mind – Noel Harrison, 2003. Album – Life is a dream.

Believe – Cher, 1998.

Harden My heart- Quarterflash, 1981

Ring of Fire – Johnny Cash, song written by June Carter Cash 1963.

It's a bitter sweet symphony of life – The Verve, 2009.

Stranger Things – 2016.

Rasberry Beret- Prince, 1985.

Bjork – It's oh so quiet, 1995 Album – Post

When you say nothing at all – Ronan Keating, 1999. Album – Notting Hill

Beyonce – Single Ladies, 2009 (if you liked it you should have put a ring on it)

Walk Like an Egyptian – The Bangles, 1986. Album – Different Light.

Brass in Pocket – Pretenders, 1979. Money isn't everything Agnes- The Gilded Age, 2020.

Allan hadn't at all been sympathetic about my Sabena situation but rather tried to involve himself in the settlement case with respect to Freddie and Mum's house, however he also embroiled me into helping him with his affidavit and providing him with an affidavit from myself on his behalf about visitations with his grandkids and Brendan, his son refusing to allow him contact with them issue.

Love sometimes actually is not just enough and can't fix all the problems and issues. Sometimes it can't make it all better but ironically even further complicates matters instead that you don't even know what your needs or wants are or what your striving for, but that being communicative, supportive and co-operative so that travelling the road together seems to bear a lighter load.

Finally I elected to cut myself off from the insidious and inappropriate toxic circumstances and drop them all to salvage what was left of my life almost like deadheading roses so the dead end resprouts.

Murder on the dancefloor – Sophie Ellis Bextor, 2001. Album – Read my lips

Your xxxxx etc. is like a manufactured sausage cheap in every way and that terrible aftertaste lingers and won't ever go straight away!

A frenzy of flashbacks flickered through my thoughts fleeting glimpses of the past in my mind. I wondered why those curious flashbacks of memory were of value but obviously they were because they were encrypted on my mind as somewhat precious. I thought of the St. Kilda people back in the Lindentree and Rebar days. Mum named them slaggies or slaggie baggies because they appeared weird, loose and lazy even if they were not but none of them were ever rude or disrespectful to me.

Behind the Lindentree flat apartments Joe White, who 'd lived there for many years was the caretaker and concierge for many years for my dad and then Freddie, he was a straight down the line retiring gay man until in his twighlight years he moved on. Paul Hester was another strange controversial character who rented the flat above the kitchen, and saw him going up and down the stairs from the kitchen door. He wore loud Purple flared trouser suits from the 60's with bright colourful paisley shirts and open necked large collar, something out of Rowan and Martins Laugh in, his face and hair reminded me of Austen Powers, 1999 – The Spy who shagged me (Yeah, Baby! Yeah, baby!). He was a comical looking, Mike Myers who somehow lost his mojo after separating from his wife and kids, was now slumming it in St. Kilda he once worked in an office but now operated a small business from the flat. It was called Polyester, it might have been music and bands but moonlighting sidelines and other stuff too. We curiously saw many youngish looking girls going up and down the stairs day and night, all hours dressed up in school uniforms, also made up with high heels, so we sussed he might have been photographing or filming sorts of porn material but no-one disturbed him, complained or battered an eyelid as he was very humble, compliant and well mannered. He went about his weird business ironically calmly and peaceably without a bother.

Later Dean and Greg came along who were also estranged from their wives but also on the dole who stayed in the cheaper accommodation outhouses in the back car park and casually helped out in the bar when we were short staffed. The Michelin man body builders who occasionally came in for a drink and were sometimes doped up who shared house together Dave T was from Tassie to the big smoke, Puffy Dave who was more streetwise and their trainer friend boss Bazza or Barry. The Russian lesbian bisexual who left her Alsatian outside, Lizzie the petite lesbian who followed me around until I told her I wasn't a lesbian. Mild Maori Godfrey, the pro whisperer who tried to appease everybody, sucking it up when life gives you messiness, Godfrey's gives you cleanliness.

In Rebar times Koda and the Indian boys who followed Freddie everywhere and were his push around to do lackey slaves. Freddie going to the Grand Prix almost every year but I never once did. How Freddie would drink the cream from those little plastic bottles and licked his mouth off, like the Cheshire cat, the butter he would eat with a knife as if he was eating a block of tasty cheese, the Chocolate Ice Magic that was buried deep in the kitchen freezer for yonks and expired which he downed in front of me without a care, and I tried to stop him but it was too late, he was a cast iron guts in his younger days.

How I missed going to see the tour of Pompeii at the end of the cruise because my cards were maxed out, how I might have been ripped off in Mumbai India with the silver Sapphire jewellery I bought and the cute spinning dolls on sticks at Kochi, Kerala that sold out before I could get to the wandering beach vendor, how the quality of the Gold Sapphire jewellery in Colombo, Sri Lanka was much finer than those of India and the stones more precious and valuable.

The patient who tried to crack onto me, there were one or two others when I was younger before Sabena was born who I shrugged off. This new patient came to the clinic in about 2009, as I was working part-time at the rear of Mum's house. He was very attractive, charming, toned, tall, blonde and middle aged English entrepreneur well heeled who moved to Australia with his wife and family. Will came several times with his children after school for their various VP and fungal treatments my receptionist Simone was then in attendance. He then made an appointment for himself after work, word in the area must have been that I was now an available woman without a child and that I might require nurturing. Will flirted with me and it was flattering but I asked about his marriage to Celia, he said they became very estranged after moving to Australia and would have nothing to do with him intimately at all. She apparently hated his guts and stayed away from him as much as humanly possible via the kids.

I said I empathized with him but what must he have done to irk her so much. He said he was oblivious to it and I suggested he try to reconcile with her, impossible he answered. I finished up his treatment and placing the instruments on the autoclave I turned around with his face down into my mouth about to kiss me and accost me around the waist with his flaying arms. I pulled away I had met his three small children and however tempting a catch he thought he might have been I wasn't a mistress or a home wrecker.

I giggled so he wasn't annoyed at me and said it those that John West rejects that make John West the best, in other words some misguided opportunities are more worthwhile dodging than accepting. It totally smacked to me of a few night stand rompy bomp in the hay, to get his socks off, it was secrets of my five-mile high sex romp with Ralph Fiennes loo scandal creeped me out. Suffice to say he was so taken aback and insulted by my unflinting blatant rejection of his attractions and embarrassed by my response to it that I never saw him or any of his three children as my clinic patients again after that. I wondered what happened to that Lisa Robertson, the former Qantas flight attendant after the 2007 fling that launched a million fantasies, now says the incident had probably ruined her life. It hasn't enhanced it in any way Robertson told The Age, not financially, personally or in any other way. My mum said she had done it as a stunt to be big noted. Simone asked me one day what ever happened to that lovely Will guy patient, I didn't answer He was probably incredulous to the fact that I was just not interested in the sexual gifts he had to offer.

Carpe Diem – Seize the Day

Extracts Court Orders

Family Law Act 1975

In the Federal Circuit Court of Australia

At Melbourne

No. (P) MLC6845/2007

Order 23/03/2015

Before: Judge Stewart

The Court Orders that:

1. *The court orders that pursuant to Section 68L, of the Family Law Act 1975 an Independent Children's lawyer be appointed for the child Sabena Francesca born 28 August 1999and Victoria Legal Aid is requested to facilitate such appointment as soon as possible.*
2. *Upon notification of the identity of the Independent Children's Lawyer, each party shall forthwith provide to the Independent Children's Lawyer a copy of all documents filed by them in the proceedings.*
3. *The proceedings are adjourned to 22 April, 2015 at 9.45 am for mention in the duty list.*

Lampe Family lawyers for the Father.

Mckean Park Lawyers independent Children's lawyer

Mother Self- represented

Order 27/05/ 2015

Upon Applications made to the court pursuant to sub-rule 15.10(2) of the Federal Circuit Court rules 2001 being considered in chambers and their being no need for an appearance by or on behalf of the parties.

The Court Orders that:

1. That leave is granted to the Independent Children's Lawyer to issue subpoenas to produce documents on short notice to:-
   (a) The Royal Children's Hospital; and
   (b) Dr. Stuart Coull, MedicalOne Sydenham:

Provided always that such subpoena are issued and served by 12.00 (noon) on 29 May 2015.

Order 03/06/ 2015

Upon application made to the court by both the applicant and the respondent both appearing in person and Mr. Lovering of counsel for the Independent Children's Lawyer.

The Court Orders That:

1. Liberty granted to the Independent Children's Lawyer to peruse the documents produced by subpoena from Professor Alasdair Vance, and/ or Ms Jo Winther and/ or the Royal Children's Hospital, and remove any documents which, in her view has the capacity to impact detrimentally

on the welfare of Sabena and place them in a sealed envelope and clearly marked with the following:-

Not to be opened unless permission is granted by further order of this court for such documents to be disclosed to the mother and/ or the father.

Extract Mother's Scribbled Notes.

March, 2015 Initial Hearing. Appointed ICL – Ms. Maria Kourtis – VLA. April, 2015 – Hearing – Lampe Lawyers – VLA for Father, Melissa Scarfo. ICL – Ms. Helen Vickers

Outline: Rice and Asplund argument.

Mother's Notes ends here.

22.04.2015 – Current orders upheld, Interim Orders with a no contact order for the mother.

The hearing in April, 2015 my memory is somewhat fragmented in parts and yet some of the proceedings are indelibly etched forever. There are none of my detailed notes of the proceedings, I suspect I was too nervous, anxious and emotional to write them and likely preoccupied with documents and court preparations etc.

There is an outline of case document submitted by the Independent Children's on the 12th May, 2015 by Ms. Maria Kourtis, ICL. Court Date 13 May, 2015.

I do however remember having to prepare heavy affidavit documents to be lodged to the ICL and that I delivered them by hand and it was a raining cats and dogs, miserable overcast gloomy grey day, to ensure that they would arrive by the deadline date and that Judge Stewart not long after that ordered for the ICL to interview with Sabena in person. Affidavits filed on 26/ 05/ 2015.

Outline: Rice and Asplund argument (1979) FLC 90-725per Evatt, CJ at 78, 905.

Court Date: Wednesday 3rd June, 2015.

I don't think that Norma was with me on this court date because there were testimonies of Dr. Alasdair Vance and Jo Winther which were cross examined by myself from questions that I pre prepared for this court date for them and then later for Eddie and Bronwyn to address on the witness stand. I'm not certain why Bronwyn wasn't appearing on the witness stand, she may have refused or perhaps the Judge deemed it not required or maybe Eddie would not permit it. It is unclear. I must have been so very befuzzled and bamboozled by myself self – representing so that multi – tasking of the higher executive order is extremely difficult when suffering scrambled eggs.

I know with me in a small similar to lawyers carry –on suitcase was heaped with documents from the previous court hearings, affidavits filed, my Scout Logbook folder, Mims Medical Medicines bible, Therapeutic Guidelines – Neurology and Developmental Disability references, references from Drs. Specialists, psychologists, Annexures of photos (Some of which some were not returned of Sabena's Bells Palsy), that I noticed long after the final hearing as I never opened the suitcase after that day again for many years after, Sabena's pictures of her previous early and now more current stylistic model manga bunnies versions, cards, letters etc. There was also my black with red glitter Hello Kitty carry bag rope library tote with urgent access to documents that I prepared for the court. It was a long drawn out one and a half days as I recall and Judge Stewart facilitated my navigating the hearing and would pull me up should I not understand the limitations of the court process being solely self – represented.

Eddie constantly maintained that Sabena wished not to speak with or see the mother, this was also the feedback and stance from the ICL. Eddie's affidavit contained information from the

Distance Education Centre Victoria of proof of Sabena's enrolment on 17th February, 2015 with support Teacher Lisa Eldridge with mathematics not yet allocated. Dr. Alasdair Vance maintained his stance that Sabena was albeit slowly delayed in improving but however making some progress nonetheless with Jo Winther backing his complete testimony up. Most remarkable to me in his affidavit was pages and pages of literally many millions of huge and smaller more numerous hospital grants and donations that he and sometimes with collaboration with Jo Winther acquired, he was obviously an absentee practitioner who's aim was to accrue as much funds as possible at the expense of patients. I was also told by a pharmaceutical friend that these medications were encouraged in young people as they would no doubt be hooked on them for at least forty- five years or for the rest of their lives.

It felt like the Twilight Zone of the Salvation Army conspiracy and corruption against me all over again on repeat. They seemed to be all ganging up against me and Sabena was coached by Eddie. I was glad that Norma hadn't wasted a day on all that nonsensical drivel that was supposed to be believed. I however also believed in the professionalism of the Judge and that she also being youngish for a person achieving of that stature about middle-aged would be intelligent enough to consider Sabena's current and future best interest utmost above all else and not rely on past orders.

Extract – Outline Maria Kourtis, ICL dated 12/ 05/ 2015.

Further Matters

In the case of SPS & PLS (2008), FamCAFC 16, the court considers the Rice & Asplund principle, including its rationale and application in cases. One of the matters canvassed is how the rule applies when it is considered at a preliminary stage or as part of a final hearing. His honour observes (at paragraph 59) that if the rule is addressed as a preliminary matter and proves determinative of the application, then all these purposes are served. The purposes referred are discouraging endless litigation (Paragraph 56); avoiding the psychological harm inflicted on the parents as well as the child (at paragraph 57, quoting Nygh J); avoiding judges substituting their opinions for those already given by another Judge (paragraph 58).

His honour continues that there are cases where the issue ought be dealt with as a part of a final hearing, where say the evidence about the best interests of the child and the material change in circumstances overlaps.

Extracts from Distance Education Centre Victoria (Practitioner Referral Form)

Your Details

Jo – Ann Winther

Patient/ Client Details

Sabena Lazar

How long has your patient / client been under your care? 1 ½ years

Which diagnoses are relevant to your patient's/client's attendance at DECV?

Social Phobia, Generalized Anxiety, Depression, ADHD- Inattentive

What support systems do you believe will be useful for the supervisor?

Regular contact to check work Progress checking she understands the work given to her – as her anxiety prevents her from asking for assistance.

Practitioner Stamp: Jo Winther Clinical Psychologist / Co-ordinator CAMHS and Schools Early Action (CASEA) Program Developmental Neuropsychiatry Program (DNP) The Royal Children's Hospital Mental Health.

Dated: 10/2/15

At the end of the day, the court case in a nutshell for me there wasn't much in it, it was a simple question of the law *should be* utmost in the best interest of the child's future life not the parents. I saw the drastic change in circumstances as Sabena's deterioration on an everyday downward spiral and a waste of a young person's future whole life in the balance whilst she continued in Bronwyn and Eddie's care. There would have to be a significant change or intervention in Sabena's life or change of residence environment and care in order for her to ever be a functioning capable motivated young adult not an emotionally passive submissive, disabled dependent cripple.

To me it was an SES rescue situation.

Both Norma and Dr. Helen Grogan, my dear friends who knew Sabena from years before wrote Affidavits for me that were included in my evidence with the exhibits of photo's, drawings etc. My potential witnesses weren't called for some reason.

Eddie's testimony and cross examination was so long, tediously painful and he babbled incoherent, indecipherable continuous verbal diahorrea. His body and hands were shaking and trembling, I would have struck him out as a non credible and incompetent witness neither was Sabena in my opinion in this current state to make her father's decisions to the ICL about what she wanted for her own independent life. I deemed Bronwyn the most competent of all three but yet obviously biased towards keeping Sabena in custody and residing with them but she was never even a witness or cross examined.

It was uncanny how Judge Joanne Stewart (I don't know how I found out her first name, I must have researched something or other), resembled Bronwyn they could have been sister's from another father. It was so unnerving with her pinch mouth and her beady eyes subconsciously it registered.

Extracts Outline of Case Document submitted by the ICL.

Applications

2. The mother does, by her Initiating Application filed 16 December, 2014 seek a raft of Orders including for specific time with the child, and input in and access to information about the child's medical issues.
3. The father's response to Initiating Application filed 24th April, 2015 seeks that the mother's Application be dismissed, an order for costs and a prohibition on the mother issuing further proceedings without the leave of the court.

The principle in the Marriage of Rice and Asplund (1979) FLC 90-725 as arising from that case, and subsequent case law provides that where final orders have been made in relation to parenting issues, the applicant must establish a change of circumstances since the orders were made sufficient to warrant variation or discharge of those orders. The change in circumstances has been described in various cases as a *startling new circumstance a substantial change or a material change.*

The Independent Children's Lawyer submits that the applicant mother has not demonstrated such a change in circumstances.

So far as the Independent Children's Lawyer can ascertain from perusing the mother's the alleged material change in circumstances can be distilled to the following:

1. The deterioration in the child's mental health and the treatment received by the child.

2. The fact that the mother has spent time and communicated with the child.
3. The father's attitude to the mother and the mother's contact with the child.
4. The mother's diagnosis of Multiple Chemical Sensitivities Syndrome.
5. The mother's attitude to the allegations that the father sexually abused the child.

Extracts Dr. Helen Grogan Affidavit filed 2nd June, 2015.

Sad to say, once your on the scary Ferris Wheel - of the Family Court System, you simply can't get off and the only one's that care are those whose children are already regrettably caught up in the cross - wires of a failed, fatally flawed system with respect to their own children.

Hoppers Lane

28/05/ 15

I have known Linda Warschauer since we five years old when we bothe went to school at Genazzano Convent in 1966.

She was a bright happy outgoing child articulate child as a little girl at that time living with her mother after her parents separated. I went out with her and her mother on a few occasions, the most memorable being a trip to Puffing Billy when she was 6 or 7 years old.

I am sure via Linda that Eddie was happy for us to go out there and Linda several times contacted him about date and time so that Sabena would be ready to leave.

When she came out of her room she was not dressed. I do not know if this was because she did not know of the plans or she had thought we were not coming.

She in the end did get dressed and come out to the restaurant and I believe enjoyed seeing us both.

When we returned to the house Eddie did say he was happy for Sabena to come out again.

Signed: Helen Grogan

24 2 Hoppers Lane, Werribee Vic. 3030
Tel: 8731 6500 Fax: 8742 2188

www.hopperslane.com.au

Extract Norma Flowerday (Justice of the Peace) Affidavit filed 26th May, 2015.

1. *I have known Linda Warschauer for nearly 12 years and see her every 8 weeks.*
2. *In the early years mum and daughter came to me home for a birthday party, Sabena was very playful and an outgoing young girl.*
3. *While at Linda's practice every 8 weeks there has been lovely drawings that Sabena has given to her mum along with some bright and smiley photo's of mum and daughter.*
4. *The last couple of years, no new drawings and no new photo's.*
5. *Last year I drove Linda out to Sabena's for her birthday. <r. and Mrs Lazar knew we were coming.*
6. *Sabena was still in bed when we arrived (after lunch), but when she saw her mum and me. She was happy to come for a walk in the park with us.*
7. *Next we went to a shopping centre for coffee and some intimate apparel for Sabena, her mum went in with her but nothing was bought.*
8. *We talked about art and colours (I also referring to her early drawings); I suggested she could paint her sneakers or embellish them, which she was keen to try.*
9. *As a mum myself, I have seen teen girls rooms, messy clothes everywhere, walls full of their music or movie stars, there was nothing like that in Sabena's room.*
10. *Sabena has lost her sparkle in her eyes, lost her goals in life, and this happened in the last few years, so sad.*

Extracts Mother's Log Notes

August, 2014 – Sabena appears drastically worse after her birthday and her father begs me to visit her and come to their home. I hope there is enlightenment for him and I visit around her birthday and again in late October, 2014 with my best friend Norma Flowerday and my primary school friend Dr. Helen Grogan. We are shocked to see Sabena is dishevelled in appearance at 2.30 pm in the afternoon and is just got up from bed, he hair is matted, is heavily sedated, she refuses to go outside and we convince her to come for a walk and some afternoon tea and a bite to eat.

She is pleased to see us and we have a pleasant afternoon and she starts to show a glimmer of her real self again.

Mother's Affidavit filed on the 26th may, 2015.

1. *That I am self- employed and work (part-time).*
2. *That I seek to rely on my previous affidavits which were affirmed on the 15th December, 2014 and 5th May, 2015.*
3. *That my previous request for orders to be granted in the Initiating Application affirmed on the 15th December, 2014 be upheld or that the default be, if this is too difficult to adhere to for both parties due to practical reasons such as distance, etc. then orders made in favour of the said mother for the child to be accommodated at my residence for either a trial temporary stay for 6-12 months at the Magistrate's discretion to be reviewed after this time or alternatively commence permanently.*

   In my care she shall be encouraged to have fair freedom of contact and visitation between either household.

   If neither of these proves a satisfactory resolution that Foster Care be considered or Community Housing for disadvantaged youth.

4 (b). That I worked with helping youth of various ages for at least the previous (7 Years) and for 29 years in my professional work duties. In various capacities and have a lot of patience and empathy for them.

I started a support group for teenagers called TEEN TALK from February, 2014 and it is well received and a growing cause amongst youth.

Extracts Mother's Outline of Arguments dated 27.04.2015

1. *Mother cannot reasonably comply with the orders.*

   The mother cannot comply with the orders if the child is chronically and severely ill.

   The mother feels torn between the loving bond to care and help her daughter and the Separation – Anxiety Disorder, she struggles with everyday and loss of precious mother-daughter moments, for the previous seven years which are gone forever.

   That the father either punishes the Sabena for enjoying time spent with her mother /Parental – Alienation Syndrome and discourages all contact or alternatively dictates contact on his own terms forcibly which are not practical but burdensome and difficult for the mother to comply with ie. Mother to visit their home 2 hours each way, with a supervisor.

   A visit to their home is 2 hours each way and the mother does not feel safe attending either on her own, or travelling the distance often due to her allergic respiratory illness and also some days feeling just unwell due to her condition.

Also Sabena should now be mature enough to visit independently without her fthaer's or stepmother's permission, and this would encourage confidence.

2. *If the orders no longer reflect actual arrangements for the child.*

   In March, 2009 Dr. Robert Adler obtained agreement for both parties for a basic parenting plan. Ie. I would call Sabena either Saturday or Sunday each week, and we would have visits every few months to then he recommenced gradually introducing and resuming a regaulr family contact regime with the mother, during the next 6-12 months after, of every fortnight or weekend staywith the mother and some weeks during the holidays. A standard contact regimen. This gradual resumption of contact never happened and the onus is on the mother to call Sabena or Sabena to ask her father for permission to see her mother. This parenting plan which was requested by Sabena from Dr. Adler contradicts the previous orders that the father have total discretion regarding contacts.

3. *The previous argument at the final hearing and Appeal no longer applies, in that the father maintains that the mother's stance is aggressive, intransigent and entrenched that the father will continue to sexually abuse and violently intimidate Sabena for years. This is no longer the case since 2009, since during counselling with Dr. Betty Kotler, the mother eventually reconciled with her fears and accepted that the abuse was never likely to reoccur due to the full –time presence of the stepmother and due to Sabena's increasing maturity, growth and ability to defend herself /disclose / report or voice her objections in response to impending various types of physical, emotional and sexual abuse from her father. Dr. Kotler encouraged the mother to focus on rebuilding her own life, friends and contacts.*

In fact during these years despite her illness the mother achieved personal goals and contributed a great deal to her community.

4. *Even after a few years the precedent in the argument is that ircumstance's change in people's lives, this is particularly the case with children. Since 2010, Sabena was struggling emotionally as her believe at the time was residing with her father would be just temporary for 6 months as she was told by Anna Warhaft, Family Court Mediator. The orders than became permanent in 2009. Sabena was not ordered to have grief or loss counselling as was suggested to myself. She began to show emotional fragility from 2010, as described by the principle and teacher's from then on. She loved reading and was an avid reader and always sketched designs for her mother, whilst she was in her care or on visits. She was a promising student until 2010 and then her grades and interest waned. This emotional fragility becomes compounded and worsens during the ensuing years with diagnoses of PTSD, Seperation – Anxiety Disorder, Parental – Alienation Syndrome, ODD Oppositional Defiant Disorder, Anxiety, Chronic depression, agoraphobia, self-mutilation and suicidal Idealization. She is traumatized, insecure, intimidated, fearful, feels guilt and blames herself as being bad for being punished by not being allowed to see her mother. She avoids confrontation, is submissive and shuts out feelings and painful emotions. The orders are no longer pertinent as they do not take into account her level of maturity and her wish to exert her freedom and independence of choices without being a slave or submissive/ passive to her father's dominance over her. She is rebelling against this tyranny by drawing attention to herself, desperately crying out for urgent help by ongoing self – mutilation and suicidal attempts. The maximum doses of severe anti-depressant medication contribute to her confused, deranged, drowsy, sedated, apathetic and desperately sad state. She suffers adverse*

effects whilst there is no evidence of improvements or regression of her illness. She began struggling since 2010 and her situation is deteriorating every year since.

There is no attendance of formal schooling for at least three years since and since she commenced on the medications from the Royal Children's Hospital, Professor Alasdair Vance – Supervising Psychiatrist Professor and Zoe Winther attending counsellor.

Her situation is constantly deteriorating and she is reverting into a dependant invalid.

Something in her life must change if she is not to become just another tragic statistic and it is the system's responsibility to protect the child, to provide a remedy and give her the chance for freedom, independence, and full functioning life she deserves. I asked her father if he would please have her totally medically, metabolically, physically and psychologically assessed with a second opinion, but he disagreed, to ensure she is obtaining the appropriate treatment.

5. *If the existing orders were made without all relevant information being put before the court. During the previous court proceedings the mother was struggling with a syndrome which was not officially diagnosed at the time, which caused her severe distress, anxiety and some aberrant out of character behaviours as a consequence. She was referred by the GP to to an allergist Dr. Nick Siemensma who performed testing, then he referred her for a specialist opinion at a Chemical and Environmental Allergist, Mr. Colin H. Little for testing and specific diagnosis. Once diagnosed and partially desensitized, the mother began to stabilize, learn to manage and cope better with her disability to improve her functioning and behaviour. The father claimed at this time that I was*

neglectful, ambitious, motivated, self – absorbed and hard working. That I did not love or care for Sabena, I was just an average single mum under pressure with no maintenance trying to do the best for bringing up my daughter, under difficult circumstances. I Struggled with my illness at its peak during 2008/ 2009which caused me to appear erratic, and aggressive with aberrant behaviours that were out of character like unexplained rudeness, anxiety and irritability out of context but otherwise I am usually a calm, peaceful, passive, reasonable, conscionable and patient person especially in my work. I have a working with children's permit. I have never harmed or threatened dangerous behaviour towards any person. I have never suffered with mental illness or taken anti-depressant or sedating medications.

My disability is neither better nor worse but it is stable for several years now, however I have learned how to maintain it and manage it so I have a good quality of life and function reasonably well, despite it. I work casual days and have learnt to pace myself these years.

Brave/ Touch the Sky/ Disney, 2015

Brave – Sara Bareilles, 2013

Brave – Kate Ceberano, 1989. Album – Brave.

The missing photos exhibits of Sabena's left droopy eye and face with an Elvis Pose of her right hand up and left hand on hip tilted, how she was previously when young a perfect little miss. Bella, Sabena's freakin cat who ran across my path at their house on visiting with Norma screaching. The scrawny, scungy, matted, runt of the litter – Tawny Tortoiseshell, also equally unkempt as Sabena. Prescribing rights – always use the minimum effective dose in patients to obtain the desired treatment outcome. The shrouded in mystery medical information I wasn't allowed to see.

That I was not permitted by the court to access a transcript as to what Sabena actually said to the ICL at her interview but I can guess. Wondering whether Bronwyn and Eddie were both bisexually oriented in their gender?

Release of Baz Luhrmans Elvis, June 2022.

The final hearing date was adjourned to another day, Wednesday 17th June, 2015 and I prepared my trial hearing address summary. Norma was kind enough to accompany me for this day, she might have even driven me there and I needed all the moral support I could get and also as I wanted to give this final shot of a chance to salvage Sabena from the grips of those evil monsters and have her freedom plus the likelihood that she might also recover would certainly increase if she managed to get out from under their care and parenting style or lack of it of the ding dongs.

How they managed to drag her down so much in the mud into the doldrums in the span of a few short six years was mindboggling to me. Plus mum used to say that anyone who lived with them would surely end up going Banana -ramas and that Sabena was the most competent of the three of them in those early days when she was ordered to reside there.

However anxious, fearful and nervous I felt sick to my stomach on the day as I used to also get that sick feeling walking up to the Family Court Building every time before, going through those deadly revolving doors and passing through security, once they made me take everything out of the case, like at the airport. It was a bit humiliating and intimidating, I also sometimes carried the odd metal spoon or fork wrapped in napkins in my handbag because of my allergies or in case I went somewhere to a seminar or a finger food function or event. Of course they were deemed to be weapons and I would have to sign them in and they were returned to sign out when I left the building at the front service and security counter desk.

I remember the security guard lady thinking it was an absolute hoot signing in a spoon or fork, well at least it wasn't a knife.

I was however pump full of adrenaline, Norma must have seen and felt me so spooked because she clung to me like a mother helping her child across the busy intersection street. What could be worse than having Sabena Lifeless, soulless and a fading away shadow of her former self and being powerless to do anything about it and to stop it continuing or worse. Mum also always drummed into me that warning about straightening up youth before they became 16 as after that it would be decidedly much more difficult to mould them or untangle them so they don't get into habitual bad patterns of behaviour or a lifelong rut.

Norma said later however that I was very composed, professional and that my cross – examination questions were very sound and that my final summary was heart wrenchingly super, almost fair dinkum lawyer like, well I paid enough of them over these many years. I would write it all here but it is almost eight pages long so I will abridge it somewhat in order.

Extracts from Mother's Final Day- Trial Hearing address.

Starting from the beginning, before leaving my care, at the time Sabena was residing with myself and my mother, from about age 3. I remember happy memories of Sabena. She loved attending Glamorgan kinder and her favourite teacher was Sue Hutton. She seemed to learn something every day. She also went to the National Theatre Ballet School every Saturday for Ballet classes. She also attended Stage Left Performing Arts School for singing, dancing and acting and also the The Rose St. Armadale Swim School during Summer months. Sabena asked to be involved in these activities and some of her school friends also attended them and she would see them there and socialize with them.

Sabena was a happy, gregarious, social and outgoing child, always smiling, she knew all the teachers and greeted them, when she saw them, she was well liked and accepted. She had lots of school friends who would often come for play dates and outings.

I knew she was unique, and an exceptional child from this young age, due to her extraordinary imagination, about mythical creatures and fantasy worlds. She loved fairies, angels and unicorns, she was always sketching, painting them and telling stories about them having wonderful adventures. She believed that the fairies and angels protected and guided us, and were invisible sitting on our shoulders, when we needed them. I think of her now as my angel without wings, restricted from exploring her real future abilities.

She would also dress up the Barbie dolls, in clothes that she would create herself, from bits of pretty, fancy and sparkly materials she found in my mother's sewing chest.

She also loved nature, all animals and tiny insects. Especially cats and was fascinated by the majesticness and presence of horses.

She also liked spending time with my friends, later on in age going to an afternoon Birthday party at Norma's house, in her favourite fun costume and meeting her daughter Zarah, an Art's Teacher and they made natural play dough together. Going to Gembrook with, Dr. Helen Grogan and myself, on the Puffing Billy train. My cousins from Italy called us not only mother and daughter but the Minnie Mouse twins, as we liked the same things, the same activities, and often we thought the same or anticipated each other. Cousin Carla called us le Topoline.

I would work late and extra hour or 2, 1-2 evenings per wek and I would pick up Sabena from school to deliver her to my mother but she would like to come to the clinic instead with me and play being receptionist with my office manager. She would also sketch fairies for the patients the patients and write their names on the files and help put the files away. She did not come to the clinic during

Winter, and I would come home, to find her blowing bubbles with my mother or doing her homework or reading to my mother.

Sabena during these early years was reluctant to visit on weekends with her father and did not like him picking her up after school on his days. She would refuse to attend kinder or school on those particular days and would make a terrible fuss. As Judge Brown mentions in her deliberation, I think my biggest fault in being Sabena's mother at this time was being a devoted mother and trying to protect her from harm at this vulnerable age, as her father was single at this time. However, I do feel the judgement was rather harsh and very restrictive, under the circumstances.

During the years I hoped the father would mellow and foster a normal contact arrangement for Sabena and myself and that she would cope reasonably well, with resilience and determination.

However, Sabena's current situation is worse than I could have ever anticipated in my worst nightmare. I do not even fathom how the steep deterioration and destruction of her life occurred or I suspect it was gradually accumulating during the years and came to a breaking point eventually.

I have no doubt they have denigrated me and put me down at every opportunity, during these years but I know I am a good person and have risen beyond it. I have become a role model for persevering and determination, conquering adversity despite my disabilities to achieve and strive to become a better functioning person and to give and help the community, for the benefit of our future society.

It is obvious that Sabena's current state is a tragedy beyond imagination. Her quality of life is non –existent in fact, her existence is a day to struggle, not even a life. Her quality of life is deteriorated, since her non-attendance at formal school for 2 years, he school friends have all but abandoned her, because she does not interact with them normally and socially. She cannot make other friends but lives in a virtual world of internet people who we don't know what their motives are or what their characters and behaviours are like.

The area at Keilor Downs – Sydenham is a growth area with young couples and small children with lots of kinders etc. However, it is very boring and lacks stimulation for youg people due to lack of entertainment and distance from facilities and activities for them to participate in, Her bedroom is spare, bare without colour.

Sabena with suffering a beating of her immune system due to stress, separation- anxiety, PTSD etc. due to the change of residence, during these years was struggling with her emotional fragility. She was continually traumatized, intimidated and tormented by various issues in her environments compounding her conditions. Her lack of happiness and gradual deterioration in functioning attest to this as evidence, of her ongoing decline. I believe her self – mutilation/ suicide attempts are a cry for help, a desperate attempt to gain attention to her mental torture, detention and imprisonment. Also perhaps to make herself unattractive, disfigured to escape life and the reality of facing each dreary day.

She is increasingly isolated, agoraphobic brainwashed by a limited environment each day, no friends, no fun, no stimulating activities or distractions, no education or limited skills, no ambition or motivation, a boring, mundane, habitual wasted life. I would be suicidal in her place any reasonably normal person would!

There are no support groups she attends with people of her age with similar problems to discuss, socialize and empathize with. There are no normal social interactions with people outside of her home like face to face friends in person, carers, teachers, instructors, coaches, craft/ hobby groups, everyday people.

There is no family inclusive therapy, such that the home environment also helps her to rehabilitate, but the father and stepmother dump her every fortnight at the RCH, hoping as if by wave of the magic wand, she will get better without any effort on their part, that is the RCH 's responsibility to cure her of all her issues with their help.

She now lacks independence, motivation and courage, and is made to believe she is an invalid. It is my belief that she will continue in this state until she is discharged from the hospital, as a dysfunctional and addicted young adult, due to her father enabling this pattern of entrenched behaviour and reinforcing it, defending it disguised as deluded concern for her well being for his own personal interests. Rather than promoting and encouraging earliest rehabilitation, and even part-time return to school and gradual resumption of normal functioning in society, which is paramount in her having a reasonably normal functioning life and future.

I have brought this application not for myself, but out of a mother's love and but a desperate attempt to rescue my daughter from what she believes she deserves and that is her fate because of the current environment which she is in, that is not conducive to her rehabilitation or healing. It is of paramountancy and in the best interest of the young developing person, young lady or young miss, to deserve and demand to have a reasonably happy and functioning life and be given the tools to form skills and independence for her future or we are doing her an injustice and disservice.

Conversely, this I believe is an alternative positive outcome, with a change of her current environment, because at times she exhibits and there are glimmers of her former character and she seems on occasion to have insight, which is somewhat reassuring.

She should have a quality of life and futue alternatives not just an existence. Her life is expiring before it even started. Her life as I see it was nothing but a horror story for the previous eight years, as with a chronically, critically ill or terminally ill child with cancer, you want them to have the best quality of life. Why is this any different? She should be given the opportunity to be weaned off all the medications and try alternative therapies, which could increase her functionality and for her to enjoy some quality of life and activities. On her current medication she could not drive or perform certain activities, due to the drowsiness and lack of mental alertness.

I believe once Sabena, sees me objectively and a lot is changed in eight years for both of us and she is given now at this mature age full disclosure and the truth about previous events when she was younger, she will have closure and begin healing.

I have demonstrated by my self- representation to be a sound, rational, caring and accomplished person and therefore should be afforded some parental responsibility and input decision making in my daughter's health, well being and education!

We have a chance to be the heroes for this young girls future? We could turn it around like the saying lemonade from lemons it is not a given, but also there is no reward without effort but if you never try you will never know.

We should not ignore the power of change and improvement, it is possible when we deliver the proper and encouraging messages to young people!

That life is just futile, we should give up, and we should just waste everyday sitting about doing nothing, with no plan, just existing every day.

That it is not important to have a life you will remember or make your personal stamp of uniqueness in contributing in your own specialness, in this society, world and for humanity!

Let us rather try to show what is achievable, and prove them wrong, when there is love, honesty, hope, determination, perseverance, and courage on your side, in your belief in what your doing is good and right and being successful in your goals!

Let us be an example of To believe is to achieve!

Woulda, shoulda, coulda but never did is not in our plan. The outcome could not be any worse than it already is, the only way up is from here, there is nothing to lose we could only gain from trying and benefit from our experiences along the way!

If you are interested in reading the entire address I would be pleased to provide you with a copy.

The point that I was trying to make was actually for the Judge, that she could be a hero for Sabena's future life. I hoped she would be a radical hero and see the compassion for the dreaded situation, break from the mould, as she was a young upcoming judge in the ranks. Become a precedent for change – do the right thing for the greater good of humanity. I was also annoyed about the contempt for climate change and my MCES (Multiple Chemical and Environmental Sensitivity) issues during these years, I would be the trail blazer Nostradamus barometer for our future health and environment. I might have worn my mask during the proceedings the exception was if I was interacting with the Judge or cross –examining the witnesses out of respect for the Judge and her court. Why people wouldn't believe about the prediction of climate change and its devastating effect on people's health and nature all over the world countries. Anyhow I thought and hoped that I had some chance to get into her insight psyche.

I felt relieved anyhow that I had done what I came to do and felt pleased in giving my all and doing my very best and putting my best foot forward. I felt a veritable Ironside, 1967 TV drama series. Viktor Frankel (Auschwitz), on giving meaning to your suffering – Dr. Phil on grave injustices.

I saw Judge Stewart's mouth moving without comprehending what she was saying in slow motion. She could not hand down a determination, deliberation or verdict on this day. Disappointed, however that this might be deliberately stalling to avoid an emotional scene but that it might also be a ray of sunshine that it wasn't cut and dried, all over rover either. Nick, my patient once said to me that a man died whilst waiting for a Family Court outcome for three years. Surely it wouldn't be that long for Sabena's emergency ambulance sake.

I am the way, the truth and the light. Jesus (John 14.6) I am the way, the truth and the life. No man comes to the father except through me.

If you read the newspaper you will always find a sad story about someone who made a bad decision. 16th November, 2015- Google.

I am the light of the world, whoever follows me will NEVER walk in darkness, but will have the light of life. (John 9:5).

During the miracle of healing the blind at birth, Jesus saying: When I am in the world, I am the light of the world.

** DOLCE - Dulce de Leche - SWEET PUDDING (NJ) (MG).*

The Final Judge deliberation, verdict address was handed down on the 11th February, 2016.

The Joint Select Committee on Family law Reform – Individual witness submission notes, 2018, hearing 2020.

11.02.2016 – Final Orders.

Final orders upheld with some variation, minor amendment 19.02.2016.

21. 04. 2020 Zoom # 467, mobile telephone hearing, at 2.30 pm for Melbourne for The Joint Select Committee on Australia's Family Law System. I prepared summary notes of my submission and recommendations for reform.

Committee Membership

Chair – Hon Kevin Andrews MP LPA Menzies Vic. Lib.

Deputy Chair

Senator Pauline Hanson One Nation QLD

Members Participating

Dr. Anne Aly MP ALP Cowan WA

Senator Claire Chandler LPA TAS

Dr. Fiona Martin LPA Reid NSW

Senator Matt O'Sullivan LPA WA

Mr. Graham Perrett MP ALP Moreton QLD

Senator Helen Polley ALP TAS

Ms. Zali Steggall OAM MP Independent Waringah NSW

The Zoom meeting was behind schedule and may have actually started closer to 2.45 pm or even 3 pm. I was certainly very anxious and nervously apprehensive about whether I would have time to get my summary of points and recommendations described and comprehended by the sitting members in what was the span of 15 – 20 minutes in total. The time passed like watching sands in an hourglass, whilst waiting for the start but then it all happened so fast almost within the blink of an eye it seemed to me.

Extracts Mother's Submission and Dissertation Presentation Notes

"Without Prejudice"

File No. MLC 6845/2007

April 2003- August 2017'

Precedent Case: Pseudonym "Licha and Wunschen, 2008.

Re: 2015, Rice and Asplund argument (1979) FLC 90-725 per Evatt, CJ at 78, 905.

The sometimes tragic waste of potential successful future live, loss of human life and the perpetual grief of never- ending tragedies and disastrous family saga's. Casualties of the terrible and horrific detrimental outcomes of Family Court processes and decisions, which might have been evaded and prevented with safety nets in the system. For eg. The Rosie Batty tragedy (12.02.2014) – Anderson the father murders his son, Luke. Arthur Freeman (37 years) murders daughter Darcy Iris (4 Years) throwing daughter off City's Westgate Bridge during peak hour traffic, (29.01.2009).

QLD Fugative Parents "The Australian "27th September, 2014.

Recommendations

- *Different levels of complex cases and categories recognized and established assessed.*
- *Safety- net for child's increasing dysfunction or parental negligence/ abuse, Independent Health and Education Family care ombudsman.*
- *Monitoring of complex cases yearly and court review 2 yearly.*
- *Child interviewed privately by magistrate from 7 years, as objective and not tainted by subjective practitioners.*
- *Post – Traumatic counselling for the child (PTSD) post change of residence or major life altering event.*
- *ICL for both parties, for fairness and equality of representation for bothe parties without bias to either party.*
- *Family Court and psychological reports / completed once internal / external and reviewed by another second opinion.*
- *Family Court Reports should never be consequentially prepared by the same Senior Court Mediator, to get another opinion.*
- *The Status Quo – not to alter orders before 16 years, continues the destructive patterns irretrievably into adulthood. – The benefit of removing the child from a dysfunctional environment outweighs the argument of disruption and upheaval.*
- *The statement the Best Interest of the Child is paramount for their future well –being and functioning as an adult.*

Initially there was a brief introduction with the Chair and then after my summary notes of Individual witness submission and recommendations blurted out at breakneck speed. The Chair then invited questions from the members, Pauline Hanson was the unique member to put forward about one and a half thoughtful and considerate questions to me. I was slightly unnerved and agitated so don't remember the exact form of the questions, but something similar to this that were food for thought provoking. *When I first noticed Sabena was being interfered with and what I had done to protect her? What was the outcome of the child after she left your care?*

Sabena was 3 years old and *he put his finger in her bottom and it hurt,* I reported it to the Department DHS (CPU) and obtained an intervention order and filed for suspension of contact in the Family Court.

The Death Nell sounded after starting residing with her Father of a consistent gradual deterioration and downward spiralling of dysfunctional behaviours.

* The Proverbial shit hits the fan ....!
* Spit the Dummy .....!
* Crack the Shits .....!

2011- Geelong vs Collingwood / Melbourne Cup Winner – Dunaden

2012- Sydney vs Hawthorn / Green Moon

2013- Hawthorn vs Freemantle / Fiorente

2014- Hawthorn vs Sydney / Protectionist

2015 – Hawthorn vs West Coast /Prince of Penzance – Michelle Payne first female jockey to win the race despite facing odds of 100 to 1. Trainer Darren Weir, Owner John Richards.

(Ride like a Girl – Rachel Griffiths released on 26th September, 2019.)

Produced by Richard Keddie; Rachel Griffiths; Susie Montague – Delaney.

Starring: Teresa Palmer; Sam Neill; Sophia Forrest

2016 – Western Bulldogs vs Sydney / Almandin – Kerrin McEvoy, Trainer- Robert Hickmont Owner – MS Gudinski.

2017- Richmond vs Adelaide / Rekindling

2016

1 January – Palliative care patient tests positive for legionnaires Disease at Wesley Hospital, Brisbane. Centre of a fatal 2013 outbreak.

4 January- Postage increase from 70 cents to 1 dollar.

Immigration minister Peter Dutton apologizes for text message, he referred to a female reporter as *a Mad fucking witch.*

Australian Stock Exchange suffers due to 7 % drop in Shanghai rocking global markets.

5 January- Dick Smith goes into voluntary administration.

6 January – 3 days of heavy rain, flooding severe worst hit Hunter Region, NSW home evacuations.

7 January- Bushfires in WA especially Yarloop.

12 January- Vic. Premier Daniel Andrews publishes a response to Coroner Ian Grays 29 recommendations from the Luke Batty inquest agreeing to implement those relevant to the government.

18 January- Clive Palmer's QLD Nickel refinery goes into voluntary administration.

22 January –NSW Gov. Pays compensation to victims of abuse at Parramatta Girls's Home for the first time.

29 January- Fed. Gov. Announces national framework to offer compensation to victims of Institutionalised sexual abuse following recommendation of Royal Commission.

31 January – Dan Andrews apologises to those who received Gay Pride March (Criminal convictions prior to homosexuality discrimination on 24 May, 2014.

3 February – Former Governor – General and archbishop of Brisbane formerly apologises to child abuse victim due to mishandling error of judgement to allow John Elliott to continue as Rector of Dalby.

4 February- 28 people fall ill from Salmonella outbreak in salad greens.

12 February - Climate Change Laws reviewed with new targets to cut emissions.

15 February- More than l Billion worth of liquid Methyl Amphetamine seized from shipment of stick on gel bras and art supplies. Biggest seizure in Australian history.

23 February – BHP Billiton reports loss, mining downturn.

Review Safe Schools programme as sexist Senator Corey Bernardi – *to imagine themselves without genitals or their attracted to someone of the same sex.*

29 February – Cardinal George Pell gives evidence via video link from Rome hotel, *He is not there to defend the indefensible.*

26 July – Royal Commission into Juvenile Detention in NT. after Four Corners Programme airs footage of abuse of detainees at the Don Dale Youth detention Centre.

28 September – SA without electricity after massive storm damages electrical transmission infrastructure.

25 October – 4 people killed at Dreamworld, Gold Coast when the thunder river rapids ride malfunctions.

4- 6 November-Bushfires flare and residents evacuated in Sydney, Hunter Valley and Central Coast (Across NSW)

21 November – Storm in Melbourne triggers thousands of incidents of Thunderstorm Asthma, resulting in at least 8 deaths.

5 December- Josh Frydenberg – review of Climate Change Policies. Emissions Intensity Scheme, generators pay for emissions above a certain level.

8 December- Vic. Premiere Andrews, Gov. To introduce 2017, Bill dealing with assisted dying.

18 December – Powerful thunderstorm lashes Sth East QLD leaving 10, 000 homes without power.

36 One Nation candidates announced.

19 December – Fed. Treasurer Scott Morrison Debt is expected to hit a record $ 648 Billion by 2026.

Market value of Ch7 plummets $ 98 Million. Executive Assistant Amber Harrison's allegations that she was paid $ 150,000 to keep quiet about affair with Tim Warner.

23 December – Australian Police raid several Melbourne properties and arrest 7 Arab Australian men, believed plotting terrorist attacks on several sites in Melbourne for Christmas Day.

Broome, WA records wettest December 226 mm of rain. Tropical Cyclone Yvette, beating previous record set in 1970.

26 December- Damaging flash floods in Central Austalia, Once in a Century Weather Event by Bureau of Meteorology.

World Events 2016

January – Hundreds of sexual assaults by asylum seekers in Cologne, Germany. Women robbed, threatened and sexually molested. The number grows over next few weeks and includes reports of other European cities.

Spread of Zika Virus in Brazil, hundreds of babies being born with severe brain injuries after their mother's were bitten by Zika infected mosquitoes. Guillane – Barre – Paralysis and miscarriages.

North Korea conducts missile and nuclear tests.

February

Reformers win big in Iranian election, setting the scene for more turmoil in the Islamic Republic.

Two former Jakarta International School Teachers are sent back to jail on sodomy charges, sends shock waves through expat community in Indonesia.

March

Us President Barack Obama arrives in Cuba for an official visit, the first president to set foot in the country since 1928.

Italy continues to pluck hundreds of immigrants ou of the sea. And thousands attempt to cross the Mediterranean as Slovenia, Croatia and Macedonia close their borders.

Terrorist attacks in Brussels and revelation to their links to Paris in 2015.

April

Hospital bombings in Aleppo, as increased Russian participation in Syrian President Bashar Al – Assad's war against rebels leaves the world at a loss.

Battle brews in Nth Carolina over Transgender Law and their rights to use public toilets.

June – Gunman opens fire at a Gay Pulse Nightclub in Orlando, Florida killing 49 people and injuring another 53.

Britons vote to quit the European Union as per British Elections in 2015.

July – Eighth terror attack in France in 19 Months.

Oscar Pistorius, light sentence of 6 Years for killing his model girlfriend Reeva Steen kamp.

August – Creepy Clowns start popping up out of the dark woods in Sth. Carolina. Pranks also occur in other states and Australia. Halloween Police issue warnings.

Strong Earthquake hits central Italy, killing at least 159 people and destroying entire towns 26 August (Amatrice – Lazio, and the centre of the food – agricultural area of Gran Sasso e Monti Della Laga national Park.)

Rio Olympics are held (5 – 21 August)

September – Mother Teresa is canonised in a ceremony at the Vatican.

November- Donald Trump winning the US Elections against all odds.

December- Assad backed by Russia and Iran claims victory in Aleppo. Thousands of rebels and civilians have perished in a relentless aerial bombing campaign. Eastern Aleppo almost completely evacuated but a solution to the 6 year Syrian Civil war is still not apparent.

World mourns pop icons – David Bowie 9 January 10, (69), 8 month battle with Liver cancer. Prince April 21, (57), Overdose of Fentanyl. Opioid Addiction Epidemic US, 78 people die everday.

Nancy Reagen (First lady), Gene Wilder, Muhammed Ali, Leonard Cohen, Alan Thicke, Carrie Fisher Dec. 27 (60), George Michael 25th December, 2016 (53).

February 19 (89) in sleep– Harper Lee *To Kill a Mockingbird* author.

Trump hosts Saturday Night Live in 2015 and is spoofed by Alex Baldwin in 2016.

Hulk Hogans successful lawsuit against gawker Media for publishing a sex tape of featuring Hogan in 2012. $ 140 Million verdict.

May 28 – Harambe the Gorilla at Cincinnati Zoo was shot, Western Lowland Gorilla (One day after his 17th Birthday) – Grabbed a young boy who fell into his enclosure.

July 6 – Nintendo releases Pokemon Go game tapping into nostalgia of adult 90's kids.

Harry Potter universe expands Jack Thorne's play Harry Potter and the cursed child.

November – Fantastic Beasts and where to find them.

Beyonce Formation protest song Superbowl Performance April (Lemonade)- 9 Grammy Nominations, Police Brutality against unarmed black citizens July statement.

Brad Pitt and Angelina Jolie Break up September 19 (6 kids).

Kim Kardashian robbed at gunpoint in Paris October, 3 retreated from public life and not updated social media accounts. ($ 10 Million in Jewellery).

Kim Kardashian leaks Taylor Swift's phone call. Kanye West about shout out in Famous. July 18, snippets on snapchat posts.

Taylor Swift rebounds with Tom Hidderstone (June to September) after messy breakup with Calvin Harris.

Leonardo Di caprio wins an Oscar for The Revenant (Best Actor Win).

June 10 – Christina Grimmie (22 year old), Voice contestant murdered in Orlando, shot her following a concert appearance *What a girl is*, brother attacked the assistant who shot himself.

Kiss singer Gene Simmons apologises after calling Prince's Death "pathetic "– 11th may, 2016.

Prince Harry begins dating Meghan Markle (Suits Actress USA).

K – Pop

I received a few short emails from Sabena during late 2015 and January 2016, probably I sent her a Birthday email and a few short emails to see how she was doing. They were one line sentence answers (Not sure if they were written by Eddie) and attached her drawings of a couple of modern fashion human stylized bunnies with stripey tops and shorts, and then later on a manga full body mermaid with her legs amputated at the thighs and drops of blood spilling out the sides, her drawings were becoming increasingly morbid and weird horror bizarre scary monstrosity fantasy creatures in peril.

I hadn't seen Sabena since after her 15th Birthday visit and the October, 2015 visit. I managed to see Sabena again in early January, 2016 School Holidays, whilst Helen was on a weeks leave from her clinic. Helen drove me to Sydenham and we might have gone to La Porchetta Restaurant nearby as most other places were closed on that day.

On this occasion Sabena was ready and up when we arrived there and she answered the door. She appeared marginally improved but still very anxious, shaky in her behaviours and even more agoraphobic so Bronwyn needed to drive her there and be her support on the outside world.

On sighting her Helen peeked at my shocked face and my eyes popping out like Popeye. I said nothing but Helen could see the horror I was feeling, sprung on me to a standstill. Very short cropped male crew cut hair, some bumfluff facial hair, black jeans with a matching hoodie with what seemed flat strapped boobs underneath a white t- shirt. The white sneekers which were thick soled and not happily decorated but still plain white. Essentially she resembled a young K – Pop boy. She explained about having weekly hormone injections, I never asked when this all started to happen the Transgender. At the restaurant she was timid and jittery, she mentioned she wanted to study nursing.

I was bothered by this revelation, as I thought instead of unpacking Sabena they were packing on more stuff without having even scratched the surface of having resolved the complex of anxiety and mental health issues. It was wrong I thought on so many levels. I remember later Dr. Betty Kotler, trying to explain to me that sometimes in desperate cases the ultimate treatment for these previously sexually abused traumatized children is to become Transgender so that they feel safe and protected in the fact that the offender would find them less alluring but grotesque and be not attracted to them at all. In hindsight I can't even begin to image what bizarre triangle of nightmares that Sabena was subjected and going through living with the ugly degenerates Bronwyn and Eddie. I could but speculate that perhaps maybe she thought this was her only way of escape. On closer inspection, she was a puffy oversized K-Pop version boy with thick dark rimmed glasses and what seemed like hundreds and thousands of tiny spotted kaleidoscope of freckles damage dotted around the bridge of her nose and upper cheeks. To think of it she was a mini me of Eddie except for the fact that she was very much more attractive in her facial features than her father, who resembled Saddam Huissen down to the Incredible Hulk bulk face, bulging eyes and saggy heavy droopy bags under his eyes. Ugly as the worst fuck as I described him in my Never, the original beginning of the first introductory autobiographical novel in a proposed sequel trilogy series.

Sabena was very dumb downed and lack lustre as I compared her to a few years ago or to the exuberant happy smiley bright young child that for which there was so much promise. Her soulless eyes and lazy posture, she appeared as if in a dreary flux of bleak that she couldn't snap out of. She was MIA and not making sensible sense during most of the hour or so, we spent together with Bronwyn and Helen, I sat next to Helen on the outer side of the bench with Bronwyn and Sabena being direct on the opposite side of me. The she versus he, her/him, Sabena will always be a she to me as she was born that way as Lady Gaga astoundingly perfectly expresses it. So I tried my best to avoid any of these apart from her name, she hadn't changed her real birth name during these times.

I thought of the quote that she wrote below a drawing of us together as glorified stick body figures with her auburn hair and my charcoal black hair at the beginning of her time with Bronwyn and Eddie, *Mummy your the star twinkling day and night throughout my life.* I brought them heaps of unexpired and lush Christmas food treats and goodies, that Sabena loved Philippa's Mince pies and star biscuits, Pannetone, Traditional Christmas cake and frozen lemon meringue pie dessert, white Christmas, caramel and rocky – road slices and candy canes and a smattering of a few other fares that I placed on their kitchen breakfast bench next to her medicines for which they never even acknowledged. Helen gave out her little token gifts at the end of our lunch to each of us, there were too many clouds in my thoughts that day that I don't remember what we ate, but you might guess. After we ate her chin was in her left hand again, her elbow slipping now and then. Helen and I both asked her some questions about her future. She seemed to brighten up a little chatting about going to college and learning to drive maybe when she was better.

Sabena wasn't anywhere close to being an ambitious, motivated, successful and proficiently capable of the Bangtan Boys BTS. Even Helen said she would have to have significantly have resolved her anxiety and mental health issues before she could even contemplate these and I also agreed. I was disappointed that her mental health issues now seemed to be on the backburner as opposed to her being Transgender excited. She spoke about her friend Amber who was a virtual younger girl from Canada whom she met on the internet and supposedly were having an online love affair relationship. This Amber girl sounded nice enough however to me it was not real but to Sabena it was. I was worried it would all end in tears, that she had no real in person friends and that she would end up broken hearted as nothing might eventuate from it over time anyhow but I never mentioned these to her but pretended not to be bothered by what I either saw or heard that particular day. It was that gift that you don't want that keeps on giving.

Sabena was no longer in possession of a mobile which I thought strangely odd for a young person, they all have mobiles but it was cancelled, she used whatsapp messenger, wechat and stuff like that. I didn't understand those things and I said I used my mobile or email. She no longer liked to speak to me on their conventional landline phone. She had not long ago started doing her drawings again and said she planned to put them up for sale on Red Bubble and things, I said I was happy for her that her interest in design returned but she refused to do a drawing for me on that day as she used to do before. Of course as per usual, my tote of Show Bag items were in tow of coloured paper, texta markers, pencils and my two different digital cameras or take a photo of us on my iphone but she wasn't having any of it and would not engage about these activities she used to like a few years ago. I wasn't offended but thought she is also becoming mature.

Around the bottom of the tote jiggling about were the first few original DVD's of Teen Talk Production duplicated from 2015 and a black T –shirt with the logo, the other TTP gift merch wasn't made yet. I told her about the cause I was inspired to begin because of her and I thought she would be proud of me for the cause I started and dedicated to her but she seemed disinterested, indifferent and apathetic about it but I handed them to her anyway as she might watch them maybe at a later date and understand about TTP. She was more preoccupied however it seemed about somehow surviving and escaping her immediate surrounds and appreciated the virtual world much more as opposed to the real world as it didn't threaten her and she was simply Stayin ' Alive - Bee Gees.

Extract Mother's Submission Joint Select Committee on Australia's Law Reform, 2018.

It is suffice to say that beyond any other reason for Parenting Orders, the child's best interest is paramount as is the overriding imperative need to protect children from Physical and Psychological harm. This statement needs to be refined and more specific in the sense of terms for eg. The child's best future interest right now, today, for the time being, in two years or the child's best future interest for their young independent adult life outcomes in their future. This is a major determinant for complex and difficult cases, where the outcome for the child's future development is severely damaged and affected by a once – off decision which moulds their entire life-long future with an ingrained pattern of dysfunctional aberrant behaviour, ruined and estranged families, life-long mental illness, from youth into adulthood, with a life –time cost of dependency on the social services, welfare systems and their scarce resources.

I'm not here for your entertainment – Pink –U+Ur Hand, 25 Oct 2009, Album – I'm not dead. Released 2006.

The Book Thief – 2013 Michael Petroni screen writer, Director – Brian Percival Producers – Karen Rosenfelt, Ken Blancato, Markus Zusak – Author.

The whole day was awkies, Sabena was apathetic, lost her bit of fierce and fight, basically given up. It was difficult for me to see this drastic deterioration and be helpless to stop or change it. I knew a part of what Sabena was going through having experienced myself her father's wrath of emotional abuse, isolation from my friends and Domination Tyranny. Eddie and Bronwyn were selfish in denial or both and not caring about anything that Sabena wanted at all. I once watched this South African Lady talk about her vanishing son to chronic illness and how she wished he might die and then he miraculously turned the corner around again after much intervention from his mum for many years. 60 minutes, Channel 9.

Helen said to me later on in the car on the drive home that regrettably most all Transgender people young people that she had treated at the clinic, all seemed to be dysfunctional in some way or other and struggled with a lot of day to day issues too.

At least Sabena might be able to get some wee bit of joy from the comfort food I brought, if she snuck in before Eddie hoed into the small packet of Haigh's Chocolates and the Baker's Delight packet of goodies, he was such a sweet tooth, Oh but now these years he was Diabetic, still nervously chain smoking and seeing a podiatrist regularly for his wonky feet.? Divine Intervention and Retribution.

I probably sent a short sentence email to Sabena to ask her how she was fairing after our visit and I received a short sentence saying she would be attending Brunswick Community College for a day or two per week in the upcoming school term. Bronwyn of course would be driving her there and back on the days she attended. It was a government –run, alternative school purposefully for young people with various issues. (Maybe written by Eddie).

Extracts of Mother's Correspondence to Attorney – General's Department, Canberra dated 2nd October, 2014.

Something needs to be altered as family units become more and more dysfunctional, parents becoming fugitives, children in danger, children and young adults self- harming, mentally ill, sedated, perpetually on welfare and unemployed, people committing crimes, entire families on welfare due to mental illness and addictions because their lives are so traumatized.

Yes, it is a complex dynamic of physical, sexual and emotional abuse, a potent cocktail of a series of consequentially unfortunate events.

Now, my daughter is 15 years of age, being with her father for the past 6 year, she never coped well with the heart wrenching trauma of leaving her loving home of her mum and her grandma years ago. After many years of struggling, she was admitted to hospital in November, 2013 suffering severe anxiety/ depression, self- harm and suicidal tendencies.

There is a non-attendance record at her school for almost two years. This is concerning for a non viable future of an unemployed, mentally ill and homeless person. Worse than that the therapy she is on is causing adverse effects to her physical health and yet because of the severity and harshness of the orders to which to all concerned were incredulous to at the time, I have no input with her care.

Precedent case: Pseudonym – Licha and Wunschen, 2008. I have thought about it a lot over the years and felt I was made a scapegoat for an overwhelmed Family Court System at the time. "I was in the wrong place for too long, at the wrong time".

My current concern is who takes ultimate responsibility for the healthcare, well – being and education of this young adult, and the potential consequences and ensuing detriment to her in years to come, particularly not being able to speak out, especially if she is suffering fear and intimidation, She is a helpless, vulnerable young adult with no voice.

Outcome: It was already organized.

Extract Order 11/ 2/ 2016 Amended 19/2/ 2016.

Amended pursuant to rule 16.05(2)(e) of the Federal Circuit Court Rules 2001.

Upon application made to the court.

The Court Orders that:

1. *All previous parenting orders be and are hereby discharged.*
2. *The Father have sole parental responsibility for the child SABENA WARSCHAUER- LAZAR born 28August 1999 ("Sabena ")*
3. *Sabena live with the Father.*
4. *The mother be and hereby restrained from contacting and/ or communicating with Sabena unless the mother has received an express invitation in writing from Sabena to do so.*
5. *The Mother be and is hereby restrained from contacting Sabena's medical practitioners (including but not limited to the Royal Children's Hospital).*
6. *The Mother be and is hereby restrained from obtaining or attempting to obtain medical information from Sabena's medical or health practitioners (Including and not limited to the Royal Children's Hospital).*
7. *Liberty is granted to the Father and the Independent Children's Lawyer to provide a copy of these orders and reasons to Sabena's treating health practitioners, medical institutions and hospitals treating Sabena (Including their legal advisors) and Sabena's school.*
8. *The appointment of the Independent Children's Lawyer is hereby discharged.*
9. *Pursuant to sections 65DA (2) and 62B of the Family Law Act 1975, the particulars of the obligations these orders create and the particulars of the consequences that may follow if a person contravenes these orders are set out in the Fact Sheet attached hereto and these particulars are included in the orders.*

10. *All extant applications are dismissed and the matter removed from the list of pending cases maintained by the court.*

By the Court

JUDGE STEWART

19 February 2016.

As a result, please find enclosed a newly engrossed order.

As a result, please find a newly engrossed order, noting that amendments have been made to:

order 2 – removing FRANCESCA from the child's name; and.

(a) *inserting order 1 – which was inadvertently not included in the previous orders.*
(b) *Please destroy the copy previously provided to you.*

Regards,

Chambers of Judge Stewart.

Francesca was named after her Godmother, Franca who I went to Genazzano with in primary school, she was a graduated Geologist from Melbourne Uni, now working for her brothers Internet Company and married to a Corporate Lawyer, Andrew then having moved shortly after to Sydney after Sabena and I attended their wedding at St. Patrick's Cathedral, East Melbourne, and it was Sabena's middle name, it was also reminiscent to me of the year I spent studying in San Francisco, California at the CCPM in 1997. SF was a good omen to me of Sabena Francesca!.

I was treating another patient's husband, introduced by his partner Lizz who was also a patient and friend, he was also kind and delivered later in December, 2016 to the Teen Talk Bowling Party at the Healthways Recreation Centre, the tiered huge Christmas cake that Lizz donated to us for the raffle prize that she made at home whilst she was doing further study and apprenticeship work as a pastry chef. After I received the orders, I said I was shocked by the outcome, at his appointment he advised to me that it was always "STATUS QUO "in cases like these to leave the circumstances being the same, and that it was predetermined. I wasn't annoyed because I thought without shit stirrers nothing would ever change or improve and nobody else cares.

Peace is expensive but I can buy it for you – The Equalizer, 2014 Denzel Washington.

A lot of ugly fuckin' shit was going down.

I thought about Duncan and what he said that it was easier to maintain the Status Quo than try to fix Sabena. He was trying to be kind and give me some solace that I could do nothing. Norma basically said the same thing her staunch view was the Law was an Ass, especially in my view these outdated draconian Family Law Rules from donkey's ages ago that failed.

Dr Betty Kotler previously said to me in my intermittent ongoing grief counselling sessions the previous year, as I explained how I was all over it exhausted trying to keep contact with Sabena as a mother's obligation but found it increasingly difficult due to Eddie and Bronwyn disruption and Sabena's current deteriorated hazy fog state for which I became more anxious and distressed after seeing her and that she made no sense at all, a total blur. Dr. Kotler suggested I should intermittently either try to keep in contact with her to give her support which she was now negative about or have a total break. Abandon all contact for a while to see if she might reach out and contact me, as she might be feeling pressured, backing –off due to her current breakdown and If I was finding the situation also too difficult and confronting for me and my own peace of mind. I said I would think about it.

As it was I was almost relieved that the situation was now taken out of my choice with the orders but the order that bothered me the most was number 4. Sabena was to write me a letter if she expressly wanted to see me. Write a letter, Sabena wasn't capable of even grasping a writing implement with her DT's and keeping it straight up between her fingers in that tragic fragile ongoing state let alone write a letter, I thought that's simply preposterous. Obviously the Judge assumed I was exaggerating and hysterical and she wasn't at all comprehending, the gravity and drastic severity of Sabena's current condition as Eddie and the expert witnesses from the RCHM played it down.

There was no contact with Sabena for 19 months or one year and seven months after the orders of the 19/2/ 2016.

Ever hopeful, I thought maybe it was for the best and perhaps she would be somewhat more recovered and more mature by the time she was 18 years old.

Deja Vu

I hoped that this Judge would have been a bit more reserved in her judgement of determination against me, instead of making a far worse deliberation than Judge Brown.

Grace Tame – Australian of the Year 2021 (Abuse Victim)

Dylan Alcott – Australian of the Year 2022 (Disability Advocate)

Maybe time will change me but I can't change time!

Just chuck a fat fuckin' Freddie – That is do absolutely positively nothing or as little as possible.

Stupidity is a renewable resource.

Quills – 2001 Author Doug Wright, Geoffrey Rush as Marquis De Sade; Kate Winslet; Joaquin Phoenix; Michael Caine. Director – Philip Kaufman.

Hunter Hunter – Horror 2020 – Director – Shawn Linden. (Skin the Deer and Bare trappers murder film).

Clay Pigeons – Thriller 1998 – Director – David Dobkin, Producers – Ridley Scott; Tony Scott; Chris Zarpas with actors Joaquin Phoenix; Vince Vaughn; Janeane Garofalo; Georgina Cates; Scott Wilson.

Circus Freak Show!

I remember the previous Family Court Lawyers, 2007 saying to me that the most favourable outcome was that all parties involved were miserable, was that Including Sabena too!

Sunshine – 1973 Drama (song Sunshine – John Denver) True Story based on the Journals of a young wife and mother diagnosed with terminal cancer. It was the most watched Television film in history and its emotional impact still resonates to this day.

Someday We'll All Be Free – Aretha Franklin, 1992 (Malcolm X).

2018 – Parkland School Shooting US and Sandy Hooks 2022.

It was kinda like a scary vampire movie with my heart being torn out vibrating and beating.

The Human Condition – as they called it from Medieval times (Melancholy) you might say that doesn't go away it persists with you every single day at the very depth of your heart pulling strings of grief and threads of twitches of pain so light yet so piercing to the soul. Melancholy with you everyday, and Never, Never, Never, Never ever goes away.

After that terrible tragic day that Sabena was stolen from me, I always began to think of things in terms of BC/AD like BS and AS, as if a great divide between happiness and tortuous pain.

It's the principal of the thing...! (F. F. Warschauer Senior my Dad).

After all these years I took it as personal offence to myself and everything I tried to do without succeeding in rescuing Sabena and try to turn her life around, after having it repeat over and over and over again in my thoughts. I now wonder looking at a different perspective whether the mini stroke/ viral paralysis on the side of Sabena's face may have obliterated and or fragmented all the precious memories of her time spent with my Mum, me and Freddie that maybe she wasn't any longer remembering me or anything that happened prior to the incident. Perhaps she was from then incapable of giving or showing her care and love emotions for me similar to a non- reciprocating autistic person. Nonetheless it still broke my heart every day since. However it still does not change the circumstance of my perpetual grief and reflection ongoing for the rest of my life and loss about what might have been.

Always look on the bright side of life – Monty Python's Life Of Brian, 2006.

Life's a piece of shit, when you look at it.

Run to Paradise – The Choirboys, 1988 Album – Big Bad Noise.

Maybe I should have cut my losses and said *Just kill her now please!* But unfortunately I actually cared. It would have saved me a lot of anguish, grief and effort but maybe not guilt. It was an abortion of a court system and these were spontaneous angry and frustrated racing thoughts, perhaps I was rather the blithering idiot not Eddie, whose imagined altruism would win above all, a wasted potential young person's future happy and successful life. So are the pure forces for good or evil? The natural order of things – why we cannot due to the earth's force field change them? How inhumanity continually fuck's up our world? I think it is God or whatever supreme being you believe in that the entire world is very sick, humanitarianly, emotionally, scrupulously – if we don't stop the shit we will kill ourselves! Negligible stuff like Critical Race Theory and what sexually you should be are individual and private for every person in the world. It's a choice! CRT – I just try to do my job and treat everybody the same. What a facocte world it's no wonder, we have climate change catastrophes, Ukraine vs Russia war and ongoing Covid and other upcoming viral pandemics. *Consequential friend knowledge, Emotional Integrity – Dr. Phil.* Buzz words!

Whiter Shade of Pale – 1967 Album –Procol Harum

You're as cold as Ice – 1977 – Foreigner

Where do you go to my lovely? 1969 – Peter Sarsted

Angel of the Morning – 1981- Juice Newton

Build me up Buttercup – 1968 – The Foundations

No One – 2018 – Jess Glynne Album – Always In Between

Don't Need Nobody – 2015 - Ellie Goulding

Drive (2011) Action/ Crime with Ryan Gosling. Director – Nicholas Winding Refn (A Real Hero)

Life Support (2007) Drama – with Queen Latifah – Director – Nelson George.

Because of You – 2004 – Kelly Clarkson Album – Breakaway

Yes, my darling Chris my first Uni boyfriend, a good Ol' country boy, he came to visit after Mum's passing, unfortunately I was not home at that time and Freddie kept his message

Life goes on!

Why am I so fucking cold? – Zusk

Smith and Nephew

From Kill Bill to Whispering Jack! From killing people to helping people.

I was walking up to the annual Wound Management seminar that was held at Milano's Brighton Beach Hotel in the elegant Conference/ Dining Room passed the Morning Melodies sandwich board ads, It might have been Emma Hirstle and Belinda Shone reps that were running the show for Smith and Nephew that day, and I sat near the large bay windows out at the colourful rainbow windsurfers that glided seamlessly back and forth across the bay with the strong winds blowing off some one's hat as they walked their dog along the front foreshore.

I scanned the file of papers that were usually familiar each year and found the glossy page, Acticoat Flex – Two Week Challenge. Immediately John Came to mind, a patient who was suffering with recurrent toe breakdown Chilblains from the cold, whose condition Peripheral Vascular Disease prevented him from healing completely or the ulcers being so fragile that the skin integrity was undermined that they were susceptible and vulnerable to re emerging.

I almost forgot about the study submitted quite some long time ago until John reminded me and said was your project ever published. So I emailed S & N enquiring about it. Nina Fan returned to me and said here it is and asked me permission for it to be published globally.

Extracts from Case Study (Published 2nd May, 2019) Smith and Nephew.

Acticoat Flex Case Study: Healing of Toe Wounds without Antibiotics.

Introduction

Prevention of recurrent infection among people who have foot wounds has the potential to improve healing, reduce the use of antibiotics, and avoid other consequences such as amputation.

He had Hypertension, Hypercholesterolemia and was an ex- smoker.

Postscript

The patient is now 84 years age. His ulcers are totally healed from being stimulated via the Acticoat – Flex, and with ongoing conservative routine management they have been solved for seven months to date, with no reoccurrence or relapse although the skin integrity is not as robust as prior to the chilling incident. His consultations are regular four weekly, to maintain, manage, treat, monitor and prevent other breakdowns.

So I successfully cured John of his plagued curse, after I asked his permission to embark on the project and to include his foot photos. He willingly participated without much coaxing and we started it on the 01. 09. 2016, John being 82 years during this time. Acticoat – Flex materials were supplied by Smith and Nephew gratis, as cost is also prohibitive unless undertaken in a subsidised hospital setting and Emma visited the clinic to give me a few tips.

Gone with the Wind

It was also during these years that the property developers were also closing their ranks on both sides in and around Mum's house and my rear home clinic. Demolition of the stately houses commenced on both the right and far left or north and Far south from the East street aspect and constructions of the multi – dwelling apartments. The Heathcote's previously lived on the left, he was a corporate lawyer and his second or third wife, his previous personal affairs receptionist, who played tennis and drove a flashy tractor, whom later on became ill with Cancer and wore headscarves with her Tennis outfit. They sold up and moved on and then the Wettenhall Estate, well established money also went up for sale with the house, Tennis Court and expansive lush fountain gardens. It was the rise of the big ugly machines taking over.

Ticky Tacky little boxes and they all look just the same.

So they paved paradise, put up a parking lot – 1970, Big Yellow Taxi – Joni Mitchell Album – Ladies of the Canyon.

Ship to Wreck - 2015 – Florence and the Machine.

Both of these were finished being built a year before the Covid Pandemic hit, but not before there were several non – zoom council and VCAT hearings and zoom pre/post covid scenarios. Both constructions went ahead with conditions on their permits and after negotiations with surrounding neighbours. The house on the close left was not yet sold to developers because John Wall was still alive until he passed in 2017, with Pam Straw his niece gaining the inheritance. It was a fabulously flashy English afternoon tea wake at St. John's Church.

I defended the house from the left impending development to rescue it with much vigour, both being self- represented and with Town Planners such as Clement – Stone, with Anthony Scarpacci and Bill Kusznirczuk his wing man to try to alter the developers covid death star wish plans of having the multi- dwelling apartments lobby and entrance on the side walkway of this house in front of my dining, galley, kitchen and office clinic windows. Worst design ever! Why wasn't the entrance facing in the front at the main road like the others, it was absolute greed to fit in extra apartments from what I came to understand much later on. The battle went on for years and then finally trialling many unsuccessful mediations with Property Lawyers and then eventually in and out of the Supreme Court before the case even ever began. The developers lodged amended plans to council and with this enabled objection, I managed with the help of Anthony to get the plans conditional for an enclosed walkway type but not love tunnel alteration and amendment condition on the permit. It wasn't what I hoped but at least there would be a barrier and a win of sorts. Before the next council meeting. I wrote an email to Councillor Matthew Koce and a few others, Matthew who personally recommended and instigated the particular condition of the side barrier construction on the permit.

It was a Ground Hog Day of the right, far left and then left developments, ultimately I must have either wore them down or they went into bankruptcy liquidation for not being commenced construction from 2018. The left, John Wall's house is still standing July, 2022.

The other developments however also created some devastating havoc to Mum's house. The right development was the first to commence construction and was being demolished, this day I went out in the afternoon to return and find the original handmade brickwork of the front driveway from the front gate to the front door fence torn down which was in reasonably good condition but the rotted rear paling broken down fence still intact at the rear aspect of the driveway. I was horrified and asked them to replace it as is, but instead ended up with a doubly abhorrent fence of paling on my side and cheap Bessa brick on their side. The deep excavations and tumultuous drilling in of the ginormous girthed pylons caused cracks, damages and destruction to this house. The midline of the house split down at the terrace driveway balcony.

Take another little piece of my heart – 1968 – Dusty Springfield – Album Dusty... Definately.

Janis Joplin, 2009.

There was the post mortem aftermath of the three legged race, similar to the bizarre Bermuda Triangle of Eddie, Bronwyn and me.

- Twisted Front Wrought Iron Gates
- Crooked Submerged Sunken Front Fence Columns
- Splitting Anchors of the side run down Paling Fences
- Uneven concrete upheaval around the rear garden and pool
- Seeping cracked and leaking pool pump
- Gutters and downpipes falling off
- Cracked, broken and fragmented roof tiles
- Electrical Power disruptions and interference
- Plumbing displacements and aberrations
- Cracks around windows and doors inside
- Cracks in walls and ceilings with water damage
- The Swinging antique heavy chunky game of Thrones Galley Door fallen off its hinges in a heap and
- The piece de resistance the 12 seater dining table now slopping and legs broken off.

I could feel sadly in my soul, the house crying and slowly dying. I'm not, *Queen of Friggin" Everything,* as was the message on a birthday card, I once saw around the house somewhere nor of the Universe, but simply my domain as Queen of Kooralbyn. So I then and there appointed myself keeper, protector and defender of my realm.

Nero fiddles whilst Rome burns.

I thought I'd break in the shoes but the shoes broke me – Former Patient.

Veni, Vedi, Vici – Julius Caesar. I came, I saw, I conquered.

Empathy and Mindfulness – Deborah (Patient)

Natalie and Bernie and their precious cats (Patients)

STA DURA – Be Strong! (Mum) IMW

Claire – the casual well mannered, old school receptionist that wore the long coat jackets and spoke on the phone saying Please be kind enough to... and knew how to divert the phone to mobile and was in the St. John's Church choir. (whilst Mum was alive).

It was my mother's dream to have Kooralbyn be an exotic Italian Villa mini mansion, of course it was her dream but I embraced it with her passion everyday as she also taught me about antiques, her decorative Mediterranean garden design with trial and error gardening tips.

Jumbled snippets of Jibber Jabber, flashbacks, hijinx and shenanigans.

The hazy brain fog creeping in, I saw the Roman inspired cement garden statues in the back four corners of the garden, of the Four Seasons scantily clothed nymphs Spring, Summer, Autumn and Winter, the cement Roman bench seat beside with anchor shaped footings and the Greek Key lock design cement garden pots strewn about the rear yard.

John's House name was called Coomaroo (an Acacia, the Wattles) on a brass plaque with later John adding above his upstairs front door a tiled ceramic WALL. This house was called Kooralbyn – Home of the (Kooralbyn) Valley of the Copperhead Snake, and I might have reached out to the Malvern Historical Society about other bits and pieces of information.

Fawlty Towers – 1975 Basil to Polly and Manuel- Don't mention the War! (German Guests).

Escape to the Chateau – 2016- DIY Reality – Lt. Col. Dick Strawbridge and his partner Angel Adoree.

You'd like to Restore the house to its former glory (Freddie, my brother November, 2019).

The rare Rosewood Burl American Antique Regency Dining Table with the three pronged two pedestal legs and the larger central with four pedestal legs that Mum and I chose together, as I drove her to Ainger's in Richmond because of Mum's driving phobia after she ploughed into a street pole learning to drive whilst she was heavily pregnant with my younger brother, Freddie. She also never learnt how to swim living in San Zenone Degli Ezzelini, a small rural village near Venice, Italy. We would help her get onto the floating lylow plastic blow up lounge and pull her around the pool.

Thank-you to Jamie Allpress from Allpress Antiques, Malvern for restoring it, during the early Covid years. Also a shout out to all the amazing tradesmen who helped me repair bits and pieces of the house before and during the Covid Lockdown years in Melbourne.

Edward Wilkins from the Council Planning Department whose concerns and recommendations for the left (Wall) Development were similar to those of our views, Clement – Stone and I, and we were aligned in agreement as to the changes in plans required for the development to proceed.

Cr. Matthew Koce, also whom I emailed all the councillors involved personally regarding my objection pleas and who listened and was kind enough to consider the amended change to the plans of the inclusion of the enclosed barrier tunnel at the section of this house's habitable windows and brought it up as a priority at the council meeting.

Tanya, my accountant whom I met coincidentally at the VCAT Building, in King St. a year before covid hit Melbourne, who was there to defend her home against an inappropriate development of a huge kindergarten complex opposite her Brighton House residence.

The paintings and many pictures of Venice, in almost every room of Mum's house. The lagoon canal in Venice where Giacomo Casanova (1725- 1798) Lived, who was The Art of Seduction chronicler. Casanova was known as the womaniser from the

19th Century. The Venice canals near the Sestiere of San Polo Casanova apartment, close to the Ponte De Rialto, the bridge home of thousands of tiny love lockets of people all around the world.

Antonio Canova (1757- 1822), The Pinnacle of Neoclassical Sculpture from Possagno in the Republic of Venice, was the greatest sculpture of the Neoclassical age. Indeed his highly sensual statue of of Venus Victrix in Rome's Borghese Gallery was actually modelled on Napoleon's sister Pauline. From an early age he showed prodigious skill in carving statues in the style of Ancient Greeks and Romans using Carrera Marble that had also been favoured by Renaissance greats such as Michelangelo. The most renowned artist in Europe of his age he worked for Popes, Prince's and even Napoleon Bonaparte.

The Museo Canova, Possagno (Established 1833), that Silvia (Feragosto, 2013) who lived in one of the side detached wings of the Villa Beltramini of my Mum's Auntie's house (Zia Romilda – Village Midwife) center wing of the Villa, who was my bouncing with enthusiasm my tour guide and friend introduced me to which was also in the province of Treviso close to my Mum's Village in San Zenone Degli Ezzelini, where they previously owned the complete aristocratic family Villa Beltramini and Via Beltramini of almost the entire tiny village main street before it was sold off into sections due to my great, great grandfather having sired 13 children and who was regrettably a hopelessly addicted gambling womaniser who sent his family bankrupt and the Villa was divided.

Tradie Nostalgia

Closer to home there was The Lindentree years (70's to 90's) when my parents were doing simultaneous repairs and renovations at this house and also their Restaurant Bar. They were absolute amazing characters, tradesmen, friends and also regular patrons of the Tree. Petite, sprightly, wiry Mitchell (His last name), the Sparky who's hair was like John (The Rat) Platten's hair of Hawthorn who retired in 1997. He was always alternative and reeked of Mary- Jane and was also very funny, I think the family used him because he was available and fast, he often joked that he shocked himself a few times into a Yahoo Serious. China Joe the Plumber, who was actually Czech but whose squinty eyes also made him look like a mini – Sumo wrestler, he could drink every other patron under the table, they also took bets on it. He was always very jolly like Santa and he often found kitchen and bathroom accessory appliances fallen strangely off the back of trucks. His wife Carol was Australian and a nurse, who rang the Lindentree to find him in concern, when he hadn't come home for several days from a binge and Joe spoke of her as being a passionate, caring, humanitarian, emotional and compulsive shopaholic and that he would probably never be able to retire as a Plumber to keep up with her. Tall German Heinz who was a lanky, giant Frankenstein Munster, who was a decorative concreter of sorts. Also a prolific aggressive boozer who was divorced a few times now single. Unfortunately he failed to take pride in his work and was lazy, turned up at all hours, taking short cuts in his work and making frequent mistakes. My dad confronted him one day about his behaviour, tardiness and workmanship as my

Father was an accurate German. The pebble mix addition around the pool was not even close to the original colour and that the Balustrades around the rear terrace patio were cracked, he took terrible offence at my Father's real scrupulous complaints and left without saying a word, leaving all his cement, sprinkled with yellow sand on the interior of the ornamental Balustrade mouldings and vanishing without return, never to be seen again. Tall Helmut, the BFG with the fine white blonde hair, smallish head to body ratio and a face of cute toddler whose hands were sadly scarred by a previous work accident, who carved the Wooden The Lindentree Plaque, pride of place at the top small bar, who also painted the Edelweiss and native German Flowers on to Mateus Rose and Liebrauwein Gothic Tower Bottles, he also might have had a crush on me, he was charming, sweet and polite as he grew up in a rural part of the German country side maybe Black Forest. He photographed me at work and then he bought a gold coloured ornate locket and placed a mini portrait of my face, head and chest like a bust statue inside it keepsake, before he was destined to wanting to return to Germany as he was so village homesick.

How my father always laughed about the English Spotted Dick Dessert that was presented to him whilst he lived in England studying. His parents trying to keep him safe during the Nazi war years and then he ended up being deported on the Dunera ship to Melbourne, Australia and later a film called The Dunera Boys was made (1985 – War/ Drama, Dad said he recognized all the main characters and people in the film and knew them personally also (Max Bruck – Goldsmith Jeweller/ Actor). My dad wasn't much a fan of Bread and Butter pudding, imagine making second hand dessert from stale bread.

The quote he always said when he felt frustrated, overwhelmed and surrounded by incompetents and idiots *in the room full of blind people the one-eyed man is the King. If you can't stand it – sit down, the Circus, why did the two – storey brothel go broke – too much fucking overhead and Don Coglioni, Semenolo from his fascination with The Godfather Trilogies, Vatican Movies and Lynda La Plante's books, The Legacy 1987, Prime Suspect (Tennison), 1973 and Bella Mafia 1990.*

Glamorous – Fergie featuring Ludacris, 2007 (Oh, the flossy, flossy).

2017

6th January, 2017 – Fed. Gov. Stops import of Green Prawns due to white spot disease.

9th January - One Nation leader Pauline Hanson disendorses, Bundambra Candidate Shan Julin, after her anti- gay social media post.

15th January – Severe storms lash South East QLd. Leaving 1,500 people without power. Chandler in Brisbane records 102 mm rain in 30 minutes. Some suburbs of Brisbane and Ipswich are flooded.

18 January – Multiple blazes burn out of control across parts of NSW and particularly Hunter Valley.

WA premier Colin Barnett rules out any attempt to ban Muslims from wearing Burkas but says he would prefer that type of clothing was not worn in Australia.

20 January – Five people killed and 30 injured, when a man drives a car into pedestrians on Bourke Street, in Melbourne City Centre.

22 January – Vic. Premier Daniel Andrews considers changes to bail laws, after Bourke St. incident Night Court for Magistrate's to hear bail requests from violent suspects after hours.

23 January - 28 year old actor is shot and killed in Brisbane during the filming of a music video for the band Bliss n Eso.

Dimitrious Gargasoulis is charged with 5 counts of murder over Bourke St. attack.

25 January – 15 Detainees escape from Malmsbury Youth Justice Centre in Victoria. Eventually all recaptured by police.

27 January – Supreme Court of Qld sentences a father to 9 years imprisonment for severe injuries inflicted on a one month old girl.

29 January- Year one students will undergo compulsory testing under Fed. Gov plan.

30 January- Susan Kiefel is sworn in as the 13th Chief Justice of Australia.

1st February, 2017- Malcolm Turnbull to keep down electricity prices admits he donat $ 1.75 Million to the Liberal Party.

8 February – PM Malcolm Turnbull calls Bill Shorten a simpering sycophant association with the late packaging Billionaire Richard Pratt (Drank French Champagne whilst selling out workers)

10-12 February- Heat Wave in SE Australia, record breaking temps and extensive power loss. 26 Blazes across NSW (Central West and Mid North Coast). Heavy rain south west of WA widespread flooding. Perth (2nd wettest day in history), 6mm short of of record set in 1992.

16 February – Police find Olympic Gold Medallist Grant Hackett in a disturbed state of mind less than 12 hours after he was reported missing on the Gold Coast.

21 February – Vic. Premier Daniel Andrews rejects state coroner push for safe injecting room.

28 February- 42 Year old man arrested in Young after trying to help the Islamic state develop laser missile detection equipment as well as their own missile arsenal.

14th March, 2017 – SA gov. Announces $ 550 Million plant of Australia's largest Grid Connected Battery. (Result of state wide blackout in Sept. 2016)

28 March – Severe Tropical Cyclone Debbie between Airlie Beach and Bowen Nth. Qld, Power outages affect 140, 000 properties across Qld.

29 March- Hazelwood power station in Victoria's la Trobe Valley taken offline after commencing operation in 1964.

(My Birthday! Congratulations 56 years)

30 March- Flash flooding as a result of Cyclone Debbie Sth. Qld and Nth. Qld. 23, 000 people ordered to evacuate.

1st – 3rd April, 2017- Ongoing floods Nth. NSW, Tweed Heads etc. 9 people dead including 3 children.

18 April- PM Malcolm Turnbull scraps 457 Visa Program. Australians should come before overseas workers.

3rd May, 2017 – Staff at Sydney Morning Herald, The Age and Australian Financial Review newspapers begin a 7 day strike after Fairfax Media announces it will cut 125 editorial jobs.

4 May- Malcolm Turnbull meets with Donald Trump in NYC. First face to face meeting since infamous phone call in February.

7 May – Celebrity Chef George Colombaris is charged with common assault after attacking a 19 year old during A – League Grand Final.

19 May- Artefacts inside a Barrow Island cave. Provide archaeologists with earliest known evidence of Aboriginal occupation dating back more than 50, 000 years ago.

28 May- 12 years after drug charges in Bali. Schapelle Corby arrives back in Australia amid a media circus.

3rd June, 2017 – Terrorist attack London. 2 Australian women 9 From Qld and SA killed and 4 among 48 injured.

14 June – Ten Network Holdings goes into voluntary liquidation after failing to obtain loan guarantee from its shareholders.

15 June – Australian actress Rebel Wilson wins a high profile defamation case against Bauer Media painted her as a liar. Trial gained worldwide media attention.

19 June- Australian Defence Force temporarily suspends air combat missions over Syria, after Russia threatened to treat any plane from US led coalition as a potential target.

29 June – Victoria Police announces that Cardinal George Pell charged with multiple counts of historical sexual assault offences.

7th July, 2017 – Tesla announces deal with French energy company Neonen to build the world's largest Lithium Ion Battery to store renewable energy in SA.

14 July – Woolworths and Coles announce nation wide phase out of single – use plastic bags by July 2018.

15 July – US Police officer murders Australian woman Justine Damond near her home in Mineapolis, Minesota after she called 911 to report a nearby assault. Reason for shooting unclear, prompting protests in the city.

30 July – Four men in Sydney suburbs arrested by Australian Police for planning an Islamic inspired terrorist attack on a plane. Delays at Sydney International Airport among others and increased security.

1st August, 2017 – Universities Australia Report. 51 % of University students were sexually harassed on at least one occasion in 2016.

25 August – A record number of Australians are enrolled on the AEC roll (Approx. 95.3 %) after enrolments close for Australian Marriage Law postal survey. Also revealed 90,000 new votes enrolled for the survey.

World Events 2017

February – Beyonce's Glorious baby bump twins post.

March – 3 people killed and 40 injured attacker rammed into pedestrians on London's Westminster Bridge.

An Islamic terrorist attack outside the Palace of Westminster in London, kills 5 and injures 507.

UK Brexit Negotiation to leave Europe.

Ninetendo Switch is released.

13 reasons on Netflix, sparked fears about how suicide depicted the meme, Welcome to your tape. Hannah high school girl (2007), commits suicide and leaves a series of tapes explaining the lead up to her death.

Handmaids' Tale adaptation on Hulu – Elizabeth Moss as Offred. (Wins 5 Emmy's) including best drama. Women wore the red robes and white bonnets to court rooms and eventually the US Capitol as a way to protest bills seen as restricting women's rights – Wake up call for women.

May – Children were among 22 killed in a suicide bombing after an Ariana Grande concert at Britain's Manchester area. Two weeks later attack on London Bridge.

Eurovision Song Contest Kyiv, Ukraine. Portugese entrant Salvador Sobral – Amar Pelos Dois.

Ransomeware Wannacry Cyber attack (150 World countries)

June – WHO – Yemen 200, 000 cases of Cholera

USA Today – Ariana Grande performed at the One Love Manchester benefit concert after a bombing at a concert in May killed 22 people and injuring 100. (with Miley Cyrus and Justin Beiber)

The melconic rise and fall of Harvey Weinstein, me too movement. Kevin Spacey, Matt Lauer and Louis C.K. were also fired from movies and TV.

Jay – Z his adultery on June's Hyperpersonal album 4:44.

Anna Farris and Chris Pratt married since 2009 announce separation in August.

August – Solar Total Eclipse seen at top of the rock observatory at Rockerfellar Centre, not seen since 1918.

Deaths – Sir. John Hurt, Mary Tyler – Moore, Dick Bruna, Bill Paxton, Chuck Berry, David Rockefeller, Don Rickles, Erin Moran, Roger Moore, Laura Biagoti, Adam West, Elsa Martinelli, Martin Landau, John Heard, Glen Campbell, Jerry Lewis.

Sabena's 18th Birthday on the 28.08. 2017.

Extracts from Mother's Submission for the JSCFLR (18- 19 September, 2019)

Mother contacts daughter for her 18th Birthday, orders are expired as child is adult, via email to see how she is fairing and to see if her thinking is more mature. Also to help her retrieve her ASG Education Fund Scholaship roll – over for further higher education use, but she refuses. Daughter returns email and says she does not want any contact with the mother or to access the ASG Fund monies for education.

Mother makes some application for some input of Guardianship for her future at VCAT, but is dismissed as daughter's adult consent is refuted to access medical and educational information.

Email contact from the mother from 28.08.2017, the Godmother and mother's friends are also rejected on her birthday.

Mother and Daughter have been estranged for 5 year. It is not even about that it is about my severe concern for her lack of future independence, poor functionality, chronic mental illness and long-term terminal unemployment and dependence. On the welfare system / or future homelessness among many other young adults of this generation in our society. I have now reconciled myself that I will probably never see my daughter again and perhaps not even before my last dying breath.

End of Submission.

It was the final nail in the coffin, everything happens for a reason (No stupid reason), thwarted again but then nobody cares. In hindsight Sabena may not have even answered the email I sent her for her birthday, wishing her a happy birthday and inquiring about her progress at the Brunswick Community School, her VCE results and that she would have to apply for herself on the ASG website to obtain the $ 3000- Education Resources Grant for either embarking or deferred for up to two years, part-time or full – time higher education study. I suspect Eddie was running the show, backed up by Bronwyn and Sabena with no say in it at all. I assume and sensed that she hadn't been doing particularly well these previous years or I'm certain Eddie would have shouted it from the rooftops. Was she still attending the BCS part- time, what about her physical and mental health, was she going to complete her VCE, what was her VCE result, was she learning driving, would she be doing further study, what career was she wanting to do further study for, was she still lost to the internet world of virtual friends, were there any real friends or school friends, was she still suffering agoraphobia and severe anxiety/chronic depression, would she see herself having a future job and career, would she still be living with Eddie? All very pertinent questions, which required answering. Since the orders were now expired I decided to make my own further investigations of the Sabena circumstance, I contacted the Principal of BCS, Ralph Gottlieb and he said unfortunately, he could make no comment about Sabena's health or educational progress for various unknown reasons. I asked my BF Norma about what she thought of it all.

She said she was refused information about her birth mother and contacted FOI – Freedom of Information Officer that helped her to find out stuff.

So I enquired at the FOI and spoke to an officer, he was a pleasant enough sounding sensible young man and he would assess my eligibility by asking questions about the circumstances for requiring information. He explained to me that because Sabena was 18 years of age and deemed to be an adult in her own right, whether she was residing with me or not that she could continue to refuse me access to documents. He said he sympathized with my concerns for Sabena's health, well- being and education plight but that even young adults are responsible for their own bad decisions and wrong choices and have to suffer with the consequences of their actions whether they were right or wrong, for example if Sabena chose to be criminal, unemployed, mentally ill, drug addicted and homeless, even if they were bad pathways, it was her freedom of rights as an adult to make her own mistakes and regrettable decisions and choices. I also contacted the IMHA (Independent Mental Health Advocacy), it was a vicious circle of responses that went round and round, like trying to get off a Ferris wheel before the ride was up. I tried to go to VCAT to get Guardianship to have some input into her future health and education and yet the irony was that because I couldn't get access to provide these basic documents that application could not be brought forward being dismissed. It was concerning to me that it wasn't actually what Sabena wanted but it was her father's coaching. I can't say I knew anything about her emotional state during this time, maybe threatened or fearful.

I received correspondence from the ASG (Australian Scholarships Group Friendly Society Limited Fund), which I enrolled Sabena in at 12 months of age, after much argument and disagreement with Eddie but It was my hard earned money, I thought it was a helpful idea at this time, so I did it anyway. Sabena was eligible to apply for her Education Resources Benefit, money that she could use at her discretion for whatever she needed or wanted, but she would have to be enrolled in a course of either part-time or full – time study to be granted the monies, they also needed to provide her health and education documents. They wrote to me because most young people reside with their parents and because the fund was applied for in my name but Sabena would be the ultimate beneficiary for the Tertiary Benefit. I wrote to the ASG concerned that Sabena would fail to try to apply for her benefit rights. Another irony was that during Sabena's early years for a few years, I became an ASG Team Member representative, and passed the requisite examination and study, because I believed in the idea of parents saving up for their children's future education, it was however very time consuming and often I would have to drive to very far outer suburban homes.

I don't remember the customer service lady except that she was attentive and tried to be helpful, she might have had an Indian sounding name but I only contacted her either on the phone or via email. She explained that Sabena needed to access the application direct for the benefit herself that I could not do it on her behalf despite the regrettable situation, terminal illness or even if she passed. This seemed to be unfair to me and unjust, so I wrote to AFCA (Australian Financial Complaints Authority), I received their correspondence and ASG 's correspondence after review that due to the specified rules and the PDS that the Fund was bound by their constitution not withstanding any leniency or unfortunate unanticipated compassionate health and family situations.

The ASG customer care lady, whom I called after receiving the correspondences, said there was nothing she could do herself, as she was bound by higher authorities on the organizations board. I asked her to be kind enough to do me an official service and write direct to Sabena from her office. She would respond to me if she received a reply from Sabena, in the end the Tertiary year would soon start, so I requested that she please defer if for two years until such time Sabena's state improved. I also asked if it could be passed or gifted to a family or friend's youth but they weren't Sabena's age. I surmised that she probably never claimed it. It was a terrible waste, she could have utilized it for so many positive things and a young adult who doesn't claim their rightful money was so very wrong. Again sadly the system failed Sabena and her transformation was complete she was one of the enemy.

Your just like my favourite song going 'round and 'round my head – Where are you now 2021– Calum Scott and Lost Frequencies.

Ralph Breaks the Internet- 2018 Walt Disney Studios Motion Pictures.

New Rules – Dua Lipa 2017

Don't call me up...Mabel, 2019 Album – High Expectations

2017 The Uncanny rise of the Fidget Spinner!

Rihanna kept photo shopping the Queen of England's head onto her body.

Lana Del Rey hexed Donald Trump.

Ed Sheeran was on Game of Thrones, July- Season 8.

Celine Dion became fetch again.

When Britney Spears posted the painting Instagram Video, heard around the world. The painting sold for 10, 000. NBD.

All four Kardashians were rumoured to be pregnant at the same time.

Megan Markle and Prince Harry released their engagement photos just like every other normal on your FB feed on 27 November, 2017 at Kensington Palace. (USA Today)

13 September 2017 – Unseasonably strong weather and strong winds see bushfires break out across NSW.

6 October, 2017 – The International Campaign to abolish Nuclear Weapons (ICAN) launched Melbourne 2007 wins Nobel Peace Prize.

1 November, 2017 – The Uluru – Kata Tjuta National Park Board votes unanimously to ban climbing of Ularu from October, 2019.

15 November, 2017 – The Australian Bureau of Statistics release result of Australian Marriage Law Postal Survey, YES 61.6 % NO 38.4 %.

7 December, 2017 – The Parliament of Australia passes the Marriage Amendment (Definitions and Religious Freedoms) Act 2017, legalising same sex marriage Austalia.

15 December, 2017 Chief Royal Commissioner, Justice Peter McClellan presents final report including recommendations of the Royal Commission into Institutional Responses to Child Sexual Abuse.

21 December, 2017 Driver rams pedestrians at corner of Elizabeth and Flinders Sts. Melbourne, killing one man and injuring 17 people in the second such attack in Melbourne, Australia this year.

Deaths – Michael Chamberlain, James Fairfax, John Clarke, Lou Richards, Geoffrey Gurumul Yunupingu, Betty Cuthbert, Drew Morphette, Dean Mercer, Peter Luck, Lady Mary Fairfax, Florence Bjelke – Petersen, Richard Cousins.

World Events 2017

20 January, 2017 – Donal Trump sworn in as 45th President of US.

19 September – Earthquake Central Mexico (7.1 Magnitude), killed 350,000, 6000 injured and thousands homeless. 11 days after another powerful Earthquake.

26 September – Devastating Hurricane season. Hurricanes Harvey, Irma and Maria sweep through Sth. East Texas, Florida and the Caribbean.

6 October – Opioid Epidemic, NYC, epidemics true cost in 2015 was $ 504 Billion. Illegal Lab made Fentanyl contributed to death of at least half of fatal opioid overdoses in 2016.

31 October – World Trade Centre memorial, NY.

2 November- New species of Orangutan discovered in Indonesia.

12 November- Earthquake 7.3 border region of Iran/ Iraq 530 Dead, over 70, 000 homeless.

22 November – International Court of Justice finds Ratko Mladic guilty of genocide, Srebrenica during 1990's Bosnian War worst massacre since WW11 sentenced to life in prison.

5 December- Russia banned from 2018 Winter Olympics in Peyeonchang by IOC following investigation of state sponsored doping.

6 December – US officially recognizes Jerusalem as Israel's Capital.

14 December- The Walt Disney Company announces that it will acquire most of 21st Century Fox and film studio for $ 66 Billion.

Deaths from September 2017- Hugh Hefner, Monty Hall, Tom Petty, Fats Domino, Charles Manson, Jana Novotna, Jim Nabors, Lil Peep, David Cassidy, Malcolm Young.

Gal Godot Wonderwoman $ 100.5 Million debut. June, 2017.

The Boss ditches arenas for an intimate midtown theatre in October's Springsteen on Broadway. Extended twice mega popular show.

Taylor Swifts comeback with Reputation, November 2017.

Window in the Closet

Extracts from IVO, 6th December, 2018 (Allan)

Magistrate's Court Family Violence Protection Act, 2008.

Application and Summons for an Intervention Order.

The Resp and the AFM were in a relationship in 2014 for about six months. There were a few years when the Resp and AM did not see each other. The AFM and Resp run into each other through mutual friends since the Resp has started harassing the AFM. The Resp is threatening that the AFM owes him money. The Resp has been sending numerous text messages and emails to the AFM. The Resp has asked the AFM for sexual favours and also sent inappropriate messages that make her feel uncomfortable and makes her feel like she is being emotionally and psychologically abused. The Resp is on heavy medication and when he forgets to take the medication he is very aggressive towards the AFM and she feels he could harm her, as she believes he is unstable. The Resp last contacted the AFM on 26.11. 18 threatening that she owed him money and if she doesn't pay he will take it further. The AFM is seeking an order for her safety and to stop the Resp from contacting her.

Date of Hearing 29/3/ 2019 at 9.30 am.

I don't remember exactly when I crossed paths with Allan again in 2018 after several years of us both going on our separate ways. It was most likely at a party of Ian's because Allan never had parties. It must have been between March and April, but I thought this time it would be different I would keep it on a plutonic occasionally going out friendship level without benefits. Having reasonable funds at this time I paid for both of us at several dinners, hoping that I would not be obligated for anything.

On the 5th May, 2018 there was an auction for the Wall house on the left, I said to Allan I would like him to attend with me and I would make him pan fried Whiting with vegetables and then Sorbet. Freddie also attended with his new partner, whom I had never previously met or seen and saw her for the first time that afternoon, they never greeted me but were on the other side of the footpath. Of course I hadn't the deposit or funds to buy the house myself but was in the hope that it wasn't going to be developers. I thought it worth a shot and I even suggested to Allan that if he would bid I would pay him off as a partner from my eventual settlement from Freddie which was ongoing, much later on. He could sell one of the Brighton properties and live next door where I would care for him. Anyhow there were very few people at the auction until five minutes before it was Asian populated. The bids went close to the asking price and then there were later private vendor/ buyer negotiations. Allan invited me for a coffee at the nearby Laurent Bakery on return it was a Sold sign. He however ironically, being exceedingly annoyed at getting a parking fine.

Soon after that on another intermittent evening out, on returning to my home in our own vehicles, Allan proceeded to try to attempt to kiss me on the lips and so I said I wasn't interested in intimacy. He would never again be invited into my home after that. Months went by after that until I encountered him in Auburn Road, Hawthorn getting into my car after picking up the DVD inserts from Laurie Barnett at Action Printing. He was also visiting a client in the area, I remarked shockingly where are all your teeth, he answered they all suddenly peeled off one day for no apparent reason. That he just bought an amazing second hand 4WD Silver Mercedes Wagon online at Gray's Online. He was currently enquiring about

Dental Implants but they cost upwards of $ 35, 000 or more. That was the last time I saw Allan until I received a few months later harassing texts, emails, calls and fake invoices for outstanding monies owed for legal services that were never rendered but it was extortion like, I was already being represented for my Supreme Court Case and he never provided legal services to me. The invoice was oddly made out to Teen Talk Production for $ 13, 000 for legal administrative services, something concocted by himself, but no disclosure cost document agreed to or signed.

Extracts Emails from Allan (Annexures).

On Mon, Sep 3, 2018 at 5.35 PM

Hi A, I have been quite ill, since Saturday and still NQR!

Monday, September 03, 2018 7.34 PM

Subject: Re: NQR!?

Hope you pick up soon and your back to your sexy self manifested by your gorgeous tits A

Sunday, September 30, 2018 12.47 PM

Hi there I want to go and see Women in Black if your interested hope your looking after those gorgeous tits cheers Allan

Extracts Further and Better Particulars prepared by the applicant (2 pages), 5.8 Statement points.

1. *Original Interim Intervention order dated 06.12.2018*
2. *Adjourned to 30.01. 2019 for mention hearing*
3. *Adjourned to 29.03.2019 for directions hearing*
4. *Further directions hearing 22.05.2019*

   Request further and better particulars by 01.05.2019 of acts relied upon in the application

Most times Allan never turned up at the hearings but I was always there and they were usually adjourned to another date. As a Lawyer (Costings), Allan was self- represented and so was I until the Magistrate suggested that the matter would be compromised should I not have legal counsel.

Allan's original affidavit was filed on the 09.05.2019 with 49 statement points and 59 pages long, which were professionally bound presumably at officeworks and the 15.05.2019 with another 5 statement points.

15. 05. 2019 Orders

The registry is to serve two affidavits sworn by the Respondent on 9th and 15th May 2019 to the applicant today by post.

OTH order:

Application for adjournment due to rail line closures, refused.

Extract Allan's further affidavit (Sworn on 3rd October, 2019)

Annexed Emails

Officeworks Elsternwick (319)

Sent: Sunday 14April, 2019 2.52 PM

To: officeworks Elsternwick (319)

Subject: Re:?????

On Wed, Feb 25, 2015 at 6.29 PM

Thanks for your email, however having thought about things sort of I really just want to motor along on my own for the time being, I have lots of things to deal with, and am somewhat fragile and really don't want to have to be keeping anyone else happy. Cheers Allan.

On Wed, Feb 25, 2015 at 6.11 PM

Hi Allan,

I have a few issues about our current arrangement or lack of it, Please call me if you would like to continue and discuss it further in person.

Mahalia Bromfield of Pentana Stanton Lawyers was very understanding and empathetic, from Legal Aid which I then later repaid their fees by instalments for the next 12 months after the case was sent for final orders, reprepared my Original affidavit of Further and Better particulars on the 5 December, 2019

Extracts of Affidavit witnessed on 6 December, 2019. (1 - 1/3 pages) 12 Statement Points.

The Relationship

1. *The relationship lasted for five months in 2014. It was characterized by oppositional and aggressive behaviour by the Respondent.*
2. *During the relationship the Respondent would not take hid medication required for depression and anxiety, and this would result in aggressive and confrontational behaviour. During this time, I would be fearful of him and what he could be capable of. His health declined while we were in a relationship.*

Current Circumstances

3. *We reconnected a few years ago as we had mutual friends, he contacted me via telephone and email wanting to spend time together. I attempted to be friends with the Respondent, I did not want to reconcile and recommence a relationship as I was still fearful of his outbursts.*

8 There have been other emails that have similarly vulgar and explicit content. He has asked for sexual favours.

10 I am not aware if he is taking his medication but from previous experience with the respondent I fear he is no longer taking his medication.

11 There has been an incident at my property where superglue was put on my gate and the buzzer on my home. This has resulted in property damage that has been reported to the police who are investigating this.

12 I am fearful that the Respondent is not in a rational frame of mind due to his mental health issues. He knows where I live, and believe that unless there is an order put in place to protect me then I am at risk of harm from the Respondent. I am of ill health and have respiratory issue as such I am vulnerable.

Extracts Original Further and Better Particulars (prepared AFM 01.05.2019)

5.3 The AFM tried to just be fiends with the Respondent but did not want to re- enter being intimate at all.

5.4 The Respondent was sending numerous harassing and stalking texts and emails since earlier 2018.

I often would not respond, hoping he would move on, just once I responded indicating I was unwell.

5.5 The Respondent during the late 2018, was threatening that the AFM owes him money. It appears that this was a method of having further contact with the AFM on this premise and also a vengeful forceful behavious for not wanting to accept and rejecting the unwanted sexual advances and approaches toward the AFM.

Orders dated 19.11.2019

The Applicant file and serve Further and Better Particulars upon which intends to rely on or before 9 December 2019. The Respondent to file and serve any response on or before 23 December, 2019.

Adjourned to 16/01/2020

Adjourned Reason: CONTESTED HEARING

Magistrate/ Registsrar S. ARMOUR

Remarks AFM I/ P Resp: Mr. Knight.

I vaguely remember attending or maybe it was adjourned from that week to two weeks after. Allan attended in person and I was with Legal Aid appointed counsel, who asked if I was concerned about Covid because I was wearing my respiratory mask in court. I said I was very concerned about it and that these diseases could potentially even spread exponentially from hundreds to even thousands.

I arrived at the court with Norma as my court support and we sat at the Women's Legal Service alcove out of his view. He weaved up and down the foyer frantically, trying to get a glimpse of me. In court he looked very unwell dishevelled in appearance and deranged with his front hair lock poking up unruly, his clothes crinkled and unkempt and a very huge tatty frayed suitcase in tow. He looked as if he'd come off homeless from the street. His shirt tails flapping about, under the grubby suit jacket. He tried to get the magistrate to order me to sign an undertaking that the proceedings that I detract and the proceedings be dismissed but I refused. I don't remember know how the cross- examination worked but the magistrate steered the hearing and she was fair. Allan's behaviour was appalling to the Magistrate, he was very rude and chauvinistic towards the mature female Magistrate, I could see her disgust, I was my usual suited passive self at court always respectful to the Magistrate. I was incredulous to the fact that she was tolerating his aggressive, demanding and dominant outbursts. I guess it was out of respect for him being a Lawyer and a bit embarrassed and ashamed for him at the time. I was quite an ordeal to be there seeing him make such a terrible klutz of himself in court. The Magistrate however levelled and forgave all, I tried to request another 12 months but was not granted it. He was however in no certain terms told by the Magistrate not to bother this lady any further with leave for me to reapply as necessary and the matter was dismissed.

Extract Email Allan

Tuesday, October 09, 2018 9.11 PM

I have taken my tits elsewhere
u will have to forbear

Invoice Emailed from Allan Dated 26 November, 2018

TO: Professional costs as follows-

Estate matter, May 2014	*$ 12,320.00*
Teen Talk	*$ 1, 155.00*
Total Amount Due	*$ 13, 475.00*

It was like an acrimonious divorce on the day of the Contested Hearing and I previously joked when I made the original application at the Registry Office on the 6th December, 2018 to the attending young lady officer of the court that this IVO story would have made a hilarious B grade Hollywood movie even if it wasn't true. Allan demanded at the end that the Magistrate make orders for me to pay the Invoice and his costs for the day. The Magistrate said that her orders dealt with the IVO and that he would have to undertake Civil Proceedings about the payment of monies he was requesting.

Mrs. McGillacutty eat your heart out – Hey, Hey It's Saturday – John Blackman voice over.

Pyjama Party – My father (F. F. W Snr) was gravely ill, 1994 and would spend mostly all day in his Pyjamas and Brown/ Yellow large Checked corded dressing gown even walking to the shops, doing errands, going to the Doctor, going to appointments and even paying bills, it was a bit worrying.

Money Can't Buy Me Love – The Beatles 1964 Albim – A Hard Day's Night.

Don't Go Chasing Waterfalls – TLC 1994 Album – CrazySexyCool

You're just like my favourite song going 'round, and 'round my head – Lost Frequencies, Calum Scott

Album – Where are you now? 6th August, 2021.

MotherFatherSon – BBC 30 January 2019.

Prodigal Son – Fox 23 September, 2019. 21 May, 2020 Cancelled.

Another One Bites The Dust – Queen 1980 – Movie Bohemian Rhapsody

The Crack –Up – LW & CN (1984)

Leonardo Da Vinci 1503 – Mona Lisa

Swedish DJ Avicii dies at 28. 20 April, 2018 Wake me Up – True 2013, Levels 2011.

Swedish House Mafia 2012– Don't You Worry Child Album – Until Now

Anything Goes! – 1934 Cole Porter, Chicago, Liza Minelli

You've Tried the rest, now try the best – Houseboat (1958) Sophia Loren, Cary Grant.

Daddy Cool – Eagle Rock 1971 Album – Daddy Who? Daddy Cool!

You've lost that loving feeling – 1964 – The Righteous Brothers, Phil Spector

What have you done for me lately? Janet Jackson, 1986 Album – Control.

Money, Money, Money! – ABBA 1976 Album – Arrival

Humpty Dumpty!

Don't go looking for what you haven't lost – My Mum. (IMW).

Sorry! Justin Beiber, 2015 Album - Purpose

Beans, Means Heinz!

Like most men I later discovered that they don't know what they've got until it's gone. Deceiving Cheaters, bringing home diseases. He was just another person like Eddie that I wished I'd never met. Money Munching Monsters. Lost husbands on the scrapheap of life, looking for things they won't find. I will not be sacrificing or dying for any man, especially those specimens not even worthwhile thinking about. For the dear boys in my life, why is your time more precious than my own. I don't know which is worse their 15 mins of fame, or my near death experiences. He won't bend the knee, so he's not for me. If you want a harem, you have to pay for them. Wanna root buy a prostitute, get a rubber and buy a scrubber. Start a new law, don't reward bad behaviour.

Ukrainian Vera, part – time receptionist at my clinic in Carnegie 2007, for a short while, *it is much more preferable if the man is more in direct interest of you.*

Angela, (work friend since from the Lindentree years) *if men looked after you like they looked and cared after their own mother's, it was a good sign in a partner.*

The Handmaids Tale – LW – White colour of purity and innocence cancels out Red, even if it is the colour of strong Power.

Veronica Guerin (2003) Director – Joel Schumacher, Walt Disney Studios Motion Pictures, Touchstone Pictures, Based on the true story of Irish journalist Veronica Guerin (Cate Blanchett), a reporter for the Sunday Independent who exposed some of Dublin's most powerful crime barons and drug lords in 1996; later that year at 37 years age, she was gunned down by assassins hired by the same criminal drug lords exposed. Veronica Guerin (5 July 1959-26 June 1996), believed in revealing the truth about drugs and crime in Ireland. Continuing to write her revealing articles even in the face of numerous threats. The murder changed Ireland, she was survived by her Husband Graham and son Cathal (6 Years age). Whistleblowers! – BC.

Wonder Park - Dream Bigger (2019) Animation, Paramount Pictures Director – Dylan Brown, Producer – Josh Appelbaum.

L. A Story (1991) – Comedy, Tristar Pictures, Steve Martin; Victoria Tennant, Director – Mick Jackson.

Oh, the window in the closet! In my Mum's House, the English Tudor inspired and modelled off Grand English home upstairs squeezey walk in closet, off the south- west corner bedroom, which is currently my own bedroom, a bird made a mad dash into it, so it was a bit holey and draughty. The Swedish handyman Adam, 2019 *Herdy Gerdy (The Muppets 2011), only boring people have tidy houses* and who dangled himself like an acrobat at the circus on the Telescopic heavy based ladder and replaced it with Perspex, so it would not happen again. I remarked silly English people who'd have thought, why having a small window in a closet, definitely not European, for what reason, I thought It must be for the secret nookie they were having whilst looking at the outside rear garden view from the closet window. English people, windows in closets!. Ralph Fiennes memories again.

The Lion, the Witch and the Wardrobe – C.S. Lewis (1950-1956) Author, adaptation Fantasy Film (Chronicles of Narnia: The Lion, The Witch and the Wardrobe 2005).

It's a long way to the top – Bon Scott – Vocals / ACDC 1975. Abbreviation. Electricity. Alternating current or direct current. Lead Guitar Angus Young, the little school boy a bit like Yahoo Mitchell.

Bon Scott (33 years age) died on 19 February, 1980, in a London street in his own parked car.

When and how did the world become so horrendous! LW.

The Carnival is Over!

I reunited with Freddie as my brother after four years, for a time, still forever loving him, but still wary of trusting him as before. I also thought what if we all died of Covid, before ever speaking to him again begrudgingly. It was before the official first person diagnosed, launch of the Corona Virus in Australia January 25 2020, that I called his mobile that I was worried about Mum's house and the Wall development next door Neighbours.

Neighbours – ceases production after 37 years, Fremantle Media 3 March, 2022 from 1985- June, 2022, citing funding problems following Channel 5 's departure as its UK broadcaster (Channel 10 aired it in Australia).

The Corona Virus must have already been in Melbourne, November/ December 2019 because the VCAT meeting was on Zoom and Freddie came to the house that day for it against the developers with Anthony Scarpacci's (Town Planners) help. We attended the meeting via Zoom on my ipad in the kitchen and I remember Freddie was wearing a black cloth mask, I thought it looked Zorro Ish. It was like the years we worked at The Lindentree together, we were a united front for the common good. I began to also write Birthday cards again and I used my fancy Calligraphy pen and colour inks.

I think it started with Father's Day that year that I wrote Freddie a card, I don't remember whether he told me about his two year old baby and new partner or I found out from someone else that we mutually knew. So we intermittently chatted now and then, as I called to find out how they were coping.

Freddie came to see me a few times that year and together we tidied the garden and he helped me mow the front, back lawns, naturestrip and reverse blow vac the pine needles in the back yard, changed the Kitchen water filter, Replaced the round fluoro tube of the Kitchen Light that blew and he came a late afternoon with his baby and Steve the tradesman to review the broken tiles and leak in the hallway ceiling during these early Covid months. That day later on he went for a swim with his baby Idelma, called after after our Mum. I previous had several other Tradies look at the leak without being able to find the source of it and then during lockdowns Tradies weren't available. Most times I made Freddie and I both Lunch or Dinner, after his doing a few minor chores and then a few laps around the pool. We usually spent either a half or entire day together and it was like the good ol' Lindentree times.

Happy Days

Jamie Oliver – Happy Days with his fast comfort meals, filming during the Covid at his home wearing the Light blue T-Shirt with Keep Calm and Carry On with a Royal Crown printed in white at the front.

Happy Days – 1974 Sitcom, genre 1950's – 1960's Milwaukee, with the Fonz, The Cunningham's (Howard Marian, Ritchie, Joanie), Potsie and Ralph.

The day that Rosemary (a mutual friend of Ian's who was a Librarian and also was a patient for a time) and I spent Cup day at the Mt. Erica Hotel for lunch and the horse Vow and Declare won on the 5th November, 2019. We discussed various topics from about her taking leave from the Library to renovate her house, about her son and the interesting book she was reading, *The Library Book by Susan Orlean. The library fire that ignited an author's imagination, on April 29, 1986 the Central Library in downtown Los Angeles caught fire and burned.*

I ransack public libraries, and find them full of sunken treasure – Virginia Woolf

If you have a garden and a library, you have everything you need- Marcus Tullius Cicero.

The only thing you absolutely need to know is the location of the library – Albert Einstein.

I wrote Freddie a Caligraphy, Birthday Card on his Birthday 22 March, 2020 and in the front of the sealed pouch were lots of coloured confetti. I always wrote previously in fountain pen, around the 28th August 2018, I sent a Birthday Card to Sabena for her 19th Birthday, I created the customized card from a neutral genderless patterned card and bought a few other cards to cut out decorations and the numbers one and nine to make up age nineteen. I received no response whatsoever from this card. So I then a year later I sent her another birthday card for her 20th Birthday from a quaint Disney Fairies card with stuck on decorations and the numbers two and zero. I received whatsoever no response from this card also. I wrote an email to both Helen and Franca (Sabena's Godmother) around August 2020, about whether we should do something special or a last ditch effort to get a response from Sabena for Sabena's 21st Birthday or let it go by, as none of us received responses from emails to her for years since she was eighteen. Why not, it was worth a good college try any hoo! We thought it would be a real treat for her, if all three of us would send her a proper mailed 21st birthday card and see what might happen. I also sent a proper express post parcel separately. I eventually bought a female 21st Birthday card because there were only male and female versions at the Newsagent and in the male versions the sentiments in them were not particularly appropriate for the circumstances and also I hadn't seen her or spoken to her since 2016, that I wasn't sure about what the situation was now exactly. I don't know what Helen and Franca sent her. I also thought that it was how I remembered her personality from 8 years ago when she was still living with me and I refused to acknowledge after that any photos of her after she left my care on the 13th September, 2007 when she was taken from me, so there are only framed photos' of her in the house pre 2008.

In the funky supposed to create a cheeky grinning smirk parcel which was supposed to have brought back fond memories of her childhood was again my Felix Bag of tricks mixed with a Melbourne Show Bag hybrid. Enclosed there were random photo's of Sabena at school, at home, with family, with me or Franca and Helen also at fun places like Puffing Billy, Anarkie Fairy Castle or Franca's bringing Sabena the hugest ever Easter Egg or at the Como House Park Swirley – Whirley slide, all photos of Sabena whilst she was in my care, some of her early drawings, fairy stories and cute little notelets to me. Favourite pages torn out from her Felicity Wishes collector Journals and Disney Character Journals and doll collectables, pages of Belle. The Buddhist Booklet and the Canary Yellow Gold Buddhist Scarf that Masako gifted me some years ago before her sudden passing of a stroke in June 2018. I thought it must have been fate because I don't think Masako would have coped at all well with the covid Pandemic and my Mum neither for various different reasons. I thought perhaps she could use the scarf doubling it as a pretty mask or headband and certainly maybe chanting might be helpful for her whatever other issues she might be struggling with that I wasn't aware of at this time.

The folded coloured Party Hat Crowns and Party favours that I found in a Christmas cracker from a singles Christmas Dinner years ago (Dinner at Eight). At a previous Melbourne Conference for my clinic work, pre covid of course, I collected some samples of various Dermatological Gels for Scars, Strataderm Scar Therapy Gel, Dermascar, Epicrinal Gel and I included all these in the goodie bag, something for everything that might be helpful for her. It was a treasure trove of precious memories.

Extracts from the 21st Birthday Card and from the 21st Birthday Card, enclosed in the parcel duplicate.

Gaining of Wisdom, the Key to Adulthood.

Reach out if you need help, support or want something I am always here for you

On my 21st Birthday, I got a car and my Uni friends came to a party at my Mum and Dad's The Lindentree Restaurant and I got lots of presents.

(Stuff about Helen and us at the Puffing Billy and the Anarkie Medieval Fairy Castle, Franca her Godmother, Sophie and her friends from Loreto, Her best 5th Birthday Party at the Fairy Shop that was in Armadale).

Hope your keeping well and happy?

You used to love blowing bubbles and reading chapter books to my mum.

Freddie's got a two year old daughter called Idelma.

Be excellent to each other and party on.

I hoped that the mini time capsule of Sabena's early childhood might bring back fond memories for her of being in my family's care. I also hoped that all of the assorted mix of Glittering and Sparkling Colourful Party Confetti (Tiny Happy Birthday word plaques, big and small Stars, Balloons, Gems that I included both in the covered with pretty tiny stickers of butterflies, flowers, bees, hearts, stars covered both the envelopes and parcel with a Winnie the Pooh stamp for the back of them too. I wondered their reactions watching the confetti spill out all across the floor randomly for them to be scattered around, to have to pick them all up.

Oh, Oh sometimes I get a good feeling – Good Feeling – Flo Rida 2011 Album – Absolute Hits 2011.

The Thrill is gone – 1969 – B.B. King Album – Completely Well B-Side – You're Mean.

It was during these Covid times that it was all a bit random that my ex- patient Kathleen whom I treated since way back in the days of the Carnegie clinic always sent me a Xmas card note every year. Not long after the first lockdown, she began to work from home and cancelled her April, 2020 appointment and also began to intermittently write me notelet cards about how she was coping with life during covid, I have not seen her since for a treatment. I guessed she was also struggling with covid anxiety and stress. She was an attractive middle – aged bookkeeper, sort of like Sandra girl next door type In Grease. She was studying to improve her skills and previously worked for a private Japanese Tree Company, then struggled with breast cancer to then go to work for The Government Defence Dept., in the city. They were very flexible about her illness and allowed her to work from home two days per week. She was married to Shingo her Japanese husband. Thoughtful, kind, and sincere, previously she brought me coloured papers from Japan to gift to Sabena from her as she met Sabena many years before at the clinic and knew all about the dreaded horrific saga. She wrote in her short notes about them starting a market garden behind in their small patch at the unit, how at work there were frequent zoom meetings, how she rarely ventured out these days and that she was negotiating prior with her boss about having to return to the office at least two days per week. She was a very conscientious worker but we often laughed together about guys in her office who were a bit slack. I always returned her notelet cards with my own responses and some even fully written in Calligraphy. Kathleen, keen on pen man ship, so thought she would get a kick out of it.

Olivia Newton – John dies, 73 at South California Ranch, USA. 9th August. 2022. In notoriously famous for Grease and Xanadu fame. Long- standing battle with breast cancer.

I wrote a Caligraphy card for Idelma, named after our Mum Idelma Maria (Freddie's, 2 year old baby), 25th September, 2020. It was rather a large card with lots of cute teeny bunnies at a birthday party up to all sorts of mischief and delights. Among Sabena's books I found some books and clothes to pass also onto Idelma, and I found a mini Disney Pixar Cars (2006), comedy family animation, mini paperback book, Freddie said to me how Idelma weirdly was fascinated with cars and things in motion rather than static things like dolls and soft toys. I thought it must be all the fast paced and tech things that the kids were watching these days on Netflix, Disney Channels and Nickolodeon like Sonic the Hedgehog (January, 2020) action film remade from a Japanese Video game). So there was enough space in the envelope so I popped the booklet in too. Before I actually met Idelma in person, I was sent a photo by her mother, Emily in December, 2019. Freddie often spoke to me about his cabin fever and how he liked to come and see me also as an excuse to get out during lockdowns, away from the claustrophobic hysterical girls. I previously not met Emily in person before, until I suggested that we have a Pescatarian BBQ at Mum's house on the Tuesday 2nd November, 2020.

It was a very warm day with everyone except me in shorts and bathers. I asked them to place a small bet for me as I don't know how to bet online. Freddie apparently met Emily at the Laika Bar, St. Kilda in the later years after 2015 when he was exiled to St. Kilda to reside in his apartments block there. She was married previously before and had lived in Canada, she worked in a pharmacy for a time and thought she knew almost everything there was to know, a bit of a smart- ass mouth like Meghan.

At first I liked her because she seemed a level above his previous wives but felt uneasy about something sinister lurking behind. She was pleasant enough and more than attractive enough, she wore a long loose white blouse, that just covered her shorts up to her bottom curves and a big flouncy straw hat attached and tied with a long black crepe de chin scarf and thick dark sunglasses reminiscent of a Hollywood movie star entrance. She resembled a Greek Ava Gardner the most, with smatterings of a brunette Betty Ruth Grable and Jean Merilyn Simmons expressions in a Greek tunic.

I was worried that she was maybe smug and that she was also too smart for herself. Freddie raved about her fabulous cooking and that he put on so much weight since his radical diet many years ago.

She brought Salmon pieces, made a special Greek Salad and hommus dip. I contributed with some sorbet dessert, panettone, sparkling wine and rose. I have to say she would have been up to a Masterchef standard.

Freddie went for a swim with Idelma before firing up the Barbie, I found Idelma a change of clothes and some of Sabena's books for her to take home. She was a fierce, defiant little girl a bit like Lucy Van Pelt from Charlie Brown, Peanuts fame. Well I preferred that at least to lie down dog, give up your guns, the submissive Sabena with no fight left in her these days.

She played with the musical Leap Frog toy, I found for her with all the Bells and Whistles, flashing coloured lights and sounds again, again, again, again and again till we all became sick to death of it, with her on the kitchen carpet floor. She became bored and then began dragging her plump little body and puffy legs up each step and wooden railing on the entire hallway staircase and down again several times, but the piece de resistance was when she was on the staircase landing peeling off the Maroon Brocade Trim of the antique Cleopatra Chaise Lounge with her tiny, long, sharp, brittle spiky mini fingernails.

Well she was a toddler after all, I bought some glue in the ensuing weeks and glued it all back on. Her mother barley noticing what she was doing or pretending even disciplining her at all. Also I lost all the two dollar bets I placed on nearly every horse except the one that won which was Twilight Payment on the 3rd November, 2020.

After Melbourne Cup day went reasonably well. Freddie invited me for Dinner a few weeks later on late Saturday afternoon at his apartment. Freddie was very proud of the improvements he made to St. Kilda and he gave me a tour and showed me around the old Lindentree stomping grounds. I was also proud of his innovativeness and left- handed creative ingenuity. I met Emily's mother, who brought back Idelma from a Babysitting session and walk in the nearby park. She was a nice placid lady with orangey – red streaks through her short hair, and you could see in her eyes that she worked hard as a dog her whole life, was divorced and worked in a regional age care facility. She delivered Idelma to the Rebar where me and Freddie were sitting chatting. Freddie joked that Emily wouldn't hardly have bought her own mother's lunch after she babysat most of the day for her. I began to have new ideas about working together with Freddie again in some ventures. Her mother went home and we went up to the apartment, Emily was dressed in a tight bustier, figure - hugging cotton stretch dress with huge white polka dots on a bright flaming red background, very loud. She took her time beginning to prepare dinner of creamy seafood pasta, so I sipped rose whilst I played with Idelma and then we read together on the floor, who then bossily demanded to watch her favourite show, PAW PATROL.

I mentioned to them about the White Tesla that seemed to be tail-gating me as I drove on Fitzroy Street, until I turned left at Acland Street. Freddie pointed to the homeless food trucks that were on the opposite side of the street at The Cattani Gardens, we could always go there for dinner if Emily took too long to cook it. Emily prepared something from a Tupperware and Idelma instinctively threw it to the ground, I then tried feeding it to her myself and she ate a few more morsels. Idelma fell asleep soon after and then we eventually finished dinner. The bossy me side of Emily then emerged, about that I should sell the house and move to regional Victoria. Maybe she could boss Freddie but not me, I was nothing to her. I began to be resentful of her bossing my life and I was certain it was not going to be in my best interests to listen to her advice or her ruling my future life. There was a mild drunken argument and then I immediately left, I don't think she was either going to be a good friend or an ally together against Freddie but Freddie and I were our usual selves regardless. It was quite dark by then and me in a bit of a huff, then and I lost my white cotton gloves in the car park behind the Lindentree. I had been bossed by Mum, Dad, Freddie and the worst Eddie, no more.

I decided it was too much too soon and to distance myself a bit. Freddie called about what I was doing for Xmas Day and that I was welcome, that Emily's mother and some other family would be there. Instead I prepared a huge hamper of frozen fish in Tupperware, Pannettone, Xmas Puddings, Lemon Myrtle and Ginger shortbread, a mixture of Koko and Haigh's Chocolates, Sabena's young fairy costumes, clothes and more books. I dropped it off in St. Kilda on Xmas Eve at dusk. I apologized for not being able to attend on Xmas Day, I thought it for the best for several reasons, Covid, I wasn't familiar with her family and I was also tired from having attended a dinner out the night before. It was as if someone was micro- managing me from far away, like a puppet doll.

It was such a long time since visitors came to Mum's house and visitors were restricted during lockdowns. I thought I would let loose this year and invite 10 of some of my dearest and loyal friends to an outside picnic lunch/ swim party in the rear garden on the frosted glass and steel framed legs outdoor table on the Tuesday, 29th December, 2020. Admittedly it was short notice but there was also covid fear still in the atmosphere – Aroma of Corona. It was a sultry warm sunny day and I was RSVP by four other people. I ordered several Sushi Platters of Seafood and Vegetarian fare the day before and people were to also bring their own plate. It was to start from 4 pm that afternoon, Rosemary arrived too early by mistake and called me erratically on the mobile saying she needed Dental work done and was embarrassed to come but she was at the local shopping centre, I rang her some time later asking if she was done shopping she could come straight here, but no she went home. Nick and Mel arrived around 4.30

pm and Norma in skirt denim overalls with a checked shirt and cowboy themed hat, Norma was always a bit flamboyant and spontaneous like that, Mel wore a bright colourful casual jacket of turquoise, yellow and orange with patterns of birds and flowers splashed across with denim jeans. Mel brought a special mixed ancient grain salad in a huge colourful Italian ceramic bowl dish, it was very good I ate it for many days after, giving Nick the dish at his next appointment. Norma brought gourmet dips and gourmet crackers and I brought out the assorted Sushi Platters. It was a very nice pleasant friendly chatting afternoon and Nick mentioned that he also was barely on speaking terms with his own brother as I described my distancing also. I provided dessert of Lemon Custard Liquor Cream filled Pannetone and Sorbet. Nick and Mel brought their own white Moscato wine to share and I cracked open a Valdobaddiene Regional Prosecco. I joked and asked if Nick and Mel had been fed sufficiently enough.

It was not long after in January, 2021 that Freddie moved from his apartment in St. Kilda because I called him as I was in the area with a friend for a walk and maybe we could all go to lunch together. It was all a bit bizarre and abrupt, as he wouldn't tell me where he moved to. He said to me things were looking up at the bar and he'd received lease offers for some of the shops. I asked him many times for Emily's mobile or email in an emergency if something terrible were to happen, but he would not provide it cagily nor would she. He said he'd caught Pneumonia during early December and that he was very weakened physically by it, I thought it was an elderly persons disease but Freddie was only 55 years old. It must have been then when he opened up honestly and broke it to me. The mother is the last to know. He asked if I had seen Sabena these years, I said not since she was 15 years, that final time. I asked if he'd seen her, he said he hadn't personally but that someone he knew that also knew Sabena encountered her at Watergardens Shopping Centre and spoke to her briefly. He said she was now a short, full bearded male specimen. It was horrible and confronting, that Sabena wasn't a very attractive man either. *Very unattractive man – Victor from Fast Forward in Moscow Tonight. Victor and Svetlana from the News Skit, 2011.*

I was actually relieved I hadn't yet ever seen her because I might have gone into total spasmodic shock. I don't think I ever wanted to see her like that because I might never recover from the devastating effect of seeing her so totally transformed for always and remembering the very girly tizzy fairy princess. As long as I didn't try to visualize I was ok with it, it wasn't indelible encrypted.

Helen said she wasn't at all surprised it finally went that way. No response from Sabena, wasn't as hurtful as a perhaps bad response and I left it at that. *Let It Go! song from Frozen – Idina Menzel – Disney, 2013.*

The Possum Earthquake

It was many months later, after another scrambled eggs few months after the outing of Sabena. It was the 22nd September, 2021 and I was expecting a tradesman to arrive to repair the front driveway gate corner alcove and side gate office locks at 9.30 am. He was to text me on his departure to alert me. I was still in my double bed upstairs at the time and at 9.15 am I was awoken by what I thought must be gigantic possums in the ceiling that often fought, rumbled and screeched from time to time. The four pronged crystal chandelier swung from side to side like a pendulum and the ceiling was blurred in slow – motion the bed floating almost rocking up and down like a magic elevation. Those dirty great giant possums populating I thought and fiercely fighting over fighting over their territory in the roof again. It lasted barely seconds to mins. Peter arrived a bit latish almost 10.00 am and said he felt the earthquake in his car driving this morning. Peter laughed as I told him about the Dirty, Great Giant Possums that were jumping and bouncing about in the ceiling.

2021 Mansfield Earthquake 53 Km SSE of the town of Mansfield in the Victorian Alps at 9.15 am local time of Magnitude 5.9, the earthquake caused minor structural damage in parts of Melbourne and left one person injured.

The Peaceful Protester

I received an email invitation to attend the Screen and Stage Summer Party – Eventbrite on Friday 26 November, 2021 at the St. Kilda Town Hall. It was not long after the Melanoma Day Surgery of the 20 October, 2021 for the rare not garden variety presentation of it buried deep underneath my right big toe. It seemed forever since I ventured out for an evening, let alone having to go out during the day to do stuff. I felt I was couped up and subdued for so many years now that I deserved to have a bit of a treat.

I just started dating a new boyfriend earlier this month but decided it was too early to invite him yet.

The plan was to have a light late arvo meal of smashed avo, an open sandwich with whatever toppings there were in the fridge, and then to arrive early and leave early before the crowds arrived. In hindsight I could have trammed it there but thought it a good deterrent for me not to drink too much that evening. I never drink and drive, especially if I haven't eaten a proper meal. I wore my favourite orange cocktail v- neckline, body hugging dress with a sheer black tie up wrap top and matching orange/bone two tone, two knots platform peep toe sandals that I bought near Fortitude Valley or New Farm in Qld, when I was babysitting Angela's house and her two student boarders. I went to get a haircut the day before so my hair was looking shiny black blow waved and straight.

It was still daylight and warm, my under wrist was stamped and entered the town hall mostly distancing from all people. There were a few large round tables only at the very back which was the stage. The room was sparsely populated at the back so sat at a table opposite a lady who I acquainted an artist lady whose name was Penelope Le Petit, she made lithographic prints. I asked how she came to be here her girlfriend, was an Indie producer. She spoke about her artistry and I looked it up on my phone. I thought her art alternative but strikingly capturing. Artists are the true dream makers. She wandered off to find her friend, who was gone some time after going to the car park food trucks which weren't there when I arrived earlier yet. There were three tiny cocktail stand up bar tables with assorted cheese and crackers, some sparse frozen finger food and a few dips. I elected not to eat these because of my allergies and also because as I passed them to get a drink it was all gone so fast. There were lines of people at the food trucks now, so I wasn't keen on waiting there, so I decided to sip on the red. It must have been cheap because of the taste it was also so undrinkable. I eventually swigged it down to get rid of it and then tried a glass of sparkling slightly less innocuous and then the white which was the least atrocious so stuck to that for the night.

I suspected the little food I ate a lot earlier was starting to wane too.

The crowd was mostly youngish, St. Kildaish and weird, so I wasn't going to network or even attempt to work the room. I was shocked to see straight- laced, Dr. David Bornstein there, crossing my path a world away from his clinic (TVMC). My dad always said he should have been a professional musician rather than a doctor and I also agreed on this. This evening he was a shadow of his former –self and I hardly recognized him. Later I told Freddie and he said it was probably him because he'd seen him around St. Kilda a lot. The rumour was that he left his long standing wife to have an affair with a St. Kildarite. I began to feel a bit woozy and overcome suddenly and so went outside for some fresh air at the terrace entrance columns, I thought I would come good and then go home as it was getting very busy. Then something or an apparition entered my body and I let out a huge meltdown. I screamed out the word NEVER at the top of my lungs, I was probably venting all the horrible stuff that happened to me, happening in the world and also the pandemic. I grieved for the allergies, climate change, decimation of nature and animals, and all the horrible diseases coming up. I must have sounded something like a whimpering Sea Lion in some kind of dire distress and unbearable pain. A few minutes passed and it happened again and again and again and again, it must be how when cutters feel such relief that they continue to do it without a thought instinctively. It was rather funny however I thought the stares, and strange expressive reactions of the people surrounding and entering that I was also conscious of. It might have gone on for 10 – 20 minutes until a very pleasant, calm and mild mannered huge Maori Security Guard asked me nicely if I would like to walk to my car with him. I passively agreed and we did. I was so sorry for reeking the havoc and I sat in the back driver's seat of my car. He said you can't drive and can you ring somebody to help you get safe home. I agreed it was the most sensible suggestion, I rummaged about in my canvas bag in the passenger seat and gave him some TTP merch of buttons and pins to thank him for his kindness. I was embarrassed but at least I vented and was feeling somewhat better. He stayed with me and the driver's back seat door open until Freddie arrived quirkily in a thick white hotel swim bathrobe and was naked underneath maybe with black undies or bathers. He spoke amicably to the Security Guard.

He then nonchalantly and princely ordered another Uber to drive us to mum's house. He poured me out of the Uber, grabbed my black canvas bag and he stumbled me to the front door. He began to walk away and I motioned him back and said, *wait a bit, and brought back from the kitchen despite being woozie, a packet of Phillipa's Gourmet Mince Tarts, to thank him* (after all it was late November already and I always used to be prepared before then), as the light wooden framed Diamond - shaped leadlight glass pre-door billowed wide open again with the gusty night breeze and I stood aside and behind what was the GOT heavy, chunky rustic solid wood door. I shrieked *Even though the birds sing so very sweetly everyday and at the dawn, be careful, close the door gently and don't let the B's (Birdie's) sneak inside the house to reek havoc.* It happened to me once or twice before and I was unawares that they snuck in. Maybe they were drawn and attracted to the reflections of the glass in the leadlight door and saw themselves as another bird friend. Anyhoo, funnily he answered *But their asleep at this time now!.* Strange that I hadn't ever before thought of Birds actually sleeping like human beings but perhaps just resting themselves with closed eyes on a perch. He then left and took another Uber back to the City Hotel, where he told me Emily booked a heavily discounted weekend holiday for the three of them. I wondered that I sent them also the link for the free tickets for the Party but the email was never answered, whether they might go or not because they were only around the corner. Freddie said to me when he left that he would pick me up late Saturday afternoon to pick up the car. He never called me back, so I wouldn't bother him any further I trammed and walked it first thing on Sunday morning and picked up the car. It must have been so hot that I arrived home having to park in the street because the battery in the remote also had a meltdown but it worked again hours later. My defence is also well I'm not a saint! I'm only human after all like every other heathen on earth.

Whoa, Black Betty (Bam-ba-lam)- Black Betty – Ram Jam 1977 Album – Ram Jam.

Catso di Testa! – Dickhead – Jamie Oliver, Italy.

Archie Roach dies 56 Years (RIP 31.07.22)

Annus Horribilus 2021

It however still broke my heart everyday none the less – LW

Let us see what Gran Capitale they win! – LW

Eye of the Tiger (Rocky 1,2,3) – Rocky III – Survivor 1982

You were amazing, we did amazing things – Alex Lloyd 2001 Album – Watching Angels Mend

Ain't that a kick in the head – 1960 Dean Martin

Dolcezza di fare niente – David Williamson

Hula – Bula the Distraction Phase Mish Mash

The time that Dr. Ian Anderson, our family doctor in the 80's and early 90's until he became so ill he stopped practising, who came to my dad's rescue immediately when we called him in the early hours of one morning that dad had collapsed next to the doorway at Mum's side of the bed in the south – west corner of their room he had contracted Spinal Meningitis, Dr. Anderson diagnosed him on the spot and he was sent direct to the hospital for urgent strong antibiotic infusion. It was also probably the late 80's that Dr. Anderson was at the Hilton in the City during the day and that he suffered a meltdown incident where police were called and he asked them to call my dad, who went to his immediate aid, rescue and fixed it. The thing about Dr. Anderson was he married three times to very eccentric wives the last of whom he met in a mental hospital that he eventually removed her from.

Stephen Tucker a college friend from the mid 80's, who was besotted by another girl in our class who was model beautiful but it was unrequited love as she always used, totally ignored and dismissed him. We called him Brains from Thunderbirds are go because he was a mirror of the character, short, nerdy, wiry, brainy, good with money, sometimes stuttering, sometimes painfully shy and timid. I eventually tried to be kind, felt his pain and said, she thinks you're not good enough for her. He finally recovered from his delusions about her and the reality of his true heartbreak. It was never to be. The upside was that after he began working, he met a Greek girl who was totally devoted to him and him to her, both being very happy. Many years later on he became involved in administration at the RCHM, I tried to contact him there to get advice about Sabena, I think I left him a few messages but he never returned them which was unusual for him as from time to time over the years we helped each other with advice about work and other stuff when I encountered him at conferences and such events. Ironically he loved dancing and was there in his element his favourite dance floor boogie songs were Don't Stop till you get enough and Billie Jean 1982 – Michael Jackson.

The Indian helper who was Freddie's laky and also worked in the bottle shop next to the Rebar before Freddie sold it. His name was Koda, who brought and met his wife from India, very enterprising, helpful and ambitious, he worked various other jobs too – Skoda Simply Clever.

The Tea and Oils stains which plagued me and that I could never get out of my front tops.

When Penelope Le Petite so adorable said, why is there nothing on the back of your Business Postcard?

Sushi Gallery Tony who was always generous, helpful and kind who organized the several special Sushi Platters of only Seafood and Vegetarian fare and made them up with extra prawns and tuna.

Masako's daughter Jeka, who I met for the first time at her mother's deathbed in the hospital whom I tried to console and befriend. I gave her a Buddhist prayer booklet that Masako had given me to help me about Sabena. Masako always berated Jeka's profession to me working as a measly nurse at the RCHM, of course Masako didn't think much of Doctors which she also knew I didn't agree with. She wanted Jeka to leave and do something like her older brother a lawyer or her other brother the Music Producer. I knew they were conflicted on this issue but I said to her follow your career heart. Perhaps they were angry because I never attended her funeral in protest and never saw them again.

The time I saw Matt Preston from Masterchef, at the Jam Factory Cinema together with his young sons who apparently was during this phase of inappropriate development, about his own house.

Dr. David Bornstein, whom I saw his son playing in a band once at a Brighton Hotel, and also many years ago, when Dr. Bornstein was at the Post Office and he was to collect an important parcel, I was in the line behind. He rocked up strangely without any ID, so I was kind enough to step forward and ID him. He fervently thanked me. I was renowned, for these little random acts of kind humanity.

The English Aussie Chris, whom I met on the singles phone chat line, before they closed them down, from near Orange in N.S.W. I started this with him for a few times in 2018, then stopped and then reconnected with his mobile number after found it on a piece of paper during 2019 Covid. He seemed adorable but was a perpetually loner single guy. He liked general chat then wanted more phone sex chat but I definitely did not. After several chats I asked to meet him in person sometime but he was not that forthcoming about it. I gauged the distance was an issue but I thought that if he was committed to our friendship, he would eventually make an effort to attend and meet me. I however became bored with the all the broken promises and I stopped calling him also, as I wasn't in favour of phone sex.

Emily, third time lucky? who one day randomly sent me a huge heavy email in December, 2021 of Idelma in a burgundy fairy dress tutu standing between pretending feeding these two static reindeer statues with Santa in a sleigh above looking on.

The silly adorable endearing stuff that spontaneously only Freddie would ever do. Like the day he came for a swim and then used the clinic hand sanitizer also on his scalp for some unknown reason. It immediately started to burn and sting, so I said quick have a shower and wash it off straight away.

The Christmas Installation that he set up in the empty Rebar in late November, 2019 that he proudly showed me that night that I came for dinner at his apartment. There were big blown up toy sleigh, Santa, reindeer and such other Christmas Paraphenalia that you could see from the Rebar window.

This inspired me also to do a mini installation of Alice in Wonderland in the front garden bed of Mum's house that you could spy through the wrought iron gates. I thought of even using some of mum's broken porcelain and crockery to place in between but decided that might be too dangerous for a Mad Hatter Party. So I bought these mini assorted different sized garden figurines of Alice, bunnies, magic mushrooms, fairies, mermaids, artificial potted mini orchids and a curious bust of a young dark haired bob cut style girl with a cat mask attached at the very front left side of her face.

The Walkie – Talkie Radio Security phones that I found of Freddie's whilst trying to declutter during covid that I showed to Freddie that day he came for a swim and like a naughty school boy begging for toys, asked if he could take them and that he wouldn't take them to the apartment as Emily hated unnecessary clutter of items and she would most likely kill him if she knew he had them.

Joel Silver for Caulfield signs that I saw everywhere I drove around the area, where he looked so the opposite of what I remembered with his Beatle like short freaky black dyed haircut and thick black nerdy glasses. It was a far cry from the hip, trendy, fashion conscious M&M, Silverchair and Caprio.

The St. Kilda Film Festival of Tuesday 13 August, 2019 that I attended with Masako before her untimely passing of a stroke at 69 Years. We ate at the Sister of Soul Vegetarian Cafe in St. Kilda before it started. Our favourite film was Ghostbear, Director / Producer Paul McDermott Producer Justine Kerrigan. Brett Stanning of the Screenplay writers course at RMIT gifted our class Free Tickets.

Sabena's Gecko mini kids mobile phone that I found during a Covid Lockdown in the crate of the Family Law Legal documents.

I wondered if maybe Emily was invidious of me living in mum's house and rudely whether she might be killing Freddie softly with his song maybe not purposefully because she was about 20 years his Junior and always wanted to get him to do more fun stuff, believe me Freddie already knew how to do fun stuff he had been doing it all his life since his time as a young boy at the St. Kevin's Boys Club.

On the flip side of it, Freddie throughout the later years, a few years even before mum's passing started to shaft me with several property partner investments that my mum financed for me, and I always came off decidedly second best, with him usually keeping my profits and me always perpetually without a house of my own, so I was now wary of becoming embroiled with his finances.

Franca once said before she was married, to me if I was to have to choose between the husband or the child, her choice husband and my choice child. Maybe now these days it depends on the husband and the child?

Why the world now tastes fuckin' shit and why we've got to shovel and eat it?

I once saw in a movie that men have short fucking memories and it was officially true.

Steel Magnolias 1989 Drama Comedy. (Strong Women) *Up there with Elizabeth Taylor.*

Cast Julia Roberts, Shirley Maclaine, Sally Field, Dolly Parton and Olympia Dukakis.

Lemony Snicket's A Series of Unfortunate Events- 2004 Fantasy/ Adventure Director Brad Silberling, Paramount Pictures.

Killing me softly with his song – 1972, Roberta Flack.

For the carnival is over and we may never meet again- Wild Rover 1963 Album – Introducing the Seekers. Judith Durham dies 6th August, 2022.

Oh, she's sweet but a psycho A little bit psycho, Ava Max 2018. Album – Sweet but Psycho

Phantasmagoria – Mary Shelley 2017 Romance/Drama Always See! (hands over opposing eyes)

Monster Galvanized Frankenstein.

Madame Bouvarie – 2014 Drama Director- Sophie Barthes Warner Bros. Pictures

Happy Feet! 2006 – Comedy Director – George Miller, Warner Bros. Pictures.

Epic Films – The Gladiator 2000 Action/ Drama – Russell Crowe Director – Ridley Scott, Universal Pictures.

Ogni Belle ballo stuffa – IMW (My Mum)

Rogering – MW (RIP)

The Eternity Man –Arthur Stace, from 1930's, Chalked the word eternity 500,000 times in over 35 years on Sydney's walls and footpaths.

Splendour in the Grass Festival, NSW 6th August, 2022- Sydney man infected with Meningococcal disease.

Keep your own places and no beebies! (TM)

Emma! (DB)

Auspices and husband surprises! (SR)

The best and worst moment – Smiths Ad. 2022

Housecleaning – you have to do it all again in 6 months. Phyllis Diller (IA)

Housecleaning, it might not kill you but why take the risk? Jessica Rowe

Someone left the cake out in the rain I don't think that I can take it ' Cause it took so long to bake it And I'll never have that recipe again Oh no!... All the sweet green icing flowing down – MacArthur Park, Richard Harris 1968 Album – A Tramp Shining

Mr. Doobie, Romper Room – 1953-1994.

The Messenger: The Story of Joan of Arc. -1999 War/Drama Director- Luc Besson, Gaumont

Your body is a wonderland - John Mayer, 2001 Album- Room For Squares

Marilyn Monroe and JFK – when it's all blown over and the fuss dies down – Speak Freely!

Mutti – Because when you know you know! Sauce ad, 2022.

I've got so many pictures in my head why don't you turn on the projector – Westlife, 2007,

pictures in my head

Dancing in the Dark – The Boss, Bruce Springsteen, 2011 – Dancing with Courteney Bass Cox.

Super Freak – Rick James 1981 Album – Steet Songs.

Minestrone

Why? Because there's so many different yummy things in it and so it's also delicious and nutritious.

My Daddy's little girl, My daddy, daddy, daddy, daddy Never before until his heart valve trouble Never cheated on my mum it was a short of lifetime freaky crisis. Before these times whatever Mum wanted she got from the Tim Tam genie, furs, jewellery, wrought iron fence, Parliament House lights and concrete lions, were hers for the asking, which people in Singapore believe are the guardians and protectors of the territory. He showered his devoted love for Mum, like the Taj Mahal Emperor who built it for his wife. Mum couldn't swim or drive with phobias of both during our lives. We weren't that athletic and I was a pudgy tomboy, but Dad taught us his German breast stroke. I was never however able to grasp Freestyle after that, Freddie learnt Freestyle at St. Kevin's lessons.

Wandai represents seriousness, thought, intuition, intent and wisdom.

My dad a very adorable incurable romantic Virgo, also bought expensive classic night attire and sexy but classy elegant lingerie for my mum who was very timid about her sexuality but passionately hot. My dad was a one man woman – Madonna like.

My dear mum was equally devoted strictly monogamously to my darling dad being brought up conservatively in a Small Italian

Village, San Zenone, TV. When my father passed she said I never want another man in my life or another man to ever replace him, she was also a one man woman. God knows Dr. Anderson between wives tried very ferociously to flirt with Mum after dad's passing.

Please remember when these love doves married that their income was a total sum of five pound between them.

The Italian light Grey Marble tiles with the black and white lightning streak veins and splashes, in the main bathroom upstairs which were especially ordered from imported Italian Marble stone and that were also in my clinic downstairs which was previously a lounge /sunroom/ rumpus /playroom for us as young kids. Their name was aptly Sognio Grigio. It will spoil it, if I translate it for you. The Rosegold taps and fixtures, the gold power points with black switches and the toilet and bidet twin set alcove. Every Mum's birthday, children's births, Easter, Christmas and their annual marriage anniversaries dad bought something of commemorative and memorable significance of his love for Mum, usually a piece of jewellery, a fur or fancy lingerie.

After much deliberation and investigation into the loving investments made to Mum's house, I surmise and believe my parents were a REAL true love story before dad became gravely ill and his soul sadly lost the family plot.

The Italian plasterer who tried to argue that his Hallway to Kitchen middle crooked arch was precisely correct on both sides and I kept saying but it was lopsided longer on the right side and stopped shorter on the left. He was so stubborn that he never corrected it and we let it go, but to this day I wonder if he was just stubborn or there was perhaps a practical technical building reason.

Dancing in the Moonlight – Boffalongo 1970, Please Stay 1969 B-side Endless Questions.

We built this city on Rock and Roll – Starship 1985 B- side Private Room Album – Knee Deep in the Hoopla.

Hopelessly Devoted to you – 1978 Olivia Newton - John B-side Love is a many splendored thing.

Love Story – 1970 with Ryan O'Neal and Ali Mc Graw Director – Arthur Hiller

Put a smile on your face – Dolly Parton, 9-5 2018-2022

Monty Pythons Flying Circus – Life of Brian 1979 Always look on the bright side of life...

The Italian Job 1969 – Michael Caine

NAB – Its more than Money!

Hey, I love you darling no matter what?

Don't get mad get everything Darlinks – Ivanica Trump dies 14th July, 2022 (73 Years).

Romantic crazy notions were dashed.

Want a happy life buy a wife!

If it's free it costs a lot of money (YM)

If you can't be good be good at it (PN)

Love grows where my Rosemary goes – Tony Burrows with Edison Lighthouse 1970

HANSARD! (RM)

The Semenolo (FFW senior and Junior Re: TZ and others).

I can't keep a wife, if I have no money to look after her...(TZ)

The MS Syndrome – (CN), Polygamy?

Soleinacqua (sun in the water, sky glare)

Umberto Pizzi's Rome Paparazzi Photo's The Allure of Audrey Hepburn 1981 at Villa Borghese Gardens of Roman Holiday 1953 with Gregory Peck. The photo of Elizabeth Taylor, Richard Burton, Sophia Loren and Carlo Ponti Snr having dinner together in Rome. Cleopatra 1963 – Elizabeth Taylor. 1968, Movie Star Richard Burton dazzles wife Elizabethe Taylor – and their legions of fans – when he buys her a 69 –carat Cartier Diamond ring costing $ 1.5 Million. Elizabeth Taylors Emerald and Diamond necklace. Gina Lollobrigida – Bulgari, Rome.

Largo di Torre Argentina is a square in Rome, Italy, with four Roman Republican Temples and the remains of Pompey's Theatre. Upon whose steps dictator Julius Caesar was betrayed and killed in 44BCE. It is in the ancient Campus Martius.

Famous for the now many stray cats, which inhabit it and the Gatti Di Roma Cat Sanctuary. Newly abandoned cats are named, registered in the shelter's log, examined and eventually desexed. Cat Ladies in Rome – The Gattare, person female who feeds stray cats – Charming Italy. Anna Magnani was a fan (Gattara). Today, volunteers care for approximately 130 cats most of which are disabled or suffer from illness.

My Dad's Italian friends connections, Othello, Tesoriero, Scomparin, Sir. John (as my dad coined him), the builder and his wife Anna – Maria, Tony and Cenzina.

Dad's German Dunera ship connections, his flatmate before marriage Philon, who fancied and asked my mum to dance before my dad did and then danced with my Auntie Wilma, younger than my mum as the default.

Philon, after recovering being rejected by my mum eventually married Marie and their fur baby cats whom they always had to be home in time to feed them at six or something terrible would happen, the coach would turn into a pumpkin with mice in it. Harry, with his ultra thick glasses Benny Hill soldier and Mr. Magoo lookalike with his house full of cats, whom Dad went to live with for a time having his late life crisis of sorts.

My Auntie Angelina married to my mother's brother, Evelino who secretly tried to crack on to my dad whilst her husband was at work and my dad was at their house for some reason, but Dad divulged it to mum.

My Dads's secretary, plain but an efficient Jane, with loose morals who had frequent extramarital affairs with various people behind her husband Bill's back and everybody knew except him, my godmother Ethel who also tried to crack onto my dad but it was nothing personal it was just business, Mum also knew about that. Ethel eventually moved on to a business associate of Dad's Italian Tony who were also rumoured to have been revealed on her office desk at Dad's Real Estate company, Frederick and Co. Fitzroy.

The only book Freddie purported that he ever read in entirety for a book report was Charlie and the Chocolate Factory (2005) Musical, Fantasy with Johnny Depp. Director – Tim Burton in primary school at SKevvies (St. Kevins).

Tanya also advised me over the years after I was shafted by him from the proceeds of the Glenferrie Road shop/ dwelling property in 2008, and also landed up paying the CGT for years after in instalments, that I should be wary of ever trusting Freddie again and having involvement with either money or in his business affair issues.

The Legacy - Castle Black.

You chop the onions and garlic, sweat and fry them off in a saucepan with a tablespoon of olive oil then add the roughly chopped celery and carrots, add vegetable stock, any other vegetables from the fridge that you have, add the tomatoe paste, Salt n Pepa, spices to your taste, add any beans you fancy, thick - skinned are best so they don't go too mushy and then add the tiny stelline pastas.

Mum was an enterprising, pioneering woman for her time and working home keeper from since before it became the norm and probably even since her marriage in the late 1940's and also worked during all three pregnancies and three miscarriages. After their marriage mum worked and owned, her own Knitwear and Dressmaking shop, Tedesco of Venice in Collingwood during the day with her sister Wilma and Auntie Angelina, they even made piece work for jumpers, cardigans and twin sets for the then Myer stores. Dad would pick us up from school to go there be fed, watered and minded.

Dad worked at his own Real Estate Company office, Frederick and Co. just up the road in Johnston St. Fitzroy, just up from Collingwood with at its peak thirty staff with a huge rental roll, and also some rural properties on offer in Ballarat and Bendigo collaborating with his long term friend and associate Peter Shone. Mum and Dad also both worked later on in the early 1970's at The Lindentree Restaurant, 11 Fitzroy St. ST. KIlda, moonlighting on the weekends their second jobs with the three of us kids in tow, my older sister hostess/ waiting, and Freddie and I sleeping on the storeroom mattress behind the top bar. Later on in 1974, I graduated to helping out in the kitchen as Entree, Salad and Dessert come Sous Chef apprentice, at sixteen I succeeded my sister's role as also hosting, waiting and band / event recruiter by eighteen I was exclusively helping mum behind the top bar. The Fuscaldo's who owned our house before us ran a silver service restaurant in Melbourne in those days. The house needed a lot of work as the Chief Fuscaldo tried to do many DIY projects around the house to save money and that were more often than not flop outcomes.

In 1985, I was 24 Years old and the TV Series Moonlighting, Comedy/Drama was showing with Cybill Shepherd and Bruce Willis. Created by Glenn Gordon Caron – opening theme Al Jarreau. Original Network ABC.

Matteo, the little svelte Italian plasterer who just imigrated from Italy before the Covid started in Melbourne in 2020, who did a marvellous job and repaired for me the small saucepan sized hole in the main bathroom ceiling approximately above the basin, due to a long- standing plumbing leak that John the Greek Plumber previously fixed for me in the ceiling roof, he could get up the manhole because he was thin enough who was currently also revolutionary, evolving and employed a young girl plumber apprentice to help him.

Maria Katsimadakos, 2008 fashionably elegant, classy, tall, professional and very brunette attractive (Gina Lollobrigida), who wore fancy flashy eccentric glasses, whom I encountered and befriended at a work conference who was in the process of retiring from her own clinic and knew someone who purposefully built clinic cabinets and she organized for it to be custom made for me and delivered to the house clinic, as I was stunned, at the organized specimen at her own practice. She eventually referred some of her previous clients to me, the first was to be Laurie, a now previous client, whom I later interviewed in 2016 for the TTP.

The incongruent Peroneus Longus tendon that went swoosh and around in the Cuboid notch that sometimes became subluxed following rare incidents. (CN)

I was made for lovin' you baby, you were made for lovin' me – KISS!979. Album – Dynasty. Gene Simmons and band OZ Tour 17th August, 2022.

The GR8 power team couple! (SK)

I'm in Chains – Tina Arena 1995 Album – Don't Ask.

I'm a believer – The Monkees 2009, Smash Mouth, 2001 – Shrek

Cold, Cold Heart – Elton John and Dua Lipa, 2021.

Stay with me – Sam Smith 2014 Album – In the lonely hour, I'm not the only one, Dancing with a stranger, Diamonds 2020 Album – Love Goes.

Maybe this time... Liza Minelli 1964 Movie – Cabaret.

Dancing on my own... Calum Scott, 2016 Album – Dancing on my own.

Ride on Time – Black Box 1990 Album – Dreamland

Joanna Lumley's Travel Adventures – 2022, Great Cities of the World.

Lillian Frank dies 92, 13th August, 2022. If something is wrong, make it right! Toorak Hairdresser and Philanthropic Socialite.

Anne Heche dies 53, 13th August, 20122 Actress US – Donnie Brasco

Italian Caught digging bank tunnel, August 2022.

The severe Melbourne Hailstorm 13th August, 2022.

I am the messenger voice prophet, why don't they listen to me (LW)

Epilogue/ Eulogy – Life goes On!

The warnings about Paedophile James Geoffrey Griffin the Launceston General Hospital ignored. Victims – Tiffany Skeggs, Kylee Pearn, Keelie McMahon. ABC News July updated 16th August, 2022.

13th September, 2022, 15 years later, after Sabena's abrupt removal from my, my Mum's and Freddie's our families home after the Family Court deliberation on 13th September, 2007 – Hallmark of That Tragic Day!

Monkey Pox – Person to person male contact, global epidemic – 5 deaths Europe, 44 cases Australia and 39,434 US. July/ August 2022. Symptoms – Immunocompromised with a rash.

Di Kershaw of Gogglebox fame dies 76 on 25th July, 2022, (I coined it Gogglefrocks – LW).

Shinzo Abe former Japanese PM shot dead, July 2022.

Boris Johnson resigns as UK PM on the 8th July, 2022.

The Coldest day in Melbourne since August 2003, 0.8 degrees, 19th July, 2022, 1 Degree.

Crisis of Hard Rubbish dumping 1st April, 2022.

The Circle of Life

Meme of the significance of circles. Aboriginal meaning of circles are the continual circle of life from beginning to end and then other new beginnings.

Monday 20th July, 2020 started writing Never and Thursday 27th May, 2021 Part 1 My Memoire Completed writing, Never of a proposed trilogy. Completed Publishing after edit, proof, photos, cover design on Wednesday 22nd December, 2021.

Come with me and you will see a world of pure imagination...

Where there are cooks there is hope... Lurpak

Sale of the Wall property next door to mum's house, from the street aspect on the immediate left,

in July, 2022 for an undisclosed sum presumably to other high-rise apartment developers no doubt.

Rebel without a Cause.

A Streetcar named Desire.

Cat on a Hot Tin Roof.

West Side Story.

Gone with the Wind – TARA

Sunday 8th May, 2022 Started writing Never After, Never Again!.

2021/2022

Rezalia (ACA- Channel 9) August, 2022 dies 6 years age from Myocarditis – consequence of Influenza A, given the incorrect diagnosis and medication of Steroids.

The murder of Ebony Jane Simpson 9 years, on the 19th August, 1992, Bargo NSW. Andrew Peter Garworth drowned her.(ACA- Channel 9) in memoriam 18th August, 2022.

Wearing white I always got so fuckin filthy! (LW)

Chris Rock vs. Will Smith and Jayda Pinket- Smith. The Academy Awards Punch, March 2022.

More than 9 Thousand Covid Cases recorded in Victoria 1st April, 2022.

Bruce Willis forced to retire and quits acting 4th August, 2022 due to a condition called Aphasia degenerative brain disease that affects speech, after Milestone Movies History.

I remember watching all the Die Hard movies with Mum and Freddie – she coined him endearingly Bruce Willy.

Don't worry, be Happy... Bobby McFerrin 1988 Album – Simple Pleasures

Fabulously Hybrid who knew! (LW)

Flashbacks, Hijinx, shenanigans, snippets and Jibber Jabber.

Nowadays single women have access to IVF (Test Tube Babies). Sometimes I wish I miscarried or aborted to have avoided what happened and the outcome.

Too Bad, Too Good doesn't sell mediocrity does!

Sweet Home Alabama 1974 Lynyrd Skynyrd B-Side take your time Album – Second Helping.

Kisses, Cuddles and Moonbeams – Monica Trapaga Released 2000 – Sabena's CD

It's my party... Lesley Gore, 1963 Album – I'll cry if I want to.

Circus Freak Show!

Mamma Mia!

Even shoes deteriorate.

Bert Newton dies 83, 30th October, 2022 complications after leg amputation on 10th May,2021.

October, 2021 Emma Watkins the first female Wiggle resigns to work on other projects.

The Perils of Penelope Pitstop – Comedy Animated TV 1969-1971.

Watch me pull a Rabbit out of my hat...Again... Presto.

The Adventures of Rocky and Bullwinkle and friends. Comedy Animation 1959.

Cosi Fan Tutti! Turandot.

Meant to be, it'll be – Bebe Rexha, 2017 Album – All your Fault Pt. 2.

John Elliott dies 79, 7th September, 2021

Andrew Peacock dies 82, The Colt from Kooyong, 16th April, 2021 at his home in Austin, Texas.

Zombie - The Cranberries 1994, You and me 1999, Album -Bury the Hatchet, Linger 1993, Album – Everbody else is doing it, so why can't we?

Walk like an Egyptian...1986, Manic Monday, The Bangles, (Bangs) –Album Different Light. 1987 – Hazy Shade of Winter Album – Less Than Zero, Eternal Flame 1988 Album – Everything.

Venus - Bananarama 1986 Album – True Confessions

Bad Habits 2021 – Ed Sheeran Album =

Rolling in the Deep – 2011 Adele, Someone like you Album – 21, Hello 2015, When we were young Album – 25, Easy on me 2021, Album –Easy on me.

Cricketer Rod Marsh dies 74, Adelaide on 4th March, 2022.

Infamous larrikin cricketer Shane Keith Warne dies 52 at Koh Samui Hospital, Thailand of suspected heart attack.

The Look 1988, Roxette Album – Look Sharp! Listen to your heart, 1987 – It must have been love Album – It must have been love but...Why? Annie Lennox, 1992 Album – Diva

Love at first sight 2001, Kylie Minogue Album – Fever, On a night like this...2008

Album – Light Years.

Glenn Wheatley dies 74 on 2nd February, 2022 of Covid Complications.

There is no challenge you are not equal to... The Gilded Age, Historical Drama 24th January,(2022), Julian Fellowes.

Firework 2010 – Katy Perry Album – Teenage Dream, Last Friday night, Roar 2013 Album – Prism.

Meatloaf dies 74 on 21st January, 2022. Bat out of Hell 1977, I'd do anything for love but...1993 Album – Bat out of hell II- Back into hell.

The Horses – 1990 Daryl Braithwaite, Album – Ride, One Summer 1988,

As the Days go by... Album – Edge.

I sold my very first Never memoire novels to my dear supportive friends Roberta 4th January, 2021, then the second to Norma 10th January, 2021 and the third to Natalie- Eva 2nd February, 2021.

24K Magic, 2016 Bruno Mars Album - 24K Magic, Just the way you are... 2010, Marry You Album – Doo – Wops and Hooligans. Uptown Funk – 2014 (Mark Ronson).

Can't feel my face... 2015 The Weeknd Album – Beauty behind the Madness, 2016 Starboy, Blinding Lights 2019.

Speed of Lightening Mutations. Aroma of Corona.

Dying for help, Annie pregnant with full body sepsis dies due to misdiagnosis and lack of duty of care. 60 Minutes Channel 9, 7th August, 2022.

Tourettes Epidemic 2020 (Tik Tok), young teen girls around the world – the power of suggestibility. 60 Minutes Channel 9, 31st July, 2022.

Duke of Edinburgh dies 99 on 9th April, 2021 at Windsor Castle, Windsor UK.

Fortune favours the brave – Virgil, Latin Proverb Fortis Fortuna adiuvat.

The Europa Cake Shop in Acland Street, St. Kilda which made the best Lemon Baked Cheesecake ever since I remember from the '80's.

Paul Green, NRL Coach dies 49 at Brisbane on 11th August, 2022.

Andrew Symonds, cricketer dies 46 on 15th May, 2022.

Don't you want somebody to love... Jefferson Airplane 1967 Album – Surrealistic Pillow.

If I were you...Mick Jagger? The Celta Course, RMIT who discriminated against me for needing wearing a mask and requiring an Hepa Filter in the classroom for my Respiratory Allergy (MCS), Deborah Randa of the DDLS (Disability Discrimination Legal Service) who was kind to assist me assert my civil rights for the course from 30th May – 11th August, 2011. Delta known as Celta on Steroids.

Men are the enemy but I also like the enemy – Renee Zellweger (Jerry McGuire).

Come up and see me, make me smile...I'll do what you want for a little while – Steve Harley and Cockney Rebel, 1975 Album – The Best Years of Our Lives. B-side Another Journey.

Come up and see me sometime! – Mae West, Lady Lou – She Done Him Wrong, Directed by Lowell Sherman (1933). Why don't you come and see me sometime, big boy? Actual Quote.

Time after Time – Cyndi Lauper 1983 Album – She's so unusual.

It's Oh so quiet – Bjork 1995 Album – Post.

I want you – Savage Garden 1997, I knew I loved you before... 1999 Album – Affirmation.

I'll stand by you – The Pretenders 1994 Album – Last of the Independents.

You can leave your hat on, 1986 Joe Cocker Album – Cocker.

Riders on the Storm – The Doors 1971 Album – L.A. Woman.

A Whiter Shade of Pale – Procol Harum 1967.

As My own Mum (IMW) – Don't go looking for what you haven't lost!

Eddie, one of the rare people that I wished I'd Never met in my life and some ghosts of boyfriends past.

Eddie the house husband (2000) who is Sabena's father that threw our bills in the kitchen rubbish so I wouldn't see them when I returned home from full time work each day and eventually became caught out when I was called about the mortgage payments at work, Incessant high Anxiety / Bipolar/Manic Depressive Chain smoker, the mobile he smashed when he placed it on the hood of the car forgot and drove off, the front door he left open one day to buy cigarettes leaving Sabena, a twelve month baby alone in an unsecured house as I arrived home, the break his arms and legs, loan sharks from playing cards at his Computer Software, Oakleigh work that he was employed for 3 months until he quit and kept pretending to me he was still going to work another 3 months after until the payroll lady from Sato called him out, the fire he started in the empty kitchen mop bucket because he was smoking inside the house which was forbidden due to Sabena's Asthma by me and he forgot he left a burning lighted cigarette on the edge of the sink dangling that dropped into the mop and bucket – Fire! I saw him trying to extinguish it as I arrived home. Steven Pugh, the psychiatrist that he saw weekly that I made payments whose wife was an out of control shopaholic. Everything but Lice and scrape the bottom of the barrel, hamburger with the absolute lot and kitchen sink. The Master of Disaster. Feigning and divulging of Mr. Bean. Some mothers do have em. Mother and Son forgetfulness, and avoidance of any responsibility. Sabena discloses to the Moorabbin Police about the child molestation that occurred over the past year on Sabena's shared care visits October, 2004.

The Notebook 2004, Romance Drama with Ryan Gosling and Rachel McAdams Director – Nick Cassavettes.

The Right one won't run – Dr. Phil.

Midnight Cowboy, 1969 Drama Directed by John Schlesinger, based on the book by James Leo Herlihy, Screenwriter – Waldo Salt, Produced - Jerome Hellman, with Dustin Hoffman, Jon Voight, Brenda Vaccaro. Jerome Hellman Productions and Mist Entertainment.

Depicts the unlikely friendship between two hustlers.

Melbourne Cup Day 2nd November, 2021 – Verry Elleegant, Incentivise and Spanish Mission.

Addams Family Values, 1993 Directed – Barry Sonnenfeld, Wriiten – Paul Rudnick, Characters by Charles Addams with Anjelica Houston, Raul Julia, Christina Ricci Produced – Scott Rudin, Distributed – Paramount Pictures.

It's the Stawell Gift!

Better be careful what you do 'cos I won't put up with you (LW) – Doesn't matter what you do, I'm still...Dragon 1978, Savoy Crackers and Arnotts Biscuits 2022.

Good Ol' Moonface – Bert Newton.

Never gonna give you up... 1987, Rick Astley Album – Whenever you need somebody,

Together Forever.

Take me to Church...2013 – Hozier. Album – Take me to Church E.P.

Dream Horse 2020 Drama/Sport– Don't judge me Jan, they're my only solace. With Toni Collette, Owen Teale. Director – Euros Lyn. Distributed – Warner Bros., Bleecker Street.

Muriel's Wedding 1994, Comedy- Drama Written and Directed- P.J. Hogan, Producer- Lynda House with Toni Collette, Bill Hunter and Rachel Griffiths. Porpoise Pit to Sydney and back again!

I can't be bought because I'm pure bitch. (Anon).

The lucky dip or booby prize, Trash or Treasure, Desperate and Dateless, stitched, Nurse and Purse, Good Will Hunting, Fill the void, The Black Spur spot, Your better off on your own, Behind the scenes, if you're on a good thing stick to it (FFW), It's raining men, Not Mr. Right but Mr. Right now, obviously I have to die of everything, Priority No. 1, Alpha Female, Honesty is the best policy, Knowledge is power, I'm the pear that wishes it wasn't the apple, The Saga Continues – the ongoing saga of life. (Faraday, JM, MM, PM, CR, IA, AM, JNT, SS, TS, DL, N Hospital Theatre Tech. Etc...).

Runaway Bride 1999 – Romance/Comedy Director- Garry Marshall, with Julia Roberts, Richard Gere, Joan Cusack, Rita Wilson. Distributed – Paramount Pictures, Touchstone Pictures.

Flame Trees 1984, Cold Chisel Album – Twentieth Century, When the War is Over 1982, Album – Circus Animals, Forever Now, 1978 Khe Sanh – Album -Cold Chisel, 1979 Breakfast at Sweethearts, Cheap Wine – 1980 Album – East, My Baby, Choir Girl, Working Class Man 1985 - Jimmy Barnes, Album – For the Working Class Man.

2020

March 1st – Australia records its first Death from Covid- 19 Pandemic.

March 3rd – Major Supermarket Chains Ration Toilet Paper after Covid triggers panic buying across the country.

May 31st – Covid- 19, 6 Million Cases Worldwide.

August 2nd – Victoria declares State of Disaster and Stage 4 restrictions. Police enforce curfew 8 pm and 5 am.

August 10th – Confirmed Cases WW 20 Million.

August 22nd- Death Toll Worldwide exceeds 800, 000.

August 26th – Amazon CEO Jeff Bezos, first person in history to have a net worth exceeding $ 200 Billion according to Forbes.

Feb 1st Pamela Anderson and Jon Peters split two weeks after their secret Malibu Wedding.

Deaths – Kirk Douglas, Robert Conrad, Max Von Sydow, Kenny Rogers, Tim Brooke-Taylor, Brian Dennehy, Little Richard, Vera Lynn, Joel Schumacher, Carl Reiner, Olivia De Haviland.

Feb, 24th – Harvey Weinstein is convicted and sentenced to 23 years prison.

March 25th – Bindi Irwin and Chandler Powell, married Australia Zoo.

June 25th – Top Gun Maverick Hits theatres.

July 17th – Princess Beatrice and Eduardo Mapelli Mozzi (Property Tycoon), private wedding.

August 30th – MTV Video Music Awards many Face masks – Lady Gaga, Ariana Grande, weeknd.

August 27th – Katy Perry gives birth and Orlando Bloom's Baby Daisy Dove Bloom.

Sophie Turner and Joe Jonas – Willa

Grimes and Elon Musk – XAE A-12 Musk.

Cameron Diaz and Benjii Madden – Raddix

2019

7th Jan. A mass fish die off occurs on the Lower Darling at Menindi Lakes. Up to 1 Million fish including endangered species. Largest fish die off in Australian History.

26th Jan. Following lifting of a suppression order Cardinal George Pell had been convicted in Dec. 2018 of sexually abusing two choirboys in 1996.

June 23rd – Ash Barty wins the 2019 Birmingham Classic No. 1 ranked WTA Tennis Player.

June 24th – Parts of the Darwin CBD are evacuated after the city is impacted by a 7.2 Magnitude earthquake originating in Indonesia.

26th Oct. Climbing Uluru is banned by The Uluru –Kata Tjuta National Park Board.

30- 31st Dec. Bushfires across NSW South Coast, SE QLd and in Victoria's East Gippsland.

Deaths – Chris Wilson, Mike Willesee, Geoff Harvey, Bob Hawke, Anne Hamilton – Byrne, Bill Collins, Peter McNamara (Germany), Margaret Fulton, Mick Miller, Tim Fischer, Paul Cronin, Ivan Milat, Bill Waterhouse, Clive James, Stuart Fraser, Greedy Smith, John Cain Jr. Verna Bloom, Carol Channing, Emiliano Sala, Albert Finney, Jan Michael – Vincent, Karl Lagerfeld, Peter Tork, King Kong Bundy, Luke Perry, Larry Cohen, Bibi Andersson, John Singleton, Les Murray, Peggy Lipton, Doris Day, Grumpy cat, Niki

Lauder, Claus Von Bulow, Antonio Reyes, Franco Zeffirelli, Gloria Vanderbilt, Etika, Eddie Garcia, Arte Johnson, Rip Torn, Valentina Cortese, Rutger Hauer, D.A. Pennebaker, Jeffrey Epstein, Peter Fonda, David Koch, Valerie Harper, Carol Lynley, Robert Mugabe, B.J. Habibi, Eddie Money, Jacques Chirac, Karel Gott, Diahann Carol, Harold Bloon, Abu Bakr al Bagdadi, Pim Verbeek, Rene Auberjonois, Carroll Spinney, Marie Frederiksson, David Bellamy, Anna Karina.

2018

Deaths – Aretha Franklin, Anthony Bourdain, Tom Wolfe, Philip Roth, Joe Jackson, Burt Reynolds, Claudio Scimone, Charles Aznavour, Jamal Khashoggi, Montserrat Caballe, Sondra Locke, Bernardo Bertolucci, Stephen Hillenburg (ALS Disease), George H. W. Bush, Penny Marshall, Dame June Whitfield, Billy Graham, Stephen Hawking, Steven Bochco, Winnie Madikizela Mandela, Milos Forman Barbara Bush, Avicii, Margot Kidder.

23rd Feb. - Voluntary recall of Rockmelons is started after several deaths from Listeriosis contracted. 20th March – 19 Infections and 6 deaths linked to Rockmelon Listeria.

22nd May – Adelaide Archbishop, Philip Wilson guilty of covering up child sexual abuse cases of 1970's. 4th June – Woolworths eliminates straws and plastic packaging wrapping on fresh produce. 8th August – NSW Gov. Announces entire state is in drought.

15th September, 2018 QLD. Gov. Announces $ 100.00 reward for information leading to the arrest of a person responsible for for contamination of Strawberries using needles and pins. Following cases of contamination across QLD, NSW, VIC and later WA grown Strawberries.

Deaths- Cornelia Francis, Harry M. Miller, Conway Savage, Bob Jane, Ron Casey, Quentin Kernihan, Ian Kiernan, John D. Lamonde, Larry Pickering, Bonita Mabo, Penny Cook.

4th March- Former Russian double agent Sergei Skripal and daughter Yuliaare poisoned by Novichok Nerve Agent in Salisbury, England UK. Specualtion of Kremlin behind the incident. 19th March- The world's last male white rhinoceros dies in Kenya, making sub-species functionally extinct. 24th March- In over 900 cities Internationally against gun violence and mass shootings calling for stronger gun control – In March for our lives. 18th April – Cinemas open for the first time since 1983 with US film Black Panther chosen as first to be screened. 8-12th May - Eurovision song contest Lisbon, Portugal won by Israeli Netta Barzilow – Toy. 19th May - Wedding Prince Harry and Meghan Markle St. George's Chapel England with an estimated global audience of 1.9 Billion. 25th May- Ireland referendum to repeal ban on abortion 66.4%to 33.6 % for repeal side. 19th June –Canada becomes first industrialized country to legalize cannabis for recreational use from October, 17. 24th June – Saudi Arabia allows women to drive. 1st August – West African Kivu Ebola Epidemic outbreak. 2nd August- Apple Inc. Becomes the first public company to achieve a market capitalization of 1 Trillion. 10- 20th August- Severe floods in Indian state of Kerala the worst in a century. 14th August- Part of the Morandi Bridge collapses after a violent storm in Genoa, Italy – 43 Fatalities. 6th September – The Supreme Court of India decriminalizes homosexuality. 28th September- 7.5 Magnitude Earthquake hits Sulawesi, Indonesia causing a Tsunami kills 4,340 and injures 10, 679. 17th October- 700,000 people march through Central London demanding a second referendum on the final Brexit deal. 8th November – The Camp Fire ignites in Butte County, California the deadliest and most destructive wildfires. 28 November- Chinese Scientist, He Jiankui at Hong Kong conference announces he altered the DNA of twin human girls beorn earlier in the month to try to make them resistant to the HIV virus and possible pregnancy of another gene – modified baby. 19-21st December- Gatwick airport drone incident.

A Star is Born – Bradley Cooper and Lady Gaga. Mark Whalberg and Michelle Williams pay disparity comes to light, Gender pay disparity. Toys R us closes. Oprah Winfrey receives the Cecil B. De Mille award at the Golden Globes. First black woman to receive the award presented by Reece Witherspoon. Frances McDormand wins Oscar for Three Billboards outside of Ebbing Missouri. Wedding of Miley Cyrus and Liam Hemsworth. The Greatest Showman soundtrack was No.1 – Hugh Jackman. Yodelling kid – 11 years Mason Ramsey- Illinois Walmart (Lovesick Blues). IHop becomes IHob, (June 11, 2018), pancake chain flipping it's P upside down. Netflix tweeting brb changing my name to Netflib, a week later we'd never turn our back on pancakes. The entire incident was a joke, of course it was.

2019

1st January- Same sex marriage becomes legal in Austria. 15th April- During Holy Week a major fire engulfs, Notre Dame cathedral in Paris resulting in the roof and main spire collapsing.

1st May- King Vajirallongkorn of Thailand marries his personal bodyguard. 6th May- First report since 2005 (IPBES) Biodiversity loss is accelerating with over a million species now threatened worldwide with extinction. The decline of the natural living world is unprecedented and largely a result of human actions. 8th May – A British Teenager Isabelle Holdaway 17 first patient to receive a genetically modified Phage Therapy to treat a drug resistant infection. July – CRISPR gene editing was first used to experimentally treat a patient with a genetic disorder. 24th July- Talaq muslim man to legally divorce wife by uttering word Talaq (The Arabic word for divorce 3x in oral, written or electronic form. 30th July – India Bans Triple Talaq. 1st August – Danish Polar Research Institution polar portal reports a large spike in Greenland ice losswith 11 Billion Tonnes melted in one day and 197 Gigatonnes during the month of July. 27th September – 500,000 people march in a climate change protest led by activist Greta Thunberg, 16 years and PM Justine Trudeaux in Montreal, Canada. 4 Million people go on strike around the world. 30th September – The Republic of Ireland promises to plant 140

Million treesin 20 years to combat climate change. 18th October – NASA astronauts Jessica Meir and Christina Koch conduct the first all female spacewalk outside of the International Space Station. 23rd October – The bodies of 39 people are found in a truck container in Essex, England 25year old North Ireland man arrested on suspicion of murder. 5th November – 11,000 Scientists from around the world publish a study in the Journal of Bioscience, warning clearly and unequivocally that planet earth is facing a climate emergency. Air pollution in parts of India hits record levels. 14th November – Italy declares a state of emergency in Venice following record flooding. 2nd December- The Covid -19 Pandemic begins in Wuhan, Hubei, China. 16th December – Pope Francis abolishes pontifical secrecy in sex abuse cases. 19th December – A locust plague devastates 173,000 acres of crop and grazing land in Ethiopia and Somalia. 20th December – The Dutch Supreme Court affirms Dutch Government is responsible for management of Carbon Dioxide emissions for the country and is bound to protect human rights. The ruling reiterated from the court of appeals is that, every country is responsible for its share of emissions. 29th December – China informs WHO of a novel corona virus in Wuhan, the ninth most populous Chinese city...

The Masked Singer launches in the US. The Reveal of the College Admissions Scandal- Lori Laughlin. Luke Perry death – Beverly Hills 90210 and Riverdale Star, stroke at 52. Jennifer Lopez and Alex Rodriguez get engaged. Kim Kardashian and Kanye West, 4th baby Psalms. The world meets Royal baby Archie, already crawling. Prince Archie Harrison Mountbatten – Windsor. The Big Bang Theory signs off after 12 years. Euphoria, black mirror worried parents of teens – Miley Cyrus. The world meets Forky from Toy Story 4. US women's soccer team wins world cup against the Netherlands. Old Town Road breaks chart records Billie Ray Cyrus and Lil Nas X. Miley Cyrus and Liam Hemsworth separate after 8 months. Kylie Jenner singing rise and shine to daughter Stormi. Selena Gomez returns with (lose you to love me and look at her now). Revival of Charlie's Angels. Billie Eilish Grammy history youngest person in 4 categories. Frozen II returns from Disney 6 years later. Fleabag season 2 Amazon comedy. Harry Styles broke the internet. Mays met gala lacy black see through top, pearl earrings and high heels. His one direction is towards androgyny. Chernobyl – HBO mini series 1986 meltdown. Senorita – Shawn Mendes and Camilla Cabello streamed more than one Billion times on Spotify (50 Million hours).

Vanity Fair 2004- Drama/ Romance Director- Mira Nair with Reece Witherspoon, Gabriel Byrne. A woman with opportunities and without a hump may marry who ever she likes. William Makepeace Thackery. I thought her a mere social climber, but now I see she's a mountaineer. Two men and two men only will enter my bedchamber, My husband and the doctor. Are you trying to steerme to an indiscretion, no man has managed it yet.

Notting Hill 1999, Romantic/Comedy-Directed- Roger Michell, Screenwriter- Richard Curtis, Producer- Duncan Kenworthy, with Julia Roberts; Hugh Grant; Hugh Bonneville. Distributed – Universal Pictures. A famous American actress who happens to walk into his London Bookshop.

Truth is sometimes stranger than fiction.

Pretty Woman 1990, Romantic/ Comedy Director – Garry Marshall with Richard Gere; Julia Roberts; Jason Alexander. Adapted from Pygmalion. Distributed- Touchsone Pictures and Walt Disney Studios Motion Pictures. A rich entrepreneur hires an escort for his business trip and they try to bridge the gap between the two worlds after he falls in love with her.

Absolutely Fabulous 1992- Sitcom with Jennifer Saunders and Joanna Lumley. Based on Modern Mother and Daughter by Dawn French and Jennifer Saunders.

Thwarted, but Nobody cares, but nobody cares, but nobody cares, but nobody cares!

Fannulone!

It was a bit brutal but my mum once said if you're going to give away your free love at least you must at least charge a fee and make them pay for it, to make it worth your while. Putana!

We're all going to hell and don't hold the horses!

Sorry Folks, sometimes I'm a bit Facklopte!

My brother Freddie writes left-handed chicken scrawl scratch, they tried to convert him at St. Kevins but they soon gave up as he always reverted to back to form.

Whose Slovakia now!

Stayin' Alive – Bee Gees 1977 Saturday Night Fever. American Dance Drama. Directed – John Badham, Producer- Robert Stigwood with John Travolta and Karen Lynn Gorney. Distributor – Paramount Pictures. Manero trapped in his working – class ethnic neighbourhood. Stayin'Alive...

Stay - April, 2017: Zedd and Alessia Cara ..... Just take your time, the clock is ticking, so stay

All you have to do is wait a second

Your hands on mine.........

Never - Moving Pictures, 1984: Film - Footloose

Never gonna not dance again........ - Pink: November, 2022

Royal Variety Performance 2022: Royal Albert Hall recorded 1st December, 2022 and live on the 20th December, 2022.

Dance all over me ....George Ezra Album: Gold Rush Kid, 2022.

Queen's Tribute music arrangement for her birthday, 2022. Sing: Gary Barlow, Gareth Malone and Andrew Lloyd Webber. Sing: 2012 Gary Barlow,

What a wonderful world!...1967 Louis Armstrong B- Side Cabaret. I see trees so green, Red Roses too I see them bloom for me and you...

Vaterland

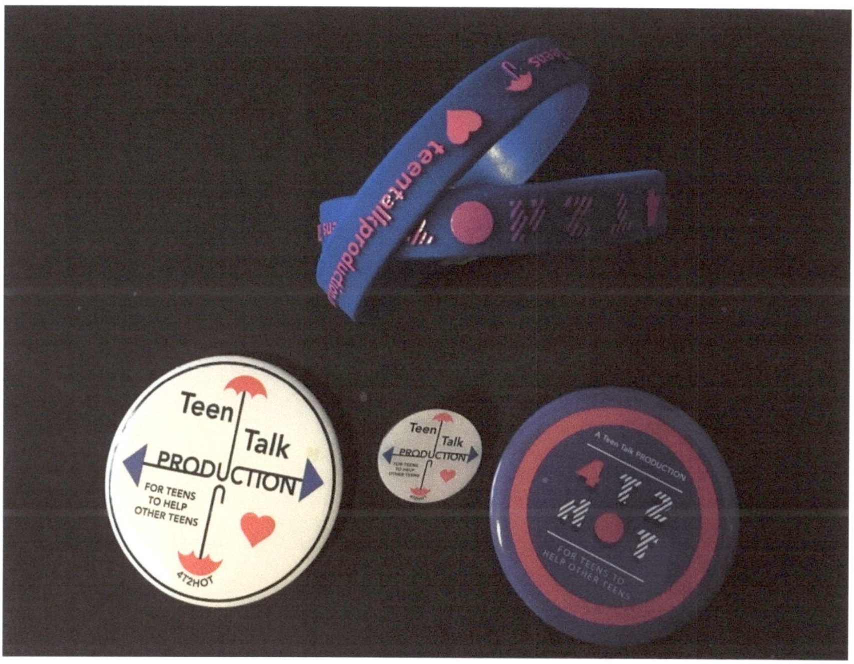
Teen
Talk
PRODUCTION
FOR TEENS
TO HELP
OTHER TEENS
4T2HOT
A Teen Talk PRODUCTION
FOR TEENS TO
HELP OTHER TEENS

The Lindentree

2016 HIGGINS COMMUNITY SERVICE
AWARD

J.P.
FOR VICTORIA
To Mummy,
10/8/13

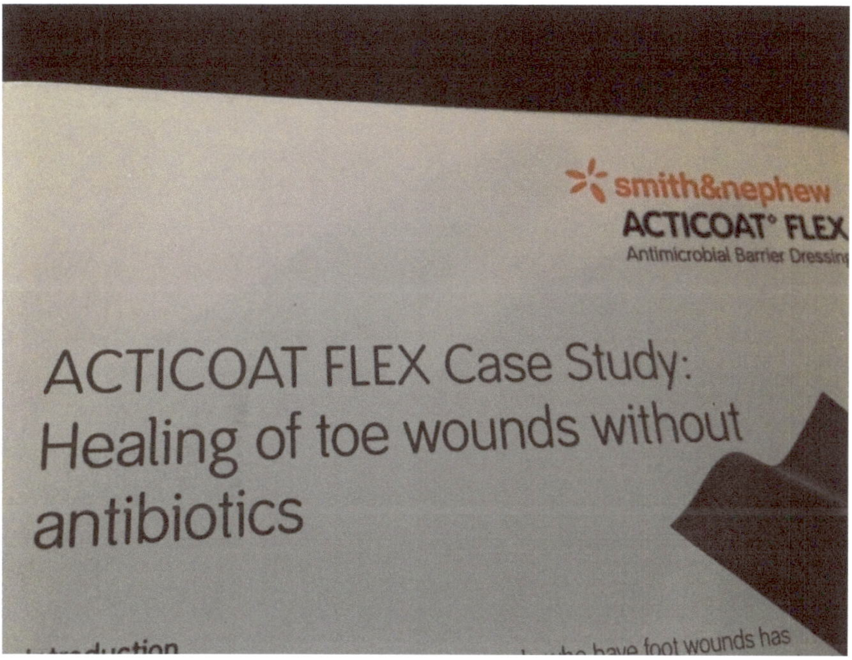
smith&nephew
ACTICOAT° FLEX
Antimicrobial Barrier
ACTICOAT FLEX Case Study:
Healing of toe wounds without
antibiotics

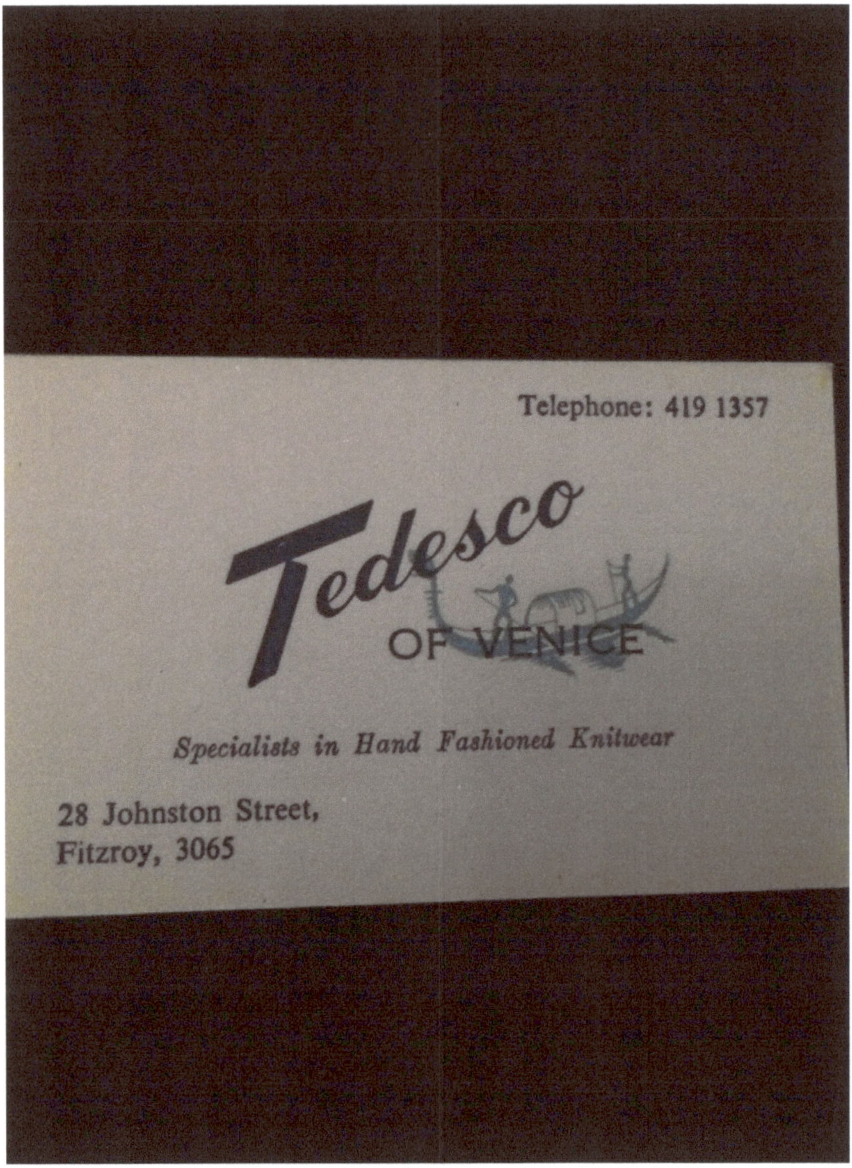
Telephone: 419 1357
Tedesco
OF VENICE
Specialists in Hand Fashioned Knitwear
28 Johnston Street,
Fitzroy, 3065

WINE DINE DANC
CUISINE INTERNATION
REASONABLE PRICES ... 944 58

Teen
Talk
PRODUCTION
Teen
Talk
PRODUCTION
Teen
Talk
PRODUCTION

A Teen Talk PRODUCTION
4T2HOT
FOR TEENS TO HELP OTHER TEENS
Teen Talk PRODUCTION
FOR TEENS TO HELP OTHER TEENS
4T2HOT

To Mummy,
with love
from Sabena
30/3/13
Freddie
フレディ
リンダ
Linda
HAPPY
EASTER!!!
うさぎ
Usagi
Rabbit

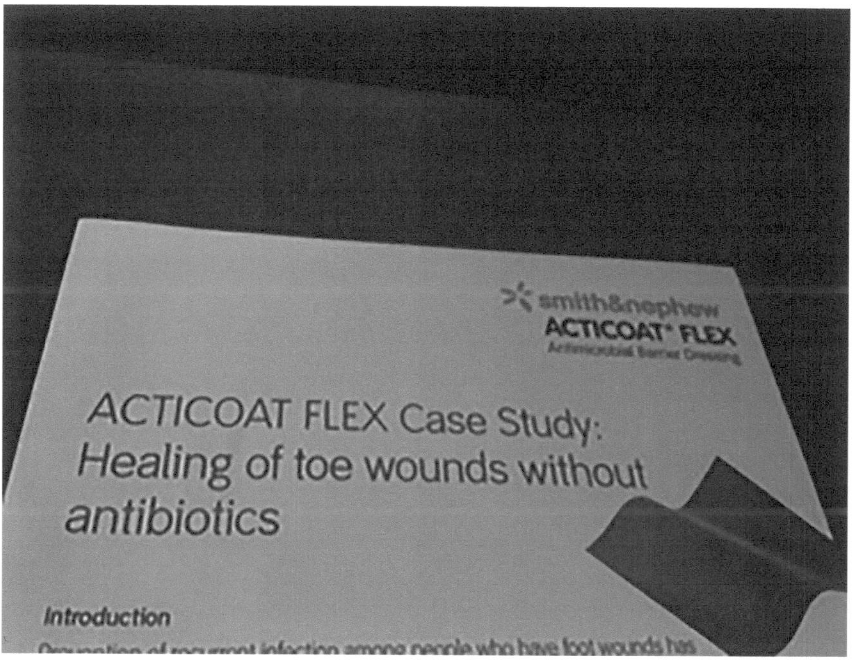
smith&nephew
ACTICOAT* FLEX
ACTICOAT FLEX Case Study:
Healing of toe wounds without antibiotics
Introduction

HEY!
DAUGHTER PRESSES
TEEN TALK

SUPER HERO APPEARS
HERO COMFORTS CHILD
OR
HERO APPEARS
WITH

BIO OF VERITY

WINE DINE DANCE
CUISINE INTERNATIONAL
REASONABLE PRICES... 944 588

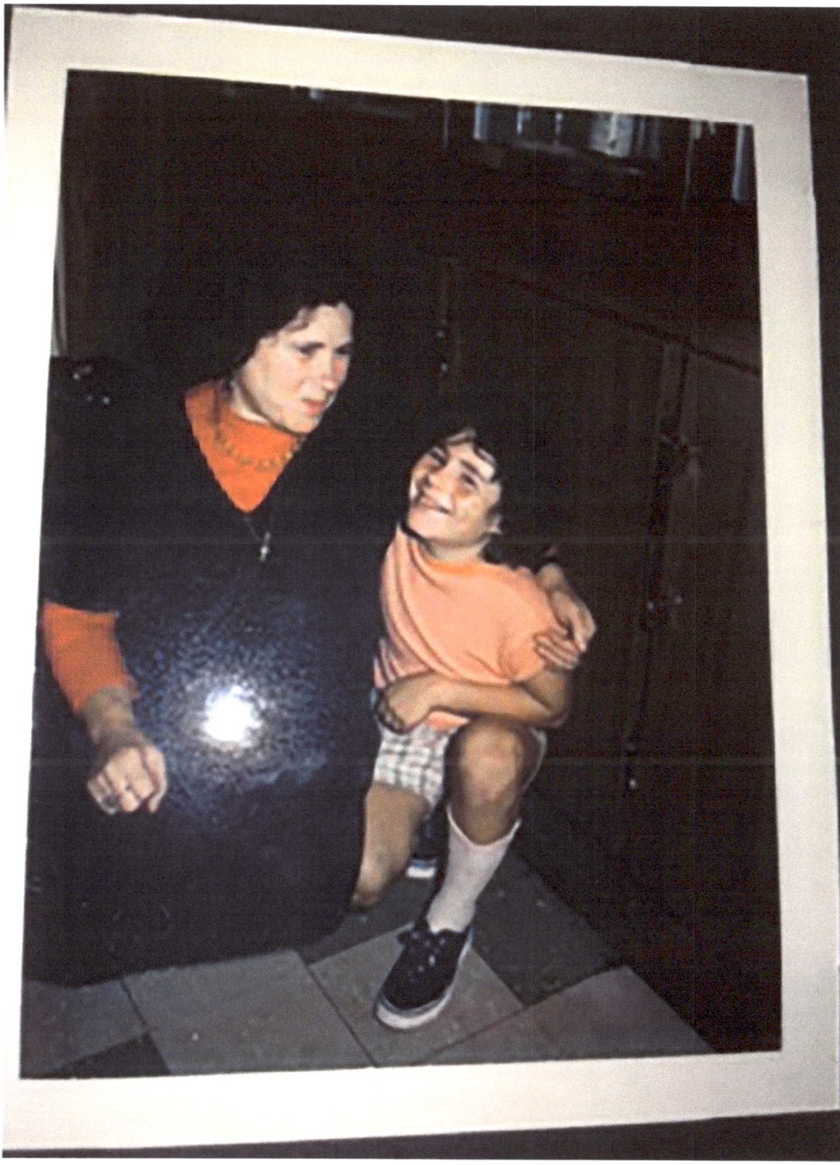

WINE DINE
CUISINE INTERNATION
REASONABLE PRICES

FRENCH
SKI
SCHOOL
4
3

The Lindentree

25/8/2012
Adorable
Adoree
ははは
だいたき
です。
Mummy, I love
you

To Mummy
with LOVE
15/12/2012
Merry Christmas

一 二 三 四
六 八
To Mummy,
with love-
Sabena
5/5/12
HAPPY MOTHERS DAY!
Love

Sat. 04th August, 2012.
I LOVE YOU
日本人
Sabena
サビナ
リンダ
Linda
みどり
Green

I love you Mummy
and you're the star twinkling happily through my life Day and night

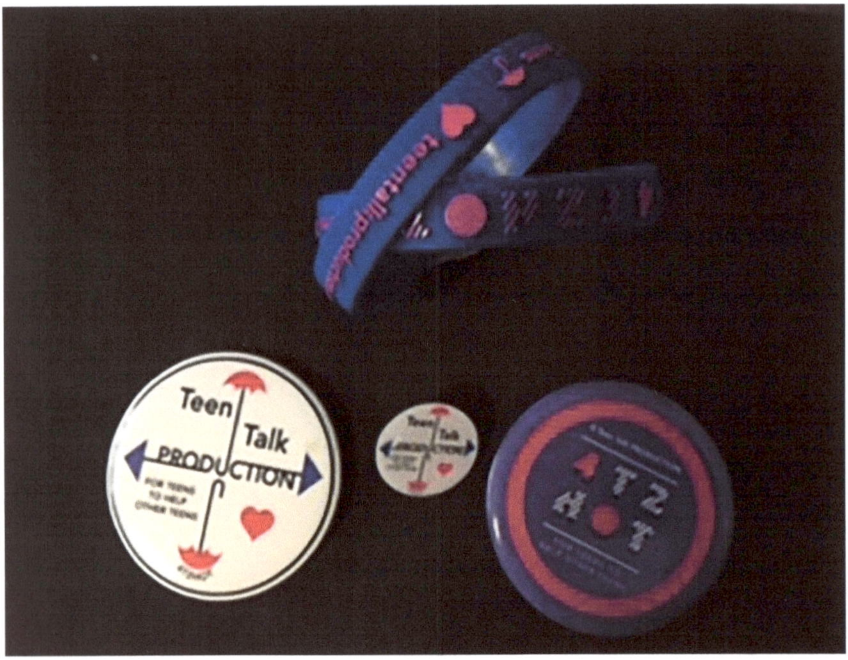
Teen
Talk
PRODUCTION

Teen
Talk
PRODUCTION

Biography

This is the sequel of the contemporary autobiographical story that I was compelled to write, during the COVID pandemic. I hope that it is a message for our community and all around the world about caring for our utmost precious future assets - "Our Children".

It includes the emotional crusade to give a voice to our youth by bringing attention to to their needs and thoughts for future change, to ensure they are given the chance to become the "Best Adults" possible for their future lives.

It is the "REAL" true journey of a young teenage girl from being a vibrant successful hostess of a kitsch late Nitespot, to her adventures in the USA and studying surgery in San Francisco, California. On returning home to Melbourne to begin a new life and professional career, only then having to embark on a the greatest epic tragic crusade of her life to fight for the protection and future life, for her only daughter of so tender years. Finally inspiring her mother to create a Youth Documentary/ Lifestyle TV series, TEENTALK.

A previous Full - time health practitioner for 27 Years and then Part- time for 10 years after being diagnosed with a severe respiratory allergy disability and MCS.

Despite struggling with this condition and being traumatised by my daughter's diagnosis of severe mental illness, self- mutilation and suicidal idealisation from 12 years of age.

I started creating a passion project Pilot, youth alternative Indie Documentary - Teen Talk Production was born. Having tried to enlist help for months about my idea concept but having no experience or connections in the TV / film industry as of November 2013, I became an Indie Director, Producer, Writer, CEO and Founder of my own Film project.

Teen Talk Production - TTP. "Please Teen Talk!" due to my daughter's suffering in silence. The Pilot episode was scripted, produced and directed by myself, in January, 2015 to visit millennial youth issues. TTP, youth voice documentary/ lifestyle program with average youth aged from 7-29 years, some special adult guests, entertaining for the whole family. Self taught scriptwriter, director, producer, and sometimes camera person filming with the crew on occasion.

"Your Star Sparkling Bright in the TeenTalk Light"

Commenced CTV broadcasting from June 2015, twice weekly with successful ratings.

Pre- production, filming, editing and post- production occurring for each 12 weeks season of episodes during 2015 - 2019.

2016 broadcasting nationally on CTV Adelaide, SA and Perth, WA upon their request. Youth audience popularity demand increased in these states, other states do not have CTV at this time. TTP - 14 Seasons, 170 Episodes and 41 DVD's.

2016 - HIggins Community Service Award presented to TTP by Kelly O'Dwyer, MP.

From 2019, TTP international Free TV streaming platform channel online of current episode content from 2017 - 2019. Https: // teentalkproduction.okast.tv.

2019 - Completed script writing course, RMIT (Brett Stanning).

2019 - Completed memoir writing course, RMIT (Sian Prior).

Written 3 Film / TV series scripts, 1 treatment from 2019 - 2021.

ScreenForever Conference Melbourne 2019, 3 professional pitches, round tables and networking groups with Dan Jinks (USA), Stuart Baxter (Eone UK), ITV - Ben Ulm (Aus), Brown Johnson (Sesame Workshop, USA), Que Minh Luu (ABC Aus.), Lizette Atkins - (Unicorn Films, Aus.), Clelia Mountford (Merman, UK), Jason Taylor (Futurism Studios, USA).

2021, 22nd May, Part 1 Original Memoire Completed "Never" of a proposed trilogy, published December 2021.

2022, 21 August, Part 2 Sequel "Never After, Never Again!" Completed.

NEVER
Dr. Linda Frederica Walsh

It is the REAL true journey of a young teenage girl from being a vibrant successful hostess of a kitsch late Nitespot, to her adventures in the USA, studying surgery in San Francisco, California. On returning home to Melbourne to begin a new life and professional career, had to embark on the greatest epic tragic crusade of her life to fight for the protection and future life, for her only daughter of so tender years... Inspiring her... to Create!

"It's Kinda Fun to do the impossible" – Walt Disney

I dedicate this book to my mum and dad, Sanae Winston, Masako Todo, and my friends Helen, Franca, Mike, Norma, Nick and Mel, Roberta and Neil and those friends who gave me their kind help and support.

René Magritte, "Those who cannot remember the past are condemned to repeat it."--George Santayana, The Life of Reason, 1905. From the series Great Ideas of Western Man., ca. 1962, gouache and pencil on paper mounted on paperboard, Smithsonian American Art Museum, Gift of Container Corporation of America, 1984.124.194

CPSIA information can be obtained
at www.ICGtesting.com
Printed in the USA
LVHW072312010323
740706LV00001B/1

* 9 7 8 0 2 2 8 8 8 4 4 1 5 *